Timothy Demkiw Grayson

Every Canadian's Guide to Common Contracts

The Essential Reference for Business Owners, Managers, Entrepreneurs and Consumers

HarperBusiness
HarperCollins*PublishersLtd*

EVERY CANADIAN'S GUIDE TO COMMON CONTRACTS:
THE ESSENTIAL REFERENCE FOR BUSINESS OWNERS,
MANAGERS, ENTREPRENEURS AND CONSUMERS

http://www.harpercanada.com

HarperCollins books may be purchased for educational, business, or sales promotional use.
For information please write: Special Markets Department, HarperCollins Canada,
55 Avenue Road, Suite 2900, Toronto, Ontario, Canada M5R 3L2.

Further information regarding Blakeney Duguay may be obtained by calling 1-800-394-1815.

The contracts reproduced herein are the property of their respective owners and are used by permission.

The following trademarks and registered marks and names are the property of their respective owners:
Federal Express, UPS, Coca-Cola, Time-Life, CIBC, National Leasing Group, Apple,
Shelter Canadian Properties Ltd., Insurance Bureau of Canada, Insurance Council of Canada,
Kentucky Fried Chicken (KFC), Microsoft, Lotus, Aldus, McDonald's, IBM Activa, Ziebart, Candu.

First edition

Canadian Cataloguing in Publication Data

Grayson, Timothy Demkiw
Every Canadian's guide to common contracts:
the essential reference for business owners, managers, entrepreneurs and consumers

HarperBusiness ed.

ISBN 0-00-638597-4

1. Contracts – Canada – Popular works. I. Title.

KE850.G62 1999   346.71'02   C99-930450-X
KF801.G62 1999

99 00 01 02 03 04 TC 6 5 4 3 2 1

The material in this publication is provided for information purposes only.
Laws, regulations, and procedures are constantly changing, and the examples given are intended
to be general guidelines only. This book is sold with the understanding that neither
the authors nor the publisher is engaged in rendering professional advice.
Personal services of a competent professional should be sought.

Printed and bound in Canada

Sic itur ad astra

To the many who doubted and underestimated,
and to those few who believed and supported: this is for you

Acknowledgments

It is curiously difficult to narrow down for acknowledgment those people who have particularly contributed to the creation of this book. Some provided inspiration; others support; and even more, real practical assistance. Many clients, lawyers, and friends—those groups not being mutually exclusive—encouraged me to develop, promote, and write this book when it was simply a "somebody oughta . . ." idea.

Nick Logan, of National Leasing Group; Raymond Petz, of CIBC; and Richard Blair, of Shelter Canadian Properties Limited, provided actual in-the-field contracts for use in the book; and Randy Bundus, of the Insurance Council of Canada, graciously agreed to provide insurance standards. I thank all of you for your personal and professional assistance. Thanks also to the people at those organizations who provided front-line assistance, as well as to Susan Kennedy, who reviewed the manuscript for the "accuracy not precision" of my interpretations and description. At HarperCollins, who took a chance on the marketability of this project and endured my artistic pretensions, is a veritable pride of people who contributed to its completion. My wonderful editor, Don Loney, with his trusted charges, managed to turn my cumbersome prose into something eminently readable.

I feel the need to acknowledge everybody that ever complained, criticized, doubted, knocked, or otherwise punched a hole into this or any of my other ideas, thoughts, notions, and writings. Without knowing it—and doubtlessly without intending it—you have made my work better. If success entails rising to a challenge, and if I have indeed risen to such challenges, then each of you *challengers* deserves and is given my thanks—even if we don't like each other. After all, *fas est et ab hostedoceri*.

But the most thanks I have are reserved for the often last-acknowledged person: the guy who went to the libraries, read every chapter draft, made suggestions, and corrected my misunderstandings. The same fellow who, I think, really wanted (and was disappointed when he didn't get) his children to go to law school: my dad, the real lawyer in the family.

Linda and Cathryn: it should be understood and go without saying that I could not have done this without you. Thank you for being mostly patient, generally tolerant, and wholly supportive—even when my computer came on vacation with us.

Contents

Foreword

Very early in my career at the Department of Justice in Ottawa, I was assigned to a senior lawyer to assist with a government procurement file where the contract to be negotiated and awarded was in excess of $300 million. Naturally, with a senior lawyer leading the file, I was more excited with the opportunity rather than feeling a sense of paranoia at the prospect of understanding the hundreds and hundreds of pages of contract clauses and appendices until, as it turned out, with one day's notice, I ended up alone, as solicitor, at the negotiation table across from a seasoned contracts law specialist in Vancouver who was prepared to negotiate and finalize the contract on behalf of the company he represented.

We were being asked to change most of the essential conditions of the contract and opposing counsel was assuring me these were only minor changes. Our meetings lasted nearly a week and, at every break (many that I called), I was on the phone with Ottawa and my senior counsel to seek assurances and guidance as to the contract issues. It was the most law I had ever learned in such a short period of time and it all happened in a phone booth. That was my first introduction to understanding a complex contract. Happily, my subsequent dealings and learning experiences have been in more pleasant and roomier surroundings.

The reason for my telling you this is because it *is* possible to read and understand contracts. Most people feel that contracts are impossible to understand. Well, actually some contracts are, like real estate agreements that contain never-ending sentences, written in archaic language, and repeated over and over again for certainty's sake. However, these type of agreements are the exception. Most contracts in ordinary commercial relations can be understood even if one is not a seasoned contracting specialist.

In business, you must know what you are doing and why. In order to manage commercial risks, you must understand, at a minimum, the binding and enforceable commitments and promises you are making to third parties and you must also know those commitments and promises that are being made to you. Even if you can afford to have a full-time lawyer by your side, it is still important to know and decide on those issues that give rise to unusual commercial risks.

Assessing the unusual commercial risks in any transaction and making sure that they are identified is the true nature of most commercial contractual inquiries. In my practice of law, it is the cornerstone of sound and practical legal/contractual advice. Whether it was advice I gave in Europe in one of the world's largest claims involving the Channel Tunnel, or to assess the simplest of commercial issues, the test remains the same. To assess the unusual commercial risks, the agreement must be read and *understood*. There are rules to assist in interpreting a contract, which are not self-evident on the face of an agreement, and neither are any surrounding circumstances written into the agreement (except for preambles, which capture a few).

For these reasons alone, I appreciate why many people feel it is impossible or too time consuming to truly understand a bargain. That is why there are circumstances when specialists in contracts law are required to review agreements or when the commercial or financial risks are significant enough that counsel ought to, in all cases, review the documentation before commitments are made or contracts signed. Nevertheless, whether you choose to consult counsel, or you are reviewing a contract yourself, you ought to be empowered with the basic skills to appreciate the importance and significance of issues. Also, you must address the more important provisions, which are usually: price, payment, delivery and scope of work and/or services. This is not to say that other unassociated provisions of a contract are unimportant, for in many cases they are very important.

What I am in essence saying is that to avoid nasty surprises and disappointments—not to mention nasty and expensive litigation—understand what it is you sign and always know what unusual commercial risks you are being asked to assume. If you are having your agreements read by a lawyer, then make sure he or she tells you about any unusual commercial risks particular to your situation. That is the most important question you need to ask and receive an answer to.

Most books you will read on the subject of contracts and contractual relationships primarily address principles of law. As a result, for many, such books and other similar literature are difficult to read and understand. This is so, mostly because legal authors and scholars are preoccupied with defining the law and naturally, in the area of contracts, they endeavour to explain principles of law at the expense of explaining the contract itself. These books are great reading for lawyers, but for business people they are next to impossible to comprehend.

Timothy Grayson's *Every Canadian's Guide to Common Contracts* is very different. It addresses the understanding of contracts and contractual relationships without an overriding preoccupation with an explanation of the law of contracts. As a result, you need not be a lawyer or make constant reference to a law dictionary to follow the analysis.

The author has managed to present extremely well-researched materials on a wide range of typical contracting issues. He has done this in a way that business people will understand. This book presents the subject matter logically and makes understanding contracts easy. He has been able to successfully present the materials accurately and he patiently explains critical issues when needed. As an example, he manages to explain complex clauses with simple language that genuinely allows for an excellent understanding of the contracting issues at play. He balances well the need to be substantive, all the while explaining issues simply and succinctly. Perhaps the most important benefit to be gained from reviewing and reading this book, which you ought to do in several sittings, is the empowerment and better control you'll have over simple and not-so-simple contractual arrangements.

We live in an era of self-reliance. More and more business people are on their own, or are teamed with others in nontraditional revenue-generating arrangements. In these situations, many look to what they can accomplish themselves, rather than relying on their employer or expensive consultant services to see them through the basic issues. Reading Timothy Grayson's book will empower the reader to be better equipped to assess commercial risks.

This book will likely be beneficial, too, for those who interact with lawyers on all contractual dealings, for the knowledge gained will serve to highlight what issues a lawyer may want or ought to review. I cannot overemphasize the importance of understanding the contractual issues and understanding your proposed bargain in advance of a commitment or signature. Knowing and managing your commercial risks and legal liabilities are imperatives in our present business climate.

Finally, a most interesting feature that you may have already noticed if you have thumbed through this book is the cross section of sample agreements and pertinent clauses within them, such as: sale contracts, lease and rental contracts and licensing agreements accompanied by ordinary, easy-to-understand language. His use of model contracts in explanations he provides for these particular commercial situations will be important reading for those who are exposed to this subject matter. This book should better prepare you for those contracting situations.

Every Canadian's Guide to Common Contracts is an excellent reference material, which will assist you in understanding complicated contractual issues. And most refreshing of all is that the author actually writes sentences under 75 words.

Finally, do not be surprised to find this book in your lawyer's bookshelf. Except for the most seasoned contracts law specialist, lawyers will learn from this book too. And remember, if you choose not to buy the book, carry a little change in case you need the phone booth!

Marc Duguay, B.C.L., LL.B.

Introduction

I am not a lawyer. I have spent my entire life in the company of lawyers and was even accepted to a very good law school. But, at least so far, it is not to be. Obviously that has not stopped me from writing on a subject that might commonly be considered the exclusive domain of the legal trade. My hope, as it may be yours, is that so long as I am able to read books and ask questions, I will be able to understand and become relatively proficient at whatever I choose. Consider the gourmand who cannot cook but knows all about good cooking, or the patient who researches a disease, syndrome, etc. (with very strong personal reasons) and becomes more expert than his or her doctors in that field. Similarly, I have, without the benefit of legal training, gained a small understanding of contracts.

I would not presume to suggest that I am an expert nor that I could do the work the lawyers do in the drafting and cobbling together of precise contract language. For the needs of a business person, whose vocation is in so many ways the creating and fulfilling of contract after contract, however, I believe I can hold my own. And I think that there is in my knowledge something to be gained by others, especially from my "working level" generalizations, parallels, and oversimplifications.

Thus I have written a book whose impetus was a simple question to myself at a time of need: Why isn't there a book that contains samples of and explanations about basic contracts (actually, I—my client—had a very specific need, but . . .)?

In my years of working as an employee, and even more years in private consulting to primarily small and mid-size business, I have had the opportunity and need to deal with many contracts: leases, employment agreements, licenses, purchases and sales, and a raft of others. Through it all I studied and learned some law regarding contracts to be better prepared when it came time to negotiate and formalize the deal in an agreement. Sometimes I was directly involved; other times I watched how my clients and their attorneys, or my colleagues, would deal with contractual issues. The lawyers were usually quite knowledgeable and talented. Too many of the others were their own worst enemy.

This book is for the people who neither have the time nor the inclination to study and learn the details of contract law. In my humble estimation, most business people are out of their depth when it comes to contracts. And why not? It is neither their job nor their reason for getting into business. Fortunately for some, they are employees of larger corporations that have legal departments or a law firm on retainer to take care of those matters. On the other hand, the people with the most to lose—small and mid-size businesses and their owners—seem to have the most trouble with contracts and the fewest legal resources. These entrepreneurs will often go without legal advice in their contractual arrangements for a variety of reasons:

- they can't afford or don't want to pay the legal fees;
- they are presented with "boilerplate" (see later) by the other side and go along; or
- they believe that long, lawyerly contracts are unnecessary except for the "important" stuff. (Which raises the question: What's important?)

Regardless of the rationale for neglecting to use well-prepared commercial contracts, most business people I encounter who avoid properly and thoroughly dealing with contracts do so because they do not understand them. In fact, they tend to be at least a little intimidated by them. One fellow I worked for operated under the misguided belief that if he read only the headings and capitalized text, he would obtain all the important information he needed. Eventually he got into a contract dispute and was bankrupted. So much for that theory. I also had a client who specifically demanded that the contract for a $250,000 transaction be kept to a one-page, four-paragraph document that was not even reviewed by a lawyer because a longer version "would be too binding." Lesson number one: A one-sentence contract will bind as well as a 20-pager, but it is the 20-pager that shields one from potential problems.

On the other hand, the world of commerce is heavily represented by business school graduates—with some of whom I studied—who were compelled to endure a few credit hours of commercial law in their degree programs. Today, I encounter plenty of these business people, and it is always surprising how little they choose to recall of those studies. Most are comfortable with their extremely limited level of competence and (ironically, quite rightly) consider the detail to be for the lawyers. One might think that their studies would have better prepared them to deal with contracts. The reality, however, is that we were taught the basic principles of commercial legal matters with an emphasis on the theory and development of commercial law. The lesson is good, but not particularly practical for the business person facing a mass of legalese who must decide how to proceed. (Nevertheless, in the opening chapters I have included some of the theory as a grounding or refresher.)

Any commercial law primer, regardless of its length or depth, can be quite impractical for the active business person. While the key principles and fundamentals are necessary to know, does one need or want to keep searching the 200-plus pages in popular textbooks that cover all aspects of commercial law, such as *The Law and Business Administration in Canada*?[1] Would one remember all the information provided, and how it might apply to the current situation? Is there a purpose to it? I would suggest that there is a practical but limited, day-to-day referential value to the theory-based legal primers, and propose this volume instead.

This book is for the average, overworked business person. The background and theory are confined to the basics, in large part providing a foundation for understanding how and why contracts work as they do. It is not a textbook, and makes no such pretense. In the interests of practicality, it is necessarily incomplete compared to a textbook. That should not be considered a failing so much as a time-saving feature. After all, we have already established that the busy business person really does not need to be an expert in contracts, but does need to be aware of the legal principles and able to recognize certain vital features.

The first requirement is a functional literacy in the language of contracts, so we will familiarize ourselves with some of the legal dialect relating to them. Most of this new vocabulary will be featured in the first few chapters, which provide a solid overview of how and why contracts work: what makes a set of promises a contract, the difference between the form and the substance of a contract, etc.

The remaining, lion's share of the book is dedicated to agreements and contracts commonly used in commercial transactions. It is, in essence, a field guide to commercial contracts that allows its user to compare and contrast "in the field," hopefully providing greater insight, understanding, and appreciation of written agreements. Some of the forms we will dissect are precedents of agreements taken from a published forms resource for lawyers; others are standard contract forms obtained from insurers, lenders, lessors, etc.

Boilerplate agreements such as those presented here usually arrive as a *fait accompli*, as often as not in preprinted multiple-copy form purportedly encompassing all the terms of the deal being made. That these agreements are usually broader than necessary, incorporate terms that were never discussed (but are, we are told, "standard"), are used in a million other situations that bear only passing resemblance to this deal, and have a noxious bias toward the presenter of the contract contributes to why boilerplate contracts are rarely read and even more rarely understood. Before binding oneself to a contract, it is imperative to understand its effect. To understand requires that the document be read, and to read it demands that one know what all the words mean. I strongly recommend reading a contract with a dictionary handy.

Some cautious business people send everything to their lawyer; others send only the "big" things to the lawyer for interpretation. Here is some advice:

1. Your lawyer will advise you on the legality of the text presented to him or her; he or she may interpret the commercial meaning as well, but the lawyer may not know the details of the deal you made or whether the contract properly reflects it. Also, a lawyer is generally not concerned with the commercial *value* of the contract—i.e., whether it is a good/the best deal for you—but with whether it legally reflects the deal you made.

2. Regardless of whether you send the "legal" stuff to your lawyer, you, the business person, should know what is written down to represent the deal.

In this book, then, what we are concerning ourselves with is primarily the written form of contract. Ideally, in reading and using this book, you will make specific reference to clauses and paragraphs in contracts with which you are familiar to get a fuller understanding of their meaning. A basic form of contract is provided in later chapters, be it a lease, insurance, employment agreement, etc., that provides an overview of that particular type of contract. Be aware, however, that these samples are not the last word. Lawyers will usually have their own forms and customize the contract to suit a specific purpose. So the contract before you may only bear a passing resemblance to that provided here.

What you will not get out of this book is the ability to eliminate legal counsel. The possibility that this thin volume of information could provide any business person with more than a basic awareness of contractual law is remote. Commercial lawyers are trained at length in the development and status quo of contractual law; they are regularly educated about and informed of changes to the law of contracts as a result of either judicial ruling or statutory amendment. Moreover, they are completely immersed in the language and nuance of contracts. The smart businesswoman does not try to outsmart her lawyer; she does, however, find out as much as possible before consulting her lawyer so that (1) she can ask the right questions, and (2) she doesn't incur more legal time (and cost) than necessary.

As I have said, it is not my intention to suggest that you can do without a lawyer, despite the humour I've tried to inject into the book occasionally at their expense. To the contrary, your lawyer is a *very* important advisor. You can make your lawyer much more efficient and helpful if you (1) generally understand the nature of contracts and (2) can communicate clearly about them. I do not presume to know as much about this area of the law (or any area of the law for that matter) as a lawyer. But the intent of the book is not to provide expert reference. It is to provide *general*, practical knowledge and understanding. Unfortunately, lawyers have a more difficult time doing that because their training and livelihood depends on qualifying every statement and striving for perfect accuracy. Mine doesn't. And, since my needs vis à vis contracts are essentially the same as yours, I believe I have worthwhile information to share with you.

It would be impossible to present anything that is close to definitive on the subject matter without losing the focus and utility of this "field guide." Besides, the underlying statutes—provincial sale of goods, consumer protection, insurance, and other such acts—sometimes differ between jurisdictions. Any attempt to get specific will certainly make the subject more confusing, causing my attempt to generalize to come up short. Hopefully, this book achieves the goal I set for it at the outset: accuracy, not precision. The details should be left to the lawyers who know them and have the resources to confirm every applicable point of law.

Finally, this book is not simply a set of forms for the business person to use in writing his own business contracts. There are books available that provide precedents and forms. These reference books vary from the extensively detailed (for lawyers) to the curiously *over*simplified for the layman. In either case, I would suggest that if the contract is important to you or the future of your business, these books should only be used as a guideline for providing information to your lawyer.

> As one who has had to prepare and deliver written contracts that reflect oral agreements at the least add-on legal cost, I have developed a process of preparing the contract myself, by including clauses and paragraphs that have been previously drafted by my lawyers for other situations and altering them to suit the current needs. I then send the entire draft to my attorney with an explanation of what I had intended to achieve. Not surprisingly, the process is efficient and effective for both me and my lawyers.
>
> On the other side of the coin, when a written contract is presented to me by the other side, I read it through, comparing each clause to similar text from other agreements, then summarize for my lawyer what I understand, do not understand, or am unsure about. We then discuss the document to determine whether I misunderstood it or if the words on paper are wrong. Again, the amount of time and frustration this saves is extraordinary.

*   *   *

Contracts as written by lawyers are created for the eventuality of disaster. A good lawyer will prepare a contract that shields her client from a variety of unexpected adverse conditions. That is, many contracts will contain "what ifs" for most all possible futures. Thus, they get long and scary. Commercially, however, the goal is to make sure both parties get what they bargained for from the contract. Knowing and understanding the language of contract law will increase the likelihood of successful agreements. As a professor once told me about doing tax returns: "You may never have to fill one in yourself—that's what accountants are for—but you have to know how to do it so you can be sure it's done right." The same holds true for dealing with agreements and contracts. Ignorance generally is no excuse under the law, so we are trying to make ourselves a little more knowledgeable. The goal is to save on legal expense both at the outset and at the end.

The concepts and laws surrounding the making and breaking of contracts, as presented in the remainder of this book, have been simplified significantly for general understanding. As stated earlier, the goal is accuracy, not precision. But the devil is in the details, as it were, and the single most important shortcoming of this book is that it omits many details germane to contract law, not the least of which is an extended review of statutory law. Thus, I issue to you now for the first time, and periodically throughout the book, the caveat that *the information presented herein is necessarily incomplete.* **In any contractual dealings, do not rely solely on the explanations and information presented herein: seek the advice of a lawyer to be certain there are no legal pitfalls within your contract.**

Chapter 1
Contract Basics

Capacity, Offer, Acceptance, Consideration, Intent

A contract is an exchange of promises enforceable at law. That is as simple as it gets. Of course, the catch is the last three words. What makes a promise enforceable at law? Around that matter is built a mountain of common and statutory commercial law that deals with the area of contracts. Law students cover the period since the beginning of time learning about how that mountain was formed, and why. (Or so it seems. After all, what real similarity is there between the commerce of 17th-century England and the international affairs of our modern, Western business system?) Business people, by and large, need that information very little. Do you really need to know about *Carlill v. Carbolic Smoke Ball Company* ([1892] 2 Q.B. 484) and its effect on the law of contracts?[1]

Case law is for lawyers. What if, instead, we simply laid down the basics of what a contract is, how it is constituted, and what—generally—makes it a promise or set of promises enforceable at law? Would that not be both educational and save everyone a lot of time?

In most of this book we concern ourselves with written contracts. Primarily we are looking at the written form of contract because it can be viewed with relative ease, certainly more easily than any oral agreement. But the written contract, all formally laid out in numbered paragraphs with plenty of WHEREASes, NOW THEREFOREs, and NOTWITHSTANDINGs, is only one *form of contract*. The form must never be confused with the concept or *substance of a contract*, which need not be written. So, let us first address ourselves to the nature of the contract itself.

THE CONTRACT

As stated at the top of this chapter, a contract is a promise or set of promises that create binding obligations on the parties to those promises. Thinking of a *contract* as a *concept* rather than as a physical item—a written document—will help. If you and I make a promise to one another or I make a promise to you, under certain conditions that we will address later, we have created a contract. That contract may have been *written*, it may have been *oral*, or it may have been *implied*. Regardless of its form, it is a contract and is binding. The main differences between those forms of contract—written, oral, and implied—is the ease of interpretation and enforcement presented by each and certain issues of compliance with statutory requirement in some situations, such as for the sale of goods.

We make promises every day and sometimes have to break them ("I will pick you up at 8:30 for the meeting." "Sorry, I got caught in traffic; I guess we missed the meeting."). Nobody considers these promises contracts. Rightfully so, since they usually are not. Sometimes we make more serious promises that we do not keep for one reason or another ("You can have my baseball tickets."), which also are not contracts. The times and situations in which we make promises to others are endless. If all of these promises were enforceable (and enforced) contracts, we would all be in serious trouble—except the litigators. In the simple illustrations above, something is missing in each promise that precludes it from being enforceable, meaning they are not contracts.

Promises that become enforceable contracts have certain features or ingredients that make them special. The basic requirements of legal contracts as made between parties that have the legal right ("capacity") to contract are:

1. A definite and precise offer
2. An acceptance of that offer
3. Value (known as "consideration") to the promise(s)
4. Intent to create a legally binding agreement

Using the characteristics noted above, we could say that a contract may come into existence when a specific tentative promise (the offer) that carries value (consideration) is made by one legally capable party to another (capacity), and that offer is agreed to by the other party (acceptance). We presume that in offering and accepting promises of value, both parties do so with the specific plan that these promises will be kept (intent).

Note the use of the word "specific" in the first sentence of the preceding paragraph. It will reappear several times, most especially in relation to offers. This is because, in addition to the four key factors of contracts as noted above, the courts have ruled that there must be "certainty" in contracts. Anything in a contract left "to be agreed" or determined subjectively reduces "certainty," and may have the effect of reducing a contract's enforceability. An offer must be "certain" in the sense that it makes specific what is being offered to whom and for how much. So, while a court may interpret or read into an agreement where certainty is unclear, drawing up a document that is specific, certain, and clear from the outset is a wiser approach.

> With regard to certainty in contracts, here is a word to the wise: When you agree formally to agree *later*, you are not agreeing to anything and therefore the agreement is worth nothing—legally speaking. If some term or condition may be meaningful to your deal in the future, sort out the way that is to be determined before the contract is made. If it is not *certain*, it does not matter.

Before we move on to the four specific requirements of a contract in greater detail, let us examine two types of contract: unilateral and bilateral. For the most part, commercial contracts are of the latter sort, likely because the courts tend to interpret disputed contracts as bilateral wherever possible. In this book, we will be mainly concerned with bilateral contracts. But unilateral contracts appear occasionally, and since the difference between the two forms of contract is significant, it is worth considering them.

The Unilateral Contract

As the name suggests, the unilateral contract is one comprising a promise made by one party to the agreement in exchange for some act of the other party. The offeree must satisfy her obligation by some act in order to accept the contract; only then is the offeror bound to keep his part of the bargain. By thinking about the situation of each party for a few minutes, it is easy to see that the contract is not equally risky to both sides. Let us say that you told a local artist you would pay $500 for a new painting if there were one available to be hung in your new office for the Grand Opening festivities three months away. In the absence of a formal commission (contract) with the artist, which would be a bilateral agreement, the artist can only accept the contract by delivering a new painting on or before the date specified. You could, technically, revoke your offer at any time before the delivery of the painting without any penalty. (On the other hand, the artist could refuse to create the new painting and you would have neither a painting for the Grand Opening nor recourse for not having it.)[2]

The courts generally will imply a promise (subsidiary contract) on the part of the offeror that he will not revoke the offer while the work is being done. But that implied subsidiary contract, which would likely be inferred in the preceding example, can be negated by specific terms of the basic agreement. Take another example, such as you offering $200 to *anyone* in the cafeteria who can deliver to you the briefcase you lost at a trade show last week. Because you did not make the offer to a specific person or people, there could be no subsidiary offer (which would have to be made, we will see later, with a definite and specific offeree or offerees). So, any time before your offer is accepted (by your briefcase being delivered), you can revoke your offer. Anyone who has gone off looking, regardless of the expense to which they have been put, is out of luck.[3]

The Bilateral Agreement

The bilateral agreement, on the other hand, is a contract comprising promises made by each party to the other. It is a contract situation that, regardless of the equity in the swap, binds both parties from the moment the contract is made. Consider the second most ubiquitous commercial contract: that of employment. When the contract is written, the employee is promising to provide the employer with a good-faith effort to provide her ability to the employer's human resources pool. In return, the employer promises to provide the employee with a certain amount of compensation in the form of money, paid vacation, and other benefits.

The bilateral agreement is usually a more equitable form of contract, because both parties oblige themselves to the other in some manner. What's more, unless you are completely unscrupulous or dealing with a complete naïf, most agreements entered will be bilateral, because few business people are willing to perform work that could be for naught on some ridiculous grounds with no recourse for damages. The truth of the matter is, we live in a litigious society.

Given that most agreements are bilateral contracts, in which both parties are promisors and promisees, we now need to examine in some detail the five principal requirements of a legal contract that make a contract legally binding.

CAPACITY

Although the four principles of common law contract examined below determine the enforceability of a promise or set of promises, thereby creating binding contracts, *capacity* is an important determinant of the legality of the contract. Put plainly, there are simply some people and things that do not, in the eyes of the law, have the ability—generally the "competence"— to enter into a contract for one reason or another. The reasons why these designated entities do not have the capacity to contract are many, and extended explanation would, for our purposes, be little more than time-consuming. We will simply list some of those incapable entities and note the significant effect of their incapacity on you, the person considering contracting with any one of them.

1. Minors

Even though the legends of great commercial heroes—usually as told by themselves—often begin with an industrious youth, getting into contractual relations with precocious children can be problematic. The law is seriously skewed toward the minor—that is, any person who has not attained the legal age of majority. In essence, the law believes that a contract between an adult and a minor is not "mutual," because the minor does not have the capacity to make an independent decision to contract. *The rule of thumb is that a contract with a minor is not enforceable against the minor but is enforceable by the minor.* The exception to this rule is contracts for *necessaries* and *beneficial contracts of service*, which are enforceable upon the minor.

Even the exceptions are in place to protect the minor infant. Contracts for necessaries, which are defined as food, clothing, lodging, medical attention, and a few other items such as transportation to and from work are enforceable to persuade service providers who might otherwise not oblige themselves to a minor, to do so without fear of repudiation of the contract. In the case of beneficial contract for service, which essentially amounts to apprenticeships and other training-oriented employment, the law apparently still holds these contracts enforceable on the minor for her own good!

Do not fall into the trap of believing that the parent or guardian will be liable. He, she, they, or it are not liable and cannot be bound to any agreement made by or with their child unless the parent or guardian is made a guarantor of the child's obligations. Oddly enough, it seems that, by and large, parents cannot be bound or liable for anything their child does on its own or allegedly on their behalf, including shoplifting.

In the event that you should enter into a contract with a minor on the cusp of legal adulthood, that passage to "capable" status confers with it certain requirements on the minor's part. In some contracts of an ongoing nature, the new adult must *explicitly repudiate* the contract upon attaining majority or it will become binding upon him. In other cases, generally the shorter or finite contracts, the minor must *ratify* the contract upon attaining adulthood for it to become binding upon her. This ratification is really nothing more than the creation of a new contract with a person of capacity to contract. The new contract is therefore binding.

2. The Insane and the Intoxicated[4]

The bottom line here is that if the party to a contract can prove she was, or be proven to be or to have been, *non compos mentis* (not of sound mind)—perhaps so drunk or stoned as to have been unable to think rationally to bind herself to a contract—the contract is unenforceable, because she did not have the capacity to enter into a contract. It pays to be vigilant in contracting with those who may be of unsound mind, particularly with the prevalence of Alzheimer's disease and rehabilitation for those declared legally insane by reintegration into the community.

The good news for you is that the "I was too drunk" and "I was temporarily insane" claims to void a contract are weak ones. To start, the burden of proof is on the allegedly drunk, stoned, or insane person to prove that (1) he was in fact out of his mind and did not know what he was doing and (2) that you knew it at the time. The paradox implicit in the situation should be abundantly apparent. If the other party really had no capacity to know what he was doing, how can we trust his judgement and perceptions about the time when he was so incapacitated? That is, without an independent witness to corroborate that he did not know what he was doing and that you did, how could he possibly have known then how you perceived him at the time?

In any event, the person attempting to void the contract because of mental incapacity must do so *immediately* upon regaining the capacity to reason. Somebody who buys a car, drives it around for a week, then wants to void the contract for mental incapacity on the grounds of excess intoxication is not likely to get very far toward his or her objective.

3. Others

Depending on prevailing legislation and custom in different jurisdictions, a number of others do not have the legal capacity to contract in some or all circumstances. Strictly speaking, corporations and trade unions are restricted from making some types of contractual relations under some statutes. For all practical purposes and in most normal circumstances, however, both corporations and trade unions are eminently capable of, and often guilty of, unrestrained contracting.

Among those people legally incapable of contracting due to lack of legal capacity are *enemy aliens*, a concept that is a holdover from wartime. We do not have too many enemy aliens to deal with now, although for the United States the nations of Cuba, Iraq, and Libya fall under this rubric as embargoed states. Before conducting business internationally or with extranationals, it would be wise to obtain information from Canadian Foreign Affairs regarding any prevailing restrictions on trade.

Aboriginal people living on-reserve do not have the capacity to contract in many instances—particularly when the contract involves property on-reserve—because of their persisting status as wards of the Crown.[5] This status is rapidly changing, and although it may be unwise to buy a property on a reserve from its resident or deliver a durable good there without some added payment coverage, doing business and making contracts with Aboriginal entities such as Band Councils—which are obliged to incorporate—should not be discounted on this presumption of incapacity. Aboriginals living off-reserve have the same capacity to contract as any other person.

Until discharged, *bankrupts* have limited capacity to contract, particularly in matters of credit. By and large, we are referring to credit sales contracts in reference to the capacity of a bankrupt. Only businesses that deal with consumers directly, such as retailers, would usually have cause to concern themselves with such a contract, and in conducting a proper credit check the bankrupt status will be brought to your attention. Govern yourself accordingly.

Obviously, capacity to contract is a prerequisite to creating a legal contract. In theory, if that requirement were removed, the four key features of a legally enforceable contract are the offer, acceptance, consideration, and intent. We will now examine them in turn.

THE OFFER

An offer made by one party to another is not immediately binding. It is merely a promise made by one to another that is subject to the agreement (and corresponding return promise) to some condition of that offer. For instance, by offering to sell your company's widgets (in a formal quotation or by saying it over lunch) to a potential customer, you have not bound yourself to a contract. You have only made a tentative promise to carry out some action.

In order for that tentative promise to move along the way to becoming a contract, it must be accepted by the other party. At that point, all other things being equal, you have bound yourself to a contract. You will have to fulfill your promise because it is no longer idle talk; it is enforceable at law.

But is every offer really an offer? Oddly enough, there are circumstances in which an offer is not really an offer, and the other party's acceptance is not an acceptance but really an offer. Huh? In some circumstances, such as advertising or the display of wares, your showing or putting out the merchandise with a price tag is not an offer to potential customers. Instead, what you have done is made an *invitation to treat*. In other words, the potential customer has been provided the opportunity to make an offer to you for that product. You then have the choice of accepting the other person's offer and creating a contract, or not.

Say, for instance, you are showing your software product at a trade show. You have posted a notice that the program sells for $499 and that you have a volume purchase discount program. This is not an offer. It is an invitation for any interested wholesaler or retailer to offer to buy the software from you, at which point you begin negotiating—or, if there is no negotiating, filling out forms to complete the offer and acceptance.

In some circumstances, communication of the sort described above may be considered an offer rather than an invitation by virtue of its wording or the explicitness of the offer. If, instead of simply displaying the price, features, and discount program, you had additionally written that 100 units in the display booth were available, first-come-first-served, for the show price of $295, chances are you have made an offer that you will have to fulfill to those people who accept it. You have not invited; you have made a specific *promise*. (There is that word "specific" again.)

Let us assume an offer is intended to be made. How can one tell an offer is an *offer*? Basically, any statement becomes an offer when it is specifically communicated in clear terms. For example, "We'll buy all your used parts for fifty cents on the dollar" is an offer. You have in this statement made a tentative promise to do something for value. Doubtless, when the deal progresses, other issues will arise, but for the sake of argument, this is a genuine offer upon which the other party can act through acceptance or rejection.

Offers may be made orally or in writing; they may also be made by an action taken. Holding one's hand up to bid at an auction is a classic example of an offer being made without words. It is still valid, and may be accepted by the other party.

Regardless of how an offer is made, it is a valid and binding offer only if the offeree knows about it. Practically speaking, in most commercial settings in which an offer is made, the targeted party will know of it, *or* the offeror will stand by her commitment even if the offeree was unaware of the offer. Consider a restaurateur who places a Mother's Day Special ad in the paper. The first 50 customers who buy mom brunch over $20 can take home a bouquet of roses. If a customer came in unaware of the offer and ordered more than $20 of brunch, chances are mom would still get the flowers. While technically not required to make good on the offer, it is simply bad business for the restaurateur not to do so.[6]

Standard Forms

Some invitations to treat are made with specific conditions, sometimes on a *standard form*, under which the offeror must make her offer without any input into the terms and conditions of the ensuing contract.[7] Courier bills of lading and airline tickets are examples of this kind of invitation to contract. Federal Express or UPS, for instance, provide an invitation for anyone to offer to use their courier services by way of promotion and advertising, and a preprinted waybill. To have the courier take an envelope to its destination, one completes the waybill and gives him or her the envelope.

In this act, the courier has been made an offer. The catch is that the offer is made strictly on the courier's terms, which are listed on both the front and the back of the waybill. The offeror has no option to alter the terms; to have the package delivered, accept the terms as written—even if, as most people, you do not bother reading the relevant conditions.[8]

Standard-form contracts, such as that mentioned above, are usually used in situations where there will be little or no bargaining. For the most part, even though the scale is often weighted in favour of the organization that prepared the form, these contracts simplify business and generally have no negative effect on you in the long run. Who needs the aggravation or has the time to negotiate the terms of the carriage contract with the courier every time they come to get an envelope? Would it be reasonable to use the drop box at 4:30 pm and still expect overnight delivery if the courier had to negotiate every contract?

There are actually two significant conditions demanded by law for the use of standard-form agreements. First, the terms of the contract must be clearly and definitely drawn to the attention of the offeror by the party making the invitation. Whether that means that the terms are provided on the stub of the ticket or the waybill, with suitable notice to the offeror to read those terms, or that they are posted nearby with sufficient direction for the offeror to be aware of and read the conditions, the invited offeror must be specifically and abundantly made aware of the contract's terms and conditions.

Additionally, *the terms and conditions of a standard-form contract must be reasonable and reasonably expected in the circumstances.* Many such contracts demand that the offeror sign or initial it. There is a good reason for this. **When you sign a standard-form contract, you are assumed to have read, understood, and agreed to its terms**. And later recourse from terms and conditions that might be considered somewhat "unreasonable" begins rapidly evaporating when a signature is put to a standard-form contract.

What about tender offers, such as those requested by large companies or government agencies? What is actually happening?

Essentially the tender notice is a request (invitation) for offers from a select or general group of potential suppliers based on specific circumstances and commercial requirements. A company analyzes and then prepares an offer to do the work or supply the product to the person who has requested the offers. If the company is notified that it has won the tender, the implication is that the requester has accepted the offer and both parties are bound to the terms of the contract (see the section "The Acceptance" below).

Alternatively, the tender request may be made for an ongoing requirement such as catering or occasional security service. In this circumstance, the requester may have indicated a periodic need and that it is seeking *standing offers* for future service. There is no winner of the tender. The requester may, at any time in the future until an offer is *rescinded* (see the discussion of revoking an offer), accept a standing offer and force the offeror to do the work at the specified price.

In any event, it is a good policy to time-date any tender offer or quotation. Most experienced product and service providers qualify their price estimates (offers) in some way or other, including the use of an effective date.

I think we could all imagine the following scenario (some of us would dredge it out of actual experience). We make an offer only to realize later that we miscalculated and will be unable to satisfy our offer—or, we will lose money by fulfilling the promise. Nevertheless, the offer has been made, and if the offer is accepted, we are bound by its terms. Obviously, we do not want to get into a contract that is not good from the word go. To solve the problem, we need to *revoke* the offer.

Revocation of an offer is fairly simple: tell the person or people that the previously made offer is no longer valid. The dicey matter is that a revocation or withdrawal is only valid when it is specifically communicated to the offerees *before they have accepted the offer*, otherwise nonperformance of the accepted offer would be a breach of contract. Additionally, a withdrawal invalidates an offer only when it has been received by the offeree, which creates a window for an interesting possibility. Imagine that you have made an offer and chosen to revoke it by calling the offeree. In the meantime, but unknown to you, she has accepted the offer by putting an acceptance letter in the mail. Because, according to contract law principles, her acceptance was made before your revocation (see the principles below regarding the timing of when an acceptance is effective in various forms), you remain on the hook.

We make offers for different reasons to different people at different times, all the time. Some of these offers are made under conditions that have changed, and would no longer be of value to us for one reason or another. Nobody wants to be liable to performance on a contract created out of an offer that is no longer operative because the circumstances have changed. Fortunately, under certain conditions offers lapse of their own accord.

An offer that has lapsed need not be honoured, and is not enforceable. *The best way to determine the exact time when an offer lapses is by setting a deadline within the offer itself.* When the deadline passes, the offer is no longer valid and the offeror must renew the offer to the offeree for reconsideration. Alternatively, one may choose either to accept the offeree's late agreement to the offer (which amounts to a new offer, actually) or not to, at one's discretion, should the offeree respond after the initial offer has lapsed. The most important benefit of a lapsing contract to you, the offeror, is that unlike revocation of an offer, *the offer lapses and becomes worthless whether the offeree knows it or not*. That reduces exposure from an offeree's acceptance of a dated offer, or promises that may have become less favourable due to changed circumstances.

There are two circumstances that cause an offer to lapse even if an effective date has not been set within the offer. First, the offeree must respond within a *reasonable* time. That reasonable time is dictated by the context within which the offer is being made: essentially to be commensurate with the urgency of the offer. Second, an offer lapses if either the offeror or the offeree becomes insane or dies prior to acceptance; however, death is not always enough to lapse an offer. An insane person cannot be bound to a contract (lacks the *capacity* to contract), so there is no point in the offer standing; and, generally, a dead person cannot perform his part of any bargain, so offers by or to dead people are usually lapsed upon death. I have used the words "generally" and "usually" because some offers and bargains between parties do not depend on the act of the offeror and can be fulfilled after his death. In such special circumstances, some courts have deemed that death does not prevent acceptance until the offeree is notified.

In a later chapter we review the *option agreement*, which is an undertaking on the part of the offeror to keep an offer open without the possibility of revoking it or of otherwise preventing the offer from being fulfilled. The option agreement, a separate contract that usually has a cost and is always finite in duration, is the only way to guarantee an offer will remain open during a period while the offeree determines what it will do.

An example of an option occurs when one has negotiated the purchase of an asset of some sort that is being sought by others—a license to bottle Coca-Cola in a specific territory, for instance.[9] Although there is agreement on most of the big-picture items and you want the license, you are not sure about your ability to be successful in this particular market or to obtain all the financing. There are others equally interested in the license, and Coca-Cola is willing to deal with you but not willing to wait for you. To buy some time, it would be reasonable to have the Coca-Cola Company grant you an option giving you exclusive right to obtain the license under the basic terms negotiated, for a set period of time. An option is not free, but the price would be a fraction of the cost and liability to which one would be bound upon signing the license.

THE ACCEPTANCE

Once the offer is made, it is conditional and tentative until accepted by the offeree. An offer may be accepted in writing, orally, or by conduct that explicitly and exclusively indicates acceptance of that offer.

By this broad definition of acceptance, it might seem that almost anything would satisfy the legal requirements of a proper acceptance of an offer. But this is not entirely true, since the one underlying principle of acceptance, required in all but one instance, is that a proper acceptance must be *positive* in nature. That is, the actual acceptance of an offer, regardless of the form, must be an act of accepting rather than not not accepting.

To clarify the concept a little, consider it this way: an offer is made and floats around waiting for you to grab it; you have to reach out and take the offer. It will not bounce into and stick to you. One does not enter into a contract by default if the offer is not specifically accepted. As a general rule, one cannot be bound to a contract by remaining silent.[10]

Earlier, we noted that there is one exception to the rule of positive acceptance. Silence can be a valid form of acceptance if one or both of two conditions are met.

1. The offeror and offeree have agreed beforehand that silence will indicate acceptance of the offer.
2. The offeror and offeree have a history of using silence as a form of acceptance.

The most common instance of *negative acceptance* is mail-order book and record clubs, which fulfill both of the above conditions by the terms of their contracts and enrollment invitations to potential members. Thus, silence (not returning the book) is acceptance. Some cable television companies recently tried, to disastrous public relations effect, using negative acceptance for having their subscribers add new cable channels (and monthly costs) to their service. Ultimately, they were forced to back down by a very angry public.

What if you have received something by way of offer that you do not want to accept, and have no interest in returning because of the cost or hassle? By your silence, are you accepting the item if you do not return it? Actually, unless the offer has been made in fulfillment of the two conditions required of silent acceptance, you will not be accepting the item by not returning it. The caveat is that you must not use the product—even to inspect or test it. That is a positive action that could be construed as acceptance of the offer. Time-Life is a familiar name among many companies that operate in this manner. Order—or receive as a "no-obligation gift" for that matter—a single, specific videotape or book from the Time-Life series, and it is reasonably likely you will begin receiving videos or books that you did not order. Because (1) you presumably have not agreed to accept their offer of other wares by your silence and (2) you have no history with them that indicates silence as a form of acceptance on your part, as long as you let those videos and books pile up in a corner you are not liable for them. Do not open a single one, or you may end up buying all of them. *But* check any terms that come along with the "no obligation" sampler that address future mailings to you. You may be agreeing "negatively" to accept those books unless you notify the company that your silence in the future does not indicate acceptance or agreement.

The general rule is that proper acceptance must be positive, and must be communicated to the offeror. Usually this makes good sense in commercial situations. Sometimes, however, the offeree need not communicate acceptance to the offeror. If the offeror has made an offer, via a broadcast medium to an indefinite number of people who need only perform some act to fulfill their acceptance and part of the contract, that offeror has eliminated its right to require acceptance be communicated to it.[11]

Going back to the issue of acceptance, generally it must be communicated to the offeror. When does that happen? If we are sitting across the table from each other and I say to you, "You've got a deal," that is it. Acceptance has happened in a fixed place at an easily determined time; it does not require any further act of putting it in writing (unless—and this is spurious—the offeror demanded that the acceptance be made in written form to be valid). Similarly, if I put a letter accepting the offer into your hand, acceptance has been made right then and there. A formal, lawyerly contract with plenty of paragraphs, is just that: a formality.[12]

Unfortunately, business dealings are usually not quite so clear-cut, and the two parties are not at the same place—sometimes not even in the same time zone. And, since the time and place of acceptance is important for a variety of reasons, not the least of which is to possibly determine the legal jurisdiction of the contract, there are specific rules for determining the time and place of acceptance.

First, acceptance of an offer, when the parties are not in the same place, must be made in the form specified by the offeror. If written acceptance is demanded, acceptance must be in writing—generally by post, although speedier forms of transmission may be employed. If no specific form of acceptance is demanded by the offeror, the accepted rule is that the acceptance should be made in the same form as the offer. If the offer was made by post, acceptance by post would be reasonable. In all situations in which the form of acceptance has not been specified by the offeror, reasonableness is the watchword.

Generally, any stipulations placed by the offeror on the form and timing of acceptance are valid, and although an offeree may make an acceptance without complying with those stipulations, she will have no chance of making the contract binding unless the offeror takes some further action that indicates that the previously set stipulations on acceptance have been waived. So, if the offer is made with the demand that acceptance be made by way of yodelled verse over a megaphone, tune up your pipes, because although the demand is not necessarily reasonable it is not illegal. You may, however, want to reconsider with whom you are contracting.

The general rules regarding when and where acceptance is effective are:

1. *By post.* The offer is accepted when a properly stamped envelope containing acceptance is dropped in the mailbox; it is deemed to be made in the offeree's jurisdiction.
2. *By courier/messenger.* Acceptance is complete when the envelope is dropped in the courier's drop box or picked up by the messenger; it is deemed to be made in the offeree's jurisdiction.

3. *By facsimile.* Acceptance is complete when the transmitted acceptance arrives in the offeror's possession (which is effectively the same time the offeree is making the acceptance); it is deemed to have been received in the offeror's jurisdiction.
4. *By telephone.* Acceptance is complete when the transmitted acceptance is received by the offeror (and is actually the exact same time that the offeree is making the acceptance, give or take a nanosecond); it is deemed to have been made in the offeror's jurisdiction.

CONSIDERATION

Let's assume that you and some other person have swapped promises in the appropriate manner such that your proper offer has been properly accepted by the other person. You would think, on the basis of the preceding discussion, that there is a binding contract. That may be correct. But the effectiveness of the contract is dependent upon the nature of the consideration involved.

Consideration is a legal term that means "value." It is not to be confused with the common English definition of the word, the practice of which is more often than not absent in contractual matters. In the legal sense, consideration is essentially the price of the promise. For instance, say you agree to sell to a small-town newspaper a license to use your page layout software for $3,000.[13] Your promise is to deliver and install the program on the paper's computer; the value or consideration paid for that promise is the delivery of $3,000 to you. Alternatively, if you were to trade that software license for a "lifetime" subscription to the paper, your promise would remain the same but the consideration, or value, in exchange for the promise is now the lifetime subscription to the paper (which, on the basis of the shorter of the paper's life or yours, can presumably be reduced to dollars and cents if need be).

Without consideration as a fundamental element of an exchange of promises, there is no contract. What exists without consideration is essentially a *gift* of a promise. In legal terms, a "contract" with no consideration is a *gratuitous promise.* That is, a promise by one party that has not been offset by anything of value from the party receiving the benefit from that promise. Transactions arising from gratuitous promises are valid (and benevolent, in many cases), but because they are not contracts they are not enforceable at law. This is the distinguishing feature between a contract and a gifted promise.

Consider the following example. I say to you: "When I buy a new notebook computer, you can have this older one." Though generous, this offer is not strictly a gift, because I have not given the computer to you, nor is it a contract, because you have not provided consideration for the computer. It is, therefore, a gratuitous promise. If I should change my mind, forget my promise, or use my computer as a trade-in on its replacement, the bottom line is you are out of luck. Because there is no contract, you have no way of enforcing my promise.

Because consideration is a requirement of a contract, and situations arise when there simply is nothing of tangible value to exchange for the promises (such as promised gifts and agreements relating to intangibles such as confidentiality, which are dealt with in some detail in Chapter 11), a lawyer might change my gratuitous promise by *writing* it down in one of the following ways.

- *Option A.* The promise will be turned into a conditional sale by the following addition: "When I buy a new computer, you can have this notebook computer *for one dollar.*" We have now added consideration to the promise(s), rendering this a valid contract and enforceable in the future.
- *Option B.* The lawyer will add text of the following sort to the agreement: "*In consideration of the mutual covenants contained herein and other good and valuable consideration, the receipt and sufficiency of which is hereby acknowledged by each of the parties hereto,* Grayson will deliver to YOU . . ." Again, in this scenario, consideration ("good and valuable," no less) is provided, creating a fully enforceable contract.

This should prompt two questions:

1. Why is one dollar suitable consideration?
2. What makes consideration "good and valuable"?

Bear in mind that the courts attempt not to interpret or intervene in assessing the "fairness" of commercial and contractual transactions. What this means is that the law has no interest in what kind of bargainer you are or what kind of bargain you have struck. If you are willing to sell your business for one dollar, so be it. Because of the nature of contract law as it has developed over the centuries, the law is concerned primarily that there be some kind of consideration involved. Nobody expects you to pull out a dollar and give it to the other person, nor will anybody question the "good and valuable" consideration you and the other person have *mutually acknowledged*. The acknowledgement that there has been consideration is sufficient to satisfy the law and turn a gratuitous promise into a binding contract.

> The requirement of "good and valuable" consideration is the agreement of both parties to it and the imagination of a clever lawyer many years ago. The law requires consideration in a contract but, on many occasions, no "valuable" consideration is exchanged (because the transaction is really a gift, or the contract is the result of a noneconomic promise—i.e., to retain information in confidence). So the clever solicitor created the fiction of nonexistent "good and valuable consideration" to which both parties agree and acknowledge "receipt and sufficiency." (The observant reader will begin to see how law is like Russian Marushka dolls: every time one is opened, another is found inside, which is reason enough to leave the real legal work to the lawyers.)

It would be prudent to add that if an agreement, within which the bargain is obviously and almost absurdly unbalanced, is disputed and brought before the court, the court will seek corresponding evidence of fraud or duress suffered by the disputing party. Such findings may ultimately render the contract void at the disputing party's discretion. Under legitimate circumstances, however, adequacy of consideration is immaterial to the law.

Contracts, it should be understood, are present- and future-tense concepts and documents. That is, a contract is based on promises, which by their nature are as yet not concluded. The import of this information bears directly on the issue of consideration. Specifically, value that has already passed hands (an act that is concluded, such as your having given me a fax machine when I started my business, out of gratitude for which I have now promised you my laptop computer sometime in the future) is not valid consideration for a new contract. The act completed, which was a gift, is called *past consideration*. A promise made by the recipient of a past consideration is not binding because *past consideration is insufficient consideration for a new promise*.[14]

Let's return to the original example of a gratuitous promise I made to you at the start of this section. Basically, I have made a promise to give you my laptop computer when I have bought a new one. It is, for lack of consideration—whether I feel obliged because you set me up with a fax machine a few years ago, or not—not an enforceable contract. I have merely promised a gift, and as we know, if I change my mind or cannot complete my intention, you have no recourse. On the surface, this is an unfortunate situation, but one we encounter every other day. Not all promises can be kept despite the best of intentions.

Let's expand the example a little further. What if I had also told you that I was actively looking for a replacement computer and would make my purchase within the next month or so. On the basis of that information, and my assurance that I would give you my Apple PowerBook Duo 2300c you went out and found and purchased the docking station and a monitor so that when you got the PowerBook you could use the computer as a desktop station as well. That kind of forethought and action is reasonable and common. You were relying on a promise, which you believed in good faith would be kept, to enter into other contracts that put you to some expense—expense, we might add, that you would not have incurred if you had not relied specifically on my promise.

Strictly speaking, as mentioned above, we have no contract and if I do not come through with my gratuitous promise, too bad. Because such situations have occurred and have been disputed in the past, the courts of equity have entered the fray and created a body of common law that deals with the issue of your injury based on the reliance you placed on my promise. The principle is known as *equitable estoppel*, which grew out of *estoppel* based on fact, and it allows the court to prevent a promisor (me) from denying the binding effect of my gratuitous promise when I have led you to rely, and your subsequent reliance on that promise has caused you injury. By way of background, estoppel based on fact, the progenitor of the equitable estoppel, prevents me from denying a statement of fact (that is, what I *believed* to be fact) regardless of whether I was ultimately right or wrong.

The English common-law principle of *equitable estoppel* is matched in many jurisdictions of the United States with a similar principle that Americans call *injurious reliance*. For the average nonlawyer, this title and effect of this principle is easier to decipher. Its effect is similar.

The *burden to prove* that one has been injured by reliance on a gratuitous promise, along with many other factors in law, serves to complicate the issue beyond the scope of what we are doing here. So, to repeat, if there is a circumstance in which you believe *equitable estoppel* should be considered, take all the facts to a lawyer for a proper analysis and evaluation of your position and options.

INTENT

The last of the four principal features required of a set of promises to be a valid and enforceable contract is the matter of intent. The question it asks is: "Did all parties to the bargain make their promises with the explicit intent of making it a binding contract?" In regard to commercial arrangements, the courts interpret and the law generally answers yes, which is a fair assumption since it would be pointless to make business deals with no intent for them to create legally binding relationships.

For the most part, the law will assume intent by all parties to leave the integrity of commercial affairs where it should rest—in business. That said, there might be one reasonable defense for a claim that intent to form a legal contract did not exist: the possible trifling or spurious nature of the contractual matter in question. If, for example, you promised to show up at a fundraising banquet and speak "for a few minutes" at an invitee's request, for which a donation would be made in your name to a charitable organization, there would appear to be a contract because of the offer, acceptance, and consideration. Let's add to the context by further assuming that the invitee did not make much of the banquet and speaking engagement; it seemed to you to be a "come if you can" sort of invitation. Certainly you were unaware you were a sales attraction for the promoter, who sold tickets at least in part because you would be attending. (Let us assume that you are not Tom Peters, Bill Gates, or Henry Kissinger.) If you were to not show up, there is a good possibility the promoter would suffer damages in the form of lost donations from disgruntled ticket purchasers. Thus, there may be cause (from the invitee, not the charity, which is not a party to the contract—an issue addressed in the next chapter) for you to be sued for breach. In this instance, you may have a justifiable defense that on the basis of your knowledge of the arrangement, you did not intend to form a legally binding contract from your promise. Therefore, there was no contract. It may or may not work, because the court will decide according to what it feels your intent to have been, but this is the type of unspecific situation where intent would be of the greatest import.

In making its decision about a disputed situation such as this, the court typically employs the notorious "reasonable man" test. That is, in this case, would a reasonable man, privy to all the information presented by both sides, see that there was intent to make a contract?[15] If, looking at the situation with that kind of detachment, the court finds that it is reasonable to assume you intended to bind yourself to a legal agreement, the contract stands and you are liable for damages.

The Four Pillars of a Contract

What we looked at in this chapter are the five requirements of a contract from the perspective of the agreement being legal and binding. While extremely important to anybody entering contractual relations, these criteria do not really address the practical details of most commercial arrangements. The four cornerstones of any contract, which always have to be negotiated and should be stated explicitly in an agreement are *price*, *quantity*, *payment*, and *delivery*. While other factors may impose themselves on the commercial agreement, you should make certain that these four are fully addressed.

• *Price* — This must be in any legal contract in some form because it is the *consideration*. But, price has many looks, and it's imperative that both sides understand the same way exactly what has been bargained. Is the pricing per unit, and if so what is the volume (see below)? is it a total? does it include taxes or discounts? in what currency is it denominated? Nail it down so there is no confusion.

- *Requirement and Quantity* — The volume of product or service to be provided must also be addressed as it can affect the total commitment and its value. What is the total volume being committed? What exactly are the services to be provided? over what period? Does volume affect the pricing? (i.e., are there price breaks?) Is there a minimum? a maximum? What about time overages?

- *Payment* — As we all eventually become aware sooner or later, the nature and timing of payment can make any deal a little better or a little worse. It may even be a trade-off for a concession. When is payment due? in what form (trade credit, cash, certified cheque, letter of credit)? in what currency, and is there a conversion factor involved? What about discounts for early payment? interest on late payment? What can be done if the payment terms are not met?

- *Delivery* — Delivery can often be a trigger for other events, not the least of which is payment. Nailing down the delivery can avoid timing problems and settle some issues before they arise. Consider questions such as: Is there a deadline for delivery? How should delivery be effected (i.e., by what mode of transport)? Who pays for the delivery? Can it be partial or must the entire quantity arrive together? Where is it to be delivered?

Most of these questions and details are or should be part of the negotiation or your commercial transaction. But, as with everything else, it is well worth ensuring that they are addressed specifically in the agreement made whether it is in the form of a written contract or an oral agreement.

Chapter 2
More Contract Basics

Legality, Privity (Novation, Vicarious Performance, Assignments, Mistake),
Undesired Contractual Obligations (Misrepresentation, Undue Influence, Duress),
Ending the Contract (Frustration, Agreement by the Parties, Court-Ordered Termination, Breach)

In Chapter 1 we examined the principal requirements for the formation of a legally binding contract: *offer, acceptance, consideration,* and *intent.* In addition, we reviewed the legality of contracts in the sense of the contracting parties having the legal *capacity* to bind themselves to a contract. From that we should have a fair understanding of what constitutes an enforceable co[...] ...t from a merely gra[...] ...ise.

The law of contracts is co[...] ...les, restrictions, and requirements as one gets deeper into a con[...] ...the common-law development of contracts and all but avoid s[...] ..., nevertheless, very important. But this is the business and bai[...] ...need to know a little bit about the parameters of the law, but a[...] ...cal for us to become expert. Thus I would again suggest that y[...] ...n of where you stand vis à vis any contractual matter.

That notice made, in th[...] ...ty of a contract, privity of contract, assignability of rights, mi[...] ...end—naturally or otherwise. All of these issues deal with exis[...] ...nt effect on any agreement. That is to say, the fundamental requ[...] ...l factors may affect the legality, status, or life of the agreement.

LEGAL CONT[...]

We examined, in the las[...] ...cts. This is different from the *legality of the contract.* In the for[...] ...tracts whereby enforcement is ensured by law. In the latter, the issue is whether the [...] number of instances where and how the legality of a contract is questionable, but for immediate illustrative purpose[...] consider the following example. You and I make an oral bargain with serious intent that for $25,000 you will import and deliver to me a fixed amount of cocaine on a day we agree on at a place we have previously agreed to meet. Unquestionably, there is a contract that has fulfilled all the requirements of offer, acceptance, consideration, and intent (and since we are both Canadian businesspeople of the age of majority and of sound mind, we have the capacity to contract). There is only the small matter of the transaction itself being illegal; thus the contract is illegal and hardly enforceable by law.[1]

This blunt example is undoubtedly not a surprise to anyone. The underlying general rule regarding the legality of a contract is that a legal contract must (1) be made within the confines of the statutory laws of the jurisdiction(s), and (2) not "offend the public good," which simply means that the object of the contract must not oppose some public policy or another. For instance, a contract to import goods from a South African business during the apartheid-related embargo of that nation would likely have been deemed illegal had the Government of Canada enacted a law making it a criminal offence to do such business—such as the United States has done in regard to Cuba.

There are various specific instances in which contracts are considered illegal in Canada and in other common-law countries. These vary by jurisdiction, and are subject to the pressure of societal change. If you have any doubt about the legality of a contract, it would be best to ask a lawyer whether it would be deemed illegal before you proceed. One common situation in which contracts tend to be illegal is when an agreement is struck to hide, hedge, protect, or eliminate assets by moving them among entities. Transferring assets from one entity (company, person, trust, etc.) to another within the context of and suspiciously close to a bankruptcy may cause investigation that warrants a court to deem the transfer a *fraudulent conveyance* (deceitful transfer) and strike the contract (not to mention leaving one open to criminal charges). Using one's imagination and considering circumstances such as those surrounding the Bre-X's principals' various transactions as that roller-coaster neared its crash, it should not be too difficult to think of examples of legally shady contracts.

It's worth remembering that (1) the law presumes all contracts to be legal until evidence is provided to the contrary and (2) a contract is found to be illegal only if a dispute among the parties brings it into contact with the legal system. While you may have a reason for creating an illegal contract, and neither you nor the other party to the agreement has reason to believe your deal will not work, there is substantial risk in such agreements. My only advice is to recognize that fact and conduct yourself accordingly, because a contract dispute could end up being the least of your worries.

Privity of Contract

Privacy among and of the contracting parties is the interpretation of this principle of contract law. *A contract benefits and binds only the parties to the contract.* In other words, only the parties who have specifically contracted with one another can enforce terms of a contract, or have those terms enforced upon them. This seems to be obvious and implicit, but what it implies is that certain actions and activities are not as clear-cut as they may seem.

Here's an example. I have a friend whose company cleans leather garments. It is subcontracted by several drycleaners to clean leather goods brought in by the drycleaners' customers. A lady brought her coat to a drycleaner for cleaning, and the drycleaner forwarded the garment to my friend's cleaning company. The drycleaner was and had been very late in paying my friend's company for ongoing service to the extent that this drycleaner was warned several times that his credit would be cut off and merchandise would not be returned without prompt payment. It ultimately came to that action and my friend's company cancelled the drycleaner's credit, refusing to return merchandise until satisfactory payment arrangements had been made. Unfortunately for the lady with the coat, mentioned above, her garment was one of those being held hostage. What could she do?

Her contract was not with my friend's leather cleaning company, but with the drycleaner. As a result, she had no claim against the leather cleaning company and could get no satisfaction until the drycleaner brought his account in order (because the drycleaner's contract with the leather-cleaning company provided for this type of remedial measure). In contract law, the lady could have sued only the drycleaner for satisfaction. The drycleaner, in turn, would have to make payment arrangements or litigate under its contract. This is unfortunate for her, but such is the privity of contracts.[2]

There are instances in which an injured party (the lady in the example above) is truly injured and has no recourse against the party directly causing that injury. A good example would be when a manufacturer's product is purchased through a retailer and subsequently harms the purchaser. The contract is between the retailer and the purchaser, and the injured purchaser—or worse yet, anybody else who has relied on the purchaser's own warranty of the item—has no recourse against the manufacturer *under contract law*.[3]

There are some exceptions to the general rule of contract privity. Insurance contracts, land sales and other such transactions, and some special cases in which the law sees an obligation between parties that are not strictly contractually bound are usually exempt from the privity rule. For example, while the contract of insurance is between the insurer and the insured, the beneficiary of a life policy is considered a gratuitously "interested party" and may enforce a claim under the contract. Also, an insurer may "step into the shoes of the insured" and sue for damages in which it has paid out a claim to the insured and believes that an action for damages resulting from a contractual breach between the insured and the other party to the contract are warranted.

Novation

This legal word means that the contract has been struck anew, or, in other words, "by agreement we replaced the contract we had with a contract we want." Novation happens in one of two ways:

1. The existing parties to a contract change a major term of the contract, in essence striking the old contract and replacing it with a new one that contains the replacement term. This normally happens quite informally, but the fact is that a new contract is created in the eyes of the law.
2. A new party to the contract replaces one of the existing parties, so that a new contract with the same terms and conditions as the existing contract is written among new parties to the contract.

Vicarious Performance

Performance done vicariously, or "through someone else," is most common when a business contracts with another to perform some task or other. Subcontracting is a form of vicarious performance. For instance, when a lawyer or accountant gets a new client, in a large organization there is a very small likelihood of that professional doing all the day-to-day work on the client's account. (That is what associates and articling students are for.) Thus, the client's work will be done *vicariously*. The contracted professional would presumably ensure that the work is correct and of suitable quality before releasing it to the client. Vicarious performance of the promise made in the contract does not absolve the contracting professional from personal liability for negligence in performance of its contractual duties. The same applies to situations in which a company has so much work it must farm out its jobs to subcontractors.

The only situation in which vicarious performance is not permissible is where the contract is made for personal performance. That is, if your deal with the professional in the above example called *specifically* for that person's activity, she would have to perform. Attempted vicarious performance of an employment agreement likely would not get very far with your employer (even if you think that some parts of your job could be done by a clever 12-year-old).

Assignments

An assignment of contractual rights is a mutually agreed-upon transfer of the benefits and obligations of one contracting party to a third party. Assignments are quite common and there is nothing particularly special about them. Receivables, among other contractual rights including share certificates and so forth, are often assigned in the course of doing business. Lenders regularly require conditional assignments of patents, trademarks, and other valuable intangibles as part of loan agreements.[4] Sticking to the fundamentals of assignments, what does the business person really need to know?

1. As an assignor and an original party to a contract transferring your rights to a third party, you should be aware that unless you have transferred all your rights, you may remain liable to the other party if the new "third party" to the agreement does not fulfill all its obligations.
2. As the assignee (i.e., the "third party"), you should know that you are receiving the assignee's part of the contract "as is" with no better "equities" than the original party to the contract possessed.
3. As the other original party to the contract, you should be aware that you must be advised of the change, especially if you have no control over the assignment. That is, when an assignment is made by the other party to your deal, especially if it is a total *statutory assignment*,[5] you have an old relationship with someone new. That new party may be "better" than the old one; or you may now have a source of irritation, trouble, and despair. Your contractual rights, in any event, remain unaltered.

Some contracts require that mutual consent be obtained before an assignment can be made. Others prohibit assignment, using words such as "This agreement may not be assigned." In these cases, you have to tread carefully when considering and effecting an assignment of rights. In other cases, providing notice of an assignment is required, but consent from the other party is not. For example, consider the internet service provider (ISP) with a number of contractual subscriptions. Its business assets are bought by a competitor. All the subscribers' contracts are assigned to the new owner. The subscribers are notified that their contract is now in the hands of a new owner and will be honoured until it expires. At that time, the subscriber can continue with the new ISP or switch. The subscriber's consent was not required.

Mistake

As you are probably aware from experience, once you have a binding contract, "Oops" is not suitable cause for extricating yourself from it. Generally, a bad bargain is something we have to live with and learn from unless the other party is willing to renegotiate. However, if one has made a genuine "legal" mistake, the meaning of which is covered below, in the creation of a contractual relationship, there may be a valid opportunity to get out of the agreement. What is considered a *mistake* in the legal sense, however, is somewhat more restrictive than "Oops."

A *mistake* in contract law generally occurs when there has been a misinterpretation of either the language of the contract ("This is not what I agreed to"), or an error in the underlying assumptions or information upon which the contractual relationship is based ("But I was led to believe in all our discussions that the property was on Industrial *Road*, not Industrial *Lane*. It's an easy error to make.") We will consider these two potential causes for mistake individually.

When there is a problem in the understanding of the language of an agreement, there are only two possible causes, both of which can be valid reasons to seek release. First, the actual words can be confusing without either party being sneaky. Have you ever agreed to something where your ongoing act would be made *biweekly*? Say, for instance, you have an agreement to update the financial accounts of a client biweekly for a sum of money per month. You may have undertaken the relationship because the money was good for doing the books every two weeks. Your client, on the other hand, may have thought he made an excellent bargain for having his accounts done twice a week. This is a mistake, since you both are right but have different interpretations of a term of the agreement. Even *The New Merriam-Webster Dictionary* carries both definitions for the word "biweekly."[6]

The other type of language mistake is what can be called a transcription error that typifies the saying "something got lost in the translation." Perhaps what had been agreed upon in negotiations was different when it hit the page, or a decimal place was different ("The minimum volume is *what*?"). This also is a mistake. It is more difficult to obtain *rectification* for this type of mistake, especially in written contracts, since one is assumed to have thoroughly read and checked the document before signing. There are instances, however, in which an error occurs in the text of a contract between drafts that nobody looks at because it was correct before. In these cases, there may be greater likelihood of rectifying the error by providing supporting documents that prove it truly was a reasonable oversight.[7]

Mistakes in assumptions or the knowledge foundation for a contract are a different story. They generally occur less frequently, and must be part of a bilateral understanding or discussion. That is to say, when a contract negotiation is based upon certain understandings that are in fact not operative when the contract is actually made, that is a mistake and the law will attempt to correct the situation. An example might be my agreeing to purchase your beautiful office building on the banks of the Red River just south of Winnipeg. After weeks of consideration and discussion, finally, while our families are vacationing together in Europe during late April 1997, I agree to buy your property at what is a fair price. We defer the transfer until our return home. Unknown to either of us, while we were away your/my building became a submarine in The Flood of the Century. Our contract could be voided as a mistake because the underlying premise and assumption about the condition of the property would no longer be valid.

UNDESIRED CONTRACTUAL OBLIGATIONS

There are times when a contract is formed but one of the parties is not happy with it, and desires to be released from the obligations of the agreement. In circumstances such as fraud or *misrepresentation* by one party, or when a contract has been coerced by *undue influence*, or perhaps when one party signed an agreement under *duress* (which is slightly different than at the hands of undue influence), a contract may be either void or voidable. For the most part, what is at issue here is the validity of the *intent* to form a contract. We will consider these three reasons for seeking to relieve oneself of undesired contractual obligations.

We have again encountered the terms "void" and "voidable" in reference to a contract. They are not the same—voidable is not merely a more elegant variation. The differences are significant.

To say a contract is void (*void ab initio*—elegant Latin variation) is actually an acceptable oxymoron because a voided contract is deemed to have never existed in the first place. See what I mean? If it never existed, it could hardly be voided. Suffice it to say that once explained most everyone accepts the literary inaccuracy.

The effect of a contract being voided is usually fair: both parties "Return to Go." If I am buying a building and have given you a deposit or down payment, following which the contract is found to be void, you give me back my money and take back (the promise to provide) the title. We lose only what it cost to negotiate and are otherwise left in our original positions.

A voidable contract, on the other hand, is a recognized, properly formed contract that the court has determined *may* be voided (i.e., not necessarily voided but possible to void, just as an apple might not be eaten but is edible)—often at one of the parties' choosing. In finding a contract voidable, the court will attempt to restore the parties to their original positions.

Of course, there may be complications such as a secondary sale of transferred property. Circumstance dictates the remedy to some extent, although there is a general rule regarding the equitability of the reversal of a contract on all parties. Smyth et al. summarize the matter of void vs. voidable, particularly as regards third parties, suitably for our purpose: "[W]here a contract concerns only the two original parties, it may not matter whether the court declares it void or merely voidable. In either event, the court may order the return of property that has passed between parties. But if the property has passed to an innocent purchaser, the original owner may recover it only if the original contract is declared void."[8]

Misrepresentation

The line between innocent mistake and misrepresentation is a fine one. Under the law of torts, a party that purposely misrepresents to secure a contract with an innocent party could (and should) be guilty of fraud. In contract, the consequence is often less dire.

One may misrepresent a circumstance by commission, omission, or error of a matter of *fact*. Generally speaking, opinions are not assertions of fact and, if genuine, are not a factor in matters of contractual misrepresentation.[9] In the first two situations the misrepresenter asserts a falsehood that changes how the other party might understand the facts, thereby inciting agreement to the contract, or he neglects to provide substantial information that might have a deterring effect on the other's decision to enter into the contract. In *erring*, the misrepresenter ignorantly asserts as fact something that may not be so. In this case the erring party is bound to reveal the truth once it is known to her, or she may be correctly found guilty of misrepresentation. Remember at all times that being an idiot in business dealings does not give you special treatment; you must have *reasonably* been unable to discern that you were being subject to misrepresentation. (The old saw of buying a bridge from an unknown vendor comes to mind.)

Regardless of what other punishment may be given to a defrauder, an innocent party to a contract has a few remedies. First, the contract may be set aside and the law will try to put you, the innocent, back where you were before the contract was struck. If the contract has caused you expense, you may be entitled to some compensation. But, by and large, that is the total recourse available to the innocent. Additionally, the court's assessment of how to handle a misrepresentation will be dependent on how *material* (i.e., how important, significant, and substantial) the misrepresentation was to the agreement.

One is always well advised to remember that contracts are made with the express presumption of good faith on the part of all parties involved. This presumption may or may not accurately reflect common practice, but the value of making and relying on contracts as a commercial device would be undermined if we could not reasonably expect good faith from everyone involved. As this relates to the issue of misrepresentation in which one party is privy to "special knowledge" that could have an effect on the other party's decision to join in a contract; it is the knowledgeable party's duty to inform the other. An excellent example of this is in applying for and obtaining a loan from a lending institution. A person would be culpable for misrepresentation if he knew his business would soon be in a debilitating cash flow position because of a large refund to a customer or the impending loss of a material contract, and did not share that information with the would-be lender.

Undue Influence

For argument's sake, let's say we grew up together. And since I was a nice enough boy (and humble), I always had an excellent relationship with your parents. In fact, once you moved and lost touch with them over your out-of-faith marriage, they became quite reliant on me. Recently, while you were struggling as an entrepreneur on the other side of the country, your father, the family scion, died, leaving to your mother his majority interest in the large business he had founded many years before. In addition to being devastated, your mother also happens to be a charmingly naive woman with no idea of the wealth left to her. Before the funeral I went to see her. By the time I left, her signature was on an agreement to sell me her interest in the company for a fraction of its value. (Did I mention that I had become quite ruthless?) Despite your mother's initial satisfaction with the deal, upon your reconciling with her and informing her of what happened—if she acts fast enough—there may be cause to have the contract examined and deemed voidable at her discretion because of my *undue influence* over her.

Such is the nature of undue influence. It generally occurs in cases wherein one party has a special position of influence relative to the other. Additionally one party may have undue influence over another if the latter is in a circumstance in which he cannot make a reasonable choice. The typical victim's post mortem on this kind of transaction is "I don't like the deal, but I had no choice." Nevertheless, in all cases, it is up to the victim to prove with evidence that he or she had succumbed to the pressures of undue influence, because the law's first presumption is validity of the contract.

Smart businesses take precautions to ensure the other party does not have the opening to claim undue influence (or misrepresentation, or lack of intent, or mistake, etc.) by insisting that the other party seek independent legal counsel or acknowledge ignoring that recommendation or waiving counsel and renouncing all right to dispute the contract on that basis. Because of the nature of a transaction and the circumstances within which it is happening, one might insist within the contract itself that independent legal advice be sought and verified.

Duress

Duress is undue influence in the extreme—just ever-so-slightly shy of extortion.[10] If one party to the contract can make a case that the other party (or someone related to that other party) implied or threatened the possibility that the victimized party, or some person or entity related to it, would physically, mentally, or financially suffer if the contract were not made, there is a case for duress. The remedy, if duress is proven in court, is to make the contract voidable at the victim's discretion.

ENDING THE CONTRACT

As with all other good things, contracts must come to an end. The initial intent when a contract is formed is for it to be completed and *discharged* by performance. That is, each party did what it was supposed to do, so the contract's purpose is complete and its life over.[11] Hopefully that is what will happen. But the best-laid plans, as Robbie Burns put it, "Gang aft a-gley" and some contracts have a different demise. The most common ways contracts come to an end, apart from performance, are:

- They are *frustrated.*
- They are *terminated* by agreement among the parties.
- They are *deemed void* or *voidable* by a court.

Frustration

Like people, contracts can become frustrated and the law says "Ah, to hell with it. Let's call the whole thing off." The law does tend to be a little bit less casual about the issue. If, after a contract is struck between us, a force beyond the control of either of us alters the circumstances of the contract so that performance by one or both of us is materially different from what was intended or contemplated when the bargain was struck (to the point of its being meaningless), the contract may be considered frustrated. Neither party is culpable for or liable toward the other for nonperformance; unfortunately, expenses incurred are the responsibility of the party that incurred them.

Frustration is somewhat similar to *mistake* except that a mistake is the result of a misunderstanding of fact that existed before the contract was formed, whereas a contract is frustrated by an event that occurs *after* the contract exists. Parties to a contract have a responsibility to prevent frustration from terminating a contract. First, the law generally ignores a party that *induces* frustration in a contract. Second, to frustrate a contract the performance of material terms must be radically different or impossible. If performance is merely harder, or more costly, the contract is not frustrated. For example, you enter into a contract to supply maple syrup from your orchard to buyers during the 1998 season. Nature, however, prevents your operation from generating the syrup in any kind of volume by warming up and then putting a three-inch layer of ice on your trees. There is absolutely nothing you can do about this situation, and it is not merely harder, it is impossible for you to comply with your contractual obligations. Thus, the contract is frustrated.[12]

Agreement by the Parties to Terminate

At any given time during the life of a contract the parties to it can agree among themselves to terminate their contractual obligations. An agreement to terminate a contract can arise for any number of reasons, not the least of which is that the parties no longer wish to continue with their relationship despite their continuing performance. Regardless of the reason, all parties must agree to *waive* the contract's terms and obligations. This waiver is itself a contract, and so there must be consideration. If none of the parties have fulfilled their obligations under the agreement, the waiver contract is effectively the reversal, and each side's agreement *not* to perform or demand performance is adequate consideration. On the other hand, if one of the parties has performed all or part of his obligations, his agreement to waive the contract may require other consideration. Some form of suitable compensation would most likely be required to obtain the other party's waiver of the contract terms.

> A good rule to follow is to create a formal mutual waiver *and release* from rights and duties for and between both you and the other party when agreeing to terminate a contract early.

Many contracts are drawn up to provide for early termination. Usually contracts that have anticipated lengthy durations or automatic rollovers, and employment agreements, provide an escape hatch that allows either party to terminate the contract under some specific conditions including a notice period and possibly some type of compensation to the other party for early termination.

Remember also that a contract can be terminated by agreement because it is being replaced with another contract. This concept—novation—was dealt with earlier in this chapter, under "Privity of Contract." Should some part of an existing contract need to be changed, the entire contract is effectively voided by replacement with a new, correct contract.

Court-Ordered Termination: Breach of Contract

A court may order a contract terminated if an action on the contract is brought before it. Notwithstanding the various reasons listed earlier for why contracts may be brought before the court, the most common reason for a contract to see the inside of a courtroom is because one party brings action against another for *breaching* a term or terms of the contract. In the most basic sense, breach is about failure to deliver on a contractual promise.

The most common contract breaches occur when the breaching party:

- Performs its obligations in a way unacceptable to the other party, or does not meet the obligation it had originally promised (i.e., it provides substandard performance),
- Acts in a way that would inhibit or prohibit proper performance of its obligations, in effect self-frustrating the agreement, or
- Directly indicates that it will not perform, expressly repudiating that term of the contract.

While technically any noncompliance with the terms and conditions of a contract by one or either of the parties is a breach of that contract, not all breaches are equal. In order for a breach of contract to give rise to a justifiable legal action, the breach must be a major one and the term being breached must be essential to the agreement or specifically cause harm to the other party. When a printer, for example, is to provide a set number of annual reports to fill a mutual fund's printing order, and instead of delivering 100,000 pieces delivers only 98,750, that would be considered a relatively minor breach of a key term. But since it is unlikely to have caused the mutual fund company serious damage, action on this breach would probably be considered spurious and likely not get very far.

In the first form of breach we noted above, one party fails to live up to its part of a bargain, either by complete nonperformance or by inadequate performance. In the case of nonperformance, the issue is fairly cut-and-dried. There was a term and Party A did not fulfill that term. Party A is in breach of contract. Where performance has been made, but is inadequate, the issue gets a little more cloudy. The breaching party may have made a genuine effort to fulfill its obligations but did not perform as required. It may have put in a performance that was merely the least it felt it needed to do in order to be in technical compliance with its obligations, but well outside the spirit of the bargain. It may have performed in a way substantially less than what was expected by the promisee, for a variety of reasons and in a variety of ways.

In contract law, there is a rule of thumb known as the *doctrine of substantial performance*. It states that a party to a contract can enforce the contract's terms once that party has provided a substantial performance of its obligations—complete and fully as promised, or not. In the printing example above, if the printer had delivered only 75,000 or 80,000 reports, it would have made a substantial performance of its obligations and would be entitled to enforce the obligations of the promisee (to pay), although the payment would be subject to a deduction of some amount to compensate the mutual fund company for the faulty performance of the printer (and quite possibly subject to a legal action seeking damages if there were cause). Substantial performance is designed to ensure that contracts are enforced (with deductions and other compensation to the aggrieved party, as necessary) and not brought before the courts for spurious reasons.

The partial payment noted above for part of the work is an expression of the principle of *quantum meruit*, literally meaning what the quantity merits. That is, the law believes that work done or product provided, even if it is not full and complete, is worth something, generally proportional to the full value as struck in the original bargain. In the case of services, particularly those that are provided on an hourly or "piecework" basis, the calculation of the value provided is fairly easy to make accurately.

In the event that the party with whom you have contracted gives no indication that it will not perform, but takes or neglects some action that renders its ultimate performance impossible, there is a good case for breach of contract. Assume that you contract with me for some fairly extensive consulting services, the deadline for which is the end of April. Without giving you any warning, on April 20, I go on a 10-day vacation leaving a substantial amount of the job undone. Obviously, unless I am a magician (or have a powerful, fully-outfitted notebook computer on vacation with me), there is a reasonable likelihood that I will not fulfill my obligation under the contract because I have (ostensibly) rendered full performance impossible.

Although I could, in this example, fulfill my part of the bargain to greater or lesser degrees, given the circumstances indicated above, you would have valid cause to consider the contract discharged on April 21 due to an *anticipatory breach* of contract. That is, you have cause to anticipate that I will not fulfill my obligations at the appropriate time. You would be permitted this position because, in general, parties to a contract are entitled to a continual expectation of performance from the time the contract is made until it is fulfilled by performance. In other words, if an action of one party causes the other party to *validly* not expect performance at any time, that latter party has reasonable cause to anticipate that the contract will be breached, and thereby consider the contract discharged (implying that it need not fulfill its own obligations).

The basic concepts of anticipatory breach and continual expectation are fairly straightforward common sense, but their application can be tricky. Thus, it may be best to be somewhat circumspect about whether you have a valid reason not to expect fulfillment by the other party and consult your lawyer before taking any kind of action. Caution is the watchword. If, in this case, you are too hasty and decide not to fulfill your part of the bargain, and I ultimately do, you yourself could be open to a breach of contract action from me.

The last common way in which a contract is breached is by *express repudiation* of a term or terms of the agreement by one of the parties. If the party with which you have contracted advises you in some way that it will not perform some or all of its part of the contract, it has repudiated the agreement. You may then rightfully and immediately consider the contract terminated and take whatever action is required.

Often, the party on the receiving end of a significant breach of contract will take the appropriate action such as contract-demanded arbitration or mediation, or will litigate, seeking damages or rectification of some sort. Earlier, I mentioned that in the event of an anticipatory breach of contract you could take whatever actions you deem necessary. This means you can take legal action. It also means you are free to contract with someone else to perform the obligations previously contracted with the breaching party. You could do both. In the event that you choose to litigate the breach, a variety of remedies may be sought and awarded.

Common Remedies for Breach of Contract: Damages

The foremost remedy for breach of contract is *damages*. Generally, when business people talk about broken contracts and subsequent actions, suing for money is the usual topic of discussion. Damages are sought and may be awarded by the court to compensate the victim of the breach for the direct and indirect economic costs and losses it incurred because the contract was breached by the other party. A court's primary objective is to put the plaintiff (the aggrieved party) and the defendant in the financial position they would have been in *had the contract been completed*. Despite the courts having the power to award punitive damages in certain circumstances, as a penalty for undesirable behaviour, **damages are generally not punitive**. This is why one often sees phrases like "may retain the deposit as liquidated damages and *not as penalty*" [emphasis mine] in standard forms of contract such as real estate purchase offers.

Despite the general rule that the victimized party may be offered relief by way of a damages award, one should be aware that merely being at the receiving end of a breach of contract does not end one's responsibility. The victim party is obliged to *mitigate the damage* caused to it because of the breach. For instance, assume the printer from our much earlier example established that it could not or would not deliver the order of 100,000 annual reports to the mutual fund company, and advised the customer a week before the regulatory deadline for distributing the reports. Missing the deadline would cost the fund company a hefty fine that increased with each passing day beyond the deadline. The mutual fund company would be obliged to mitigate its damages by finding another printer to do the job and pay whatever rush charges might be necessary to prevent or limit the fine (and sanction). In claiming damages against the printer, a justifiable claim would be the costs over and above those that would have been incurred by the fund company had the original printer not breached the agreement (rush charges, fine incurred, etc.). The fund company might not receive all the damages it claimed if it took no action to mitigate the breach and simply went about sourcing a new printer and putting the job into work under average conditions, letting the fine build (because its intent was to claim all those costs as damages). Furthermore, only damages that would "naturally flow from the breach" may be recovered. In this example, had the fund company decided to change a part of the report since it had to reprint anyway, it would have a tough time proving the expenses to change (and possibly part of the fine levied upon it) "flowed naturally from the breach."

The whole matter of determining if, what kind, and the value of damages in a breach of contract matter is equal parts commercial and legal. If you believe you have cause to seek damages for a breach of contract, you would naturally consult an attorney. Only a reasonably experienced lawyer will be able to advise what damages may be available to you, because the issue of damages is quite extensive and elaborate. Thus, rather than go into the details, we'll simply list and very briefly describe the nature of damages and what might justify an action.

- *Expectation damages* are based on the aggrieved party's potential profit that was lost due to the breach of contract.
- *Opportunity cost damages* are based on the costs that might be attributed to the aggrieved party's not making a contract with someone else because it chose to contract with the breaching party. (In other words, what opportunities were foregone due to the contract?)
- *Consequential damages* arise when the effect of the breach spills over into and affects other contracts. (For example, a silicon chip maker does not deliver on an order of chips that are to be installed into computers and as a result the downstream contract to supply computers is breached.)
- *General damages* are awarded by the court over and above specifically quantifiable damages to fully compensate the aggrieved party.
- *Reliance damages* may be awarded when expectation damages cannot be sought because of successful mitigation on the victim party's part. Not to be confused with a penalty, these damages compensate the victim of the breach for expenses incurred in reliance of the contract being fully performed.
- *Liquidated damages* are damages specified within the contract as compensation from the breaching party to the aggrieved party. This is not a penalty clause, and as the earlier language drawn from a real estate offer shows, such terms almost always carry the specific language that the payment is liquidated damages and *not* a penalty. Another example of large liquidated damages are the "pullout" damages that were part of the ultimately withdrawn merger agreement between the Royal Bank of Canada and the Bank of Montreal.
- *Nominal damages* are the damages awarded to the aggrieved party when it has won "on principle" but the court does not feel it deserves compensation. The apparent desire is to eliminate or reduce spurious actions (because a one-dollar award of damages, without costs, does not go very far toward legal fees).

Common Remedies for Breach of Contract: Equitable Remedies

Awarding money is not the only way the court has to compensate parties aggrieved by a breach of contract. Sometimes the victim would not be suitably compensated for its losses with a payment of cash. In such circumstances, the law provides for *equitable remedies* instead of or in addition to compensatory damages (money). There are some general rules by which the law determines whether an equitable remedy is required (or, conversely, whether such a request should be denied), but for the most part an innocent victim that acts quickly on a breach by the other party may have an equitable remedy available to it. The most common equitable remedies the court may award are listed below.

1. *Specific performance*, which is a court order upon the defendant (breaching party) to take some specific action to compensate the aggrieved party. Most likely, the specific action will be the fulfillment of its obligations under the contract.
2. *Injunction* is similar but opposite to specific performance (specific *non*performance, perhaps?). It is a court order for the defendant *not* to do something, or to stop doing it. Generally speaking, an injunction will be ordered if the contract contains a promise by the breaching party not to do something (i.e., it contains a *negative covenant*).
3. The option to *rescind* the contract—make like it never happened and hopefully be back where you would have been had that contract never happened—is the third principal option available to the court. The rub is that unlike the other equitable options available, in this case *the possibility for having both the equitable remedy and damages awarded is close to nil.* After all, if there never was a contract, damages cannot flow naturally.

Both compensatory damages and equitable remedies are court orders, and as such demand compliance. Noncompliance with a court-ordered judgement is contempt of court and could land the guilty party in jail or have it facing a hefty fine. In the case of damages, prior to a contempt action being made, however, it is more likely that the plaintiff (the aggrieved party) would avail itself of one or more of the options available to enforce judgement. The common way in which a *judgement creditor* would have a judgement enforced against the *judgement debtor* would be by obtaining another order called an *execution order*, which would permit a sheriff to enter and seize property (to be sold or otherwise) from the judgement debtor.

Similarly, a *garnishing order* permits the judgement creditor to compel an individual's employer to withhold some part of the judgement debtor's salary and turn it over to the creditor. A garnishing order can also be issued against the judgement debtor's bank account, seizing money to the full extent owing under the judgement—if there is enough money in the account. If the account does not have enough money to satisfy the debt, the entire bank account may be seized and applied against judgement.

Although there are other orders and means (and variations thereof) by which a court-ordered debt can be enforced, execution orders and garnishing orders are the most common.

Chapter 3
Basic Written Contract Form

The Customary Components of a Written Contract,
Common Paragraphs, Legal Language, Special Provisions

A written contract can be as simple as:

> Templar Strategies will provide 50 hours of service to YOUR COMPANY to prepare a business overview at a rate of $150.00 per hour plus taxes and disbursements. The job is to be complete in six weeks.
>
> Timothy Demkiw Grayson, <date>
> Accepted on behalf of YOUR COMPANY.
> Your name, <date>

I suppose it could be even simpler. The point is that the key factors of offer, acceptance, and consideration are included, and the document is dated and signed by both parties. This is a more than adequate document to properly bind both parties, all other factors being equal.

More often, however, we see contracts that run on for pages and pages, with clauses (aka paragraphs) that extend to three levels of points such as the sample provided below. Although there is no prescribed formula or format that contract drafters must employ, certain features have become commonly accepted. Variations of how those features of form are presented are usually the result of personal or law firm preference, or prevailing standards among members of a local bar association ("bar" from *barrister*, not "beer hall").

There are arguably nine required parts to a written contract of any length or detail. In this chapter we will examine the form of a reasonably extensive contract. They are explained below. Some of those nine parts, such as "Special Provisions," have common clauses that are likely to appear within any contract. In the latter part of this chapter we will present and translate some of these more common clauses.

CUSTOMARY COMPONENTS OF A WRITTEN CONTRACT

As mentioned at the head of this chapter, a written contract need only specify the parties to the contract, their promises/obligations, the consideration, and a date. The document should be signed, often on as many original copies as there are parties to the contract. Be that as it may, most contracts that come out of a law office or legal department have been "what if'ed" and expanded to address every conceivable problem that might arise in the fulfillment of the obligations. It ends up being a little longer than one paragraph, and can be quite intimidating (especially if the purpose of the deal seemed simple to begin with).

The following list is an explanation of the nine customary components of a written contract, as displayed on the annotated illustration above. While I have separated these components into discrete parts, in practice the terms and conditions—the middle part of the document—may be put together in a different way. That is to say, there will very likely not be distinct sections entitled "Conditions," "Warranties," and so forth. They may all be mixed together to suit the flow of the particular contract. I have separated them for the sake of convenience and easier understanding.

1. Date

Generally the date of the agreement will appear as the first line at the top of the first page of the contract following a few capitalized words that indicate that the document is an agreement. This is the effective commencement date of the agreement unless (a) another date is specified within the body of the agreement, or (b) the date of execution (signing of the document) is specified within the body of the contract as the commencement date of the agreement. The date line is usually similar to the following:

THIS AGREEMENT made the 21st day of April, 1998.

2. Parties

The individuals making the contract between and among themselves are listed prior to anything else in the contract (except the date, usually). There may be only two parties, or there may be several parties to the agreement, all of whom are specified. Regardless, each is listed and defined as expressly as possible so that there is little potential for confusion. Thus, one usually sees parties to a contract annotated in a form such as follows:

Timothy Demkiw Grayson,
of the City of Winnipeg, in the Province of Manitoba
(hereinafter referred to as "GRAYSON").
OF THE FIRST PART

Or

Templar Technologies Inc.,
a corporation incorporated under the federal laws of Canada, (hereinafter referred to as "Templar").
OF THE SECOND PART

In contract form, and in the law in general it might be argued, there are many archaisms that are little more than traditional holdovers or stylistic choices. For instance, the use of "OF THE FIRST PART" is really an archaism that probably was created when legal forms were printed in bulk so that they could be used for any purpose, and the body of the agreement would not require changing regardless of whose name was attached to the agreement. The reason everyone is a "party" is because everyone named in the contract plays a "part." This defining convention appears or does not appear almost at the whim of the drafting lawyer. Given that the parties to the contract are usually defined with an abbreviation of their full legal names, it hardly seems necessary to also define them as parts of the contract, but tradition dies hard in a profession built on precedent.

The full and legal names of the parties to the contract will usually be seen again only once before the very end, where they are to affix their signatures. Instead, the defined name for each party (i.e., the name assigned to the party in the "hereinafter referred to" statement) will be the operative name in the body of the agreement. Sometimes it is capitalized, sometimes not. There is no hard-and-fast rule.

3. Recitals

Following the naming of the parties to the contract, and before the "meat" of the agreement, are often found a few paragraphs of text that each commence with either "WHEREAS" or "AND WHEREAS" (or are just a series of points below a single "WHEREAS"). This part of the contract is generally referred to as the *recitals*. Webster's dictionary defines "recital" as "an act or instance of reciting: account." What happens in contracts is essentially an accounting of the circumstances and context of the contract; subjects that might later be questioned about the good faith of the agreement are usually dealt with in this section. Good recitals ensure that neither party will be able to say it did not have intent to develop and arrive at the binding agreement.

4. (a) Consideration

At the end of the recitals is a paragraph or two that commences with the words "NOW THEREFORE THIS AGREEMENT WITNESSETH THAT" or something to that effect.[1] As we are all aware, every contract requires consideration. In this section, the consideration is specified clearly so there is no mistaking it or losing it within the body of the contract. As we noted in the section "Consideration" in Chapter 1, sometimes consideration is difficult to define or to specify even though there are a variety of valid, and possibly even valuable, promises made in the contract. Thus, some clever lawyer introduced this statement, which quite often appears in some variation in the *Consideration* section of a contract:

NOW THEREFORE THIS AGREEMENT WITNESSETH THAT in consideration of the respective covenants, agreements, and undertakings herein contained and for other good and valuable consideration (the receipt and sufficiency of which are hereby acknowledged), the parties hereto covenant and agree as follows:

The meaning of this statement is that the parties to the agreement agree within the contract that they have each received sufficient valuable consideration—in addition to the promises being made—to satisfy the necessity for consideration in the formation of a legally binding agreement.

4. (b) Mutual covenants, agreements, and undertakings

Notice how in the immediately preceding example of legal text for notice of consideration, the words "respective covenants, agreements, and undertakings" also make an appearance. A contract is all about promises and agreements, which is essentially what covenants, agreements, and undertakings represent. They are elaborated upon and specified in the *Conditions* and *Warranties* sections that follow.

5. Conditions

Along with the *Warranties* (see below), this section is the "guts" of the contract. In this portion of the agreement, which can consist of as few as one or two, or as many as twenty or more, sections (each containing a variety of clauses), are spelled out the key promises and obligations to which each party is binding itself. The information provided in this part of the contract is more or less unique to each individual agreement, and therefore takes whatever form is required to communicate those specific promises. Often this section begins with definitions of words and terms used throughout the remainder of the document, as well as the governing legislations that will be referred to at various places. Its heart is the sections that deal with who will provide what to whom, when, and how often.

> Why don't lawyers simply use the word "promise" or something equally simple? Instead, a contract is full of "covenants," "mutual undertakings," "warranties," and "conditions." Good question, probably only answerable by the equally glib response: because that's just how it is. Or as the Fiddler on the Roof might say, "Tradition!"
>
> In fact, most of these words either have a specific meaning in law or indicate a relative level of gravity in the hierarchy of promises, or both. A *covenant*, for instance, is a very serious promise on the order of a "holy oath." Thus, in contracts it is used with suitable reverence to indicate that the promise is not being made lightly. *Agreements* would appear to speak for themselves, and *mutual undertakings* are agreements being made by all parties to the contract—mutually.
>
> *Conditions* and *warranties* are hierarchical definitions of promises. *Conditions* have, over the years, become defined as the essential terms of the contract. This does not mean there is anything "conditional"

about the terms, although it's understandable how that could be confusing. *Warranties*, similarly, have come to mean terms of the contract that are important enough to be included but are not essential. The term bears no relation to manufacturers' assurances provided in owner's manuals.

As it relates to a breach of the contract, naturally the breach of a more important *condition* is viewed more gravely than the breach of a *warranty*.

6. Warranties

As mentioned in the preceding point, together with the conditions, warranties complete the recitation of all terms and promises specific to an individual agreement. Most of the "what ifs" regarding non- or partial performance, collateral promises, and so forth are dealt with in this part of the agreement.

7. General provisions

In this part of the written contract, which normally is set off as a separate section entitled "General [Terms/Provisions]" or "Miscellaneous," are found a variety of rules relating to the function and environment of the relationship created by the contract that do not necessarily affect the promises being made. Later in this chapter, we will examine some of the more common general terms; but, for example, clauses that define the jurisdiction, use of gender pronouns, and severability of the contract are common general provisions.

8. Special provisions

Many contracts internally provide for resolution (e.g., arbitration), damages, indemnities, and so forth. These terms are not part of the fundamental agreement made by the parties, but may nevertheless be of importance in carrying out the termination of the agreement and/or resolution of a breach of contract, or dealing with other unusual circumstances. They are therefore included as agreements between the parties for eventualities neither party hopes will arise.[2]

9. Signatures

At the very end of the contract is a section for the parties to the agreement to execute ("put in force," not kill) the agreement. Individuals sign on their own accord, with a witness to each individual's signature being required. Each witness then completes a separate document called an "Affidavit of Execution," which is a sworn statement by the witness saying that the contract was properly signed. Corporations execute by the signature(s) of their duly authorized officer(s), and their corporate seal. An Affidavit of Execution is not required for a corporation's execution of an agreement. Signatures are dated.

The signatures are preceded by a sentence to the effect of:

IN WITNESS WHEREOF the parties have executed this Agreement.

Most often that line will continue with words that render the execution date of the agreement the same as the effective date (the date mentioned at the very beginning of the agreement):

IN WITNESS WHEREOF the parties have executed this Agreement on the date first mentioned above.

To return briefly to legal archaisms, the signature boxes are often preceded by a statement such as

SIGNED, SEALED, AND DELIVERED in the presence of:

It may actually have a space for a seal as well. The seal, most often now a small, red adhesive dot, dates back to when the monks wrote the contracts and nobody else—even most of the landowning middle aristocracy, which had cause to use contracts—could write their own name. A drop of wax was laid on the document and the "signatory" would imprint his (rarely, if ever, "her") signet (usually worn as a ring), or family crest, into the wax to indicate his act or deed. Although some would have you believe that they are necessary, and perhaps technically a seal is required in some circumstances, for all practical purposes the seal is merely another holdover from another time. Most people can make a suitably distinguishing mark in ink to execute a contract.

COMMON PARAGRAPHS AND LEGAL LANGUAGE—GENERAL PROVISIONS

The following samples of legal text have been drawn from a variety of sources, including contracts with which I have been involved. The way each statement is written may vary somewhat from text appearing in other contracts, but that is primarily attributable to stylistic differences between lawyers and law firms. Some differences, however, may change the meaning of the text substantially. It is best to use these samples as a guide only and have a lawyer confirm that what appears in the contract you are dealing with is what you think it is.

These clauses are commonly included in contracts as "boilerplate"—a term that derives from the standard, use-everywhere, patterned sheet metal used in the construction and repair of steam boilers—by lawyers who draw the text from in-house precedents. Although it is not always done, in a well-drafted contract the lawyer will make these clauses specific to the needs of each contract, as is done for the major conditions and warranties. Be vigilant and curious about whether the text and meaning of a clause is truly specific to the needs of your agreement.

The samples that follow are not meant to be exhaustive. Rather, these clauses seem to be common across a variety of contract types and the likelihood of encountering one or more of them is high. An explanation is provided beneath each.

> **Gender and Number:** In this agreement, the singular includes the plural and the masculine includes the feminine and neuter and vice versa unless the context otherwise requires.

This paragraph probably exists (1) for convenience, and (2) because somewhere, a lawyer once tried to use incorrect pronouns as a loophole. ("But this says '*he* shall' and my clients are *three women*.") It might also be an attempt to be politically correct.

> **Force Majeure:** Neither party shall be liable to the other for any failure to perform any obligations under this Agreement due to causes which are beyond their reasonable control and of a nature which neither has the power or authority to remedy, including without limitation, acts of God, acts of civil or military disturbances, fires, floods, epidemics, wars, and riots. In the event of such an occurrence, the party claiming relief thereon shall give prompt written notice thereof to the other party and any time for performance of an obligation shall be extended by time equal to the length of delay attributable to such occurrence.

Force majeure is from the French, and generally translates into a "great power" beyond man's control—i.e., an act of God. This clause, sometimes written to apply to only one party—if that party is *doing or producing something* as opposed to paying for something, "prevents" a breach due to "greater forces" beyond one's control. It does not discharge the contract or absolve the party from performing its obligations. The effect is to delay. The second sentence specifies that the party seeking relief under this provision (1) must immediately notify the other party or parties, and (2) will be provided with a time extension equivalent to the time lost due to the force majeure. This is a clause that inserts fair treatment into the agreement should greater forces arise to the contract's detriment.

> **Waiver:** Any failure of either party to insist upon strict compliance with any of the terms and conditions of this Agreement shall not be construed as a waiver of such terms and conditions and agreements, or of the right of the affected party to insist at any time thereafter upon such strict compliance.

One party to an ongoing transaction may let the other party get away with a breach or breaches of contract for any number of reasons just to keep the relationship going. For instance, one party may not provide a report on time, deliver late or short-ship, or possibly miss a payment date. This paragraph attempts to prevent an inch from turning into a mile. Remember that established practice ("We've been doing it that way all along") has a fair amount of import under contract law, and that if a contractual right is waived it could disappear. With this paragraph in place, the party that "goes along" for a while (1) does not waive its contractual right, and (2) can, at any point when it has had enough, demand strict compliance with the terms of the agreement.

> **Survival:** The expiration or termination of this Agreement for any reason shall be without prejudice to the rights of the parties hereto and shall not relieve the parties hereto of any of their obligations hereunder.

Sometimes contract provisions are long-lasting, or have effects designed to last longer than the contract itself. For example, a licensor's right to inspect the periodic accounts of a licensee for some years after the period has elapsed naturally lasts longer than the contract. (For example, when a license agreement expires or is terminated, the licensor may still have a set number of years to inspect the final years' books, although the contract is no longer in force.) This clause specifies that the termination of the agreement does not affect those rights, which *survive* the termination of the agreement.

> **Headings:** The headings as to contents of particular provisions herein are inserted only for convenience and are in no way to be construed as a part of this Agreement or as a modification of the scope of any terms or provisions of this Agreement.

This seems straightforward enough. At issue is that sometimes contract clause headings would imply the opposite of the textual content. In the example of "Waiver" above, the heading seems to suggest there is a waiver when, in fact, the paragraph prevents it.

> **Severability:** If any provision or part of any provision in this Agreement is found to be invalid, illegal, or unenforceable, such provision will be severable therefrom and the remainder thereof will be construed as if the invalid, illegal, or unenforceable provision or part thereof has been deleted therefrom.

Sometimes referred to as *partial invalidity*, this provision is inserted to keep the contract as a whole in effect even if some part of it is a problem that could otherwise render the agreement void or voidable. Of course, if the part that is deemed illegal, invalid, or unenforceable happens to be the key part of the contract, this clause may be immaterial.

> **Time of Essence:** Time is of the essence of this Agreement.

This single-line clause has to be my all-time favourite waste of ink. Presumably its purpose is to provide an incentive for all parties not to dawdle in performance of the agreement, and is a justification for rescission or breach action if a party does. To my untrained eye, however, it seems that the concept is implicit in the agreement. Supposedly, if "time is of the essence," any breach of a deadline or "unreasonable" delay by one party would be the breach of an important "condition" of the contract with graver repercussions than such a breach if time is *not* specified as being "of the essence."

> **Entire Agreement:** This is the entire agreement between the parties hereto and is intended to be the complete and exclusive statement of the terms hereof. No additions, deletions, or amendments may be made to this Agreement orally, and may only be made in a written document signed by all parties hereto.

This clause has the effect of giving the written agreement total force over any other earlier or ensuing oral agreements between the parties. If this clause appears, it is a good idea to make sure that nothing important in the bargain/relationship is left out of the written agreement—regardless of how insignificant it may seem—as an "understanding" between the parties. That "understanding" will not be enforceable should the time arise when it is not quite as well understood as everyone thought.

> **Term:** This Agreement shall come into force and effect as of the date set out on the first page of this Agreement and shall continue in force until <date>.

Some contracts have an inherently finite lifespan. (For example, when the machine is sold, it is sold—end of story; end of contract.) Others have an ongoing—possibly infinite—life. *Usually* lawyers will rightly suggest that a limited duration be imposed on an otherwise continual agreement. A finite term provides a natural reassessment point for both parties. Circumstances may change over the life of the agreement, and the conditions may no longer be favourable or of value to one or more parties. If the intent is to create a more permanent relationship, the finite term of the agreement may have an additional provision for automatic renewal (rollover) such as in the following example.

> **Renewal:** In the event that this Agreement is not terminated during the initial term, Party A shall have the irrevocable option to renew this Agreement for an additional term of <a certain number of> years commencing <the day after the expiration of the initial term> on the same terms and conditions as applied during the initial term (including, without limitation, the further right to renew this Agreement), provided that Party A gives written notice to Party B of its exercise of such renewal option at least <some period> prior to the expiration of the previous term.

This particular example provides an option for one party to renew under the same terms and conditions by giving notice to the other party. Other similar clauses will provide that the agreement automatically renews for another term unless specifically *not* renewed. Still others demand that the renewal be mutually accepted. (In the example above, Party B must comply with the terms and conditions if Party A renews, regardless of their value to Party B at that future date.) Although the procedure is different, the effect is largely the same.

Where they differ is in the renegotiation of terms. In this example, if Party A wishes to create a new relationship it need merely not exercise its option while negotiating. In the other case noted above, notice would have to be provided that the agreement *not* be automatically renewed under the same terms and conditions, and the new terms would be negotiated.

> **Enurement:** This Agreement shall enure to the benefit of and be binding upon the parties hereto and their respective heirs, executors, administrators, successors, and assigns.

The word "enure" means, according to *Black's Legal Dictionary*, "to operate or take effect" or "to serve to the use, benefit, or advantage of a person." This paragraph provides that the contract is made to benefit and to bind solely and exclusively those parties named in it or those other parties upon whom the obligations and rights become obligations or rights in some legal way. The paragraph specifies the nature of the privity of the contract. (See "Privity of Contract," Chapter 2.)

> **Notices:** Any notice required or permitted to be given hereunder shall be deemed to be sufficiently given if delivered, telegraphed, telexed, telecopied, or if mailed in a postage prepaid envelope by ordinary mail addressed as hereinafter set forth. Any notice delivered, telegraphed, telexed, or telecopied as aforesaid shall be deemed to have been given on the first business day immediately following the date of delivery or on the date of sending, as the case may be. Any notice mailed as aforesaid shall be deemed to have been effectively given on the tenth business day following the date of mailing. For purposes hereof, notice shall be effectively given, if delivered, telegraphed, telexed, telecopied, or mailed to the following addresses [addresses follow]:

Nearly every contract has time-determined requirements for notice of breach, examinations, renewals, lapse, etc. It may also provide for remedy periods that also have time restrictions. (The law, you may have begun to notice, has all kinds of self- and statute-imposed time "hurdles" that lend urgency to legal affairs.) This paragraph specifies how notices must be provided: in writing and by particular transfer mode. Because notice by post is always acceptable, but nobody can ever tell how long the post office may take to move the mail, this paragraph provides a reasonable, albeit arbitrary point from which to start the clock.[3]

> **Counterparts:** This Agreement may be signed in counterparts and each of such counterparts shall constitute an original document and such counterparts, taken together, shall constitute one and the same instrument.

Often parties to an agreement reside at some distance from one another and it is neither timely nor practical to travel across the country or around the world, or to repeatedly mail the same original documents to all parties to an agreement so that all original signatures appear on one (or several) copies. This provision allows for each party to sign a different original copy, *and* when all those copies are put together the documents will effectively be recognized as a single original signed by all parties. Commonly one of the law firms will hold all the originals together.

> **Assignment:** This Agreement, or any of the rights herein, may not be sold, transferred, or assigned, in whole or in part, by either party without the express written consent of the other. Such consent may not be unreasonably withheld. If assigned, this Agreement shall be binding upon and enure to the benefit of the parties hereto and their respective successors and assigns.

The first sentence of this provision prevents any party from removing itself from the agreement by assigning the contract to a third party, unless the other parties expressly consent to the change. The second sentence provides that none of the other parties can maliciously withhold their approval.[4] The last sentence reimposes the enurement clause (see above) on the parties to the contract, which would now include the new third party to whom rights and obligations have been assigned or sold, etc. Note that a total assignment *may* be a statutory assignment and remove the original "assigning" party from the agreement altogether. (See "Assignment," page 34.)

> **Law of Contract:** This Agreement shall be construed and interpreted in accordance with, enforced according to and governed by the laws of the Province of <province> and the federal laws of Canada applicable therein and each of the parties hereby irrevocably attorns to the jurisdiction of the courts of the Province of <province>, which courts shall have exclusive jurisdiction over all matters pertaining to this Agreement, including the enforcement, interpretation, and application thereof.

Just so there is no confusion about the jurisdiction under which the contract will be governed—given the rules about jurisdiction and when/where an offer is accepted—this clause specifies that all parties consent (*attorn*) to a named legal jurisdiction. It is usually in one's best interests to take the home-field advantage by having the contract construed under the laws of one's own province, because any future disputes will be resolved by those rules and physically within that jurisdiction. Sometimes this paragraph is entitled "Jurisdiction," "Governing Law," or "Construction" (from "construed").

> **Relationship:** Nothing herein shall create, be deemed to create, or be construed as creating any partnership, employer-employee, joint venture, or agency relationship between the parties hereto.

This clause, which appears in other, similar variations, is provided to ensure that for potential liability purposes there is specifically no legal relationship of any of the types indicated being created out of the agreement. Such relationships, if deemed to exist, might create unwanted tax, tort, and other exposure for one or all parties to the agreement where none is desired or should exist. Furthermore, this clause could be of particular import to the interpretation of agency or employment relationships between the parties—which create even more liabilities and responsibilities. In this case, the parties are indicating that despite the agreement at hand, they are totally independent and have neither control over nor responsibility for one another.

Remedy for Breach: The parties hereto acknowledge and agree that a breach of any of the covenants, agreements, or undertakings hereunder will cause to the other parties irreparable injury which cannot be readily remedied in damages or solely by termination of this Agreement and that the injured party, in addition to all other legal and equitable remedies, shall have the right of injunction for any breach of this Agreement by the other parties.

This clause may be mutual, as written above, or, more likely, in favour of one party over the others. It is a serious provision in which one or all parties consent to allow a party that has been subject to a breach all the normal rights to damages and equitable remedies, as well as the right to a temporary or permanent injunction (a court order to stop acting in some grievous manner) without proving need and leaving its levy to a court's discretion. Like a lot of legal language, however, its bark is worse than its bite, because "irreparable" injury does not necessarily mean "terminal" or "serious" and a party subject to breach always has the remedy of injunction available to it by order of the court anyway.

Independent Legal Advice: The parties hereto each acknowledge having obtained independent legal advice with respect to the terms of this Agreement prior to its execution, or have chosen to not seek legal advice of their own accord.

Recall that in Chapter 2 we noted how ensuring that the other party had legal advice before executing the contract could prevent that party from using its lack of knowledge of the full legal effect of the provision or condition it is disputing as an option for extricating itself from the agreement. This clause does just that.

Parties to Execute Other Documents: Each party agrees that it will execute all documents and do all acts and things as the other party may reasonably request and as may be lawful and within its respective power to do, to carry out and/or implement the provisions or intent of this Agreement.

A contract could be frustrated by one or more parties obstinately refusing to do or sign the things/documents necessary to carry out the agreement. And since the fulfillment of an agreement often includes the conclusion or implementation of other acts, parties to a contract can be reasonably expected to complete documents or actions that would (or could) not be specified in the agreement itself. In this clause, all parties acknowledge and pledge not to frustrate the agreement, and will, in fact, facilitate its implementation and fulfillment.

COMMON PARAGRAPHS AND LEGAL LANGUAGE—SPECIAL PROVISIONS

The following clauses are examples of special provisions to written agreements. They are relatively few, simply because they are common to a variety of contracts in contrast to the vast majority of special provisions that are "special" to specific contractual requirements. Like the general provisions, they are commonly included as boilerplate drawn from in-house precedents. In a well-drafted contract, these clauses will address the specific needs of the contract.

A written contract might *not* have a specific group of clauses headed by a title, "Special Provisions." It is used here to set apart special contractual requirements.

Arbitration: Whenever and wherever a dispute shall occur among the parties relating to the interpretation or implementation of any of the provisions of this Agreement, or which by the terms of this Agreement are subject to this arbitration provision, such matters shall be determined by arbitration and the following provisions shall apply.

(a) Arbitration shall be initiated by one party giving notice (the "Arbitration Notice") to the other party to the dispute of its desire to have a matter arbitrated in accordance with this section, and shall state the matter which the initiating party wishes to have arbitrated.

(b) The matter requiring arbitration shall be referred to a single arbitrator if one can be mutually agreed upon by the parties to the dispute, difference, or question within thirty (30) days of the Arbitration Notice being given.

(c) If the parties to the dispute, difference, or question cannot agree upon a single arbitrator, then each party involved in the arbitration shall name an arbitrator within a further period of thirty (30) days therefrom, and the arbitrators so named shall appoint one more arbitrator.

(d) If the arbitrators named by the parties to the arbitration cannot agree upon the additional arbitrator as above provided within thirty (30) days of the date of the appointment of the last of them, then, after the expiry of such thirty (30) day period, any one of the parties to the arbitration may apply to a judge of the Court of Queen's Bench of <province> or its successor to appoint the additional arbitrator or arbitrators to sit and hear the arbitration.

(e) The decision arrived at by a single arbitrator or a majority of the arbitrators, as the case may be, shall be binding upon all the parties to the arbitration and no appeal shall lie therefrom.

(f) The provisions of this section shall be deemed to be a submission to arbitration within the provisions of The Arbitration Act (<province>).

Litigating a contractual disagreement in court can be time-consuming and expensive. In many contractual relationships, it can be in everyone's interest to avoid going to court over a disagreement about either the interpretation or the implementation of the contract. Binding arbitration (from the same root as "arbitrary") is a less expensive and usually more rapid way to resolve an issue, which is why many contracts incorporate this form of dispute resolution within the body of the agreement. Because binding arbitration is statutorily regulated by relatively similar legislation in each province, it is an amply legitimate way to resolve disputes.

> There are several ways in which unrelated parties help resolve differences. Arbitration and mediation are two of the primarily informal—out-of-court—means to reach a resolved bargain. Many people are not completely aware of or have trouble remembering exactly how they are different, although aware that the underlying purpose is the same.
>
> Arbitration, sometimes referred to as "binding arbitration," is a dispute resolution mechanism that most closely resembles a courtroom with a judge. It is much less formal than that. But in principle, with an unrelated and disinterested arbitrator or panel of arbitrators, binding arbitration requires that each side give its version of the "facts" and provide any other information requested in order that the arbitrator(s) might provide their binding decision on how the dispute is to be resolved. (Think of how the decision is rather "arbitrary.") Generally speaking, before an arbitration panel the finer points of contract law will take a back seat to the practicality of interpreting the contract's intent and the parties' actions that give rise to the dispute.
>
> Mediation, on the other hand, does not impose on the parties a third-party settlement as does either formal litigation or binding arbitration. A mediator will channel the parties to negotiate a resolution among themselves without interfering beyond getting the disputants out of their dug-in positions to find a resolution. The mediator, in the "middle," provides the medium within which a solution is created (with apologies to the chemists among us).

In this lengthy example of an arbitration clause, the contracting parties have formally agreed to resolve disputes arising out of the interpretation or implementation of the contract by arbitration with no right of further appeal (i.e., to a formal court).[5] It also provides the protocol for both commencing a dispute and convening the arbitrator or arbitration panel. Finally, at the very end, the rules by which the arbitration will take place, i.e., the applicable legislation, is provided. In this example, and in most other situations, fairness is incorporated by starting with a single arbitrator option and a mechanism for creating an odd-numbered panel of arbitrators that is acceptable to both parties.

> **Insurance:** Party A agrees to obtain and keep in force, at its own expense, product liability insurance, with a thirty (30) day notice of cancellation provisions, from a recognized and responsible insurance company naming Party B as an additional insured and providing protection in the amount of $1,000,000. Upon request, Party A shall provide Party B with a certificate evidencing such insurance.

When the use or transfer of an asset—tangible or intangible—is at the heart of the contract, the owner of that asset may insist upon an insurance clause such as that above. Its purpose, obviously, is to satisfy the owner of the asset that its interests are covered in the event of (insured) damage arising in the future. Note that insurance may be of any sort: property, fire, theft, liability, and any other type of insurance common to the circumstance. The owner of the asset may add language to this paragraph to the effect that if insurance is not purchased by the other party, the owner may purchase it and demand immediate reimbursement from the other party.

> **Indemnification:** Party A agrees to indemnify and hold Party B, its subsidiaries, affiliates, successors and assigns harmless from any and all liabilities, damages, claims, judgements, awards, fines, penalties, or other payments (including reasonable counsel fees) which may be incurred by any or all of them arising out of any claims or suits which may be brought or made against Party B by reason of any breach by Party A of any agents or subcontractors of Party A of any provisions of this Agreement, provided Party B shall give prompt notice and reasonable cooperation and assistance to Party A relative to any such claim or suit brought to its attention. This provision shall survive indefinitely the termination or expiration of this Agreement.

This clause often appears near the *Relationship* (not creating any, to be specific) clause in contracts where some kind of arm's-length business relationship is being created or an asset is being provided by one party to another (e.g., leases, licenses, franchises, etc.). The verb "indemnify" means, according to Merriam-Webster, "1: to secure against hurt, loss, or damage 2: to make compensation for some loss or damage." Most often the clause is skewed to one party's favour, but can sometimes be mutual. Its purpose is to protect the party that is allowing its name or asset to be used by the other party in some ongoing business from the expense and trouble of protecting itself from potential liability that might arise only because the other party is using that name or asset. Note that in this case the last sentence provides that Party A will continue to indemnify Party B *forever* against liability that might arise from Party A's actions under this Agreement.

> **Liquidated Damages:** Party A agrees that if it should breach any provisions of this Agreement then it shall pay to Party B for each and every breach of any covenant the sum of <dollars> as liquidated damages and not as a penalty. Party A acknowledges that the precise amount of Party B's actual damages would be extremely difficult to ascertain and that the foregoing sum represents a reasonable estimate of such actual damages.

The key part of this clause is that the payment not be interpreted as a penalty, because penalty clauses are usually struck down by the court. In order to do so, the clause must provide a dollar amount for the liquidated damages that is somehow a reasonable estimate of real costs, losses, etc. arising from the breach. Often such clauses will not be as broad as the one provided above, instead making a provision for liquidated damages on the breach of a specific covenant or covenants. Liquidated damages are generally one-sided, although in some instances both parties may be bound to liquidated damages covenants.

Chapter 4
Contract Basics and the Quebec Civil Law
by Marc Duguay, LL.B., B.C.L.

An introduction to the way in which contractual relationships are interpreted under Quebec Civil Law

Every Canadian's Guide to Common Contracts would not be complete without a brief examination of contracts subject to Quebec civil law.

Although the Province of Quebec is part of Canada, the province is distinguishable from the other nine provinces by being the only one not to be governed under the Common Law which was derived from England. Indeed, the Quebec civil law as derived from France, governs persons, their relations, and property matters. We should point out that while Quebec has its distinct civil law, it does share with the rest of Canada what is called public law, such as criminal law, bankruptcy law, copyright, and trade-marks legislation, to give but a few examples. However, concerning contracts, the distinctive Quebec Civil Code is applicable.

The goal of this chapter is not to elaborate on all the notions of Quebec civil law as it impacts on contractual relationships and particular contracts. To do so would require no less than a book to cover all the issues. However, what we can accomplish is an introduction to the way in which contractual relationships are interpreted under Quebec's civil law. We will focus primarily on the formation and interpretation of contracts, and we will complete this review with a look at particular legislative enactments such as the Consumer Protection Act. Finally, several important provisions of the Quebec Civil Code will be examined for substantive and illustrative purposes in order that you may gain an understanding as to how contracts are interpreted under Quebec's civil law.

To accomplish this, we must first appreciate the meaning and purpose of a civil code. The notion of a civil code that contains thousands of rules is unusual for Canadians outside Quebec because the legal system applicable in the rest of Canada is founded on the Common Law. The Common Law derives its authority from laws enacted by governments as well as from judgements issued by courts in individual cases (case law). Often, the Common Law is referred to as a system that relies on case law to decide the outcome of disputes. Except for specific legislation in defined areas, Common Law jurisdictions do not have an overriding set of rules or principles that summarize all matters. In Quebec, like most civil law jurisdictions, to the contrary, has a code that contains many of the laws, rules, and regulations, both of general and specific nature, that govern the relationship of people with the state, and also people's relationships with each other. First though, here is a brief history of the origins of the Quebec Civil Code.

HISTORY AND SOURCES OF THE QUEBEC CIVIL LAW

In the years prior to 1759, immigrants who had come to Nouvelle-France were governed under the French régime. Louis XIV, in 1664, made the laws that were governing Paris at the time applicable to those who had chosen to live in the newly found territory. Those who had emigrated from France accepted this legal system drawn from the "Coutume de Paris." At the time, there was no unified system of civil law in France.

In 1763, France, after losing the war to Great Britain, gave up Nouvelle-France to Great Britain. The *Traité de Paris* confirmed this and, from then until 1774, Quebec was subject to the English law, namely the "common law" as derived from Great Britain.

The English conquest did not, however, convert or assimilate the French, and in 1774 in the Quebec Act, the British parliament restored the French language and French civil law in Quebec. Thereafter, and to this day, notwithstanding major milestones in our shared history such as the division of Upper Canada and Lower Canada in 1791, the Union of the Two Canada's in 1840, Confederation in 1867, and even the patriation of the Constitution in 1982, Quebec's citizenry has continued to be governed by the Quebec Civil Code.

Although the civil code in 1867 was inspired by the Napoleonic Code of France, today's Quebec's civil code is fully modernized and reflects that society's modern values and traditions. In fact, the civil code underwent significant reform when, on January 1, 1994, a revised version was adopted in Quebec. The reform which led to this had actually started in 1955, when Maurice Duplessis was premier.

During this time, the law was not static, and legislation modernizing most areas of provincial jurisdiction was being fully implemented. The Quebec Civil Code today, as its predecessor, is interpreted alongside legislative enactments on specific subjects. Naturally, when the Quebec Civil Code was finally adopted, the result was the codification of the previous 125 years of laws and principles of law enunciated by the courts. Robert Bourassa's government also wanted to give a new image to civil rules by updating them according to important judicial decisions and some other principles of law borrowed from various other jurisdictions. The new Quebec Civil Code represented what the then minister of justice saw as "un mouvement de société." The Quebec Civil Code revised the private law in a manner that reflected current and accepted trends in other jurisdictions although remaining faithful to the distinctiveness of Quebec's civil law values and heritage.

As was noted earlier, to properly understand how contracts are governed under civil law jurisdiction, we must review the civil law itself and particularly the Quebec Civil Code.

CIVIL LAW GENERALLY

Unlike the Common Law, where there is no consolidated book of rules or codified law, the Quebec Civil Code lays out the most important principles that individuals are expected to respect. Imagine for a moment if we were to consolidate in a series of principles all of Canada's laws and judicial decisions. The result would be similar to the Civil Code, although perhaps not identical in substance, but definitely similar in form. The Quebec Civil Code includes more than 3,100 articles and covers a wide range of issues that would normally be expected to govern a modern, free, and democratic society. All matters concerning the organization and values of society are addressed specifically or generally in the Quebec Civil Code. The preliminary provision of the Quebec Civil Code sets the stage for the rules that follow. The introduction reads as follows:

> The Civil Code of Quebec, in harmony with the Charter of Human Rights and Freedoms and the general principles of law, governs persons, relations between persons, and property. The Civil Code comprises a body of rules which, in all matters within the letter, spirit or object of its provisions, lays down the jus commune, expressly or by implication. In these matters, the Code is the foundation of all other laws, although other laws may complement the Code or make exceptions to it.

This introduction notes and confirms the primary status that the Quebec Civil Code has in determining legal issues. Although legislation on specific subjects complements the code, the courts are to look first to the Quebec Civil Code to gain direction and authority for any decision. This is in contrast to the Common Law where the courts look first to previous case law or "precedents" that have previously decided similar questions. The Quebec Civil Code is the main and binding authority. Under a civil law régime, previous court decisions are but an aid to give effect to or to refine a codified principle.

CIVIL LAW AND CONTRACTING

Before we get totally absorbed in the heart of the subject matter, I thought it would be appropriate at this juncture to express some of my personal thoughts as to the differences between the two systems of law regarding contractual relationships.

First, both systems of law strive to give effect to the intent of parties who wish to be bound by lawful contracts. Both

Quebec and the rest of Canada share many common values concerning freedom to contract. Both systems support and encourage contracting between individuals as a means of advancing personal or commercial interests. We are not, for example, comparing the common law to China's civil law system, which allows the state to dictate who can be a permissible party to a binding contract. The civil law in Quebec, particularly on the subject of contracting, achieves results that would be similar to conclusions reached under the common law. If one were to apply a series of factual case examples to determine if the two systems arrive at the same conclusion, we would find that they would in fact reach similar conclusions in many instances. How a decision is arrived at constitutes the major difference between the two legal systems in matters concerning contract interpretations.

Actually, we should not be surprised that there is in this field so much similarity because a contract, if all essential terms are spelled out, ends up being the "law of the parties" that the courts will enforce, provided it complies with the requirements of the law.

The Quebec Civil Code is divided into ten different Books and each Book is subdivided into chapters. For information purposes, the Books are as follows:

Book One – Persons (articles 1 to 364)
Book Two – The Family (articles 365 to 612)
Book Three – Successions (articles 613 to 898)
Book Four – Property (articles 899 to 1370)
Book Five – Obligations (articles 1371 to 2643)
Book Six – Prior Claims and Hypothecs (articles 2644 to 2802)
Book Seven – Evidence (articles 2803 to 2874)
Book Eight – Prescription (articles 2875 to 2933)
Book Nine – Publication of Rights (articles 2934 to 3075)
Book Ten – Private International Law (articles 3076 to 3168)

The fifth Book, as you will have noticed, concerns Obligations, and it is in this Book that we find the majority of civil law principles that apply to contractual relations. However, not all contract issues addressed by the Quebec Civil Code are exclusively found in Book Five, for there are other general principles that also apply. Take for example, Articles 6 and 7 at the beginning of the Civil Code. They read as follows.

6. Every person is bound to exercise his civil rights in good faith.

7. No right may be exercised with the intent of injuring another or in an excessive and unreasonable manner which is contrary to the requirements of good faith.

These two provisions are in Book One and they frame the interpretation of subsequent principles. As you can see, the Quebec Civil Code entrenches the principle of good faith as a requirement when exercising civil rights, including the entering into of contracts. The Quebec Civil Code also addresses the notion of good faith specifically under the general Provisions of the Book on Obligations. Article 1375 states that:

1375. The parties shall conduct themselves in good faith both at the time the obligation is created and at the time it is performed or extinguished.

Therefore, regarding contracts under the Quebec Civil Code, the contracting parties must be in good faith when entering into a contract, and when performing or terminating it.

Let's take a moment to illustrate here what is an example of differences we find between our two systems of law, the Common Law and the Civil Law. As we just saw, the Quebec Civil Code is not hesitant to lay down the broad principle of "good faith." In contrast, the Ontario Law Reform Commission grappled with the issue and expressed concern as to the applicability of good faith in pre-contractual situations. Some writers have even suggested that it would be unwise to admit a concept difficult to ascertain in advance for fear of hindering the freedom to contract. In my view, this is a good example of the fundamental difference that separates our two rich legal systems. In the case of the Common Law, we hesitate to recognize broad principles of law in the absence of a clarification tied to a similar set of facts as decided by an earlier court judgement, whereas, under civil law jurisdiction, the principles of law stand out alone in the broadest sense possible, ready to be applied by the courts in Quebec. In law school, civil law training was deductive in nature, while common law study required one to think inductively. In civil law, you start with the principle of law and affirm its application to a particular set of facts. Thereafter, reference is made to case law to confirm the conclusion. Under common law analysis, one matches a set of facts to earlier case law and from such precedent you find the principle of law.

The articles of Book Five comprise some 40 percent of the Quebec Civil Code. Book Five is made up of two broad titles. Title 1 is called OBLIGATIONS IN GENERAL and title 2 is called NOMINATE CONTRACTS. Title 1 addresses obligations in general, be they by way of contract or by general operation of the law. As we will see a little later, Title 2 identifies a certain number of specific contracts that contain particular rules for each, such as a contract of sale.

In Title 1 – OBLIGATIONS IN GENERAL we find nine Chapters that govern obligations of a contractual nature and those that are extra-contractual. They are listed as follows:

Chapter 1 – General Provisions (articles 1371 to 1376)
Chapter 2 – Contracts (articles 1377 to 1456)
Chapter 3 – Civil Liability (articles 1457 to 1481)
Chapter 4 – Certain Other Sources of Obligations (articles 1482 to 1496)
Chapter 5 – Modalities of Obligations (articles 1497 to 1552)
Chapter 6 – Performance of Obligations (articles 1553 to 1636)
Chapter 7 – Transfer and Alteration of Obligations (articles 1637 to 1670)
Chapter 8 – Extinction of Obligations (articles 1671 to 1698)
Chapter 9 – Restitution of Prestations (articles 1699 to 1707)

We will not be able to cover all the issues; however, we will address some main issues that will enable you to see how Quebec law responds to the challenge of interpreting contractual commitments. One must bear in mind that although we see "Contracts" under Chapter 2, this does not mean that the other Chapters are not applicable, for they are equally applicable to contractual matters as well as extra-contractual matters.

Obligations, which are extra-contractual, are important in the context of contracts because they have their equivalence in common law under the heading "torts." A tort is a wrong or an invasion of some legal right of an individual. Under Common Law, tortious conduct exposes one to liability and resulting damages. Examples of torts associated frequently with contracting issues are negligent misstatements and fraudulent misrepresentations. Under civil law, the broad principle, which is analogous to common law torts, can be found at Article 1457. It reads as follows:

> **1457.** Every person has a duty to abide by the rules of conduct which lie upon him, according to the circumstances, usage or law, so as not to cause injury to another. Where he is endowed with reason and fails in this duty, he is responsible for any injury he causes to another person and is liable to reparation for the injury, whether it be bodily, moral, or material in nature. He is also liable, in certain cases, to reparation for injury caused to another by the act or fault of another person or by the act of things in his custody.

The above-referenced provision is the general principle that governs civil liability. General civil liability can be triggered, for example, in a commercial context in the absence of a contractual relationship. An example of this would be a manufacturer's liability for defective goods. In Quebec, there are specific principles applicable to manufacturers and safety defects. They can be found at Articles 1468 to 1469. They read as follows:

> **1468.** The manufacturer of a movable property is liable to reparation for injury caused to a third person by reason of a safety defect in the thing, even if it is incorporated with or placed in an immovable for the service or operation of the immovable.

The same rule applies to a person who distributes the thing under his name or as his own and to any supplier of the thing, whether a wholesaler or a retailer and whether or not he imported the thing.

This provision can place a manufacturer in a position of liability even in the absence of a contract. Furthermore, a distributor, a supplier, a wholesaler, a retailer, or an importer of goods shall be liable to repair damages caused to a person by reason of a safety defect. Also, as an example of the civil law readiness to define a matter, below is the actual definition of a safety defect. It reads:

> **1469.** A thing has a safety defect where, having regard to all the circumstances, it does not afford the safety which a person is normally entitled to expect, particularly by reason of a defect in the design or manufacture of the thing, poor preservation or presentation of the thing, or the lack of sufficient indications as to the risks and dangers it involves or as to safety precautions.

Also, specific contractual liability is found at Article 1458. It reads as follows:

> **1458.** Every person has a duty to honour his contractual undertakings. Where he fails in this duty, he is liable for any bodily, moral, or material injury he causes to the other contracting party and is liable to reparation for the injury; neither he nor the other party may in such a case avoid the rules governing contractual liability by opting for rules that would be more favourable to them.

You will note that in Article 1458, a party to litigation cannot opt for rules that are more favourable. One recognizes with just a few examples that Quebec's system of civil law permits the creation of broad principles of law that are not necessarily judge-made or judge-driven, as in a common law jurisdiction. A good example of this will be seen when we review the principles of contract interpretation.

Formation of Contracts

According to the Quebec Civil Code, a contract is formed with the agreement of the parties. That agreement can be verbal or written. In some cases, the agreement, if it is to be binding, requires a particular form. For example, if Mary and John wish to enter into a marriage contract, Article 440 stipulates that such a contract be in writing and established by a notarial Act.

> **440.** Marriage contracts shall be established by a notarial act en minute, on pain of absolute nullity.

Notarial acts are written agreements that are signed under oath in the presence of a Notary in Quebec and registered thereafter.

Another example of a particular form of contract requirement can be found in the Consumer Protection Act. It requires that a contract is binding when the merchant and consumer sign it and a duplicate copy of the contract has been given to the consumer. When a contract is verbal, and if there are no specific requirements to the contrary, as noted in the two examples above, the contract will be valid and binding. However, in the case of a verbal contract permitted by law, the question is not the validity of the contract but the proof of it and of the terms and conditions agreed upon by the parties. This is equally the case in Common Law jurisdictions.

What kind of consent does Quebec law require to bind a party to a contract? The Quebec Civil Code requires that consent be given in a free and enlightened manner. It states:

> **1399.** Consent may be given only in a free and enlightened manner.
> It may be vitiated by error, fear, or lesion.

In other words, parties to a contract must know and understand the nature of the bargain and liabilities. The consent can be found invalid if error, fear, or lesion were present. For example, Mr. Smith signs a contract for a new Cadillac to be delivered in one week. Instead, the merchant delivers a used Cadillac. In this case the error nullifies Mr. Smith's consent to that contract because the error relates to the nature of the contract.

The Quebec Civil Code spells out each and every factor that may effect consent. Contracts will be valid if the cause of the contract is legal and not prohibited by law or contrary to public order. The Quebec Civil Code at Article 1411 states:

> 1411. A contract whose cause is prohibited by law or contrary to public order is null.

The reason why the parties entered into the contract is the cause of the contract. Therefore, if someone rents a warehouse to traffic in stolen goods, the lease will be declared legally nonexistent because the cause is prohibited by law. Furthermore, the contract must have an "object." The object of a contract is the legal operation that the parties agree upon. If the object of the contract is prohibited by law or contrary to public order, the contract will be null; for example, Mr. Jones hires Mr. Brown to collect money from his borrowers using threats or violence.

Interpretation and Effects of Various Contracts

The revisions and resulting adoption of the Quebec Civil Code in 1994 introduced significant changes that had been developing in legal thinking and decisions over the years. In particular, under the heading "Nature and Certain Classes of Contracts" under Chapter 2 of Title 1, there are several types of contracts singled out for special attention. It will be no surprise that we find a consumer contract listed as a type of contract that receives special attention. The other I will mention is the contract of adhesion (referred to elsewhere in this Book as standard-form contracts). Both classes of contracts have particular additional regulations under law. A contract between a merchant and a consumer is defined in the Quebec Civil Code as a "consumer contract."

> 1384. A consumer contract is a contract whose field of application is delimited by legislation respecting consumer protection whereby one of the parties, being a natural person, the consumer, acquires, leases, borrows or obtains in any other manner, for personal, family or domestic purposes, property or services from the other party, who offers such property and services as part of an enterprise which he carries on.

Also, the Quebec Civil Code defines the contract of adhesion as follows:

> 1379. A contract of adhesion is a contract in which the essential stipulations were imposed or drawn up by one of the parties, on his behalf or upon his instructions, and were not negotiable.
>
> Any contract that is not a contract of adhesion is a contract by mutual agreement.

In both these types of contracts, the law offers special regulations. It does so in this way.

Articles 1435, 1436, and 1437 address three distinct means of protecting the consumer and the adhering party. These articles read as follows:

> 1435. An external clause referred to in a contract is binding on the parties. In a consumer contract or a contract of adhesion, however, an external clause is null if, at the time of formation of the contract, it was not expressly brought to the attention of the consumer or adhering party, unless the other party proves that the consumer or adhering party otherwise knew of it.
>
> 1436. In a consumer contract or a contract of adhesion, a clause which is illegible or incomprehensible to a reasonable person is null if the consumer or the adhering party suffers injury therefrom, unless the other party proves that an adequate explanation of the nature and scope of the clause was given to the consumer or adhering party.
>
> 1437. An abusive clause in a consumer contract or contract of adhesion is null, or the obligation arising from it may be reduced.

An abusive clause is a clause which is excessively and unreasonably detrimental to the consumer or the adhering party and is therefore not in good faith; in particular, a clause which so departs from the fundamental obligations arising from the rules normally governing the contract that it changes the nature of the contract is an abusive clause.

A careful reading of these articles will demonstrate the attention and special consideration that the law attaches to parties that find themselves with less bargaining power. In particular, any clauses referred to in the contract, but not attached to it, will bind the adhering party or a consumer only if such a clause has been explained or known by the adhering party or a consumer prior to executing the contract. Also, a clause, which is illegible or incomprehensible to a reasonable person, will be declared null in favour of the adhering party or consumer if injury results, unless an explanation was given beforehand. Such contracts that contain clauses which are excessively or unreasonably detrimental can also be declared null or alternatively, the obligations imposed on the consumer or adhering party may be reduced. This could include a reduction in payment.

As you may have noted, a contract of adhesion by its very definition at Article 1379 is not considered a contract by mutual consent. As a result, such standard-form agreements receive special attention and, not surprisingly, such contracts, like consumer contracts, are interpreted by the courts in favour of the party who has not drafted the contract. In particular, the purpose for introducing the standard-form contract protection was to provide some equitable relief (based on inherent fairness) for the party that finds itself faced with a pre-printed contract where no negotiation is contemplated. We can all easily recall the many agreements we have all been required to sign from time to time where we essentially are barred from making any changes, such as insurance agreements and loans. Therefore, when the terms and conditions of a contract are not negotiable but imposed by one party on the other, the contract will be classified as an adhesion contract.

Finally, in these cases, the burden of proof will rest with the merchant or stipulant of the adhesion contract. Note that the Quebec Consumer Protection Act provides for many more protections that are well worth reviewing if you plan to purchase in Quebec or sell goods or services to consumers in Quebec.

*   *   *

The two classes of contracts reviewed above give you a flavour of how the law defines certain contracts through the application of codified provisions. It is important to examine the nature of the contract because the Quebec Civil Code will define particular rules and notions of law according to the class and nature of the contract.

While we have provided a couple of examples of classes of contracts, it should be pointed out that there are, in addition, eighteen separate Chapters under Title 2– Nominate Contracts which have special rules for each type of contract. For example, if the contract is a contract of sale Articles 1708 to 1805 will apply, inclusive of special rules regarding sale of residential property. Other important chapters address various contracts such as gifts, leasing, affreightment, carriage, contracts of employment and for services, mandate, contracts of partnership and of association, and deposit, loan, suretyship, annuities, insurance, and arbitration agreements.

Naturally doing business in the province of Quebec will likely involve a contract under the Quebec Civil Code and general and specific provisions as described above will be applicable.

Finally, please take note of the interpretation rules for contracts in general. In preparing a contract or examining a contract that could be the subject of litigation, the professional will have to ask, what was the common intention of the parties?

The Quebec Civil Code provides explicit guidelines to find the intention of the parties. These are contained in Articles 1425 to 1432 of the Quebec Civil Code reproduced below:

1425. The common intention of the parties rather than adherence to the literal meaning of the words shall be sought in interpreting a contract.

1426. In interpreting a contract, the nature of the contract, the circumstances in which it was formed, the interpretation which has already been given to it by the parties or which it may have received, and usage, are all taken into account.

1427. Each clause of a contract is interpreted in light of the others so that each is given the meaning derived from the contract as a whole.

1428. A clause is given a meaning that gives it some effect rather than one that gives it no effect.

1429. Words susceptible of two meanings shall be given the meaning that best conforms to the subject matter of the contract.

1430. A clause intended to eliminate doubt as to the application of the contract to a specific situation does not restrict the scope of a contract otherwise expressed in general terms.

1431. The clauses of a contract cover only what it appears that the parties intended to include, however general the terms used.

1432. In case of doubt, a contract is interpreted in favour of the person who contracted the obligation and against the person who stipulated it. In all cases, it is interpreted in favour of the adhering party or the consumer.

As these provisions will govern the interpretation of a contract under the jurisdiction of the Quebec Civil Code, it is wise to keep them in mind when formulating the contract as well.

JURISDICTION

Except for some contracts such as a consumer contract, it is possible for a party outside Quebec not to be subject to the Quebec Civil Code when contracting with someone living in Quebec. To do so, the parties must agree and expressly include in the contract which law will be designated as applicable. The Quebec Civil Code, in Book Ten, entitled "Private International Law," stipulates:

3111. A juridical act, whether or not it contains any foreign element, is governed by the law expressly designated in the act or the designation of which may be inferred with certainty from the terms of the act.

A juridical act containing no foreign element remains, nevertheless, subject to the mandatory provisions of the law of the country which would apply if none were designated.

The law of a country may be expressly designated as applicable to the whole or a part only of a juridical act.

Regarding conflict of laws, the application of the law is quite complex depending on the nature of the contract, on the nature of the legal document involved. At times, counsel in this field will look at international conventions and treaties to determine the law applicable.

A consumer contract is an exception to the above-stated general rule. We must refer to the following provision to understand the complexity of the matter. The Quebec Civil Code addresses this point as follows:

3117. The choice by the parties of the law applicable to a consumer contract does not result in depriving the consumer of the protection to which he is entitled under the mandatory provisions of the law of the country where he has his residence if the formation of the contract was preceded by a special offer or an advertisement in that country and the consumer took all the necessary steps for the formation of the contract in that country or if the order was received from the consumer in that country.

The same rule also applies where the consumer was induced by the other contracting party to travel to a foreign country for the purpose of forming the contract.

If no law is designated by the parties, the law of the place where the consumer has his residence is, in the same circumstances, applicable to the consumer contract.

Except for consumer contracts, parties are free to elect the governing law for the contract. The Quebec Civil Code specifies that such a clause must be in writing. Therefore, the contracting party will be able to choose, as an example, the law of Ontario to govern the contract and the rights arising from it. This is stated in the Quebec Civil Code at Article 83:

83. The parties to a juridical act may, in writing, elect domicile with a view to the execution of the act or the exercise of the rights arising from it.

Election of domicile is not presumed.

Doing business with Quebec individuals or companies does not mean that any resultant contract will automatically be governed by the Quebec Civil Code. To know whether it does, one looks first to the agreement to see if the parties have mutually selected a jurisdiction and provided for it in the contract. If not, private international law notions will apply in addition to the Quebec Civil Code. The Quebec Civil Code provides that no matter how the parties communicate, the contract is formed when and where the acceptance of an offer is received. The Quebec Civil Code states the following at Article 1387:

1387. A contract is formed when and where acceptance is received by the offeror, regardless of the method of communication used, and even though the parties have agreed to reserve agreement as to secondary terms.

This is the "Reception Theory": that is, the contract is formed when and where the acceptance of an offer is received. It should be noted that when there are counteroffers, such might have an effect as to when and where the contract is formed. This could have the impact of changing what legal system would be applicable. The Quebec Civil Code addresses this matter in Article 1389, which states:

1389. An offer to contract derives from the person who initiates the contract or the person who determines its content or even, in certain cases, the person who presents the last essential element of the proposed contract.

A counteroffer that effects when and where the contract is formed must concern an essential element of the contract such as price or the like. One ought to keep detailed records of contractual negotiations generally, and especially if your negotiations involve the risk of another jurisdiction applying to the contract.

*   *   *

This has been a very brief outline of the major points of the law of contracts in Quebec. Although in many cases we find corresponding principles in the Common Law jurisdiction, the procedures and mechanics to interpret contracts under the Quebec Civil Code are different. It should have given you enough of an insight into the important legal principles and provisions which govern this area. This description should not be taken as legal advice but rather as an introductory background so that you can feel somewhat more at ease when dealing with contracts subject to Quebec jurisdiction.

Chapter 5
The Sale and Purchase Contract

Conditions Implied by the Act, *Title, Sample Purchase and Sale Contract, Description of Terms*

The contract of sale (and, obviously, purchase) is arguably the most common commercial contract. It is the workhorse of business agreements, quite often not given the respect and time accorded some other contracts such as employment agreements, licenses, and such; but it is always there doing its job. Despite its implied presence in the smallest of purchases (gum) right through to major contracts (to supply fighter aircraft), it can be easy to overlook—particularly in small-dollar-volume or repetitive transactions.

Governments have not overlooked contracts of sale and purchase, having enacted legislation to define and specify the exact nature and prerequisites of the exchange. All common-law provinces in Canada have enacted what are essentially duplicates of the British *Sale of Goods Act*, and these laws govern the sale of goods throughout Canada. The original British act set into the legal code the prevailing common law regarding sale and purchase. Although its underlying premise is the well-worn maxim *caveat emptor*, or "Let the buyer beware," the Act implies and demands certain minimum standards of conduct on the parts of both the seller and the buyer.

Goods are, as defined specifically within the Act, all personal chattels excepting choses in action and money. Thus, the Act does not apply to real property (real estate) or to transactions in which the property being sold is a "thing" (from the French *chose*) that derives its value by the binding obligation or right it represents or is a negotiable instrument—choses in action. Moreover, the Act does not apply to transactions that are barter; money must be exchanged for goods in order that the Act be applicable. It does, however, apply both to actual sales, when title and possession pass to the new owner, and to agreements or contracts to sell, when the transfer of title is to pass later.

CONDITIONS IMPLIED BY THE ACT

The following are, briefly, some of the more important things to know about the *Sale of Goods Act* as reflected in most provincial acts of the same or a similar name. They are, generally speaking, conditions (major terms) of the contract, the breach of which would be considered major.

• *Implied right to title*
There is an implied condition that the seller has title to the goods and the right to sell them. We simply expect that the person selling us merchandise has the right to do so. But there are times, such as when goods are stolen or otherwise do not belong to the seller, that our expectations are dashed. In most circumstances, one would not ask the seller, "Oh, by the way, do you have title to this merchandise and can you legally sell it to me?" It is implied by the seller in her offer to sell.

• *Implied correspondence to description*
If the goods are being sold by description, there is an implied condition that the actual merchandise will correspond to the description provided. Mail order merchandise, or custom goods purchased on the basis of a description or plan, are excellent examples of when this condition is effective.

• *Implied fitness of goods*
The goods are implied to be fit for the use which the vendor specifies and the purchaser intends for them. Wise sellers

clearly identify acceptable and unacceptable uses for their goods; and the cautious purchaser questions whether the merchandise will be fit for her intended use. This condition may be waived if the purchaser uses the goods for an unspecified and unanticipated purpose without advising the seller in advance.

• *Implied correspondence to sample*

When goods are sold by sample, the sale contract has a condition that the actual, delivered merchandise will correspond with the sample. Consider how manufacturers sell clothing to retailers. A sample line is created that represents the final product, and a representative takes orders for the product. Six to nine months later when the bulk order is delivered, if it is not the same colour, size, fabric, or finish as ordered, the retailer can reject the order. More likely the purchaser will accept the goods with some incentive such as a discount.

• *Delivery of goods*

The quantity and time of the delivery of the goods purchased are usually conditions within the contract. Technically the purchaser may reject the merchandise if the volume delivered is higher or lower than that specified in the agreement. As mentioned in an earlier chapter, there is an element of reasonableness to be exercised. If the delivered volume is practically close to that ordered, the purchaser may have a tough time repudiating the whole order. However, only what is provided is generally paid for if there is short-shipment; over-shipments are returned, discounted, or not paid for depending on the circumstances. Also, if a delivery is late (and, sometimes, if it is early), the purchaser may repudiate the order and rescind the contract. A date and place for delivery must be specified in order to avail oneself of this condition; if delivery is ASAP, delivery within a reasonable time must be accepted.

> ## Exemption from Implied Conditions
>
> A contract can be prepared that specifically provides for the sale to be exempt from the conditions implied by the *Sale of Goods Act*. If one agrees to such a contract, the terms and conditions of the signed contract supercede the *Act*'s implied conditions, and the purchaser can no longer avail herself of the protection afforded by the *Act*.

Payment timing is considered a warranty, and as such a buyer's breach of meeting the payment deadline would likely not be considered a major breach. Thus, if you sold a computer to me and I missed the payment date (say, "Net 15"), I would be in breach of a minor term of our contract. You would not, therefore, have as an option the right to rescind or void the contract. You have to fight it out the hard way; unless, of course, our contract provided for some other remedy in the event of late payment.

Title

A key issue in the sale of goods is the determination of when the title of ownership passes between the parties. Because the transfer of ownership is not necessarily coincidental with the change in possession of the goods or with the payment for the goods, the *Act* has provided several rules regarding the passage of title.

> Responsibility and liability are probably the most significant reasons for being sure of when the title has passed between you and the purchaser/vendor. It is not unusual to have merchandise in transit between parties, or have purchased goods awaiting shipment in the vendor's warehouse. What if something happens to destroy that merchandise? Whether title has passed determines who is responsible for the goods, and therefore who is liable and has incurred a loss. It is worthwhile making sure of when title passes.

The first four of the *Act*'s rules for determining when title passes pertain to *specific goods* (i.e., existing merchandise that has been *specifically* set aside for the purchaser), and the last to *unascertained goods* (i.e., merchandise that has not been earmarked for the purchaser, or has, in fact, not yet been manufactured).

1. Title passes *immediately* when an unconditional contract is made for specific goods, regardless of payment or delivery terms. For example, say you buy an IBM Aptiva *from off the floor of the computer store.* Regardless of whether it is to be delivered or picked up and taken out, whether you pay cash or on credit, you own it immediately upon the sale being made.

2. If the vendor must alter or augment the specific merchandise purchased, title does not pass until those changes are made and the buyer has been notified. For instance, if you buy a car off the lot subject to it being Ziebart-coated, title does not pass until the dealer does the job *and advises you*—even though you may have paid for the car.

3. If the vendor must weigh, measure, test, or otherwise probe the specific merchandise being purchased in order to determine its price, the title does not pass until those tasks are done and the purchaser is advised. Consider a situation in which you are purchasing several rods of plutonium for your backyard CANDU reactor, and the scrupulous international arms trader has to test the plutonium grade and weigh out the rods to give you a price. Even though you have made the purchase, title does not pass until those activities have been completed and you have been properly advised.

4. If specific merchandise is provided "on approval" or other such terms, title passes to the buyer (a) when approval is signaled to the vendor in word or act or (b) when the purchaser has retained the goods past the return deadline (or a reasonable time if no deadline has been set) and has not specifically rejected the goods.

5. Title to merchandise passes to the buyer who has made a contract for the purchase of unascertained goods when (a) suitable merchandise is appropriated to the contract with mutual consent of both buyer and seller or (b) suitable merchandise has been appropriated and placed in transit to the purchaser, so long as the seller does not retain the right of disposal. For example, a retailer purchases from a manufacturer shirts to be produced before a set delivery date. These unascertained, future goods would become the property of the retailer either (a) when they became mutually acceptable specific goods or (b) when the manufacturer put the goods for the retailer's order on a carrier's truck.

A SAMPLE SALE AND PURCHASE CONTRACT

The following is a sample sale and purchase agreement that might be used for a reasonably large transaction. It is not a form that anyone specifically uses, but was obtained from a legal reference book of precedents.[1] The content is relatively common and general, and I have left some of the "blanks" open with descriptions of how they would be completed. In this kind of agreement, many of the terms and conditions are purely the subjective choice of the drafting party, who will include terms needed to effect the desires of the parties to the agreement.

I would remind you to use the sample contract and comments as a guide and reference only. Consult a legal professional when dealing with your own contracts.

The Contract

THIS AGREEMENT made this 11th day of April, 1999, between Big Seller Ltd., of the City of Fredericton, a corporation incorporated under the laws of New Brunswick (the "Vendor") and The Real Superbuyer Inc., a corporation incorporated under the laws of Canada (the "Purchaser").

WHEREAS:

1. The Vendor is the owner of <description of goods to be sold> (the "Assets");

The significant factor to notice in this recital is that the nature of the goods being sold should be described suitably so as to cause no confusion about them, and they are described as being the vendor's property to sell.

2. The Vendor wishes to sell, assign and transfer and the Purchaser wishes to purchase the Assets on and subject to the terms and conditions of this Agreement:

IN CONSIDERATION of the respective covenants and agreements contained in this Agreement and for other good and valuable consideration (the receipt and sufficiency of which is mutually acknowledged), the parties covenant and agree as follows:

1. **Definitions**

As used in this Agreement, unless their subject-matter or context is inconsistent, the following terms shall have the following meanings:

(a) "Agreement" means this Agreement of Purchase and Sale of the Assets and all instruments supplemental to it or in amendment or confirmation of it;

(b) "Assets" means <description of goods to be sold>;

(c) "Closing" means the completion of the sale to and purchase by the Purchaser of the Assets by the transfer and delivery of documents of title;

(d) "Closing Date" means the 30th day of April, 1999, or another date as the parties may agree as the date on which the Closing shall take place;

(e) "Closing Time" means 10:00 a.m. (Fredericton time) on the Closing Date or an earlier or later date as the parties may agree as the time at which the Closing shall take place;

(f) "Parties" means the Vendor and the Purchaser, collectively, and "party" means any one of them;

(g) "Person" means any individual, corporation, partnership, unincorporated syndicate, unincorporated organization, trust, trustee, executor, administrator, or other legal representative; and

(h) "Purchase Price" means the amount as set out in paragraph 2(2) in this Agreement.

2. **Purchase and Sale**

(1) *Purchase and Sale.* Subject to the terms and conditions of this Agreement, and in reliance on the representations, warranties and conditions set forth in this Agreement, the Vendor agrees to sell, assign, transfer and deliver to the Purchaser and the Purchaser agrees to purchase from the Vendor the Assets.[2]

(2) *Purchase Price.* The Purchase Price for the Assets shall be the sum of fifty thousand dollars ($50,000).

(3) *Payment.* The Purchaser shall pay and satisfy the Purchase Price as follows:

(a) as to twenty-five thousand dollars ($25,000) by delivery of an initial deposit payment made the 11th day of April, 1999, the receipt and sufficiency of which is acknowledged by the Vendor;

(b) as to the balance of the Purchase Price, together with any interest on the unpaid balance, payment as set out below: $15,000 plus interest accrued 30 April 1999; $5,000 plus interest accrued 15 May 1999; $5,000 plus interest accrued 30 May 1999.

If the transaction contemplated in this Agreement does not close due to default by the Vendor of any of its obligations, or due to the non-fulfillment or non-performance of any of the conditions set forth in paragraph 4(1), the deposit shall be repaid to the Purchaser. If the transaction contemplated in this Agreement does not close due to default by the Purchaser of any of its obligations, the Vendor shall be entitled to retain the deposit.

Always follow the reference "links" from paragraph to paragraph. In this case there is a reference to paragraph 4(1), which defines the conditions required of the vendor before the purchaser's obligations under this agreement become effective. The last sentence of this clause essentially provides for liquidated damages to the vendor's benefit if the deal should not close.

(4) *Interest.* Any balance of the Purchase Price unpaid as of the date of this Agreement shall bear interest at the rate of 4.0% per month.

3. **Representations and Warranties**

(1) *Vendor.* The Vendor represents and warrants to the Purchaser that:

(a) the Vendor is a corporation duly incorporated under the laws of New Brunswick;

This sub-clause is a little repetitive, since it was established under the listing of parties to the agreement. Probably it exists here as a "warranty"; that is, a misrepresentation would be a technical breach of a minor term of the contract. In any event, it applies only to corporate vendors and would be different if the vendor were a person.

(b) the Vendor has all necessary corporate power, authority, and capacity to enter into this Agreement and to perform its obligations under the Agreement;

Such a representation and warranty is significant to ensure that the vendor (if it is a corporation) has the requisite power to contract for this sale inasmuch as there could be prohibitions upon it as set by statute or the vendor's own corporate bylaws, or by its shareholders, lenders, or other related parties.

(c) this Agreement constitutes a valid and binding obligation of the Vendor enforceable against it in accordance with the terms of this Agreement, subject, however, to limitations with respect to enforcement imposed by law in connection with bankruptcy, insolvency, or similar proceedings relating to creditors' rights generally and to the extent that equitable remedies such as specific performance and injunction are in the discretion of a court of competent jurisdiction;

The vendor and the purchaser agree in this paragraph that in the event that there is a bankruptcy or some such similar proceeding taken upon the vendor, this contract will become subject to the laws and practices that apply to such situations.

(d) the Vendor is not a party to, bound or affected by, or subject to any indenture, mortgage, lease, agreement, instrument, charter or by-law provision, statute, rule, regulation, judgement, order, writ, decree, or law which, with or without the giving of notice or the lapse of time, or both, would be violated, contravened, breached by, or under which default would occur as a result of the execution, delivery, and performance of this Agreement or the consummation of any of the transactions provided for in it;

This representation and warranty, similar to paragraph (b) of this section, specifically applies to any form of claim upon the assets being purchased, or other such prohibition or rule that the vendor's selling of the assets would breach (or would, in fact, prevent the sale in the first place) and void the agreement.

(e) the Vendor is the absolute beneficial owner of the Assets, with good and marketable title, free and clear of any liens, charges, encumbrances, or rights of others (other than statutory liens for taxes, assessments, and other governmental charges the payment for which is not yet due and owing) and is exclusively entitled to possess and dispose of the same;

This term is implied by the *Act* in a contract of sale. In this contract, however, it has been made a specific warranty.

(f) as far as the Vendor is aware, no person has any written or oral agreement, option, understanding, or commitment, or any right or privilege capable of becoming an agreement for the purchase from the Vendor of any of the Assets;

The vendor is representing that *to the best of its knowledge* nobody else has already purchased the assets in question.[3]

(g) as far as the Vendor is aware, there is no proceeding in progress or pending or threatened against, relating to, or affecting the Vendor in connection with the Assets which might be expected to have a materially adverse effect on the Assets;

The purchaser is getting covered every which way from Sunday, with ever-more-specific variations on the same theme, i.e., that the assets are free and clear to be sold to the purchaser. In this case the concern is already-commenced legal proceedings against the vendor that would have an impact on the vendor's ability to sell the assets.

(h) the Vendor is not a non-resident of Canada for the purposes of the *Income Tax Act*, R.S.C. 1952, c 148; and

I am not entirely sure of the purpose of this paragraph, but would suspect that tax assessment and collection are the underlying reasons for its inclusion. That is, tax as applicable to the sale must be collected and the Canadian purchaser could be held accountable if it is not collected and remitted to Revenue Canada.

> (i) no consent, authorization, or approval of, or exemption by, any governmental or public body or authority, or by any Person, whether pursuant to contract or otherwise, is required in connection with the execution, delivery, and performance of this Agreement by the Vendor or of any of the instruments or agreements referred to, or the taking of any action contemplated.

The effect of this warranty is to strip the vendor of any conditions to the final sale of the assets. That is, it removes from the vendor the right to claim it cannot complete its obligations due to some other party's withholding of consent to complete the transaction and fulfill its part of the agreement.

> (2) *Purchaser.* The Purchaser represents and warrants to the Vendor that:
> (a) the Purchaser is a corporation duly incorporated under the laws of Canada.

Refer to comments pertaining to Section 3(1)(a).

> (b) the Purchaser has all necessary corporate power, authority, and capacity to enter into this Agreement and to perform its obligations under the Agreement;

Refer to comments pertaining to Section 3(1)(b).

> (c) this Agreement constitutes a valid and binding obligation of the Purchaser, enforceable against it in accordance with its terms, subject, however, to limitations with respect to enforcement imposed by law in connection with bankruptcy, insolvency, or similar proceedings relating to creditors' rights generally and to the extent that equitable remedies such as specific performance and injunction are in the discretion of a court of competent jurisdiction;

Refer to comments pertaining to Section 3(1)(c).

> (d) the Purchaser is not a party to, bound or affected by, or subject to any indenture, mortgage, lease, agreement, instrument, charter or by-law provision, statute, rule, regulation, judgement, order, writ, decree or law which, with or without the giving of notice or the lapse of time, or both, would be violated, contravened, breached by, or under which default would occur as a result of the execution, delivery, and performance of this Agreement or the consummation of any of the transactions provided for in it; and

Refer to comments pertaining to Section 3(1)(d). In the case of the purchaser, one must assume that this paragraph relates specifically to prohibitions on the purchaser's owning such assets as are part of this agreement or on its transacting such purchases at all. This is possible for a variety of reasons.

> (e) no consent, authorization or approval of, or exemption by, any governmental or public body or authority, or by any Person, whether pursuant to contract or otherwise, is required in connection with the execution, delivery and performance of this Agreement by the Purchaser or of any of the instruments or agreements referred to, or the taking of any action contemplated.

Refer to comments pertaining to Section 3(1)(i).

(3) *Survival after Closing.* All statements contained in any certificate or other instrument delivered by or on behalf of a party pursuant to or in connection with the transactions contemplated by this Agreement shall be deemed to be made by that party under this Agreement. All representations, warranties, covenants, and agreements contained in this Agreement on the part of each of the parties shall survive the Closing, and the execution and delivery of any bills of sale, instruments of conveyance, assignments, or other instruments of transfer of title to any of the Assets and the payment of the consideration therefor; . . .

Note that the agreement and all its terms survive the closing of the deal. The basic purpose of this term is to ensure that any provisions or obligations, such as payment or the representations and warranties made, do not come to an end when the sale closes and the agreement is effectively completed and terminated by "performance." Those terms would, in the absence of this clause, quite possibly be unenforceable in court or otherwise by the other party.

. . . provided, however, that all representations and warranties contained in paragraph 3(1) and (2) of this Agreement shall survive only for a period of three (3) years from the Closing Time, after which time, if no claims shall, prior to the expiry of that period, have been made by a party with respect to any incorrectness in or breach of any representation or warranty made by that party, the party shall have no further liability with respect to that representation or warranty.

Do you see how this contract provides its own "statute of limitations" on claims against either party? The need for this part of the paragraph is to close the loop that was opened by the first part of the paragraph (i.e., survival after closing). Technically, without some form of limitation, the survival of the terms of this agreement would extend forever. And there needs to be closure for everything at some point.

(4) *Limitations on Vendor's Representations and Warranties.* The Purchaser acknowledges and agrees that the Assets are being sold and purchased on an "as is, where is" basis and, except for the express representations and warranties given in paragraph 3(1), no representation or warranty expressed or implied has been or is given by the Vendor concerning the Assets.

This particular paragraph has an effect similar to the "entire agreement" general term that states something like "This document constitutes the whole of the agreement between the parties," in the sense that both parties agree that anything not specifically written into this document is immaterial. All *implied* warranties are no longer operative, which may or may not have an effect on the parties' rights as provided by statute depending on the specifics of the written warranties within the contract itself.

The clauses and sub-clauses of the section shown below refer to the "conditions" (i.e., things that must be done or must happen; not necessarily major terms of the agreement) that must precede closing of the deal as they pertain to the respective parties. The clauses provided here are samples of fairly common and general conditions precedent. Every agreement is likely to have conditions unique and specific to its circumstances. The comments made below are merely for clarification of heavy language.

4. Conditions Precedent to Closing

(1) *Conditions Precedent to Purchaser's Obligations.* The obligation of the Purchaser to complete the purchase of the Assets under this Agreement shall be subject to the satisfaction of or compliance with, at, or before the Closing Time, each of the following conditions precedent (each of which is acknowledged to be for the exclusive benefit of the Purchaser and may be waived by it in whole or in part):

(a) *Truth and Accuracy of Representations at Closing Time.* All of the written representations and warranties of the Vendor made in or pursuant to this Agreement, and any other agreement or certificate made or delivered, including the representations and warranties made by the Vendor as set forth in paragraph 3(1), shall be true and correct in all material respects as at the Closing Time and with the same effect as if made at and as of the Closing Time;

(b) *Performance of Obligations.* The Vendor shall have performed or complied with, in all respects, all of its obligations, covenants, and agreements under this Agreement;

(c) *Receipt of Closing documentation.* All instruments of conveyance and other documentation relating to the sale and purchase of the Assets reasonably requested by the Purchaser including, without limitation, bills of sale, trade mark assignments, documentation relating to the due authorization, and completion of sale and purchase and all actions and proceedings taken on or prior to the Closing in connection with the performance by the Vendor of its obligations under this Agreement shall be satisfactory to the Purchaser and Purchaser's legal counsel and the Purchaser shall have received copies of all documentation or other evidence as it may reasonably request in order to establish the consummation of the transactions contemplated and the taking of all corporate proceedings in connection therewith in compliance with these conditions;

Note especially how the approval of the purchaser's lawyer is drawn into this paragraph. This can be an important condition, as I found out quite personally. Its import is that you (in this case the purchaser) have a higher authority on whom to rely to ensure that from both legal and practical perspectives you have not made a bad bargain or one that is not right by law. In this case legal counsel's approval is required for closing documentation and fulfillment of the conditions precedent. Generally speaking, that requirement can be extended as far as desired.

(d) *Consents, Authorizations, and Registrations.* All consents, approvals, orders, and authorizations of any persons or governmental authorities in Canada or elsewhere (or registration, declarations, filings, or records with any authorities) including, without limitation, all registrations, recordings, and filings with public authorities as may be required in connection with the transfer of ownership to the Purchaser of the Assets shall have been obtained on or before the Closing Time provided that if, after using its best efforts, the Vendor shall have been unable to obtain any necessary consents, approvals, orders, and authorizations of any governmental authorities in Canada or elsewhere necessary for the completion of the transactions contemplated by this Agreement, and the Purchaser shall not waive that condition, this Agreement shall be null and void without liability between the parties; and

(e) *Bulk Sales.* The Vendor shall have complied with the provisions of the provincial bulk sales legislation.

This particular condition addresses a statutory issue regarding "bulk sales," which is, as generally defined, a sale of a portion of the vendor's business assets that will impair its ongoing business. Included might be all or most of its stock in trade, or its other equipment, fixtures, assets, chattels, and so forth. A bulk sale most often would arise in conjunction with the sale of a business. The purpose of the Bulk Sales Act in each jurisdiction (province) is to protect the vendor's creditors against their debtor's (the vendor's) business being sold out from under them and the debtor leaving them without recourse to satisfy the debts. The buyer generally bears the brunt of the responsibility to the creditors after the deal is completed, which is where this paragraph has its effect. Essentially, the purchaser here has put the onus back on the vendor to ensure that it has complied with the terms of the appropriate Bulk Sales Act that permit the purchaser to be without obligation to any creditors. Generally, this would include the vendor (1) paying off the creditors or obtaining their agreement and permission for the sale, (2) having a suitably small aggregate credit volume outstanding (e.g., $2,500 in Ontario), or (3) providing an affidavit to the purchaser that assures the purchaser that the vendor has taken care of its creditors. Additionally, the Bulk Sales Act in many provinces demands that a public notice of a bulk sale be made (a "Notice to Creditors").

(2) *Conditions Precedent to Vendor's Obligations.* The obligation of the Vendor to complete the sale of the Assets shall be subject to the satisfaction of or compliance with, at or before the Closing Time, each of the following conditions precedent (each of which is acknowledged to be for the exclusive benefit of the Vendor and may be waived by it in whole or in part):

(a) *Truth and Accuracy of Representations at Closing Time.* All of the written representations and warranties of the Vendor made in or pursuant to this Agreement, and any other agreement or certificate made or delivered, including the representations and warranties made by the Vendor as set forth in paragraph 3(2), shall be true and correct in all material respects as at the Closing Time and with the same effect as if made at and as of the Closing Time and the Vendor shall have received a certificate from a senior officer of the Purchaser confirming, to the best of his knowledge, information, and belief (after due inquiry), the truth and correctness in all material respects of the representations and warranties of the Purchaser;

(b) *Performance of Obligations.* The Purchaser shall have performed or complied with, in all respects, all of its obligations, covenants, and agreements under this Agreement;

(c) *Retail Sales Tax.* The Purchaser shall have delivered to the Vendor a provincial sales tax exemption certificate and a certified cheque or bank draft in an amount estimated to be equal to the sales tax payable in accordance with <name of provincial sales tax legislation> arising from the transaction contemplated by this Agreement; and

This contract example specifies provincial sales tax but presumably a similar provision would be included if other taxes such as the GST/HST were applicable. Sales taxes are levied on the vendor, although it is supposed to collect those taxes payable from the purchaser. This paragraph ensures that the payment of the taxes is not left behind to collect later, when the vendor has the onus to remit collected taxes to the government, and the purchaser has little incentive to hurry with its payment.

(d) *Security.* The Vendor shall have received the security contemplated in paragraph 5.

Follow the thread to paragraph 5.

(3) *Actions to Satisfy Closing Transaction.* Each of the parties shall take all actions as are within its power to control, and use its best efforts to cause other actions to be taken which are not within their power to control, so as to further comply with any conditions set forth in paragraph 4 which are for the benefit of any other party.

What does this paragraph say? Each party has to do its part where it has control and help where is does not have control, to close the deal. This includes ensuring that all the conditions precedent listed in paragraph 4 are met.

(4) *Non-fulfilment of Condition Precedent.* In the event that the Vendor or the Purchaser fails to comply with any condition precedent set out in paragraph 4(1) or (2) required to be complied with at or before the Closing Time and the Purchaser or the Vendor, as the case may be, does not waive that condition, this Agreement shall be null and void as at the Closing Time, without liability between the parties.

Repetitive for effect maybe? If the conditions precedent are not fulfilled, *and* the condition is not waived by the party to whom the condition is beneficial, the agreement collapses. Moreover, there will be no liability on either party except the liquidated damages noted in clause 2, if applicable (the vendor can keep the deposit if the deal does not close at the purchaser's fault).

In the next section, shown below, the vendor is provided with security for the payment of the purchaser's obligation. The security may take different forms, and in this example there is a personal guarantee (5(1)) from a principal of the business or some other party, and a mortgage (5(2)) on a real property asset in favour of the vendor. In other agreements where security is a term, its nature may be substantially or moderately different depending on the circumstances (size and nature of the purchase) and the parties. The security provided herein may, in fact, be a little extreme (or redundant).

5. Security

(1) *Personal Guarantee of Purchaser.* The Purchaser shall deliver to the Vendor a personal guarantee of Don McPherson in the form attached as Schedule "A"[4] pursuant to which Don McPherson shall guarantee the payment by the Purchaser, pursuant to the terms of this Agreement, of the Purchase Price and any interest.

(2) *Collateral Mortgage.* In order to secure the amounts owing under the personal guarantee described in paragraph 5(1) Don McPherson shall grant a collateral mortgage to the Vendor of the property at 125 Waterton Avenue, Fredericton, New Brunswick.

6. General

(1) *Time.* Time shall be of the essence.

(2) *Notices.* Any notice or other writing required or permitted to be given under this Agreement or for the purposes of it

to any party, shall be sufficiently given if delivered personally, or if sent by prepaid registered mail or if transmitted by telex, telecopier, or other form of recorded communication to that party:

(a) in the case of a notice to the Purchaser at <an address>; and

(b) in the case of a notice to the Vendor at <an address>; or

at any other address as the party to whom the writing is to be given shall have last notified the other party. Any notice delivered to the party to whom it is addressed as provided shall be deemed to have been given and received on the day it is delivered at that address, provided that if that day is not a business day then the notice shall be deemed to have been given and received on the first business day next following that day. Any notice mailed shall be deemed to have been given and received on the third business day next following the date of its mailing. Any notice transmitted by telex, telecopier, or other form of recorded communication shall be deemed given and received on the first business day after its transmission.

(3) *Assignment.* Neither this Agreement nor any rights, remedies, liabilities, or obligations arising under it or by reason of it shall be assignable by any party without the prior written consent of the other party. Subject thereto, this Agreement shall enure to the benefit of and be binding on the parties and their respective successors and permitted assigns.

(4) *Further Assurances.* The parties shall with reasonable diligence do all things and provide all reasonable assurances as may be required to consummate the transactions contemplated by this Agreement, and each party shall provide further documents or instruments required by any other party as may be reasonably necessary or desirable to effect the purpose of this Agreement and to carry out its provisions, whether before or after the Closing.

(5) *Entire Agreement.* The Agreement constitutes the entire agreement between the parties and, except as stated in it and in the instruments and documents to be executed and delivered, contains all the representations and warranties of the respective parties. There are no oral representations or warranties among the parties of any kind. This Agreement may not be amended or modified in any respect except by written instrument signed by both parties.

(6) *Non-merger.* The representations, warranties, covenants, and agreements contained in this Agreement or in any instrument, document, or written statement delivered pursuant to this Agreement shall survive and not merge on Closing.

Again, more repetition. I would think this was probably adequately covered in Section 3(3).

(7) *Applicable Law.* This Agreement shall be interpreted in accordance with the laws of the Province of New Brunswick, and the laws of Canada applicable therein, and shall be treated in all respects as a New Brunswick contract.

IN WITNESS WHEREOF the parties have caused the Agreement to be executed by their respective officers which are duly authorized, as of the date first above written.

BIG SELLER LTD.,
Vendor
Per:

THE REAL SUPERBUYER INC.,
Purchaser
Per:

_____
Mike Wyck,
President

_____
Don McPherson,
General Manager

Chapter 6
The Employment Contract

Sample Employment Letters and Their Terms

Arguably, the second-most-common commercial contract after the purchase and sale contract is the contract of employment. While we might tend to think of employment contracts as relating only to collectively bargained contracts with unions or management and executive employment situations, in fact every act of employment is a contractual situation. There is common law—both employment and contract law—that applies to the employment contract. There is also the overriding applicable statutory law created by the federal and most provincial governments (e.g., the federal *Labour Act* and *Human Rights Act*, and various provincial legislation for worker's compensation, labour standards, etc.).

The reason one might not initially think of the nonunionized secretarial, clerk, driver, or other such employment situation as having an employment contract is because formal contracts with such individuals are few. At best, a business may offer a letter setting out what the employee is being hired to do and for what type of compensation (money, benefits, paid vacation, etc.). This is usually followed up by some kind of published statement of the company's "employment policy." In general, the policies closely mirror the employment standards or imply the conditions of the provincial employment standards legislation into the specific contract of employment. For example, paid vacation time is statutorily required. In short, nonmanagerial, nonunion employment is often not given a great deal of thought vis à vis contractual obligations.

You may have noticed in the preceding how I specified more than once that what we usually do not consider and overlook as being contractual forms of employment are nonunion, nonmanagerial employment situations. Union employment, on the other hand, with a more elaborate and visible collective bargaining process, is marked by formal and usually exhaustive employment agreements. Lawyers and other negotiators/representatives are deeply involved in the creation of these contracts for both management and the union. It is an area of special expertise that people involved must possess, and precious little needs to be added by me here. Thus, union contracts are omitted. After all, it is only fair to assume that the lawyers are well versed in the law of employment contracts and are providing adequate information to you, their clients/employers.

At the other end of the personnel spectrum are executives. Businesses that have "executive" and "upper management" layers are, I assume, abundantly aware that such employment is also made under the fairly exacting—and expensive—terms of employment contract. Later in this chapter we will look at a management employment contract. But due to the very specific nature of upper-executive contracts, detailed examination those employment agreements will be left to books and texts better suited for the topic.

All employment, at the bottom and at the top, is ruled and regulated by the several acts of legislation mentioned above. The employer and employee should be aware of at least the following facts:

> • Employees cannot be terminated without just cause ("just," of course, in the sense of "justice" not "merely," although this semantic mix-up could be interesting), unless given reasonable notice or compensated in lieu of notice. Typically, the commercial world works by the "one-pay-period notice" rule, which is almost universally two weeks or thereabouts, where the notice period *has not been otherwise differently specified*.

The minimum amount of notice that has been provided in law is, ironically, used for the sake of convenience and may not be justified. Its origin is in the reasonableness of requiring a full term's notice in ongoing terms of employment. That is, one would assume that people paid biweekly are being employed for continuing two-week periods, the end of each completing the contract of agreement and automatically rolling over into a new two-week contract. However, for all practical purposes, people are hired, *unless otherwise specified by contract term*, for indefinite periods and are merely paid in regular installments for the sake of convenience and regularity. A question thus raised is: If a two-week contract reasonably requires a two-week notice, is two weeks really reasonable notice for an indefinite, ongoing position? Conversely, an employee is required to provide to his or her employer the same notice of termination he or she would expect to be given. If the employment "contract" is indefinite and ongoing, should the notice be of equal term?

Obviously, there would be a problem in administering and planning for what amounts to a calculus problem ("As my job term approaches infinity . . .") So the two-week/one-pay period provision is applied by statute.

- Both employees and employers can terminate the agreement between them "with cause" without any termination notice required. Generally, across Canada, each province's act will specify what conditions are considered to be "just cause" in that province. Here are some key reasons for immediate termination with cause:
- *Workplace safety.* An employee may terminate the employment agreement without notice if the work environment is not suitably safe, as the contract of employment has an implied term whereby the employer will provide a safe place in which the employee will work.
- *Illegal work.* If an employee is asked to perform work that is illegal or otherwise unreasonable in the circumstances, the employee may terminate the agreement without notice.
- *Insubordination or misconduct.* The employer may dismiss the employee with cause immediately in circumstances in which the employee has either been grossly insubordinate or has carried on activity that has affected or will adversely affect the relationship of trust between the employer and the employee. Justifications and their reasonableness are relative issues that depend on the situation.
- *Incompetence.* Obviously, an employee who has taken on a contract of employment and is unable to perform substantially as he or she had indicated at the time of the formation of the contract (i.e., at the time of hiring) may be dismissed for incompetence. Having said that quite definitively, there is apparently a lot of case law (law created by judges deciding on lawsuits brought before the court) that says the employer must serve notice on the employee to become competent before the employer can terminate. Incompetence, in this context, specifically means inability to perform a job as required, and makes no judgement on mental abilities. Employers should be advised that, as in all other situations in which there has been a "mistake," the contract problem must be addressed quickly; it gets more difficult to claim employee incompetence the longer an employee remains on the job.
- *Illness.* An employer may terminate an employment contract without notice if an employee's chronic illness has caused repeated absence and inability to perform the employee's duties. Although there may be some moral issues about cutting loose a person who is ill, in the law of employment agreements it is valid and permissible.

THE CONTRACT

Basic Employment Contract Letter

The following sample is a friendly and chatty little employment agreement that might be used for lower- to mid-level employees. It is not particularly specific and relies to a great deal on statute. My commentary is relatively sparse as the letter is fairly straightforward.[1]

May 1, 1999

Dear Ms. Walton:

We are pleased to confirm our offer of employment and your acceptance on the following terms:

You will be starting with us on May 15, 1999, as a Customer Service Representative.

In this capacity you will be responsible for all direct customer service needs including enquiry, complaints, and other duties as assigned.

You will report directly to Jack Friendly, Customer Service Manager, and will work closely with Sheila Whittaker, Senior Customer Service Representative.

We have agreed that your salary will be paid twice monthly on the basis of $24,000 per year. In accordance with standard company policy for all personnel, your employment is probationary for the first three (3) months. The purpose of a probationary period is to provide the employer with the opportunity to assess your skills and suitability in the position of Customer Service Representative, and your ability to work in harmony with others in the organization. During this period the employer retains the discretion to terminate your employment for any reason without notice.

You will be entitled to participate in those benefit plans made available by the company to personnel at your level. A booklet describing the current insurance program is enclosed. Holiday pay and vacation entitlement will be in accordance with company policy. The current policy is set out in the enclosed booklet.

It is always difficult to consider termination just when a new relationship is starting out, but it is important that you be aware of, and agree to, our corporate policy in cases of termination. Once the probationary period is completed, employees receive one (1) week's notice of termination, or, at the employer's discretion, pay in lieu thereof, plus all payments or entitlements prescribed by the Manitoba Employment Standards Act, including notice of termination, or at the employer's option pay in lieu of notice, and severance pay if applicable. The provisions of this paragraph will not apply in circumstances in which the employee resigns from employment or is terminated for cause.

Jennifer, we look forward to your joining us, and given everything you have told us about yourself, we have no doubt this will prove to be a very successful relationship.

You will be required to sign and return our standard Confidential Information Agreement, which is attached to this letter.

Should you wish to accept this offer of employment on the terms and conditions set out in this employment agreement, please sign, date, and return this letter to me on or before May 6th. The extra copy of this letter is for your personal files.

Sincerely,

<signature of employer>

EMPLOYEE'S AGREEMENT

I have read, understood, and agree with all of the foregoing. I have had a reasonable opportunity to consider this letter and the matters set out therein. I accept employment with the Employer on the terms and conditions set out in this letter.

<date>   <signature of employee>

This letter is reasonably clear and straightforward. Note that it adequately covers all relevant matters without excess formality. The notice period is specified within the body of the letter along with reference to the company policies. The contract does not elaborate on much besides the absolute basics of the employment relationship, which leaves just about everything to be interpreted within the statute-based implied terms. The letter notes that holiday pay and vacation entitlement are subject to the company policy. This may well be so, but both these issues are set out and regulated by applicable federal and provincial labour legislation. The company policy may be more generous, but in any event must be consistent with the baselines set by the law.

Of particular note:

- The agreement requires signatures and dates in the appropriate places from both the employer and the employee.
- It incorporates the company policy manual as an integral part, although those policies can change at any time at the employer's sole discretion—so long as they are within the law as set by statute.
- In this agreement, the employer is largely without obligation except payment of salary and abiding by the statutory requirements of employment.

Formal Employment Agreement Letter

This second sample, although somewhat more specific and detailed, is also generally applicable to lower- and mid-level employees. Its slightly greater degree of formality lends it an air of greater authority. As always, this contract is subject to the maxim of reasonableness, particularly as it relates to the matter of notice period. Some comments are provided where the text is heavy or a special note is warranted.[2]

> June 7, 1999
> Dear Mr. Jones:
> This letter agreement (the "Agreement") will confirm the terms and conditions of your full-time employment with the employer (the "Employer"), effective as of June 21, 1999.

> 1. **Employment**
> (1) You are employed by the Employer in the position of Accounts Receivable Manager. You agree to be bound by the terms and conditions of this Agreement during your employment with the Employer. In carrying out your duties you will comply with all reasonable instructions as may be given by members of management of the Employer. In your position, you are responsible for the proper and timely recording, control, management, and collection of accounts receivable in accordance with prevailing company policies and procedures.
> (2) You acknowledge and agree that the employment relationship will be governed by the standards and terms established by the Employer's policies as they are established from time to time and agree to comply with the terms of such policies so long as they are not inconsistent with any provisions of the Agreement. You undertake to inform yourself of the details of such policies and amendments thereto established from time to time.

This paragraph serves to make the agreement and terms of employment subject to the company's statement of policy as provided in the published manual. The phrase "so long as they are not inconsistent" in clause 1(2) is an interesting hole in the agreement that leaves room for interpretive wiggling, grandfathering (exempting the employment agreement from a company policy change because the agreement existed first and its terms are not "inconsistent" with the new policy), or unanticipated alteration.

> (3) You agree that your reporting relationships, duties, and responsibilities and the geographic location of your employment may be changed unilaterally by the Employer as the Employer deems appropriate. You agree that any of the changes which may occur pursuant to this paragraph will not affect or change any other part of this Agreement.

The word "unilaterally" comes up in circumstances such as these fairly often. It is the word that can most alter the nature of the employment agreement short of changes in company policy. It is a word to which special attention must be paid.

> (4) You understand and agree that the first three (3) months of your employment shall constitute a probationary period, during which time the Employer may terminate your employment as set out in paragraph 7(3) of this Agreement.
> (5) As you will be employed on a full-time basis for the Employer, your hours of work will vary and may be irregular

and will be those hours required to meet the objectives of your employment. Accordingly, this Agreement constitutes your consent to working greater hours than those provided in any applicable employment or labour standards legislation. In addition, it is expected that you will devote yourself exclusively to the Employer's business and will not be employed or engaged in any capacity in any other business without the prior permission of the Employer.

This paragraph essentially devotes the employee's full commercial efforts to the employer without a ceiling on the amount of the employee's time it may take to do so. Given that with this paragraph the employee waives any right to overtime pay or recourse to legislated standards of work-week duration, this paragraph is the leading cause of the super-long work weeks that reduce employees' compensation per hour to the equivalent of a Third-World brand-name shoe manufacturing serf (at least at some places I've worked).

2. Remuneration and Benefits

(1) In consideration of your performance of the obligations contained in this Agreement, the Employer will:

(a) pay you a starting salary of $26,000 per annum payable in biweekly installments, in arrears, subject to the normal statutory deductions.

"In arrears" is the elegant way to say "with a one-pay-period lag", so that the employee works one full month before seeing a cheque. More generously, it could simply mean that the wage will be paid at the end of the work period.

(b) you will be entitled to participate in the Employer's insurance benefits package after the completion of three (3) full months of employment with the Employer. You understand and agree that the Employer reserves the right to unilaterally revise the terms of the insurance benefits package. Please note that benefits will be provided in accordance with the formal plan documents or policies and any issues with respect to entitlement or payment of benefits under the insurance benefits package will be governed by the terms of such documents or policies.

This, of course, would be one of the changeable company policies to which this agreement is subject (Sections 1(2)).

(c) you will be entitled to ten (10) days of vacation per annum.

(2) You understand and agree that, on providing thirty (30) days' advance written notice, the Employer has the right to unilaterally introduce changes to your compensation arrangements and that such changes in your compensation arrangements will not affect the application of this Agreement.

Here's where that word "unilaterally" shows its teeth. The happy and optimistic reading—for the employee—of this paragraph is that forthcoming pay raises, increases in vacation time, and so forth will not be affected by what's written here. The cynical reading is that those same things can be reduced on 30 days' notice with no recourse for the employee except to quit.

3. Confidential Information

(1) You acknowledge that as an Accounts Receivable Manager and in such other position as you may hold with the Employer, you will acquire information (the "Information") about certain matters which are confidential to the Employer, which Information is the exclusive property of the Employer, including but not limited to, the following:

(a) trade secrets;

(b) lists of present and prospective customers and buying habits;

(c) purchase requirements;

(d) pricing and sales policies and concepts;

(e) financial information;

(f) business plans, forecasts, and market strategies; and

(g) discoveries, inventions, research, and development, formulas and technology (the "Works").

(2) You acknowledge that the Information could be used to the detriment of the Employer and that its disclosure could cause irreparable harm to the Employer. Accordingly, you undertake to treat confidentially all Information and not to disclose it to any third party or to use it for any purpose either during your employment, except as may be necessary in the proper discharge of your duties, or after termination of your employment for any reason, except with the written permission of the Employer.

(3) You acknowledge that the Employer owns all Works that may be developed by you during the course of your employment with the Employer and you agree to waive all moral rights to any such Works.

The "Works" comprise everything the employee does to create long-term value: inventions, patents, etc. On the one hand, the employer was paying for the employee to do these things for it, and should have the right to those things. On the other hand, does the employer own the employee and the employee's mind? Consider this: What if the employee is at home, after hours, tinkering at her workbench/chemistry set/computer/etc., and comes up with a brilliant idea (not necessarily related to the work being done at the office). She continues to work on the idea at home— never on office hours, and ultimately files a patent on this revolutionary idea. Who owns the "Work"? In the contract, the employer may have cause and right to it. (See Chapter 11 for a better, more equitable way of dealing with this issue.) It would be best for us not to get hung up on this issue, because the boilerplate clauses about inventions and such would probably not appear in this context within a real employment contract.

(4) All notes, data, tapes, reference items, sketches, drawings, memoranda, records, diskettes, and other materials in any way relating to any of the Information or to the Employer's business produced by you or coming into your possession by or through your employment shall belong exclusively to the Employer and you agree to turn over to the Employer all copies of any such material in your possession or under your control, forthwith, at the request of the Employer or, in the absence of a request, on the termination of your employment with the Employer.

All in all, this confidential information clause is fairly standard and not unwarranted on the company's part.

4. Non-Competition

(1) You acknowledge and agree that as an Accounts Receivable Manager for the Employer you will gain a knowledge of and a close working relationship with the Employer's customers, which would injure the Employer if made available to a competitor or used for competitive purposes.

(2) You agree with and for the benefit of the Employer that for a period of six (6) months from the date of termination of your employment, whether such termination is occasioned by you, by the Employer with or without cause, or by mutual agreement, you will not, within the geographical area of Lethbridge, Alberta, directly or indirectly, either as an individual or as a partner or joint venturer or as an employee, principal, consultant, agent, shareholder, officer, director, or as a salesman for any person, firm, association, organization, syndicate, company, or corporation, or in any manner whatsoever, carry on, be engaged in, concerned with, interested in, advise, lend money to, guarantee the debts or obligations of, or permit your name or any part thereof to be used or employed in a business which is the same as, or competitive with, the business of the Employer, including but without limiting, any business relating to hog processing.

This kind of noncompetition clause appears regularly in employment agreements for all but the most pedestrian of jobs, and even then it tends to show up as a matter of course. It sounds ominous, but may have less teeth than it shows. That is, depending on the circumstances and the reasonableness of the specific terms to be inserted and imposed (time, geography, kind and breadth of business endeavour, employee's position with the former employer, etc.), it may or may not stand up in court should it be pursued that far. While both parties knowingly agree to the terms of the noncompetition clause, an ex-employee's right to earn a living cannot be *completely* taken away for the sake of noncompetition.

(3) You agree with and for the benefit of the Employer that for a period of six (6) months from the date of termination

of your employment, whether such termination is occasioned by you, by the Employer with or without cause, or by mutual agreement, you will not, for any reason whatsoever, directly or indirectly, solicit or accept business with respect to products in which you traded on behalf of the Employer from any of the Employer's clients or customers, wherever situated, with whom you had direct contact in the six (6) months preceding the termination of your employment.

Just like Section 4(2), this clause may be a little overzealous. For the employer to insist that after termination the ex-employee not *solicit* the employer's clients or customers is reasonable. To demand that the employee not accept business from the former employer's customers is a restraint of trade that might not hold much water, since it attempts to impose a condition upon a party (the customer) that is a stranger to the agreement. In short, if the customer willfully chooses to go to the ex-employee rather than the employer, he or she should be free to do so.

5. Non-Solicitation

You further agree that during employment pursuant to this Agreement and for a period of six (6) months following termination of employment, whether such termination is occasioned by you, by the Employer with or without cause, or by mutual agreement, you will not hire or take away or cause to be hired or taken away any employee of the Employer for the purposes of employment in any business related to or competitive with the business of the Employer.

It is one thing for the employer to terminate or lose the employee to another business. It is another thing altogether for the employer to lose more personnel to the former employee's poaching from the employer's labour pool. Again, to induce another employee to leave the employer is one issue; to accept that employee's offer to work is another. Presumably the way to defeat this (from the former employee's perspective) is for the poached employee to quit her job with the employer and then approach the former employee for a new job. It all seems like more trouble than it's worth to all parties concerned. After all, if the conditions of employment with the employer are so lacking—in opportunity, growth, pay, morale, etc.—that other employees want to follow the first one who left, the problem may be larger than the first employee to go to a competitor.

6. Injunctive Relief

(1) You understand and agree that the Employer has a material interest in preserving the relationships it has developed with its customers against impairment by competitive activities of a former employee. Accordingly, you agree that the restrictions and covenants contained in paragraph 3 "Confidential Information," are reasonably required for the protection of the Employer and its goodwill and that your agreement to same by your execution of this Agreement are of the essence to this Agreement and constitute a material inducement to the Employer to enter into this Agreement and to employ you, and that the Employer would not enter into this Agreement absent such inducement.

(2) You understand and agree that the restrictions and covenants contained in paragraph 3 "Confidential Information," paragraph 4 "Non-Competition," and paragraph 5 "Non-Solicitation," shall each be construed as independent of any other portion of this Agreement, and the existence of any claim or cause of action by you against the Employer, whether predicated on this Agreement or otherwise, shall not constitute a defense to the enforcement by the Employer of such covenants and restrictions.

The two paragraphs immediately above (Sections 6(1) and (2)) are little more than recitals that set up the hammer blow of injunctive relief that follows in sub-paragraph (3). They are really legal "posturing" for any litigation that might arise pertaining to the issue of confidentiality, noncompetition, and nonsolicitation.

(3) You understand and agree, without prejudice to any and all other rights of the Employer, that in the event of your violation or attempted violation of any of the covenants contained in paragraph 3 "Confidential Information," paragraph 4 "Non-Competition," and paragraph 5 "Non-Solicitation," an injunction or other like remedy shall

be the only effective method to protect the Employer's rights and property as set out, and that an interim injunction may be granted immediately on the commencement of any suit.

This paragraph is the contractual relief afforded to the employer for the employee's breach of the three covenants noted. In any event, if these clauses were deemed by a court to be reasonable in the event of a breach action brought against the former employee, court-ordered injunctive relief would be afforded the employer. This contract term, however, gives the employer the right to obtain a temporary injunction against the former employer *without* the court's consideration. In this respect, it is a strong term, because the employer may obtain an injunction pending a court order *regardless* of the reasonableness of the contract's terms or justification in the specific circumstances. Although the former employee might eventually win in court, the employer has benefitted in the interim with an injunction that restrains the former employee's actions.

7. Termination

(1) You may terminate your employment pursuant to this Agreement by giving at least one pay period of advance notice in writing to the Employer. The Employer may waive such notice, in whole or in part, and if it does so, your entitlement to remuneration and benefits pursuant to the Agreement will cease on the date it waives such notice.

Most employees, and some employers, do not consider the full potential impact of this clause when an employee gives notice of termination. The employee is obliged to provide the requisite notice period, and most employees count on working and earning for that period. But the employer can accept the resignation and say "Okay, goodbye. There's the door." The employee walks out the door and receives not a nickel more than what he has earned up to that moment.

(2) The Employer may terminate your employment pursuant to this Agreement without notice or payment in lieu thereof, for cause. For the purposes of this Agreement "cause" shall include:
(a) any material breach of the provisions of this Agreement by you, as determined at the sole discretion of the Employer;
(b) consistent poor performance on your part, after being advised as to the standard required, as determined at the sole discretion of the Employer;
(c) any intentional or grossly negligent disclosure of any Information by you, as determined at the sole discretion of the Employer;
(d) your violation of any local, provincial, or federal statute, including, without limitation, an act of dishonesty such as embezzlement or theft;
(e) conduct on your part that is materially detrimental to the business or the financial position of the Employer, as determined at the sole discretion of the Employer;
(f) personal conduct on your part which is of such a serious and substantial nature that, as determined at the sole discretion of the Employer, it would injure the reputation of the Employer if you are retained as an employee; and
(g) any and all omissions, commissions, or other conduct which would constitute cause at law, in addition to the specified causes.

The interesting part of this list is how much of it rests in the employer's discretion. Yet the employer cannot be capricious in exercising its discretion because of (1) employment standards legislation, and (2) the doctrine that requires subjective actions be "reasonable."

(3) In addition, the Employer may terminate your employment pursuant to this Agreement at its sole discretion for any reason, without cause, upon providing to you one (1) week of notice of termination, or at the Employer's option, pay in lieu of notice, plus all payments or entitlements to which you are entitled pursuant to the Alberta Labour Standards Act, including notice of termination, or at the Employer's option, pay in lieu of notice, and severance pay, if applicable.

The one-week notice period in this sample is probably somewhat out of line with common practice, which generally commands one pay period of notice.

(4) Pay in lieu of notice will be calculated on the basis of your annual base salary as of the date you receive notice of termination. Bonuses and other forms of additional compensation will not be considered part of your annual base salary. Your rights and entitlements under any performance bonus shall terminate effective as of the date of your termination of employment, or as at the date you receive notice of termination, if pay in lieu of notice is provided.

(5) Pay in lieu of notice will be provided in regular biweekly installments and shall be subject to all deductions and withholdings required by law.

8. Notices

Any notice required or permitted to be given to either party must be delivered by hand or personally to the party's address last known to the other party and will be deemed to be received on the date of hand delivery or personal delivery to such address. Personal delivery shall include delivery by a commercial courier.

9. Severability

In the event that any provision of this Agreement is found to be void, invalid, illegal, or unenforceable by a court of competent jurisdiction, such finding will not affect any other provision of this Agreement, which will continue to be in full force and effect.

10. Waiver

The waiver by either party of any breach or violation of any provision of this Agreement shall not operate or be construed as a waiver of any subsequent breach or violation.

11. Modification of Agreement

Any modification of this Agreement must be in writing and signed by both you and the Employer or it shall have no effect and shall be void.

12. Governing Law

This Agreement shall be governed by and construed in accordance with the laws of the Province of Alberta.

13. Independent Legal Advice

You acknowledge that you have read and understand this Agreement, and acknowledge that you have had the opportunity to obtain legal advice about it.

Please review this Agreement carefully. If, after reading it and considering its contents, you are prepared to accept employment with the Employer in accordance with the terms and conditions contained therein, please indicate your acceptance by signing your name where indicated. The photocopy is for your personal files.
Yours very truly,
<signature of employer>

I have read, understood and agree with the foregoing. I have had a reasonable opportunity to consider this Agreement and the matters set out therein. I accept employment with the Employer on the terms and conditions set out in this Agreement.
SIGNED in the City of Lethbridge this _____ day of June, 1999.
<witness>   <signature of employee>

Formal Employment Agreement for a Manager

This following sample is more common of managerial- and junior-executive-level employment contracts. It provides for considerably more contractually determined obligations on both parts, and is optically much more serious than a letter agreement. The sample is not meant to be completely realistic, and is (like the other samples in this chapter) a legal precedent rather than a form used in actual practice.[3]

> THIS AGREEMENT made as of the 29th day of August, 1999, between SunRay Corporation (the "Employer") and Alvin Dunlap, of Windsor, Ontario (the "Employee").
> WHEREAS:
> 1. The Employer is engaged in the manufacture, marketing, and distribution of home appliances; and
> 2. The Employer and the Employee have agreed to enter into an employment relationship for their mutual benefit;
> THIS AGREEMENT witnesses that the parties have agreed that the terms and conditions shall be as follows:
>
> **1. Employment**
> (1) The Employee represents and warrants to the Employer that the Employee has the required skills and experience to perform the duties and exercise the responsibilities required of the Employee as a Marketing Manager. In carrying out these duties and responsibilities the Employee shall comply with all lawful and reasonable instructions as may be given by superiors representing the Employer.

The premise for any employer to employ a manager or executive is a tacit understanding and representation from the employee that he can do the usually "subjective" job he is being given. This paragraph is important, inasmuch as it provides a foundation for removal of the manager for the "cause" of incompetence and/or misrepresentation of abilities if the manager is not able to handle the role.

> (2) The Employee specifically undertakes and shall be responsible for the following:
>   (a) sales and marketing;
>   (b) planning and budgeting;
>   (c) supervision and training;
>   (d) <etc.>
> (3) The Employee agrees to comply with and be bound by the terms and conditions of this Agreement.
> (4) In consideration for the Employee's agreement and the Employee's performance in accordance with this Agreement the Employer employs the Employee.
> (5) The Employee acknowledges and agrees that the effective performance of the Employee's duties requires the highest level of integrity and the Employer's complete confidence in the Employee's relationship with other employees of the Employer and with all persons dealt with by the Employee in the course of employment. The Employee is required to ensure that he at all times conducts himself in a professional, businesslike manner, appropriate to the Employer's corporate image.

This is another one of those subjective "out" opportunities, at least on the surface before the lawyers get involved in a disagreement. Basically, it says that the employee must play nice and fit in, or the employer can use it to dismiss the employee.

> (6) It is understood and agreed to that the Employer plans, at its discretion, to involve the Employee in national sales matters with a view to his being able, if so directed, to assume full responsibility for national sales.

This paragraph is nothing more than a possible growth plan for the employee, and notice that the employee will be expected to take on work and responsibility outside the specifics detailed earlier in this agreement.

(7) It is understood and agreed to by the Employee that the Employer is a nationwide operation and that in the course of his employment the Employee's assignments may be unilaterally changed by the Employer and consequently, the Employee may be transferred to any new location or new assignments deemed appropriate by the Employer. Any major change in the location of the Employee's employment will be subject to reimbursement in accordance with the generally applied policies of the Employer at the time of the change.

2. Exclusive Service

(1) During the term of employment the Employee shall devote himself exclusively to the business of the Employer and shall not during the term be employed or engaged in any capacity in promoting, undertaking, or carrying on any other business, without the prior written approval of the Employer.

This is fair. It is often abused these days, but is nevertheless fair.

(2) The Employee will be expected to work on a full-time basis exclusively for the Employer. The Employee understands and agrees that his hours of work will vary and may be irregular and will be those hours required to meet the objectives of his employment. Accordingly, this Agreement constitutes the Employee's consent to work greater hours than those provided in applicable employment or labour standards legislation.

See my comment about this type of clause in relation to the previous letter agreement of employment (page 53). For management and executive personnel this type of clause is commonplace and is not going to go away. Still, I consider it to be an open opportunity for an employer to coerce from the employee the work that might more reasonably be done by one-and-a-half or two people for the price of one. It's just the way of the world in the West.

Regarding the Confidential Information and Non-Competition clauses, discussion of which follows, see my comments in the previous letter agreement of employment. Specifically, see page 54.

3. Confidential Information

(1) The Employee acknowledges that as Marketing Manager, and in any other position as he or she may be appointed to, the Employee will acquire information about certain matters and things which are confidential to the Employer, and which information is the exclusive property of the Employer including, without limitation:
  (a) product design and manufacturing information;
  (b) lists of present and prospective customers, and related information;
  (c) pricing and sales policies, techniques, and concepts;
  (d) list of suppliers; and
  (e) trade secrets.

(2) The Employee acknowledges the information as referred to in paragraph 3(1) could be used to the detriment of the Employer. Accordingly, the employee undertakes to treat confidentially all information and agrees not to disclose same to any third party either during the term of his or her agreement, except as may be necessary in the proper discharge of his or her employment under this agreement, or after the date of termination of the Employee's employment, however caused, except with the written permission of an officer of the company. The Employee also agrees that the unauthorized disclosure of any such information during his or her employment with the Employer will constitute just cause for the Employee's immediate dismissal from employment with the Employer.

(3) The Employee acknowledges that in addition to any and all rights of the Employer, the Employer shall be entitled to injunctive relief in order to protect the Employer's rights and property as set out in paragraphs 1 and 2 of this section.

4. Non-Competition

The Employee acknowledges that as Marketing Manager for the Employer he or she will gain a knowledge of, and a close working relationship with, the Employer's customers, which would injure the Employer if made available to a competitor or if used for competitive purposes. The Employee agrees that, for a period of eighteen (18) months from the termination of employment pursuant to this Agreement for any reason or cause, the Employee will not be employed by another employer engaged in a business which is in competition with the Employer, in a position the duties of which are the same or similar to those duties performed for the Employer pursuant to this Agreement.

5. Remuneration and Benefits

(1) The Employee acknowledges and agrees that the Employer reserves the right to unilaterally introduce and amend various salary or commission arrangements designed to remunerate the Employee.

See page 52 for my comments about the nature of unilateral actions, and one's need to look closely at the statements surrounding this word.

(2) In consideration of the Employee's undertaking and the performance of the obligations contained in this Agreement the Employer shall pay and grant the following salary and benefits:

(a) A salary of $80,000 per annum, payable in arrears in equal biweekly installments, subject to an annual review on or about January 1 of each year of this contract, the first review to be on or about January 1, 2000.

Notwithstanding all the other parts of remuneration that are provided for the manager/executive, below, this is the first true deviation from the samples we've seen earlier. The salary level is effectively fixed at the indicated amount until the review is conducted. It says that a decision—leading to increase, decrease, or no change in salary—is scheduled for a fixed date. Depending on the result of that review, the employee can fix a time for his or her own decision to stay or leave. Sections 9(1) allows for unilateral amendment of the salary itself by the employer.

(b) The other benefit programs as are made generally available by the Employer pursuant to the provisions of this Agreement.

(c) The reimbursement of any expenses authorized and incurred pursuant to the Employee's employment in accordance with the Employer's generally established practice as applied.

(d) An automobile allowance of $500 per month, plus reimbursement for gas and repair expenses generated by use of the automobile on behalf of the Employer. The Employee shall insure the automobile at his or her expense in an amount satisfactory to the Employer and shall produce proof to the Employer when requested to do so.

(e) In addition to the compensation specified above, the Employee will be entitled to participate in the Employer's Bonus Plan, attached as Schedule "A" and incorporated into this Agreement.[4] The right of the Employee to participate is solely at the discretion of the Employer and a bonus may or may not be paid in any given year. The Employer may at its sole discretion unilaterally discontinue the bonus scheme at any time on giving two (2) months' notice in writing to participating Employees.

6. Termination

(1) The parties understand and agree that employment pursuant to this Agreement may be terminated in the following manner in the specified circumstances:

I commented on the terms of this Sections 6(1) in reference to the letter agreement of employment on page 51. Refer there.

(a) by the Employee giving at least two (2) weeks' advance notice in writing to the Employer. The Employer may waive such notice, in whole or in part, and if it does so the Employee's entitlement to remuneration and benefits pursuant to this Agreement will cease on the date it waives such notice.

(b) By the Employer without notice or payment in lieu thereof, for cause. For the purposes of this Agreement "cause" shall include but not be limited to:

(i) any material breach of the provisions of this Agreement by the Employee, as determined at the sole discretion of the Employer;

(ii) the Employee's consistent poor performance, after being advised as to the standard required, as determined at the sole discretion of the Employer;

(iii) any intentional or grossly negligent disclosure of any confidential information by the Employee, as determined at the sole discretion of the Employer;

(iv) the Employee's violation of any local, provincial, or federal statute, including, without limitation, an act of dishonesty such as embezzlement or theft;

(v) conduct on the Employee's part that is materially detrimental to the business or the financial position of the Employer, as determined at the sole discretion of the Employer;

(vi) personal conduct by the Employee which is of such a serious and substantial nature that, as determined at the sole discretion of the Employer, it would injure the reputation of the Employer if you are retained as an employee; and

(vii) any and all omissions, commissions, or other conduct which would constitute cause at law, in addition to the specified causes.

(c) by the Employer at its sole discretion for any reason, without cause, upon providing to the Employee two (2) weeks' notice of termination, or at the Employer's option, pay in lieu of notice, plus all payments or entitlements to which you are entitled pursuant to the Labour Standards Act (Ontario), including notice of termination, or at the Employer's option, pay in lieu of notice, and severance pay, if applicable.

The notice period provided in this sample may be out of line with common practice for a negotiated notice period. Nevertheless, the period above should probably parallel the notice period required of the employee, as specified in clause 6(1)(a).

(2) The parties understand and agree that the giving of notice or the payment of the Employee's regular salary in lieu thereof by the Employer to the Employee on termination shall not prevent the Employer from alleging cause for the termination.

For one reason or another, the employer reserves the right to give the departing employee notice grace without prejudicing its position of having terminated the employee for cause. This act and provision can defuse one line of attack from a disgruntled former employee alleging that the employer "did not really have cause because it provided the notice grace period afforded to discretionary terminations."

(3) The Employee authorizes the Employer to deduct from any payment due to the Employee at any time, including from a termination payment, any amounts owed to the Employer by reason of purchases, advances, loans, or in recompense for damages to or loss of the Employer's property and equipment save only that this provision shall be applied so as not to conflict with any applicable legislation.

In the remuneration section (5) above, we see that there are various types of payment to be made to the employee, including some that are irregular—such as expenses. With an automobile benefit and with expenses, and so forth, there will be some final accounting to be done to determine compensation due to the departing employee. And, since it is possible that the employee has taken a loan or a salary advance from the employer, bought products from the employer, or has not returned (or has returned in damaged condition) some of the employer's assets—perhaps a laptop computer or pocket dictating machine—it is also possible that the employee owes something to the employer. Thus, this paragraph provides for a netting of any amounts owing to the employer from salary and other remuneration due to the departing employee.

7. Assignment of Rights

The rights that accrue to the Employer under this Agreement shall pass to its successors or assigns. The rights of the Employee under this Agreement are not assignable or transferable in any manner.

The issue of assignment of performance should take us back to Chapter 2, where we discussed vicarious performance and indicated that where personal service is anticipated (which is the essence of employment), assignment of that personal service or vicarious performance of it would be unacceptable.

8. Severability

In the event that any provision or part of this Agreement shall be deemed void or invalid by a court of competent jurisdiction, the remaining provisions, or parts of it, shall be and remain in full force and effect.

9. Entire Agreement

This Agreement constitutes the entire agreement between the parties with respect to the employment of the Employee and any and all previous agreements, written or oral, express or implied between the parties or on their behalf relating to the employment of the Employee by the Employer are terminated and cancelled and each of the parties releases and forever discharges the other of and from all manner of actions, causes of action, claims, or demands whatsoever under or in respect of any agreement.

10. Modification of Agreement

Any modification to this Agreement must be in writing and signed by the Employee and an officer of the Employer, or it shall have no effect and shall be void.

11. Governing Law

This Agreement shall be governed by and construed in accordance with the laws of the Province of Ontario.

12. Headings

The headings utilized in this Agreement are for convenience only and are not to be construed in any way as additions to or limitations of the covenants and agreements contained in this Agreement.

13. Notices

(1) Any notice required or permitted to be given to the Employee shall be sufficiently given if delivered to the Employee personally or if mailed by registered mail to the Employee's address last known to the Employer or if delivered to the Employee via facsimile.

(2) Any notice required or permitted to be given to the Employer shall be sufficiently given if delivered personally or if mailed by registered mail to the Employer's head office at its address last known to the Employee or if delivered to the Employer via facsimile.

(3) Any notice given by mail shall be deemed to have been given forty-eight (48) hours after the time it is posted.

IN WITNESS WHEREOF the Employee, Alvin Dunlap, has duly executed this Agreement this 29th day of August, 1999, in the City of Windsor, in the Province of Ontario.

SIGNED, SEALED, AND DELIVERED
in the presence of:

_____   _____
Witness   Alvin Dunlap,
                                 Employee

<requires an affidavit of execution>[5]

IN WITNESS WHEREOF the Employer, Sunray Corporation, has by the signature of a duly authorized officer executed this Agreement this 29th day of August, 1999, in the City of Windsor, in the Province of Ontario.

SUNRAY CORPORATION
Employer
Per:

_____
Robert McKenzie, Chief Executive Officer

Chapter 7
Borrowing and Lending Contracts

Sample of Standard Credit Terms and Their Meaning,
Including Business Improvement Loans and Bankers' Acceptances

Businesses borrow and lend value in a variety of ways: by large formal borrowings/lendings in the debt and money markets with debentures and corporate paper; through financial institutions in the form of loans and other credits; and to/from customers and suppliers in the form of trade credit.

Broadly, these are all forms of lending and borrowing, although in trade credit it is not money that is being credited. Additionally, trade credit is usually short-term and unsecured, meaning that it is not registered as a debt and the creditor does not have a collateral interest in the debtor's property to secure the credit. Thus, we will ignore trade credit.

On the other hand, issuing debentures or bonds is a formal process performed in and by the capital markets with the assistance of lawyers, accountants, corporate finance professionals, and brokers. Furthermore, debentures issued by small to mid-sized companies have a hard time being floated, as the market is more interested in the debt of large companies. (That's not to say that smaller companies do not issue debt, or that credit-risky debentures—"junk bonds"—are not a large part of corporate borrowing and lending. Rather, it's an area of specialty beyond the scope of this book.) It is not a simple and common contractual relationship such as any of the others examined within this book. So, despite its relative prevalence and importance to corporate finance, this form of borrowing is omitted from our discussion as well.

Most businesses obtain credit at one time or another, to greater or lesser degrees from financial institutions such as banks, trusts, credit unions, near-banks, and so on. These credits appear as term loans, revolving lines of credit, overdraft protection, and company credit cards, among other types of secured financing. For most small and mid-sized businesses, bank credit is often the only way to expand and grow without obtaining more cash equity. For all businesses, using bank credit is the best way to smooth the irregular highs and lows of periodic cash requirements. For these and other reasons, bank credit is ubiquitous in most business. (For the sake of simplicity, and because of the contract sample that follows, we will use "bank" to represent all credit-giving financial institutions.)

The essence of borrowing has been the same since before the Romans popularized it: I give you money now; you pay me back later. My benevolence will generally not go unrewarded. My money, after all, has time value, so you should pay me for that time when my money is in your hands rather than mine: we call it interest. That's the nub of it regardless of whether the lender is a loan shark or a chartered bank. But I repeat myself.

What does it mean to borrow on secured credit? Essentially, the lender provides money to a business or individual, in return taking a "security" on an asset or assets that the lender may seize—generally without additional intervention by the court—and possess for liquidation in the event that the borrower defaults on any term of the loan credit. Secured creditors have priority rights to the collateral asset or assets over unsecured creditors such as trade creditors.

Credits must be registered with a provincial registrar to be properly secured. Creditors intend and hope to have no overlap of securities with other creditors on any of the borrower's assets, and registry assists in that effort. Among secured creditors there are differing levels of security and priorities depending on the covenants within the credit agreements and the order in which the securities were registered by the creditors. This is a concern to you, the borrower, while your business is a thriving going-concern and you are borrowing to finance your asset purchases or operations. It may also be a concern to you if things get a little rough and you are having trouble meeting all your credit obligations. But when your business is in dire straits, it is no longer your concern: it is the creditor's problem. A fact which does not go unheeded by creditors who, as we will see, reserve the right to protect themselves at the earliest warning of possible trouble in the future.

> Here's a little bit of security registering information and jargon to expand your borrowing/lending vocabulary as it relates to chattels. A security is registered and protected against claims by other creditors in a three-step protocol.
>
> First, the security is *created* by the writing and executing of a credit such as a loan to purchase an asset. For instance, obtaining a chattel mortgage loan from a bank to purchase a new computer system creates a security interest within the system in the bank's favour.
>
> Second, the security interest *attaches* to the asset when the bank and the borrower fulfill their respective parts of the bargain. In this instance, the bank provides the money to purchase the computers and the borrower pays the supplier for the system and has it installed in place.
>
> Third, the security interest is *perfected* ("perfect" by whose standards, one wonders?) when the lender registers the loan with the appropriate provincial registry by filing a financing statement.
>
> Priority in security goes to the first creditor to *perfect* security interest in a particular asset, which may or may not be the first to create or attach an interest in the asset. This goes a long way toward explaining why creditors move so quickly in registering securities.

The business of lending is all about the mitigation or elimination of risk. This gets into the theory of interest, which, very briefly, suggests lending money is always subject to some risk and that risk is reflected in the rate of interest being charged to the borrower. In practice, on the open market, "risk-free" credits are equated to government T-bills and then grossed up to the *bank rate* (the rate of interest the Bank of Canada charges the chartered banks for overnight money), and again to the *prime rate* (the rate of interest the banks allegedly charge to their most preferred customers). For most businesses, the interest rate is then pushed up some degree with a risk premium on top of prime.

Lenders may, and often do, attempt to secure credits with more than the asset being financed. This is particularly true in the circumstance in which the credit is a revolving operating line of credit that is at least partly provided on the basis of the business' standing and creditworthiness. In such circumstances even highly creditworthy customers will be asked to provide a variety of securities, possibly including insurance, guarantees, pledges of various additional assets such as inventories, receivables, intellectual properties (patents, trademarks, etc.) and so forth. What is finally secured is the subject of a negotiation between the bank and the borrower, and since there is a strong likelihood that the borrower needs the money more than the bank needs to make the loan, guess how much negotiating is going to take place.

Regardless of how the credit agreement is arrived at, the typical form for most small to mid-sized businesses obtaining a variety of common credits from a bank is in an engagement letter that sets forth the particulars of each type of credit, be it a credit card or an operating line, including interest rates and terms. Attached to the letter is a standard schedule of covenants between the bank and the borrower that lay out quite distinctly the nature of the credit agreement. The CIBC has generously provided a sample of this schedule for reproduction as a fairly common example of the broad terms of a lender/borrower agreement between a bank and its customer. The covenants in this schedule are remarkably consistent with those of the other chartered banks, and with those of the vast majority of lending institutions in general.

CIBC SCHEDULE—STANDARD CREDIT TERMS

ARTICLE 1—GENERAL

1.1 Interest rate. You will pay interest on each Credit at nominal rates per year equal to:
  (a) for amounts above the Credit Limit of a Credit or a part of a Credit or for amounts that are not paid when due, the Default Interest Rate, and
  (b) for any other amounts, the rate specified in this Agreement.

The nominal rate of interest is the "named" interest rate for a given period. It will appear in the letter to which this schedule is attached, coupling a numeric value to the definitions in this section and other places within the document.

That rate may be based on annual, monthly, or some other periodic calculation. The important thing to watch out for in negotiating and evaluating the agreement is the *effective* interest rate, which is the true rate of interest being paid once the effect of the daily, weekly, or monthly compounding is taken into account. The effective rate of interest is rarely lower than the nominal rate. However, we have to presume that if you are at this stage with your lender those details have been discussed and evaluated.

> **1.2 Variable interest.** Each variable interest rate provided for under this Agreement will change automatically, without notice, whenever the Prime Rate or the U.S. Base Rate, as the case may be, changes.

I assume we have all seen "floating" interest rates in our mortgages. Essentially, this paragraph defines what the base for the variable interest rates would be (depending on the currency), and how changes to the variable rate are subject to change without notice.

> **1.3 Payment of interest.** Interest is calculated on the daily balance of the Credit at the end of each day. Interest is due once a month, unless the Agreement states otherwise. Unless you have made other arrangements with us, we will automatically debit your Operating Account for interest amounts owing.

Notice here that the effective interest rate is based on daily compounding (which results in the greatest difference between nominal and true annual interest rates), although it is due and charged monthly. Interest charges are removed automatically from the customer's operating account with the bank.

> If your Operating Account is in overdraft and you do not deposit to the account an amount equal to the monthly interest payment, the effect is that we will be charging interest on overdue interest (which is known as compounding).

This disclosure is quite interesting. The use of the word "compounding" seems to be accurate, yet could possibly be misleading in its somewhat ominous characterization.[1] The simple meaning of this statement is that if your account is in overdraft, the interest charged will be an additional charge to you (your account will go further into overdraft), and you will get charged interest on it in the future. No surprise there for anyone participating in the real world with a chequing account.

> Unpaid interest continues to compound whether or not we have demanded payment from you or started a legal action, or get judgement, against you.

The upshot of this term is that the bank will continue to charge interest on the debt regardless of what other (legal) action they may be taking against you. Trust me, they are not simply posturing. Having said this, however, in the event that there is litigation in which the defendant (you) succeeds, that compounded—and probably all—interest accrued from when the legal action commenced may be struck down by the court.

> **1.4 Default interest.** To determine whether Default Interest is to be charged, the following rules apply:
> (a) Default Interest will be charged on the amount that exceeds the Credit Limit of any particular Credit.
> (b) If there are several parts of a Credit, Default Interest will be charged if the Credit Limit or a particular part is exceeded. For example, if Credit A's limit is $250,000, and the limit of one part is $100,000 and the limit of that part is exceeded by $25,000, Default Interest will be charged on that $25,000 excess, even if the total amount outstanding under Credit A is less than $250,000.

In "Default Interest," the word *default* is not used in the sense of the *fallback* position. It implies the "you lose by default because you couldn't field a team" sense of the word. The default interest rate is a more onerous rate that you pay because you have exceeded your credit limit. Sub-paragraph (a) states plainly that amounts over the credit limit bear the default interest rate. Sub-paragraph (b) states that even if you have not exceeded your total credit limit, if one of the several limits (say on the line of credit) is exceeded, you pay the default interest rate on that particular credit's excess. Translation: your various forms of financing through the one institution do not lead to a cumulative and collective whole.

> **1.5 Fees.** You will pay CIBC's fees for each Credit as outlined in the Letter. You will also reimburse us for all reasonable fees (including legal fees) and out-of-pocket expenses incurred in registering any security, and in enforcing our rights under this Agreement or any security. We will automatically debit your Operating Account for fee amounts owing.

While "user pay" is not a kindly phrase in the context of socialized medicine, it is the watchword of this paragraph. The customer is hereby advised that it will pay for all costs and disbursements, including those related to suing the customer or repossessing chattels (collectively "enforcing our rights"), either directly or within the regularly or line-item-assessed fees and other charges.

> **1.6 Our rights re demand Credits.** At CIBC, we believe that the banker-customer relationship is based on mutual trust and respect. It is important for us to know all the relevant information (whether good or bad) about your business. CIBC is itself a business. Managing risks and monitoring our customers' ability to repay is critical to us. We can only continue to lend when we feel that we are likely to be repaid. . . .

This language, which, if you've read the other parts of this book, is not common legal phrasing, seems to be a thinly veiled attempt to have you, the relatively miniscule customer, understand and empathize with the relatively leviathan bank's difficult business obstacles.

> As a result, if you do something that jeopardizes that relationship, or if we no longer feel that you are likely to repay all amounts borrowed, we may have to act. We may decide to act, for example, because of something you have done, information we receive about your business, or changes to the economy that affect your business. Some of the actions that we may decide to take include requiring you to give us more financial information, negotiating a change in the interest rate or fees, or asking you to get further accounting assistance, put more cash into the business, provide more security, or produce a satisfactory business plan. It is important to us that your business succeeds. We may, however, at our discretion, demand immediate repayment of any outstanding amounts under any demand Credit. . . .

The bank at the other end of these credits lets you know in advance, in this statement, that it can and will act rapidly to protect itself in the event that there appears to be trouble in your business or among businesses collectively in your "industry" (and even rumours of trouble, apparently). The actions the financing institution can take to protect itself range from the benign through the draconian. "It is important to us that your business succeeds," it says. But given the sentence that follows thereafter, it should probably continue with, "but it is more important that we get ours back first and early."

> We may also, at any time and for any cause, cancel the unused portion of any demand Credit. Under normal circumstances, however, we will give you thirty (30) days' notice of any of these actions.

Your credit limit or any part of your finance package can be cut at any time for any reason. This provision, I think, has some merit to it considering it is the bank's money, after all. (Actually, it's the banks depositors' money, but we'll not go there just now.) The financial institution will give you 30 days' notice *under normal circumstances*, which can be important if you had plans for using that part of the demand credit. It does, however, raise the question: If circumstances were normal, why would these actions be taken?

> **1.7 Payments.** If any payment is due on a day other than a Business Day, then the payment is due on the next Business Day.
>
> **1.8 Applying money received.** If you have not made payments as required by this Agreement, or if you have failed to

satisfy any term of this Agreement (or any other agreement you have that relates to this Agreement), or at any time before default but after we have given you appropriate notice, we may decide how to apply any money that we receive. This means that we may choose which Credit to apply the money against, or what mix of principal, interest, fees, and overdraft amounts within any Credit will be paid.

The bottom line here is that the money you have in credits is not yours: it is the bank's. And, at its discretion, the bank will do with its money what it chooses. The first-glance read would suggest that you must be somehow out-of-bounds on the agreement for this remedy to be available to the bank. On further study, it would seem that the bank ultimately need only provide notice of its intent to apply the money as it sees fit.[2]

1.9 Information requirements. We may from time to time reasonably require you to provide further information about your business. We may require information from you to be in a form acceptable to us.

I think I speak for all of us when I say we can only hope this means on preprinted report submission forms or in standard financial statement form.

1.10 Insurance. You will keep all your business assets and property insured (to the full insurable value) against loss or damage by fire and all other risks usual for property such as yours (plus for any other risks we may reasonably require). If we request, these policies will include a loss payee clause (and if you are giving us a mortgage security, a mortgagee clause). As further security, you assign all insurance proceeds to us. If we ask, you will give us either the policies themselves or adequate evidence of their existence. If your insurance coverage for any reason stops, we may (but do not have to) insure the property. We will automatically debit your Operating Account for these amounts. Finally, you will notify us immediately of any loss or damage to the property.

This paragraph presents a fairly standard demand to insure, with the requirement for both mortgage payee and a loss payee clauses to be included. Over and above all this, so that the bank can feel secure, the customer must assign the *whole* of any insurance claim proceeds directly to the bank.

1.11 Environmental. You will carry on your business, and maintain your assets and property, in accordance with all applicable environmental laws and regulations. If (a) there is any release, deposit, discharge, or disposal of pollutants of any sort (collectively, a "Discharge") in connection with either your business or your property, and we pay any fines or for any clean-up, or (b) we suffer any loss or damage as a result of any Discharge, you will reimburse CIBC, its directors, officers, employees, and agents for any and all losses, damages, fines, costs, and other amounts (including amounts spent preparing any necessary environmental assessment or other reports, or defending any lawsuits) that result. If we ask, you will defend any lawsuits, investigations, or prosecutions brought against CIBC or any of its directors, officers, employees, and agents in connection with any Discharge. Your obligation to us under this section continues even after all Credits have been repaid and this Agreement has terminated.

Environmental laws are getting ever more fierce. And, while I am not entirely sure how a lender would end up at the receiving end of environmental-related litigation caused by and directed at the borrower, suffice it to say that by this paragraph the customer is prohibited from any acts that might expose itself or its lender to such prosecution. Just to be safe, the customer also forever indemnifies the lender from any repercussions in this regard.

1.12 Consent to release information. We may from time to time give any credit or other information about you to, or receive such information from, (a) any financial institution, credit reporting agency, rating agency, or credit bureau, (b) any person, firm, or corporation with whom you may have or propose to have financial dealings, and (c) any person, firm, or corporation in connection with any dealings you have or propose to have with us. You agree that we may use that information to establish and maintain your relationship with us and to offer any services as permitted by law, including services and products offered by our subsidiaries when it is considered that this may be suitable to you.

This clause gives the financial institution a blanket right to divulge to almost anyone any fact about the customer's financial affairs and whatever other information it has obtained about the customer. It also allows the financial institution to mine the customer's datafile in order for it or its subsidiaries or affiliates to direct-market more products and services to that customer.

> **1.13 Our pricing policy.** Fees, interest rates, and other charges for your banking arrangements are dependent upon each other. If you decide to cancel any of these arrangements, you will have to pay us any increased or added fees, interest rates, and charges we determine and notify you of. These increased or added amounts are effective from the date of the changes that you make.

This sounds an awful lot like "You will be charged some amount of money that will be payable in any of a variety of forms such as fees, charges, interest, and so forth. You cannot reduce your overall costs. You can only alter the balance of how that amount will be paid." That could be an unfair read, but I will let you decide. Ask your lender what such a clause might mean.

> **1.14 Proof of debt.** This Agreement provides the proof, between CIBC and you, of the credit made available to you. There may be times when the types of Credit you have requires you to sign additional documents. Throughout the time that we provide you credit under this Agreement, our loan accounting records will provide such complete proof of all terms and conditions of your credit (such as principal loan balances, interest calculations, and payment dates).

This paragraph is important, because at the top of it is an acknowledgement of a debt, which is important to the lender. The latter part of the paragraph essentially provides that the customer agrees to the lender's records of the credit history, status, etc., being the official version of the credit record, period.

> **1.15 Renewals of this Agreement.** This Agreement will remain in effect for your Credits for as long as they remain unchanged. We have shown a Next Scheduled Review Date in the Letter. If there are no changes to the Credits this Agreement will continue to apply, and you will not need to sign anything further. If there are any changes, we will provide you with either an amending agreement or a new replacement Letter for you to sign.

Do you notice the similarity of the above to a "this contract renews on the same terms and conditions" clause or perhaps a "this document comprises the whole of the agreement" clause? Actually, in a roundabout way all this paragraph says is that the agreement is effective until a change is made, at which point a new agreement or an amendment will be required.

> **1.16 Confidentiality.** The terms of this Agreement are confidential between you and CIBC. You therefore agree not to disclose the contents of this Agreement to anyone except your professional advisors.

I trust that I am not the only one who sees the incongruity between this clause and paragraph 1.12. According to this one, the customer cannot disclose the terms of this agreement to anyone because those terms are confidential. Yet under paragraph 1.12, the lender can give up this *confidential* information to just about anyone with half a reason.

> **1.17 Pre-conditions.** You may use the Credits granted to you under this Agreement only if:
> (a) we have received properly signed copies of all documentation that we may require in connection with the operation of your accounts and your ability to borrow and give security;
> (b) all the required security has been received and registered to our satisfaction;
> (c) any special provisions or conditions set forth in the Letter have been complied with; and
> (d) if applicable, you have given us the required number of days' notice for a drawing under a Credit.

> **1.18 Notices.** We may give you any notice in person or by telephone, or by letter that is sent either by fax or by mail.

1.19 Use of the Operating Line. You will use your Operating Line only for your business operating cash needs. You are responsible for all debits from the Operating Account that you have either initiated (such as cheques, loan payments, pre-authorized debits, etc.) or authorized us to make. Payments are made by making deposits to the Operating Account. You may not at any time exceed the Credit Limit. We may, without notice to you, return any debit from the Operating Account that, if paid, would result in the Credit Limit being exceeded, unless you have made prior arrangements with us. If we pay any of these debits, you must repay us immediately the amount by which the Credit Limit is exceeded.

1.20 Margin requirements. If your Operating Line is margined against Inventory and/or Receivable Value, the available Credit Limit of that Credit is the lesser of the Credit Limit stated in the Letter and the amount calculated using the Monthly Statement of Available Credit Limit.

Margin credit is based on the customer being able to borrow against inventory and receivables an amount equal to some formula-derived percentage of the value of those assets. Naturally such an asset value has to be updated to be effective, and a regularly required report is specified within this paragraph. The bank will lend the marginal value up to the maximum limit stated in the agreement letter.

1.21 Foreign currency conversion. If this Agreement includes foreign currency Credits, then currency changes may affect whether either the Credit Limit of any Credit or the Overall Credit Limit has been exceeded.

(a) See section 1.4 for the general rules on how Default Interest is calculated.

(b) To determine the Overall Credit Limit, all foreign currency amounts are converted to Canadian dollars, even if the Credit Limits of any particular Credits are quoted directly in a foreign currency (such as U.S. dollars). No matter how the Credit Limit of a particular Credit is quoted, therefore, currency fluctuations can affect whether the Overall Credit Limit has been exceeded. For example, if Credits X and Y have Credit Limits of C$100,000 and US$50,000, respectively, with an Overall Credit Limit of C$175,000, if Credit X is at C$90,000 and Credit Y is at US$45,000, Default Interest will be charged only if, after converting the U.S. dollar amount, the Overall Credit Limit is exceeded.

(c) Whether the Credit Limit of a particular Credit has been exceeded will depend on how the Credit Limit is quoted, as described below.

(d) If the Credit Limit is quoted as, for example, the U.S. dollar equivalent of a Canadian dollar amount, daily exchange rate fluctuations may affect whether that Credit Limit has been exceeded. If, on the other hand, the Credit Limit is quoted in a foreign currency (for example, directly in U.S. dollars), whether that Credit Limit has been exceeded is determined by reference only to the closing balance of that Credit in that currency.

(e) For example, assume an outstanding balance of a Credit on a particular day of US$200,000. If the Credit Limit is stated as "the U.S. dollar equivalent of C$275,000," then whether the Credit Limit of that Credit has been exceeded will depend on the value of the Canadian dollar on that day. If the conversion calculations determine that the outstanding balance is under the Credit Limit, a drop in the value of the Canadian dollar the next day (without any change in the balance) may have the effect of putting that Credit over its Credit Limit. If, on the other hand, the Credit Limit is stated as "US$200,000," the Credit Limit is not exceeded, and a drop in the value of the dollar on the next day will not change that (although the Overall Credit Limit may be affected).

(f) Conversion calculations are done on the closing daily balance of the Credit. The conversion factor used is the mid-point between the buying and selling rate offered by the CIBC for that currency on the conversion date.

This is a long paragraph with several examples that boils down to the following: Foreign currency credit limits and standings are converted to Canadian dollar values at the prevailing exchange rates in order to determine whether limits have been exceeded (1.21(b)). When the Canadian dollar declines against the currency denomination of the credit, *and* the credit limit is denominated in the *equivalent* of Canadian dollars, there is risk exposure from the foreign exchange causing the credit to exceed its limit (1.21(d) and (e)). If the credit limit is denominated in the foreign currency, only the *actual* amount in the foreign currency is relevant so there is no credit limit risk exposure (1.21(d) and (e)). Regardless of whether individual credits are over their limits due to foreign exchange exposure by virtue of how they are denominated, a customer's overall total credit limit may be exposed because the total credit limit is *always* in Canadian dollars (1.21(b)). You might want to read this explanation twice.

    1.22 Installment loans. The following terms apply to each Installment Loan.

        (a) **Nonrevolving loans.** Unless otherwise stated in the Letter, any Installment Loan is nonrevolving. This means that any principal payment made permanently reduces the available Loan Amount. Any payment we receive is applied first to overdue interest, then to current interest owing, then to overdue principal, then to any fees and charges owing, and finally to current principal.

The latter part of this paragraph is relatively easy to follow. Before getting there, however, we need to be aware of a few things such as the difference between a revolving and a nonrevolving loan. As the language above implies, a nonrevolving loan is provided for certain chattels at a fixed amount (e.g., $100,000 to purchase some machinery). As you pay the loan off, the loan's full amount decreases; or, the lender is not required to re-advance credit to the full $100,000 initially lent to you. The counterpoint is the revolving credit, such as a line of credit, which is for a set maximum amount. If you have a revolving loan for $100,000 and your current level of borrowing on it, because you've been making payments, has been reduced to $35,000, the lender will re-advance another $65,000 (to the limit) at any time.

Generally speaking, fixed-asset loans are nonrevolving, and operating lines of credit, which are to be used for ongoing operations often in the form of an overdraft, are revolving credits. The occurrence of revolving fixed-asset loans is infrequent and arises only in special circumstances such as with leasing companies that purchase fixed assets that may be purchased from them during the term of their loan with the lender.

        (b) **Floating Rate Installment Loans.** Floating Rate Installment Loans may have either (i) blended payments, or (ii) payments of fixed principal amounts, plus interest, as described below.

           (i) **Blended payments.** If you have a Floating Rate Loan that has blended payments, the amount of your monthly payments is fixed for the term of the loan, but the interest rate varies with changes in the Prime or U.S. Base Rate (as the case may be). If the Prime or U.S. Base Rate during any month is lower than what the rate was at the outset, you may end up paying off the loan before the scheduled end date. If, however, the Prime or U.S. Base Rate is higher than what it was at the outset, the amount of principal that is paid off is reduced. As a result, you may end up still owing principal at the end of the term because of these changes in the Prime or U.S. Base Rate.

When the credit conditions have an interest rate that floats but payments that are blended (principal and interest in a single fixed amount each period), it makes sense that if the interest rate declines (on average, from the interest rate used to determine the payments), you will be paying more principal each month. Thus, the loan is paid off earlier. Conversely, if the rate goes up, you are paying more interest and less principal, so the loan will still be outstanding when your scheduled payments have been completed.

           (ii) **Payments of principal plus interest.** If you have a Floating Rate Loan that has regular principal payments, plus interest, the principal payment amount of your Loan is due on each payment date specified in the Letter. The interest payment is also due on the same date, but it is debited from your Operating Account one (1) or two (2) banking days later. Although the principal payment amount is fixed, your interest payment will usually be different each month, for at least one and possibly more reasons, namely: the reducing principal balance of your loan, the number of days in the month, and changes to the Prime Rate or U.S. Base Rate (as the case may be).

Assume your loan/credit floats with interest rates and has a payment schedule that has a set principal payment *plus* interest components. The principal will, regardless of interest rate movements, be drawn down on schedule. The interest, on the other hand, will vary with each payment period due to interest rate changes, the remaining principal balance, etc. So, the total payment each month—principal on a set day and interest two days later—will vary depending on the factors noted above.

(c) **Prepayment.** Unless otherwise agreed, the following terms apply to prepayment of any Installment Loan:
  (i) **Blended payments.** You may prepay all or part of a Floating Rate Installment Loan (whether it is a Demand or a Committed Loan) at any time without notice or penalty.
  (ii) **Payments of principal plus interest.** You may prepay all or part of a Fixed Rate Installment Loan, on the following condition. You must pay us, on the prepayment date, a prepayment fee equal to the interest rate differential for the remainder of the term of the Loan, in accordance with the standard formula used by CIBC in these situations.

The interest rate differential is the "loss" the lender incurs because of early payment. It works more or less like this: the lender advances the client (you) money at a fixed rate of interest (say 8%) for a fixed term; the lender has obtained those funds at a certain cost, the *cost of capital* (say by selling GICs, at 6%); in between what they take in from you and pay out is the *spread*.[3]

If you pay off your loan early, essentially the lender no longer gets the income for the remaining period *from you* to cover its obligations and make its spread. The lender will lend that money out again to someone else. But the issue is what has happened to interest rates. If they have gone up, the lender will be able to relend your credit at a higher interest rate (thereby increasing its spread on the original cost of capital for those funds). If rates have gone down, the lender's spread will shrink on relending "your" paid-up credit. In order to maintain its original spread (profit margin) as calculated when you took out the loan, the lender would demand the "interest rate differential" (more or less the difference between your original interest rate and the interest rate prevailing on the re-lent credit now) for the planned remaining period of your loan on the declining balance. This part of the payback ensures that the lender does not have a downside.

Generally, unless you had a windfall, you would probably prepay your loan if interest rates went down (i.e., pay out the existing loan at the older, higher rate of interest and take out a new one at the lower rate). Under this contractual term, however, you should be indifferent, because you have to pay out the interest differential anyway. Notice how the lender is not required to pay out an interest rate differential for the privilege of lending the funds out at a higher rate if lending interest rates have increased and you pay back your loan early? Nice business.

(d) **Demand of Fixed Rate Demand Installment Loans**. If you have a Fixed Rate Demand Installment Loan and we make demand for payment, you will owe us (i) all outstanding principal, (ii) interest, (iii) any other amount due under this Agreement, and (iv) a prepayment fee. The prepayment fee is equal to the interest rate differential for the remainder of the term of the loan, in accordance with the standard formula used by CIBC in these situations.

Interesting demand conditions that very few can command. Demand early payment of a loan, *and* the interest rate differential to compensate for the "lost" interest on the remaining period (forgone by the financial institution's own demand, by the way). This risk/reward relationship could create a "*post*modern portfolio theory."

1.23 **Notice of Default.** You will promptly notify us of the occurrence of any event that is an Event of Default (of any that would be an Event of Default if the only thing required is either notice being given or time elapsing, or both).

ARTICLE 2—BUSINESS IMPROVEMENT LOANS

2.1 **Definitions.** In this Article, the following terms have the following meanings:
  "*Act*" means the *Small Business Loans Act* (Canada), as that Act is amended or replaced from time to time.
  "*Application*" means the application that you sign under the Act in connection with a Loan.
  "*BIL*" means a business improvement loan made under the Act.

2.2 Purpose of the BIL. You acknowledge to us that (a) the purpose of the BIL is as specified in the Application and (b) all information and supporting documents presented to us in connection with the BIL are, to the best of your knowledge, after due enquiry, accurate and complete.

2.3 Prepayment of a fixed rate BIL. You may prepay all or any principal portion outstanding under a fixed rate BIL so long as (a) you pay to us a prepayment fee equal to three (3) months' interest thereon at the rate otherwise applicable to such a loan and (b) you pay any additional charges payable under, and subject to any restrictions set forth in, this Agreement. There are no fees or charges, however, if you switch from a fixed rate to a floating rate BIL.

2.4 Default. The BIL will become due and payable immediately and without notice if any payment of principal or interest is not paid in full when due.

This is the most generous and simple part of the entire form, in my opinion. Business Improvement Loans are part of a program legislated by the Federal government.

ARTICLE 3—BANKERS' ACCEPTANCES

3.1 Definitions. In this Article, the following terms have the following meanings:

"Bankers' Acceptance" or *"B/A"* means a Canadian dollar Draft that we have accepted under this Agreement. Paragraph 3.7, below, provides a little bit more explanation of a bankers' acceptance.

"Commerce Acceptance Rate" means the variable reference rate that we declare from time to time as our stamping or acceptance fee for Drafts accepted by us.

"Draft" means, at any time, a blank bill of exchange within the meaning of the *Bills of Exchange Act* drawn by the Customer on us (in satisfactory form), but before we have accepted it.

3.2 Availability. B/As are available only with terms to maturity of between thirty (30) and one hundred eighty (180) days.

3.3 Minimum issue amount. You will present drafts for acceptance in a minimum amount of $1 million. We can change this minimum amount at any time by thirty (30) days' prior written notice.

3.4 Required notice. You may either obtain a new advance by issuing a B/A stamped by CIBC (including a rollover of an existing B/A) or you may convert an amount outstanding under another Credit to issuance of a B/A on the following terms. You must give us notice (in the form we require, including, when applicable, the date of acceptance, the amount, and the maturity date). Notice must be given by 10:00 am (local time where the CIBC Branch/Centre is located) on the Business Day prior to the requested date of issuance. You must also give us any other notice required by the Letter.

This clause applies if you wish to either roll over a maturing B/A or a different type of credit (e.g., operating line, which you might convert to a B/A because of the usually lower applicable interest rate) into another B/A. This clause provides the notice procedure required to do either of these B/A rollovers.

3.5 Special Conditions.

(a) Draft conditions. You will deliver to us the Drafts that you want us to issue. Each Draft must (i) be in a whole multiple of C$100,000; (ii) be dated the date of delivery (which will be the same date as the requested date you notified us); (iii) mature on a Business Day; and (iv) be presented to the CIBC Branch/Centre for acceptance by 12:00 noon on the date of delivery (unless you have made prior arrangements in writing with us).

(b) Maturity limitation. The maturity date of a Draft submitted to us for acceptance may not (i) be after a scheduled or mandatory final maturity or termination date for that Credit or (ii) conflict, in our opinion, with any scheduled or mandatory repayment for that Credit.

(c) Conversion-to-loan limitation. You may only convert a B/A into a loan otherwise allowed under this Agreement if the total of "A" plus "B" is less than Prime Rate existing on that maturity date, where:

"A" is the annual discount rate quoted at 9:30 am (Toronto time) by the Toronto office of Wood Gundy Inc.

as the discount rate at which it would purchase a bankers' acceptance issued by CIBC having a term to maturity of thirty (30) days, and

"B" is the annual stamping or acceptance rate applicable to a Draft accepted by us under this Agreement, as determined on the maturity date of that B/A.

In making these calculations, each of A and B is expressed as a percentage.

At maturity of a bankers' acceptance, you, the bank's customer, may not be able to repay it and wish to convert the debt (credit to the banker) to a loan. The bank will do it if the formula-set requirement to do so is beat. The paragraph above provides the formula.

3.6 Stamping fee. When we accept a Draft under this Agreement, you will pay us a stamping fee, on the date of acceptance, in the amount as set out in the Letter. The stamping fee will be calculated on the face amount of that Draft for the number of days to maturity based on a three hundred sixty-five (365) day year.

The stamping fee is calculated as an annual basis point addition on the order of 50–100 basis points. A basis point is a percent of a percent, i.e., one hundredth of a percentage point.

3.7 Reimbursement. B/As are negotiable instruments that are purchased in financial markets at a discount. Market forces determine what the discount amount for B/As is at any particular time. At maturity, the holder of a B/A redeems it from CIBC. We then pay the holder the face amount.

So there is the skeletal explanation of how a bankers' acceptance works. If your business is too small to issue commercial paper (short-term, money market debt instrument) on its own merits, the B/A is the next-best thing in this area. It usually bears a lower cost than other forms of bank credit. . . .

You will, therefore, reimburse us at the maturity date for the face amount of all B/As that we have accepted for you, unless you convert those amounts to another Credit (assuming all proper notice has been given).

On maturity of the B/A, the customer pays the bank the face value of the B/A or converts that sum to another type of credit (debt owing the bank) such as rolling it into the operating line account.

If you do not reimburse us or convert those amounts to another Credit, we may convert them to any type of loan (if available) under any Credit.

If the issuer of the B/A—the customer—does not pay on or convert the B/A at maturity, the bank has the right to convert the B/A to any other type of loan it chooses.

3.8 Signatures and safekeeping. All Drafts must either be signed by a properly authorized signing officer or bear a mechanically reproduced facsimile signature of that officer (subject to any prior written arrangements with us). Each Draft and B/A bearing a facsimile signature of that officer will be as binding on you as if it had been manually signed by that officer. This applies even for individuals who may no longer be authorized or otherwise be an officer at any time. You will compensate us for any loss or expense relating to any Draft or B/A that we deal with under this Agreement.

Any draft bearing the signature, or a mechanically reproduced facsimile signature, of a "then" authorized officer of the party issuing the draft or other document shall be binding and the customer shall be responsible for all costs and expenses pertaining thereto. This could be the lender, whose signature is required on the bank draft, etc., or the borrower, whose signature would be required on its cheques. The lender would have on file a document indicating not only whose signature was required but that a facsimile reproduction of that person's signature could be used on negotiable drafts.

We need only exercise the same degree of care in safekeeping executed Drafts delivered to us for future acceptance as if they were CIBC's property and we were keeping them at the place at which they are to be held.

The financial institution will keep drafts safe in the same manner they would keep their own documents safe—no more. They are not responsible for the documents beyond that degree of safekeeping, nor should we expect it of them.

3.9 Credit cancellation. If your B/A Credit is terminated for any reason, we may require you to pay us immediately on demand the appropriate reimbursement amount for each B/A then outstanding. We will calculate the reimbursement amount in accordance with standard practice in the banking industry in Canada. After making this payment, (a) you will have no further liability for that B/A and (b) we will (i) become the sole party liable under the B/A and (ii) compensate you if you have to pay anyone else under that B/A.

If the bank should cancel a customer's B/A credit early, the customer owes them the face amount of the B/A immediately, with the reimbursement amount calculated according to "standard banking practice." The customer is then no longer liable or responsible for the B/A, and the bank will indemnify the customer from any loss on that paid-up B/A.

3.10 Waiver. You will not claim any days of grace for the payment of a B/A. You waive any defense to payment which might otherwise exist if for any reason a B/A is held by us in our own right at its maturity.

The B/A is due and you owe the financial institution the money on the due date, period. Don't bother to ask for an extension. The likely reason for such a definitive condition is because the bank would owe that money the same day.

3.11 Obligations absolute. Your obligations for Drafts and B/As are unconditional and irrevocable. You will perform your obligations strictly in accordance with the provisions of this Agreement including, among other things, (a) any lack of validity or enforceability of a Draft accepted by us as a B/A and (b) the existence of a claim, set-off, compensation, defense, or other right which you may have against the holder of a B/A, CIBC, or another person.

Basically, the customer's obligations under the B/A (to pay the bank) must be carried out completely regardless of extenuating circumstances, especially regarding payment or authorization of the B/A.

ARTICLE 4—DEFINITIONS

3.1 Definitions. In this Agreement, the following terms have the following meanings:
"*Base Rate Loan*" means a U.S. dollar loan on which interest is calculated by reference to the U.S. Base Rate.
"*Business Day*" means any day (other than a Saturday or a Sunday) that the CIBC Branch/Centre is open for business.
"*CIBC Branch/Centre*" means the CIBC branch or banking centre noted on the first page of this Agreement, as changed from time to time by agreement between the parties.
"*Committed Installment Loan*" means an Installment Loan that is payable in regular installments but is repayable in full only upon the occurrence of an Event of Default. Such a Loan may be at either a fixed or a floating rate of interest.
"*Credit*" means any credit referred to in the Letter, and if there are two or more parts to a Credit, "Credit" includes reference to each part.
"*Credit Limit*" of any Credit means the amount specified in the Letter as its Credit Limit, and if there are two or more parts to a Credit, "Credit Limit" includes reference to each such part.
"*Current Assets*" are cash, accounts receivable, inventory, and other assets that are likely to be converted into cash, sold, exchanged, or expended in the normal course of business within one (1) year or less, excluding amounts due from related parties.
"*Current Liabilities*" means debts that are or will become payable within one (1) year or one operating cycle,

whichever is longer, excluding amounts due to related parties, and which will require Current Assets to pay. They usually include accounts payable, accrued expenses, deferred revenue, and the current portion of long-term debt.

"Current Ratio" means the ratio of Current Assets to Current Liabilities.

"Debt to Effective Equity Ratio" means the ratio of X to Y, where X is the total of all liabilities, less all Postponed Debt, and Y is the total Shareholders' Equity, plus all Postponed Debt, less (i) amounts due from/investments in related parties and (ii) intangibles.

"Default Interest Rate," unless otherwise defined in the Letter, means the Standard Overdraft Rate.

"Demand Installment Loan" means an Installment Loan that is payable on demand. Such a Loan may be at either a fixed or a floating rate of interest.

"Event of Default" means, in connection with any Committed Installment Loan (even if that Loan has not yet been drawn), the occurrence of any of the following events (or the occurrence of any other event of default described in this Agreement, in any of the security documents or in any other agreement or document you have signed with us):

(1) You do not pay, when due, any amount that you are required to pay us under this Agreement or otherwise, or you do not perform any of your other obligations to us under this agreement or otherwise.

(2) Any part of the security terminates or is no longer in effect, without our prior written consent.

(3) You cease to carry on your business in the normal course, or it reasonably appears to us that that may happen.

(4) A representation that you have made (or are deemed to have made) in this Agreement or in any security is incorrect or misleading in any material respect.

(5) (i) An actual or potential default or event of default occurs in connection with any debt owed by you, with the result that the payment of the debt has become, or is capable of becoming, accelerated or (ii) you do not make a payment when due in connection with any such debt. (This subsection (5), however, applies only to amounts that we reasonably consider to be material.)

(6) If you are a corporation, there is, in our reasonable opinion, a change in effective control of the corporation, or if you are a partnership, there is a change in the partnership membership.

(7) We believe, in good faith and upon commercially reasonable grounds, that all or part of the property subject to any of the security is or is about to be placed in jeopardy or that a material adverse change in your business operations or financial affairs has occurred.

(8) The holder of a Lien takes possession of all or part of your property; or a distress, execution, or other similar process is levied against any such property.

(9) You (i) become insolvent; (ii) are unable generally to pay your debts as they become due; (iii) make a proposal in bankruptcy, or file a notice of intention to make such a proposal; (iv) make an assignment in bankruptcy; (v) bring a court action to have yourself declared insolvent or bankrupt, or someone else brings an action for such a declaration; or (vi) you default in payment or breach any other obligation to any of your other creditors.

(10) If you are a corporation, (i) you are dissolved, (ii) your shareholders or members pass a resolution for your winding-up or liquidation, (iii) someone goes to court seeking your winding-up or liquidation, or the appointment of an administrator, conservator, receiver, trustee, custodian, or other similar official for you or for all or substantially all your assets, or (iv) you seek protection under any statute offering relief against the company's creditors.

It is interesting to note that an "event of default" is a trigger to default a Committed Installment Loan *even if* that loan has not been drawn. Special interest notes about this section begin with acknowledging that default on *any* credit could be a default trigger. Additionally, in the following referenced paragraphs, you should note:

• *Point (3): "reasonably appears to us."* A business setback that you have to fight to overcome may be just the start of your troubles.

•*Point (4): "deemed to have made."* You did not make the representation, but we will assume and accept that you did.

•*Point (5): "potential" and "is capable of becoming."* Means something to the effect of "The sky is blue, but it may rain."

•*Point (6):* In practice what would happen, one would hope, is that the new owners/partners would meet with the bank and everything would be fine.

•*Point (7):* Read this as "business is tough for you, our valuable customer, but we are reasonably no longer 100% certain of receiving principal plus interest, charges, and fees, or, moreover, 100% assured of our security, so we'll call the loan."

"*Fixed Rate Installment Loan*" means an Installment Loan that is also a Fixed Rate Loan.

"*Fixed Rate Loan*" means any loan drawn down, converted, or extended under a Credit at an interest rate which was fixed for a term, instead of referenced to a variable rate such as the Prime Rate or U.S. Base Rate, at the time of such drawdown, conversion, or extension. For purposes of certainty, a Fixed Rate Loan includes a LIBOR Loan.

"*Floating Rate Installment Loan*" means an Installment Loan that is either a Prime Rate Loan or a Base Rate Loan.

"*Installment Loan*" means a loan that is repayable either in fixed Installments of principal, plus interest, or in blended Installments of both principal and interest. A Demand Installment Loan is repayable on demand. A Committed Installment Loan is repayable only upon the occurrence of an Event of Default.

"*Intangibles*" means assets of the business that have no value in themselves but represent value. They include such things as copyright, patents, and trademarks; franchises; licenses; leases; research and development costs; and deferred development costs.

"*Inventory Value*" means the total value (based on the lower of cost or market) of your inventories (other than (i) inventories supplied by trade creditors who at that time have not been fully paid and would have a right to repossess all or part of such inventories if you were then either bankrupt or in receivership, (ii) work in process, and (iii) those inventories we may from time to time designate).

"*Letter*" means the letter agreement between you and CIBC to which this Schedule and any other Schedules are attached.

"*Letter of Credit*" or "*L/C*" means a documentary or stand-by letter of credit, a letter of guarantee, or similar instrument in form and substance satisfactory to us.

"*L/C Acceptance*" means a draft (as defined under the Bills of Exchange Act (Canada)) payable to the beneficiary of a documentary L/C which the L/C applicant or beneficiary, as the case may be, has presented to us for acceptance under the terms of the L/C.

"*Minimum Shareholders' Equity*" means the total Shareholders' Equity, minus (a) amounts due from/investments in related parties, and the value of all Intangibles, plus (b) all Postponed Debt.

"*Money Market Investments*" means instruments such as GICs, bankers' acceptances, T-bills, etc.

"*Monthly Statement of Available Credit Limit*" means the CIBC form by that name, as it may from time to time be changed.

"*Negotiable Securities*" means securities traded on a publicly recognized securities exchange in Canada or the United States, each of which has a value at all times greater than the minimum value from time to time specified by us.

"*Operating Account*" means the account that you normally use for the day-to-day cash needs of your business, and may be either or both of a Canadian dollar and a U.S. dollar account.

"*Postponed Debt*" means any debt owed by you that has been formally postponed to CIBC.

"*Prime Rate*" means variable reference rate of interest per year declared by CIBC from time to time to be its prime rate for Canadian dollar loans made by CIBC in Canada.

"*Prime Rate Loan*" means a Canadian dollar loan on which interest is calculated by reference to Prime Rate.

"*Priority Ranking Claim*" means any amount owing to a creditor that ranks, or may rank, equal or in priority to our security. These may include unremitted source deductions and taxes; other amounts owing to governments and governmental bodies; and amounts owing to creditors who may claim priority under the Bankruptcy and Insolvency Act or under a purchase money security interest in inventory or equipment.

"*Receivable Value*" means, at any time of determination, the total value of those of your trade accounts receivable, including accounts domiciled in the United States, that are subject to the security (other than those accounts: (i) outstanding for ninety (90) days or more, (ii) owing by persons, firms, or corporations affiliated to you, and (iii) that we may from time to time designate).

"Shareholders' Equity" means paid-in capital, retained earnings and attributed or contributed surplus.

"Standard Overdraft Rate" means the variable reference interest rate per year declared by CIBC from time to time to be its standard overdraft rate on overdrafts in Canadian or U.S. dollar accounts maintained with CIBC in Canada.

"U.S. Base Rate" means the variable reference interest rate per year as declared by CIBC from time to time to be its base rate for U.S. dollar loans made by CIBC in Canada.

Chapter 8
Lease and Rental Contracts

Chattel Leasing and Property Leasing; Their Terms and Meanings

Leasing, whether of an office space, property, or some kind of chattel, is one of the most prevalent commercial "acquisition" arrangements used in business today. Leasing office space is a conventional manner of housing an operation because of the low relative costs involved—especially in downtown high-rise office space. More recently, businesses have become mass consumers of leased chattel, including office equipment, automobiles, and even fleets of aircraft. One underlying reason for the growth in leasing is found in tax law. Other financial-presentation reasons (e.g., off-balance-sheet financing) have been driving the demand for lease financing. On the more practical side, the ability to register and keep track of moveable properties (unlike land and buildings, which are not prone to movement except when located near fault lines or in the path of other acts of God) has provided a means for the property owners to realistically find and retrieve their property when it has been leased to another.

In this chapter, we will examine both a chattel lease and a property lease. The standard forms we will look at have been provided by large companies in those respective businesses as samples of typical lease forms.

CHATTEL LEASING

There are essentially two types of chattel leases: the operating lease and the capital lease. The former is a rental agreement whereby for a set term and fixed installment rent payments, the lessee is allowed to use the property. The lessee takes possession and may act in every respect like the owner, but never takes title to the property. At the end of the lease term, the property reverts to the owner—the lessor. Whether it is rental cars or long term aircraft leasing, the operating lease has the same structure. For tax purposes, the periodic payments of rent for the leased property are totally expensed in the period in which the payment is made. An operating lease may have a purchase feature, but the buyout price must be (1) optional and (2) fair market value. In short, it can't be preplanned from the commencement of the lease, nor can it be a sweetheart price.

If either of these last two conditions is part of the lease contract, the lease may be deemed to be a capital lease. The capital lease is best typified by the "rent to own" idea. In essence, the lessee takes on a term lease contract from the lessor in which the intent is for the product to be financed and become the lessee's property at the end of the lease term either automatically or for a bargain price. Additionally, according to the Canadian Institute of Chartered Accountants (CICA), a lease may be deemed to be a capital lease if its term is for more than 75% of the asset's useful life, or if the present value of the rent payments exceeds 90% of the asset's value.[1]

More important than what the chartered accountants have to say on the matter is Revenue Canada's position, since the most significant difference between the operating lease and the capital lease is the treatment of the rent payments for tax purposes. Whereas the rent on an operating lease is 100% expensed in the period in which it occurs, as noted earlier, a capital lease is deemed to be a capital purchase. Thus, the asset is "capitalized" and only the allowable capital cost allowance deduction can be made from income. Generally speaking, the capital lease provides a smaller tax deduction than the operating lease during the term of the lease.

Capital leases are generally of two types: the finance lease and the security lease. The former arises when a leasing company purchases an asset on your behalf and leases it to you. In essence they are "financing" the lease. The latter is typified by GMAC leasing, for instance, in which the vendor is providing the leasing of the asset they are "selling." For the most part, there is not a great deal of difference in the net effect of these two leases to the lessee inasmuch as the lessee is paying rent on an asset and taking possession of it at the end of the term with or without a buyout. The difference is in the number of parties involved and the responsibilities of those parties.

In the finance lease, the leasing company—the lessor—purchases an asset from a vendor with whom you, the lessee, have negotiated a price. The lessor will then own the asset and rent it to you under certain lease terms. The vendor, except for its responsibility for warranties (which are technically the property of the lessor), is now out of the picture. Because of both this technical issue and a finance lessor's reluctance to hold itself responsible for what amounts to the vendor's deficiencies in the asset, the lessee may find dealing with problems that arise later to be troublesome. After all, the lessee has no contract or warranty with the vendor; it is not privy to the purchase and sale between the vendor and the lessor. That said, most leasing companies assign the warranty to the lessee, and it would seem most vendors will honour and accommodate lessees in this respect.

The most common terms in a chattel lease are as follows.

• Duration
The term of the lease is normally specified. For office equipment, anywhere between 24 and 48 months is normal. Automobile leases tend toward 36 to 48 (and sometimes 60) months. Leases for larger assets would tend to more closely reflect the useful life of the asset. Many leases will automatically renew if the lessee does not specifically return the asset to the lessor. The rental terms of the unnegotiated extension, like an overholding tenancy of a property lease, however, can be often quite unfavourable to the lessee. The purpose is to ensure that a renegotiation of a renewal takes place prior to the lease expiration. In a negotiated renewal the rent will normally be lower because of the reduced asset value.

• Rent
The periodic cost of the lease is another normal term. Most leases seem to be based on monthly payment installments. There is a minimum periodic rent for the lease to which may be added various other costs such as insurance premiums, service program charges, and taxes. Some of these costs are on-time only, while others, such as insurance, may fluctuate. All such charges over and above minimum rent are considered "additional rent." The minimum lease price will have taken into account the full cost of the asset, the term of the payments, and a lease ("interest" or "capital return") rate. Rent is typically paid in advance, and more than one period's rent (i.e., a security deposit) is often requested at the commencement of the contract.

• Insurance/repair
You, the lessee, do not own the asset; the lessor does, and it is the lessor that would suffer economic loss by the theft, damage, or loss of the asset. Thus, the lessor will typically demand in the lease contract that the lessee keep the asset in good repair and ensure that it is properly and adequately insured. This seems sensible.

• Buyout option
Most leases, even operating leases, will contain a purchase option. The buyout option for a capital lease will often be set in some way and be more favourable to the lessee than the buyout provision of an operating lease. In any event, it is a good option to have, as the lessee can leave the asset behind when the term expires, or can purchase it if that would make more economic sense.

The chattel lease agreement would seem to come with implied terms as well, not the least of which is the "quiet possession" term found in property leases. That is, so long as the lessee is in compliance with the terms of the lease, the lessor will not bother the lessee. As alluded to earlier, there is also the matter of the warranty of fitness. In the case of the vendor leasing directly to the lessee, this warranty would naturally be implied. When the lease is through a leasing company, the question about whether the lessee enjoys the benefit of such a warranty is a little hazier. From the lessor's perspective, the lessee has negotiated the price, etc. from the vendor and has merely asked the lessor to purchase the asset and provide a form of financing to the lessee. Therefore, the lessor makes no warranty of fitness. In and of itself this is reasonable, although problems that could not be reasonably foreseen at the time of purchase, or notice of the intended use, made to the vendor before purchase, may not apply or be of effect to the lessee, because the lessee is not privy to the purchase contract between the vendor and lessor. Oddly, there is not a lot of law in this area. On the other hand, as shown in the sample agreement that follows, the lessor will normally assign warranties and so forth to the lessee.

The following standard contract was generously provided by National Leasing Group. It is typical of a finance lease contract for chattels such as office equipment, communications systems, and other, similar assets. The top half of the front side of the agreement provides space for the particulars of the lease agreement (lessee, asset, price, rent, term, etc.) to be completed by the leasing agent, and provided to the lessee for consideration.

> Note that the lease agreement, which is filled in by the leasing agent, is not an offer made by the "lessor." It is an invitation for the potential lessee to make an offer to the "lessor" under the terms indicated on the contract sheet. The leasing company is not bound to the agreement until it "accepts" your offer. This is seen in paragraph 2 of the sample.

These particulars are defined within the boxes and are referred to in the contract terms that follow.

National Leasing Group Inc.
D.B.A. National Equipment Leasing
National Agri Leasing
National Medical Leasing

LEASE CONTRACT

WEBSITE ADDRESS:
www.nlgroup.ca

FastCredit

Lease No.
Customer No.
Commencement Date:

LESSEE			Telephone No.
	Marketing Contact:	Billing Contact:	Facsimile No.
ADDRESS			
CITY & PROVINCE		POSTAL CODE	SUPPLIER:
LOCATION OF EQUIPMENT (if different than above)			
LESSEE OWNS PREMISES ☐	NAME AND ADDRESS OF LANDLORD IF EQUIPMENT IS TO BE PLACED IN RENTED PREMISES.		

QUANTITY	EQUIPMENT DESCRIPTION (Include Make, Model and Serial Number(s)

TERM (NO. OF COMPLETE MONTHS)	RENT PAYMENTS WILL BE MADE IN ADVANCE	☐ MONTHLY ☐ QUARTERLY ☐ OTHER	NO. OF PERIODIC RENT PMTS. DURING TERM	PERIODIC RENT AMOUNT	P.S.T.	G.S.T. / H.S.T.	TOTAL RENT PAYMENT

PURCHASE OPTION (see Section 15.2)	OPTION DATE: the end of the term's _____ calendar month.	OPTION PRICE: ☐ Fair Market Value or $ _____

PRE-AUTHORIZED PAYMENT PLAN – National is hereby authorized to periodically draw payment under its Pre-authorized Payment Plan from the bank account specified in the Bank information section above and/or as outlined on the attached sample cheque to cover the Rent and other amounts due under this Lease. **PLEASE ATTACH AN UNSIGNED SAMPLE CHEQUE.**

Per _____   Per _____
AUTHORIZED SIGNATURE   TITLE   AUTHORIZED SIGNATURE   TITLE

THIS LEASE made by and between National Leasing Group Inc. ("National") and Lessee.

1. **Lease:** National hereby leases to Lessee, and Lessee hereby hires and leases from National, the equipment described above, together with any related or affixed parts and accessories (the "Equipment").

This is the mutual promise to lease and pay rent made to one another. Note that the "Equipment," as most other defined words encountered in the contract, is specified in the fill-in section that precedes the contract terms.

2. **Term:** The term of this Lease ("term") begins on the Lease Commencement Date to be established by National when the Lease Contract is accepted by National, but shall be no earlier than the date the Equipment is shipped to the Lessee. Unless sooner terminated by Lessor, the Term will end after the number of months specified above from the date the Term commences; provided, however, that if the Term commences on OTHER THAN the 1st day of the month, the Term shall be extended to the last day of the month in which the Term would otherwise expire. "Termination Date" means the date on which the Term ends, according to this section. If the Rent includes a cost of service or maintenance, Lessee acknowledges that such inclusion is for Lessee's convenience and Lessee will not assert against Lessor any claim by way of abatement, defense, set-off, compensation, counterclaim, or the like which Lessee might have under any service or maintenance agreement.

The contract begins on the later of: the dates the agreement is accepted by the lessor and the date the equipment is received. It then runs the specified number of periods (months, in this case) unless the lessor terminates the agreement early. This contract specifies that if the periods do not run concurrently with calendar months, then the last period extends through the whole of the month in which the term expires. If there should be a partial period of rent required due to a non-first-of-the-month commencement date, rent is prorated at the beginning of the lease as per paragraph 3 below.

The last part of the paragraph is there for a specific purpose. First, the lease rent is a fixed price equivalent to the "minimum rent" of a property lease (see below). Anything else added over and above that, such as taxes owed, would be equivalent to "additional rent." As most chattel leased properties are equipment of some form (e.g., automobiles, computers, etc.), there is a fair likelihood that the cost of the asset includes a service agreement or maintenance package—unlike real estate properties. To make life simple, the leasing company may offer to incorporate the total cost of the service program into the cost of the property (e.g., make the purchase price of the photocopier *plus* the annual service contract price for the lease period the total from which the lease payments are calculated) for the sake of having a single, inclusive, periodic payment. This last part of the paragraph says in effect that this procedure is being done for your convenience and that the lessor is not responsible for the service or maintenance package. Furthermore, you have no right to withhold payment from the lessor if you have a problem with the service program and do not want to pay on it.

3. **Rent and Rent Adjustment:** Lessee agrees to pay rent as follows: (a) if the Term commences on other than the 1st day of the month, Lessee will pay pro rata rent from the date of shipment to the end of the month in which shipment took place; (b) the Periodic Rent Payment ("Rent") for the first complete calendar period of the Term when Lessee executes this Lease; and (c) subsequent Rent in advance on the 1st day of each calendar period of the Term. Lessee shall make all payments at National's office shown above, or as National specifies in writing. National's invoice is NOT a condition of Lessee's obligation to pay Rent and/or interest charges when due. **Lessee's obligations under this Lease shall be absolute and unconditional under all circumstances whatsoever and without limitation.**

The first payment required is the pro rata rent for the current month if not commencing on the first day of the month plus the first full month's rent. The rent is thereafter to be paid in advance of each month for the remainder of the term; invoices are not required and will not necessarily be issued. The boldface text states that the lessee agrees to make the agreed payments as required without any exception throughout the contract's life.

3.1 Lessee has signed to acknowledge that Lease No. _____ has been terminated and replaced by this Lease and to consent and agree that the balance of rental of $_____ due under such replaced Lease has been prorated and included in the Total Rent Payment under this Lease herein above set forth.

This paragraph applies if a new lease is replacing an existing one. The remaining payments on the old lease are prorated and added into the new lease payments, the particulars and mathematics of which have all been specified in the fill-in section at the top of the agreement.

4. **Sales Tax:** Lessee shall pay Provincial Sales Tax, Goods & Services Tax, and/or Harmonized Sales Tax to National on and with each Rental Amount. The current applicable amounts of Provincial Sales Tax, Goods & Services Tax, and/or Harmonized Sales Tax on the one is set forth above.

The lessee must pay taxes to the lessor with and in addition to the rent each month. These amounts, as currently applicable under prevailing tax rates, are specified in the fill-in portion of the document, above.

5. **Non-Cancellable:** This Lease cannot be cancelled or terminated except as expressly provided in this Lease and will remain in force for the full Term.

This clause simply confirms that the parties agree to have the lease run its full duration, *unless*, of course, some other provision in the agreement itself allows for early termination. By the by, that "other" provision would likely be for the lessor to terminate early. This is another example of language that has to be followed through the document. The wording is accurate, but without checking to see what termination options are "expressly provided," one might infer that there is a provision that allows the lessee to terminate early.

6. **No Warranties:** National does not make any warranty or representation whatsoever as to the durability, quality, condition, or suitability of the Equipment for Lessee's purposes or as to any other matter in respect of the Equipment. Lessee requested National to purchase the Equipment from the original supplier of the Equipment (the "supplier") and to lease the Equipment to Lessee upon these terms and conditions. Lessee will accept the Equipment delivered to Lessee by Supplier. National is under no obligation to inspect, service, or otherwise maintain the Equipment. National shall not be liable to Lessee for any loss, damage, or expense of any kind caused directly or indirectly by the Equipment or its use, maintenance, or possession, or by any interruption of service or loss of use, or for any loss of business or damage whatsoever and however caused. National shall not be responsible to Lessee if Supplier fails to deliver the Equipment. Nothing shall in any way affect Lessee's obligation to pay Rent or perform its obligations under this Lease. The doctrine of fundamental breach shall have no application to this Lease.

This clause serves to effectively absolve the lessor from any responsibility whatsoever regarding the suitability or condition of the equipment, or any problems that may arise in the future which relate to the condition or suitability of the equipment. It also repeats that the lessee's obligations are unconditional, etc., just in case something does go wrong or the equipment is unfit for your purpose and you hope to extricate yourself from the lease. In this case, and in most cases, the lessor is nothing more than a financier for your purchase. As such the lessor does not want or need to get into issues regarding implied terms of suitability, etc. This type of paragraph pulls the lessor out of the loop. The important question then is, if you are not the actual buyer, do the implied sale terms of suitability and fitness for intended purpose apply? In general, it can be a tricky issue, but since you, the lessee, negotiated the purchase in the first place, there seems to be much on your side to force those warranties from the vendor. Furthermore, in paragraph 22 of this agreement, the lessor assigns to the lessee all rights to enforce the vendor's or supplier's warranties.

In special reference to the last sentence of the paragraph, the *Doctrine of Fundamental Breach* is "a breach that is so serious that it amounts to nonperformance of the contract . . . [it] goes to the "core" of the bargain between the parties . . . [and treating] an exemption clause as excusing one party entirely from performance would be repugnant to the very idea of a binding contract; therefore the clause must be struck down and the aggrieved party given a remedy in order to preserve the idea of a binding bargain."[2] In other words, exemption clauses that alter the agreement fundamentally are not valid under the doctrine of fundamental breach. What this single sentence of paragraph 6 in the lease agreement does is force an agreement from the lessee to make the doctrine not applicable to this paragraph, which is in its essence an exemption clause and precious little more.

That said, consider that an equipment lease such as this is, as noted earlier, primarily a financing transaction rather than an agreement to use equipment. It is therefore similar to a loan, whereby you (not the lender or lessor) have sourced and satisfied yourself with the equipment, and then obtained debt financing under a security agreement. A lender would have no concern for the state of the equipment, and loan payments would be required in any event. The lessor, under this lease agreement, provides the use of the equipment similarly to but more cost-effectively to the lessee than a lender in part by making the lease noncancellable. Under a normal rental agreement, if the property were not useable the lessee might claim a fundamental breach because she is not receiving the promised benefits under the agreement. In this lease situation, however, because the agreement is really a financial arrangement, that breach should not occur and affect the lessor. Thus, the last sentence of paragraph 6 is the lessor's way of making clear the fact that the condition or existence of the equipment is not a fundamental term of the lease.

> **7. Collection Charges:** Should Lessee fail to pay when due any part of the Rent, or renewal Rent herein reserved, or any sum required to be paid to National hereunder, Lessee shall pay to National, in addition thereto, a late charge of ten dollars ($10.00) for each month or part thereof for which the Rent or other sum shall be delinquent together with interest on any and all delinquent payments and amounts in default from the date thereof until paid in full at the rate of 24% per annum calculated monthly. Lessee further agrees to pay to National a returned cheque or non-sufficient funds (NSF) charge of $35.00 to reimburse National for its time and expense incurred with respect to a cheque or a Pre-Authorized Payment Plan that is returned for any reason.

Clearly, this paragraph specifies fees and charges, and interest, that would apply to late or NSF payments of rent. There is a $10 late fee *plus* $35 NSF charge *plus* daily interest at 24% per annum calculated monthly. (The effective annual interest rate on this compounding schedule is actually 26.82% per year.)

> **8. Use:** Lessee shall use the Equipment in a careful and prudent manner and not for any unlawful purpose. Lessee shall, at its own expense, comply with all federal, provincial, municipal, and other laws, ordinances, and regulations in any way relating to the possession, use, or maintenance of the Equipment. The Lessee represents and acknowledges that the Equipment is intended to be used and shall be used by the Lessee for the primary purpose of carrying on business.

Note that in this paragraph the lessee promises not to use the equipment illegally or for an illegal purpose. The equipment is the lessor's property and as such the lessor has an interest in the equipment's use. It would seem like a reasonable enough request of the lessee.

> **9. Title:** The Equipment is and shall at all times be and remain the sole property of National. Lessee shall have no right, title, or interest in the Equipment except as set forth in this Lease.

Again, in case it had escaped the reader earlier, note that the equipment is the property of the lessor, not of the lessee.

> **10. Identification:** Lessee shall at its own expense affix and maintain on the Equipment, labels, or other marks supplied by National to identify the Equipment as National's property.

This paragraph is relatively self-explanatory, although in my experience the lessor does not always provide identification labels.

> **11. Personal Property:** The Equipment shall at all times be and remain personal property and shall not in any manner be affixed or attached to any lands or buildings without National's prior written consent.

Fixtures on property, especially on leased land, can become attached to and title vested in the landlord once those properties are made fixtures. This paragraph attempts to ensure that will not happen to the lessor's property as a result of actions taken by the lessee.

> **12. Location:** Lessee shall maintain stationary equipment at the Location. Lessee shall not operate mobile equipment outside the Province of Location of Equipment without National's prior written consent. Lessee shall advise National of the Location of Equipment immediately on request.

The owner of the property justifiably wants to know where the moveable property it has rented to you is at any given time. Although personal properties are registrable, they can disappear out of jurisdiction quite easily. The issue of the equipment only being used in-province has obvious practical limitations: consider a leased notebook computer. I cannot think of too many people or companies who would advise their lessor of a business trip to another province or into the United States on which they would be taking the computer. Nevertheless, despite the lessor's usual waiving of this requirement, not so advising the lessor would technically be a breach of contract.

> **13. Inspection:** National or its agents shall have the right, and Lessee shall allow them free access, to inspect the Equipment on request.

Despite a renter's right to "quiet enjoyment" it is not completely unreasonable for the lessor to check up on the state of its property.

> **14. Repairs:** Lessee shall at its own expense repair and maintain the Equipment in good condition and working order. Lessee assumes all risk of and shall pay for any loss or damage to the Equipment. Lessee shall not make any alterations to the Equipment without National's prior written consent.

This clause is standard fare for longer-term rentals. The lessor does not have to repair the equipment, but expects it to be in a state of good repair. "Alterations" in this context, are permanent changes, additions, or removals to or from the equipment. Technically it would not be allowed, but if you wanted to add more RAM to your leased computer, nobody will stop you from doing so.

> **15.1 Surrender:** At the end of the Term, Lessee shall at its own expense return the Equipment to National's nearest office in good condition and working order. National may direct Lessee to deliver elsewhere or to dispose of the Equipment. If so, any increased costs shall be at National's expense. Where Equipment comprises telecommunications equipment, installed cable and wiring may be substituted with an equivalent amount or cost of new cable and wiring of then current manufacture and technology. Lessee shall at its expense cause the manufacturer or an authorized agent or dealer of Equipment to supervise the dismantling, packing, crating, and loading of Equipment and shall use a carrier approved by National.

The equipment must be returned in reasonable order to the lessor's nearest office when the lease expires. Should the lessor direct the equipment be returned elsewhere or that it should be disposed of, the lessor will pay the incremental costs of doing so. Installed telecommunications equipment (especially cabling) does not have to be removed, but substitute cable of equivalent quality and quantity must be provided. Only approved technicians must remove and crate equipment. This provision would generally apply to technical installations, and is in the lessee's interests to do anyway so as to limit liability for any damage sustained in transit.

> **15.2 Purchase Option:** If the Lessee is not in default under this Lease, the Lessee shall have an option to purchase the Equipment at the Option Price and on the Option Date set out on the reverse side of this Lease. The Purchase Option may be exercised by the Lessee giving National written notice to exercise the Purchase Option at least sixty (60) days prior to the Option Date and paying the Option Price, plus all applicable taxes, to National at least thirty (30) days prior to the Option Date. . . .

This part of the paragraph allows a Lessee the right to purchase the asset (Equipment) at a set price on a fixed date. Sixty days' notice is required of the Lessee to exercise this option, along with 30 days' prepayment of price plus taxes.

> If the Option Price is the Fair Market Value of the Equipment, it shall be calculated on the basis of the delivered and installed all-inclusive purchase price for the Equipment in good repair in a sale between an arm's length purchaser buying for its own use and a seller dealing in such equipment in the ordinary course of its business, as determined by National acting reasonably. . . .

This part of the paragraph applies to the determination of fair market value (FMV). In this instance, the lessor shall "reasonably" determine the FMV based on an arm's-length sale. The cynic in me infers basically "Take what we give you." I have been assured, however, that there is a lot of case law to dictate what constitutes acting reasonably in this situation.

> If the Option Price box on the reverse side of this form is blank, then the Option Price shall be the Fair Market Value of the Equipment. If the Option Date box on the reverse side of this form is blank, then the Option Date shall be the expiration date of this Lease. . . .

This section of the paragraph sets the option price if the fill-in space at the top of the contract is incomplete so there is no preset option price. The option price will be the FMV as determined by the method described above, and the option date will be the expiration date of the lease. Note that all appropriate notice and payment periods and deadlines would still apply.

> After giving the required notice to exercise the Purchase Option and paying the Option Price, the Lessee shall acquire the Lessor's interest in the Equipment on the Option Date on an "as is, where is" basis without any condition, representation, or warranty by the Lessor of any kind whatsoever.

The exercise of the option to purchase, when complete, provides the lessee with title to the equipment in exactly the same condition in which it exists currently. The lessor is not responsible for or obliged to make any repairs, alterations, or deliveries. (After all, the lessee already has possession and control of the equipment.)

> 15.3 **Continuing Lease:** Provided Lessee is not in default hereunder, this Lease will be automatically renewed on a month-to-month basis upon the expiration of the Term ("Renewal Period") upon and subject to the terms and conditions set forth herein including the periodic Rental unless either National or Lessee has notified the other in writing within thirty (30) days prior to the expiration of the Term to the effect that the Renewal Period will not be entered into. During the Renewal Period, either party may cancel this Lease by providing thirty (30) days' written notice to the other party.

This is important. The lessee is obliged to notify the lessor, at least 30 days in advance of the expiration of the lease, that the equipment will be surrendered *or else* the lease will renew on a month-to-month basis automatically. During this "renewal period," 30 days' notice of intent to terminate the agreement is required. This lease agreement does not provide for a change in rent during renewal, and carries the same consequences as the overholding provisions of a property lease[3]. Check with your lessor to see what rent payments would be required if the equipment is "overheld," and if you want the equipment under a renewal (month-to-month or otherwise), negotiate a deal beforehand.

> 16. **Assignment by National:** National may at any time assign all or any part of its interest in the Equipment or this Lease without the Lessee's consent. In the event of such assignment, the assignee shall be entitled to enforce the rights so assigned to it but shall be under no liability to Lessee to perform any of the obligations of National hereunder and the Lessee's rights hereunder as against National shall be unaffected except as herein specifically provided. . . .

This part of the paragraph likely exists in order for the lessor to pledge the lease/equipment to a financial institution for the capital needed to buy the asset (or other assets to lease). So, the lease can be assigned by the lessor without consent from the lessee. Any such assignee can enforce all the rights of the lessor (mostly for payment and care), but is protected from performance of the lessor's obligations, which remain with the lessor in full.

> In the event of such assignment the assignee shall not be liable to the Lessee for any breach of warranty or any other liability arising from the manufacture or use of the Equipment or its fitness for use for the purposes for which it was intended, the sole remedy of Lessee being against the Supplier. . . .

See paragraph 6. This is an exemption clause designed specifically for the benefit of any assignee. As in paragraph 6, it raises the privity of contract issue, since the lessee is not part of any warranties—the lessor is. But, in paragraph 22, those warranties are specifically assigned by the lessor to the lessee.

> Lessee covenants and agrees not to assert against the assignee any claim by way of abatement, defense, set-off, compensation, counterclaim, or the like which Lessee may have against National, and Lessee shall pay to such assignee all Rent and other amounts due hereunder unconditionally and shall not assert any defense against such assignee in any action for Rents or other amounts due and payable hereunder except the defense of payment, notwithstanding such assignment to assignee any warranties pertaining to the Equipment shall be available to the Lessee and National agrees to the exercise of such warranties directly by Lessee. The Lessee waives receipt of written notice of the assignment. . . .

Refer to the last part of paragraph 2; this language repeats it for the benefit of the assignee. Essentially, the lessee agrees to pay rent to the assignee without question or defense, period. In this part of paragraph 16, the lessor assures that product warranties are available to the lessee, and that the lessor will authorize and permit the lessee to exercise those warranties directly with the vendor and/or manufacturer.

Again, to repeat in case it was missed, and to make explicit, the lessee waives right to notice of any assignment by the lessor.

> 17. **Assignments and Subleasing:** Lessee shall not subject or part with possession of the Equipment or permit its use by any person other than Lessee or its employees who are qualified and competent to operate the Equipment. Lessee shall not assign this Lease without National's prior written consent. Lessee agrees to pay an assignment fee to National of $100.00 or National's actual cost, whichever is greater.

First, the equipment (in this case what would seem to be automotive equipment or machinery of some sort) may only be operated by qualified employees of the lessee. The latter part of the paragraph provides for the lessee assigning the lease by express consent of the lessor. If the lease is assigned by the lessee, at the lessor's approval, a fee of at least $100 is required to be paid to the lessor.

> 18. **Insurance:** Lessee shall obtain and maintain for the entire Term, at its own expense property damage and legal liability insurance against loss or damage to the Equipment, including without limitation, loss by fire (including extended coverage), theft, collision, injury, or death and damage to property of others and such other risks as National may specify and such other risks of loss as are customarily covered by insurance on the types of Equipment leased hereunder and by prudent operators of business similar to that in which Lessee is engaged, in such amounts, in such form, and with such insurers as shall be satisfactory to National. All such insurance shall name National and Lessee as insureds and shall be carried in one or more insurance companies approved by National. . . .

The equipment must be fully insured by the lessee to customary levels for such equipment by insurers that are approved by the lessor. Both the lessee and the lessor are to be named insureds.

All policies of insurance shall contain an endorsement that the policy may not be cancelled without thirty (30) days' notice being given to National. Within twenty-one (21) days from Lessee's signing this Lease or any Schedule, Lessee will provide National with certificates or other evidence of such insurance naming National as loss payee and providing that National shall be given thirty (30) days' prior written notice of any material alteration or cancellation of insurance. . . .

The lessor must be given 30 days' notice of insurance amendment or cancellation, which is fair given that the property being insured belongs to the lessor. Additionally, within 21 days of the signing of the lease, the equipment must be insured, with the lessor being named as the "loss payee" (party to whom payout of a loss claim is made).

> If Lessee does not provide evidence of property insurance acceptable to National, National may, but will not be required to, buy such insurance and add the cost including any customary charges or fees associated with the placement, maintenance, or service of such insurance ("Insurance Service Amount") to the Rent due from Lessee. Lessee agrees to pay the Insurance Service Amount in equal installments allocated to each remaining Rent (with interest on such Allocations up to the maximum rate permitted by applicable law).

If the lessee does not purchase insurance on the equipment within the 21 days specified, the lessor may insure the equipment and add the insurance cost plus applicable fees, charges, and interest to the lessor in equal installments on remaining rent payments. A noteworthy item to look at and weigh is the final parenthetic statement, especially the words, "maximum rate permitted by applicable law." I am not sure what the applicable law is in this instance nor what it says about interest rates, but I would bet it's not close to prime.

> Nothing in the Lease creates any insurance relationship between National and any other person or party. National is not required to effect any insurance coverage and it may terminate or allow to lapse any coverage without having liability to Lessee.

This part of the paragraph explicitly states that the lessor is *not* the insurer (which would create all kinds of obligations on the lessor) nor is the lessor obliged to insure the equipment. If the equipment is not insured by the lessee or if the lessor allows insurance it has obtained to lapse and the lessee does not reinsure the equipment, the lessee will be in breach of contract and subject to paragraph 23.

> **19. Net Lease:** Lessee shall pay all costs, fees, and taxes (other than taxes on income levied on National under the Income Tax Act of Canada or any Provincial Income Tax Act) relating to the Equipment. The Rent shall be absolutely net to National free of all set-offs or expenses of any kind.

The lessee is obliged to pay all taxes and expenses. Furthermore, the rent amount is net, and is never subject to reduction for any reason at any time, period.

> **20. Additional Rent:** If Lessee fails to repair the Equipment or to maintain insurance or to pay any costs, fees, or taxes relating to the Equipment, National may do so and any amount spent shall become Rent immediately due and payable. National will be entitled to immediate reimbursement from Lessee without prejudice to any of National's rights or remedies. All interest payable by the Lessee under this Lease and all costs incurred by National in collecting Rent, including reasonable charges for NSF cheques, shall become Rent immediately due and payable.

The way this paragraph reads is pretty much what it means. If the lessor expends any money on the equipment to maintain, insure, or otherwise administer it, that expense becomes due and payable immediately as "additional rent." This paragraph seems somewhat inconsistent with paragraph 18, which makes expenses incurred to insure equipment payable over the remaining months. But it is consistent with an immediate compensation as additional rent for *monthly* payments of insurance. When in doubt (1) anticipate the least favourable (to you, that is) interpretation or option to be the one that will apply, and (2) ask what the meaning is from someone with authority to say—never assume.

21. **Headings:** The insertion of headings in this Lease is for convenience of reference only and shall not affect the interpretation of this Lease.

22. **Assignment of Warranties:** National shall, on Lessee's request, assign to Lessee any and all warranties, guarantees, service contracts, and representations (the "Warranties") which the manufacturer of the Equipment or Supplier makes or gives. On Lessee's request and at Lessee's cost, National shall do all necessary things to assist Lessee in enforcing the manufacturer's or Supplier's performance of the Warranties. Lessee shall reassign the Warranties to National at the end of the Term.

This paragraph deals with the issue of privity of contract between the vendor/manufacturer and the buyer (lessor). The lessee must pay any costs associated with enforcing rights to warranties on the leased equipment, but the lessor will provide all assistance it is able and is necessary.

23. **Default:** National has purchased the Equipment at the specific request of Lessee for the purpose of this Lease. The Rental Amount and loss to National in the event of default are dependent upon its cost of the Equipment, the Term and the minimum return expected by National from the sale of the Equipment at the end of the Term. If (1) Lessee fails to pay any Rental Amount or pay any other sum within ten (10) days of being due and payable; or (2) Lessee fails to comply with any other obligation, term, or condition of this Lease; or (3) Lessee defaults under any other lease or other contract between National and Lessee or under any instrument evidencing any long term indebtedness; or (4) National discovers that a representation or warranty made by Lessee in connection with obtaining this Lease is incorrect; or (5) any of the Equipment is subjected to any lien, charge, encumbrance, levy, seizure, attachment, or other judicial process; or (6) Lessee sells, mortgages, pledges, or attempts to sell, mortgage, or pledge any of the Equipment; or (7) Lessee makes any assignment for the benefit of its creditors, becomes insolvent, commits any act of bankruptcy, ceases or threatens to cease to do business as a going concern, or seeks any arrangement or composition with its creditors; or (8) any proceeding in bankruptcy, receivership, liquidation, or insolvency is commenced against Lessee or its property; then, all Rental and any other payment to the end of the Term shall become due and payable on demand. . . .

This part of the paragraph is a—probably incomplete—recital of the circumstances that would give rise to a default of the contract by the lessee. Each circumstance should be easy enough to understand.

Lessee at its own expense on National's demand shall immediately deliver the Equipment to National's nearest office. National may, without notice and without resort to legal process, take immediate possession of the Equipment. National may enter the premises where the Equipment is located without incurring any liability to Lessee. Lessee's rights hereunder shall then cease and terminate absolutely. Upon termination, Lessee shall pay the total of all amounts due as Rental or otherwise to the end of the Term. Lessee shall pay National's costs of collection or possessions of Equipment or for enforcement of all of National's rights including without limitation legal costs on a solicitor-client basis. National's remedies shall be cumulative and not alternative.

The latter half of this paragraph explains what must be done and happen should the contract be placed into default by the lessee. Essentially, the lessee must—agreeably or by force—surrender the equipment, and the lease terminates. Because it is terminated by default, all remaining rent due for the full life of the lease becomes immediately due. Expenses for collection or repossession are also agreed to be borne by the lessee. Furthermore, the lessor retains the right to all of these remedies cumulatively to recover the equipment and the rent (i.e., the lessor can get the equipment, then the rent due, then the rent remaining, then the damages and costs, then . . .). In short, the lessor, like a lender, is not in an either/or equipment or rent situation and can seek to obtain both and more (as damages).

24. **Notices:** Any notices and demands required to be given herein shall be given to the parties in writing and by registered mail or delivery at the address herein set forth or by facsimile, to the facsimile numbers herein set forth, or to such other address or facsimile number as the parties may hereinafter substitute by written notice given in the manner

prescribed in this section. National and Lessee hereby agree that all documents, including this Lease, sent by facsimile or other means of electronic transmission to the other party shall be considered to be the original documents.

Note that unlike most of the other sample contracts herein, in this agreement a facsimile transmission of notice is valid and the fax is considered an original document.

25. **Pre-Authorized Payment Plan:** If Lessee has completed the pre-authorized payment section on the reverse side, Lessee warrants that the signatures appearing on the reverse hereof are those of the persons authorized to sign on the account with the Bank. The Lessee authorizes and requests the Bank to pay and debit the bank account specified on the reverse side ("specified Account") whether it continues to be maintained at the location set forth on the reverse hereof or is maintained at another branch of the Bank all payments purporting to be drawn on the Bank on behalf of Lessee payable to the Lessor, or its assignee and are presented to the Bank for payment and to pay and debit the Specified Account all amounts specified on any magnetic or computer produced paper tape that is or purports to be a direction on behalf of the Lessee to credit an amount to the payee and to debit such amount to the Specified Account. Lessee acknowledges that provision and delivery of this authorization to National constitutes delivery by the Lessee to the Bank.

This clause creates an authority for the lessor to go to your specified bank and withdraw the rent amount periodically regardless of where your account resides.

26. **Time:** Time is of the essence to this Lease.
27. **Applicable Law:** This Lease shall be construed according to the laws of the Province of Location of the Equipment.
28. **Lessee's Waiver:** To the extent permitted by law or statute and to the extent the same extends to and relates to this Lease as amended or renewed or any collateral security thereto or promissory note, Lessee waives the benefit of all provisions of any applicable conditional sales, regulatory credit, and other statutes and regulations made in any manner, that affect restrict or limit the rights of National including without limiting the generality of the foregoing, all of its rights, benefits, and protection given or afforded to it by Sections 19 to 24 of the Sales of Goods on Condition Act of British Columbia as amended, Section 49 of the Law of Property Act of Alberta as amended and the provisions of the Limitation of Civil Rights Act of Saskatchewan as amended. Lessee also waives any right to demand security for costs in the event of litigation.

This waiver is one of those boilerplate take-it-or-leave-it clauses that one might not permit under other circumstances. Essentially, the lessee agrees to waive statutory protection as afforded by the legislative Acts specified in the paragraph. The lessee also forgoes the right to demand security for costs in the event of litigation. Whether a judge would overrule this waiver as being the prerogative of the court, is a matter one could test before a judge. Having said that, given that the lessee waived that right—in writing, perhaps even having had independent legal advice—and would be deemed to have read and understood the waiver, the court might very likely pass the buck right back to the lessee. This is especially likely since security for costs is not doled out by the court, except after consideration when security for costs has been *asked* for.

29. **Credit Investigation:** National may conduct a personal investigation or credit check upon Lessee subject to applicable legislation.

As stated, this paragraph allows the lessor to make a personal credit check on the lessee. The key concern may be whether a personal credit check of the person leasing on behalf of or the owners of a company that is the lessee is allowed or warranted.

30. **Choice of Language:** The parties agree that this document be written in the English language. Les parties aux présentes conviennent à ce document soit rédigé en anglais.

31. **Execution:** This Lease shall not become binding upon National until accepted by National as evidenced by the signature of a duly authorized officer of National in the space provided on the reverse side.

32. **Enurement:** This Lease shall be binding upon the parties and their respective heirs, executors, administrators, successors, and permitted assigns.

33. **National Financing:** This Lease and the Equipment will be subject to any rights and interest in and to the Equipment granted by National under any contract or contracts to a financing institution.

This paragraph allows the lessor to finance the chattels with a bank or other financing institution. Look back to paragraph 16 regarding assignment by the lessor for concurring covenants.

34. **Financing Statement:** National may file a financing statement or similar registration with respect to this Lease so as to give notice to interested parties. The Lessee agrees to waive all rights to notice as may be applicable under any such registration of the Lease. Any such filings or registrations are not necessarily to be deemed evidence of any intent to create a security interest either under the Personal Property Security Act of Manitoba or under any similar legislation of any other province.

This clause permits the lessor to file the appropriate documentation to register the debt. It would be similar to the registration filed by the lender on any other secured debt.

35. **Severability:** In the event that any provision of this Lease shall be invalid, illegal, or unenforceable, it shall not affect the validity, legality, or enforceability of any other provision of the Lease.

36. **Interpretation:** Wherever the context of this Lease so requires, the singular shall include the plural and vice versa, and that in the case of more than one Lessee is named as Lessee, the liability of each Lessee shall be joint and several. Where an individual is a Lessee, such individual acknowledges that the Equipment is not a "consumer good" within the meaning of the Personal Property Security Act of Manitoba, or similar legislation of any other province.

I suspect that the purpose of this clause is to ensure that the leased equipment never becomes a consumer good "personal property" and thus the provisions relating to consumer goods in the *Personal Property Security Act* and the *Consumer Protection Act* do not apply to the lease.

37. **Software:** Any other provision of this Lease notwithstanding, if software is described or listed so as to constitute or appear or constitute part of the Equipment or is supplied for use therewith, Lessee acknowledges and agrees that (a) National may not have, and does not purport to have, title to or ownership of such software or the right to lease, license, sub-license, or grant possession of, or grant the right to use, same; (b) the Equipment which is the subject of this Lease consists of HARDWARE ONLY; (c) rent is payable in respect of HARDWARE ONLY; and (d) National does not, by virtue of this Lease or otherwise, purport to lease, sub-lease, license, sub-license or authorize Lessee to possess or use any software.

As mentioned elsewhere in this book, software is not sold; its use is licensed. The lessor (and anyone else for that matter) is prohibited from leasing or sub-licensing software. This paragraph ensures that at least for legal purposes (as between the lessor and the software vendor) the lessor is contractually only leasing hardware. The software is purely the lessee's license issue directly with the software licensor.

38. **Administration Fee:** At National's request, Lessee agrees to pay a contract administration fee to National of $100.00 or National's actual costs, whichever is greater, such fee to cover National's initial processing and registration costs.

39. **Entire Agreement:** The Lease, clauses 1–39 inclusive, together with Delivery and Acceptance Certificate, schedules, amendments, or additions, which are accepted in writing by National, constitute the entire agreement between National and the Lessee. The Lessee acknowledges that the supplier or its sales representatives are not agents of National and are not, therefore, authorized to waive, alter, amend, or change terms and conditions of the Lease.

Indemnity

For good and valuable consideration, the receipt and sufficiency of which is acknowledged, the undersigned Indemnifier(s), jointly and severally indemnify National and its assigns for the full and prompt performance by the lessee of its obligations under the Lease as set forth herein, including any and all monies payable under the Lease and the performance and observance of all lessee's obligations thereunder and hereby waives notice of default by lessee and the benefits of division and discussion and agrees this indemnity shall not be released or impaired by the bankruptcy or insolvency of lessee, or any extension of time, indulgences, or modifications which National may extend or make with lessee. The undersigned agrees that its liability under this Indemnity is joint and several with the lessee and that National and/or its assigns may enforce this Indemnity without exhausting its rights or remedies against the lessee or any other person.

The undersigned agrees to pay reasonable legal fees and all other costs and expenses which may be incurred by National and/or its assigns in the enforcement of this Indemnity. To the extent not prohibited by law applicable to or governing this contract, the Indemnifier(s) HEREBY WAIVE the benefit of all provisions of any applicable personal property security, conditional sales, regulatory credit and other statutes, and regulations made thereunder in any and all provinces of Canada which would in any manner affect, restrict, or limit the rights of National hereunder including, without limiting the generality of the foregoing, all of its rights, benefits, and protection given or afforded to it by Section 49 of the Law of Property Act of Alberta as amended, and the provisions of the Limitation of Civil Rights Act of Saskatchewan as amended. Indemnifier(s) also waive and assign to National the right of any statutory exemption from execution or otherwise and further waive any right to demand security for costs in the event of litigation and Indemnifier(s) hereby acknowledge notice of the waiver given by the lessee.

In this context the indemnifier is a guarantor who is indemnifying the lessor (or guaranteeing for the lessee) for performance by the lessee especially as regards rent payment. The indemnifier's responsibility for the lessee's performance under the lease is one with the lessee's responsibility. Note that the indemnifier makes an absolute indemnity to the lessor and waives various contractual and statutory rights which might apply in the circumstances, including where there might be exemptions to laws that permit the lessor to execute its rights to make a demand on the lessee or the indemnifier.

<signature of indemnifier and witness>

Delivery and Acceptance Certificate

The equipment referred to in the Lease has been inspected and was received in satisfactory workable condition and is fit for the purpose for which it was intended.

We also confirm and acknowledge that there are no maintenance, service, or other agreements which attach to this Lease.

We/I have read our/my Lease with National and are aware of and understand the terms thereof and in particular, but not limited to, "Non-Cancellable" and "No Warranties."

We/I acknowledge that National is not a manufacturer or distributor of the equipment, nor an agent of the Supplier, and that the essential element of the Lease is leasing only.

The lessor has provided a certificate that requires signature indicating that the lessee has received and accepted the equipment. Just to be safe, it has also included—for endorsement by the signature—some further acknowledgements by the lessee that repeat, in different language, important parts of the terms and conditions of the lease agreement. Whether everything beyond the first paragraph is more effective or binding than the terms of the lease itself is questionable. That first paragraph, however, is important, because by endorsing it the lessee confirms that it has inspected the equipment and that the equipment is in satisfactory condition for the purpose for which it was intended by the lessee.

PROPERTY LEASING

Leasehold tenancy has been around for a long time. Naturally, it has become fairly well defined. The fundamental aspect of this contract is that it is created when a landholder (landlord) grants a term to a tenant. A "term" in this context has a definite meaning, generally being an interest in a piece of land for a specific period of time. The two key elements for creating a leasehold estate interest in the property, giving the tenant greater rights than would otherwise accrue as a simple lessee ("licensee of the [land] property"), including many of the rights normally reserved for the landlord, are *exclusive* tenancy and *finite term* tenancy.[4]

- *The tenant must be granted exclusive possession and use of the property.* It is the exclusivity of possession and use that differentiates a leasehold tenant with an estate from another person with other lesser rights to use the land. One with a leasehold estate may prevent others, including the landlord, from using the land, and may not be put off the land until the end of the term (or if a condition of tenancy is breached). In essence, exclusivity affords the tenant almost all the rights that belong to the landowner.

Interestingly enough, the matter of exclusive use can create leasehold problems. If anyone else, including the landlord, has a right to use the land or any part of it, there is an argument against exclusivity and therefore against you having a leasehold estate. In this instance, the rights that accrue to a tenant would technically not be yours.

The moral of the tale is: Do not share your leasehold rights with anyone; insist on exclusivity or the value of your tenancy is questionable.

- *The term must be finite and definite.* A term of tenancy must have a definite start date and a terminal date that, if not definite, can be determined accurately. Because a leasehold exists for a finite period, the lease term must be finite in some way. That is not to say the lease must end on a specific date on the calendar or "in 12 months," or so forth. It could be tied to a fixed event under certain conditions (e.g., "will end in 100 years or when Canada wins the World Cup in soccer, whichever comes first").

An interesting point, which you may never come across, is that rights in leasehold estates may *never* be granted to extend beyond the rights of the titleholder. This could crop up in a lifetime estate, in which a person enjoys the title to a property during her lifetime. If a 90-year-old woman were to extend a 25-year lease to you, but her interest in the land was a lifetime estate, technically she couldn't make the deal, and chances are you could be out on your rear when the lady dies. As I said, this is an interesting point which merely suggests the importance of ensuring that the landlord leasing the land to you has and attests to her right to provide a lease term to you.

The two principal types of tenancies, not including tenancies that are unplanned or unanticipated, are *term certain* and *periodic* tenancies. The term certain tenancy has a fixed and finite term that ends on a specific day (the term is "certain"). At the end of the term, without any notice being given, the rights to the land revert to the landlord who, naturally, expects the tenant to have vacated the premises. The periodic tenancy, on the other hand, has a finite term (often a year or a month) that renews itself on the same terms and conditions unless notice not to renew is given by either the landlord or the tenant. A tenant *at will* is on the land at the landlord's pleasure and may be removed at will; there is no leasehold, and no obligation on either the landlord's or the tenant's part. Sometimes *overholding* tenants—those who stay on the premises beyond an expired term—are tenants at will.

There are arguably eight key covenants in a property lease. We shall examine them briefly in turn.

1. *Rent payment*

Rent for the term is the "cost" of the leasehold estate for a given period in time, which is why many commercial leases specify a total rent for the term that is then divided into equal periodic payments. Because of this underlying principle, rent cannot be increased during the term (unless otherwise specified in the agreement). Consider the leasehold like a car: monthly rental payments are like loan installments of a total purchase value, and once you've bought the car, the price doesn't go up so the loan payments remain the same. Generally, unless otherwise specified in the lease agreement, the tenant has limited rights to suspend or withhold rental payments—even if the property is damaged.[5]

2. *Sublet and assignment*

The tenant with a leasehold has the right to sublet all or part of the land just as the landlord leased the land to the tenant. A sublet is for a part of the tenant's term only, and the terms and conditions of the sublet agreement need not be the same as the leasehold itself. An assignment, on the other hand, is a complete transfer of the rights to the lease to another party, and the assignee is bound to the conditions of the original leasehold contract. In both cases, the tenant remains responsible to the landlord to fulfill the leasehold agreement whether that means enforcing a sublet agreement or "guaranteeing" on behalf of the assignee. Most often the landlord's consent will be required for the tenant to either sublet or assign.[6]

3. *Use of property*

The landlord and the tenant would agree, or discuss anyway, the permissible and intended use of the land prior to the lease being signed. The landlord can limit or prohibit certain uses of its property. Once the tenant has been granted the lease, the landlord can—under most circumstances—no longer interfere in the tenant's use. Even if there is no specific covenant in the lease on this issue, however, there is an implied term that the tenant will not use the property for an unreasonable purpose. The "prohibition of use" knife cuts both ways, though, with the tenant quite able to demand the landlord not lease to any others that may infringe upon the tenant's business or enjoyment of the lease. Exclusivity in a mall is one example of a tenant's requirement for approval of new tenants.

4. *Fitness for occupancy*

Generally and traditionally a lessee takes the leasehold on the property "as is," and is responsible for ensuring that it has fully examined the property for fitness for the intended purpose. There appears to be law developing, however, that places some burden on the landlord as regards fitness and suitability for use *if* the purpose to which the property will be put is specifically part of the agreement.

5. *Repairs*

Considering that property leases runs the gamut from free-range pasture land to complete buildings on a property to office space in a commercial building, the common rule regarding repairs is that the landlord is not responsible for any. In practice, most lease agreements specify how much and what repairs will be the landlord's responsibility, and which will be the tenant's. In commercial office space situations, the landlord is generally responsible for the repair and upkeep of structure and common areas, whereas the tenant is responsible for repairs to the leased space. The tenant is most often responsible for ensuring that the leased property is kept in proper order reflecting only normal wear and tear.

6. *Quiet enjoyment*

While noisy circumstances may interfere with a tenant's "quiet enjoyment," this covenant more generally refers to the tenant's right not to be interfered with by the landlord or anyone gaining a title or other interest in the land. Specifically, quiet enjoyment is the tenant's assurance that the landlord has the capacity and requisite title to lease the property. (Remember our earlier notice that a titleholder cannot lease land with greater rights than the titleholder enjoys itself.) It is also an assurance that anyone purchasing or otherwise gaining the title to the property will not disturb the tenant's rights under the lease.

7. *Insurance*

Although there are no hard-and-fast rules about who must insure leased property, in practice the landlord will require the tenant to maintain insurance on that part of the premises for which the tenant is specifically responsible. In all likelihood, the tenant would want to do so anyway, as it may very well remain responsible for rent in the event that all or part of the leased premises or common areas of a leased property are damaged. Most lease contracts will specify both what kind and the amount of insurance is required.

8. *Services and taxes.*
The circumstances of service provision and payment differ according to the lease. Where an entire building is being leased, the tenant will usually be responsible for the services and taxes itself. In the case of an office building situation, the landlord may bring in and pay for the services charging the tenant "additional rent" for its portion. The same would apply to property taxes.

The remedies available to either the landlord or the tenant for the other's breach of a covenant are several and probably more than we need to address ourselves to here. Damages and eviction/reentry are common remedies, among those which we will see in the following commercial property lease example.[7]

Property Lease

THIS LEASE made as of the 16th day of May, A.D. 1999.
BETWEEN
Commercial Property Corporation
(hereinafter called the "Landlord")
OF THE FIRST PART.
– and –
New Tenant Company Inc.
(hereinafter called the "tenant")
OF THE SECOND PART.

ARTICLE I — DEFINITIONS
Although some of the following definitions are a little difficult to read, they are readily understandable, I think, so I have not made any specific comment about them. Where necessary, within the later text of the document, the application and effect of these definitions is explained.

In this Lease:

1.01 **Architect** means the architect qualified to practise and practising in the Province of Manitoba from time to time deemed by the Landlord.

1.02 **Common areas and facilities** means those parts of the Office Complex not part of the premises set aside by the Landlord for leasing to tenants of the Office Complex, including but not limited to exterior weather walls, roofs, common entrances to and exits from the Office Complex, parking areas, storage rooms, delivery passages, malls, courts, ramps, landscaped and planted areas, retaining walls, stairways, washrooms, mechanical and electrical rooms, and all general signs, improvements, fixtures, facilities, equipment, and installations which the Landlord provides or designates from time to time for the general use by or for the benefit of the Tenant, its officers, employees, agents, customers, and other invitees in common with other tenants of the Landlord and others designated by the Landlord in the manner and for the purposes permitted by this Lease.

1.03 **HVAC costs** with reference to a specified part of the Office Complex means the cost of heating, ventilating, and air-conditioning the specified part, and includes but is not limited to the cost of fuel, electricity, operation of air distribution and cooling equipment, labour, materials, repairs, maintenance, service, and other such costs, and depreciation of fixtures and equipment used therefor which by their nature require periodic replacement or substantial replacement, reasonably attributable to the heating, ventilating, or air-conditioning of the specified part, and the reasonable cost incurred by the Landlord in making an allocation of the cost with reference to the specified part.

1.04 **Land** means the land described in Schedule "A" hereof.

1.05 **Landlord** means the Party of the First Part.

1.06 Lease Year means a period of twelve (12) consecutive calendar months during the term ending on the last day of a financial year of the Landlord, which on the date of this Lease is the last day of December, excepting that:

(a) the first Lease Year during the term begins on the first day of the term and ends on the last day of the financial year of the Landlord in which the first day of the term occurs, and may be a period less than twelve consecutive calendar months;

(b) the last Lease Year during the term begins on the first day of the financial year of the Landlord during which the last day of the term occurs and ends on the last day of the term, and may be a period less than twelve (12) consecutive calendar months; and

(c) if the landlord changes its financial year and gives notice to the Tenant of the first and last days of the new financial year, the period between the last day of the old financial year and the last day of the new financial year will be a Lease Year and will be a period less than twelve (12) consecutive calendar months, and the next Lease Year will continue consecutively.

1.07 Mortgage means a mortgage or charge (including a deed of trust and mortgage securing bonds and all indentures supplemental thereto) of the reversion immediately expectant on the term, and includes all renewals, modifications, consolidations, replacements, and extensions thereof.

1.08 Mortgagee means the mortgagee or trustee for bond holders, as the case may be, named in a mortgage.

1.09 Operating costs means the sum (without duplication) of all costs of the Landlord of operating and maintaining in good repair the Office Complex including but not limited to the total costs of:

(a) insuring the Office Complex pursuant to this Lease, and such insurance as the Landlord affects against public liability, property damage, loss of rental income, and other casualties and risks; HVAC costs, cleaning, including snow removal, garbage and waste collection and disposal, lighting, electricity (including that used for signs), public utilities, policing, supervising, traffic control, and security; the cost to the Landlord of building supplies and the rental of equipment used by the Landlord in maintenance and operating services; and depreciation of fixtures and equipment which by their nature require periodic replacement, but excluding buildings and structures and permanent parts thereof;

(b) repairs and replacements to and maintenance of the Office Complex including but not limited to the cost of maintenance and repair of paving, curbs, walkways, drainage, and lighting facilities and the cost of maintenance and repair of the roof of the Office Complex, the surface of the exterior walls of the Office Complex and the cost of gardening and landscaping maintenance, not normally charged to capital account as determined by the Landlord's auditors and/or accountants;

(c) maintaining and operating the area occupied by a central cooling system or any other service or facility used to heat or cool the premises or other parts of the Office Complex;

(d) the amount of all taxes, rates, duties, levies, and assessments of any kind including real property taxes, school taxes, municipal, provincial, or parliamentary taxes (other than income or corporate taxes), special frontage assessments, special local benefit assessments and local improvement taxes levied, rated, or charged in respect of the Office Complex and common areas and facilities and improvements thereto and the Landlord's business taxes, if any; together with

(e) an administrative overhead charge equal to a sum not greater than five (5) percent of the minimum rent payable by the Tenant.

1.10 Premises means the premises leased to the Tenant by this lease and described in Section 3.01.

1.11 Proportionate share means the ratio that the area of the premises bears to the aggregate rentable area of the Office Complex.

1.12 Rentable area where applied to the leased premises means the area (expressed in square feet) of the floor of the leased premises (whether such area be at, below, and/or above ground level) measured from the exterior face of the exterior walls and the centre line of partition walls. Where a storefront or entrance is recessed from the exterior building wall line the area of such recess shall for all purposes be part of the leased premises.

1.13 **Office Complex** means collectively the land and the building, structures, facilities, and other improvements erected or to be erected on the land and all expansions, alterations, additions, or relocations from time to time which may be made pursuant to Article X.

1.14 **Tenant** means the Party of the Second Part.

1.15 **Term** means the term of this Lease as stipulated in Section 3.03.

1.16 **The Landlord and Tenant Act** means the Landlord and Tenant Act, L.R.M. 1987, cL70, as from time to time amended or replaced.

1.17 **Unavoidable delay** means a delay in performance of an act or compliance with a covenant caused by fire, strike, lockout, inability to procure material, restrictive laws or governmental regulations, or other cause of any kind beyond the reasonable control of the party obliged to perform or comply, excepting a delay caused by lack of funds or other financial reasons.

ARTICLE II — STRUCTURE OF DOCUMENT AND INTERPRETATION

2.01 Schedules

The Schedules to this document are a part of this Lease and consist of:

(a) Schedule "A"—description of Land;

(b) Schedule "B"—plan of premises.

These Schedules are not included in the book, but would ordinarily appear at the end of the lease agreement, obviously.

2.02 Number Gender

The necessary grammatical changes required to make the provisions of this Lease apply in the plural sense where the Tenant comprises more than one entity and to corporations, associations, partnerships, or individuals, males, or females, in all cases will be assumed as though in each case fully expressed.

2.03 Headings and Captions

The Table of Contents, Article Numbers, Article Headings, Section Numbers, and Section Headings are inserted for convenience of reference only and are not to be considered when interpreting this Lease.

2.04 Obligations as Covenants

Each obligation of the Landlord or the Tenant expressed in the Lease, even though not expressed as a covenant, is considered to be a covenant for all purposes.

Basically what this paragraph attempts to do is make *everything* in the document, whether written as such or not, a promise of great importance.

2.05 Entire Agreement

This Lease contains all the representations, warranties, covenants, agreements, conditions, and understandings between the Landlord and the Tenant concerning the premises or the subject matter of this Lease.

2.06 Governing Law

This Lease will be interpreted under and is governed by the laws of the Province of Manitoba.

ARTICLE III — LEASE, PREMISES, TERM, RENTAL AND ADDITIONAL RENT

3.01 Lease and the Premises

The Landlord leases to the Tenant for the Term, the premises situate in and forming part of the Office Complex, containing 6,498 square feet as shown outlined in red on the plan attached hereto marked Schedule "B," but it is understood and agreed that, for purposes of calculation of rent set forth in Section 3.03, the square footage has been grossed up to 6,824 square feet being premises plus untenable portion of common areas attributable to premises.

Note that some part of the common space that is "untenable" because it is useless except as being adjacent to the premises, is added to the total square footage of the premises.

3.02 Tenant Covenant to Pay Rent

The Tenant covenants that it will pay the minimum rent and additional rent at the office of the Landlord at <address> or at such other place as the Landlord may designate in writing, on the due dates without any deduction or abatement whatsoever.

3.03 Term and Rent

The Term of this Lease is five (5) years, commencing on the 1st day of June, A.D. 1999, and fully to be ended and completed on the 31st day of May, A.D. 2004, subject to the right of renewal, if any, as herein provided. The annual minimum rent is seventy-six thousand seven hundred seventy dollars and zero cents ($76,770.00) payable monthly in advance at the rate of six thousand three hundred ninety-seven dollars and fifty cents ($6,397.50) on the first day of each and every calendar month during the said term, the first of such payments to be due on or before the 1st day of June, A.D. 1999.

PROVIDED THAT if, due to the failure of the Landlord to complete construction which the Landlord is hereby obliged to furnish, the premises or any part thereof are not ready for occupancy on the date of commencement of the term, no part of the rent, or only a proportionate part thereof if the Tenant shall occupy a part of the premises, shall be payable for the period before the date when the entire premises are ready for occupancy, and the full rent shall accrue only after such last mentioned date, and the Tenant hereby agrees to accept any such abatement of rent in full settlement of all claims which the Tenant might otherwise have because the premises were not ready for occupancy on the date of commencement of the term.

Note that in this covenant(!), if leasehold improvements are undertaken and not completed in time, rent abatement during that/those months (in whole or in part depending on whether part of the premises is being occupied) is the sole remedy the tenant has against the landlord for not having its premises ready and in proper order.

PROVIDED however, that when the Landlord has completed construction of the premises, the Tenant shall not be entitled to any abatement of rent for any delay in occupancy due to the Tenant's failure to complete the installations and other work required for its purposes or due to any other reason. A certificate of the Landlord's architect that the construction of the premises is complete shall be conclusive. If the premises are complete before the commencement date of the term and the Tenant occupies all or a part thereof before such date, the Tenant shall pay the Landlord a fee for such use and occupancy, calculated on the basis of 1/365th of the annual rent for each day and in proportion to the part of the premises the Tenant so occupied.

This paragraph's important part is that if the tenant moves in early, it pays rent by the day for each day it occupies the premises prior to the lease commencing.

3.04 Additional Rent and Charges

(1) In each lease year the Tenant will pay to the Landlord as additional rent:

    (a) the Tenant's proportionate share of the operating costs;

    (b) municipal realty taxes including local improvement levies attributable to the premises;

    (c) the HVAC costs attributable to the premises; and

    (d) all other sums of money required under this Lease to be paid to the Landlord by the Tenant whether or not designated "additional rent."

"Rent" is the cost of the leasehold interest in the property itself for a finite period of time. "Additional rent" consists of all those other costs and expenses that are attributable to the premises and for which the tenant is responsible over and above basic rent. The previous list contains some of the specific costs and expenses that must be reimbursed to the landlord in the form of additional rent.

(2) In each lease year the Tenant will pay as additional rent and discharge when they become due and payable, all taxes, rates, duties and assessments, and other charges that may be levied, rated, charged, or assessed against improvements, equipment, and facilities of the Tenant in the Office Complex, and every tax and license due in respect to every business conducted on or from the premises or in respect of their use or occupation by the Tenant (and any and every assignee, sub-tenant, concessionaire, licensee, and other persons conducting business on or from the premises), other than such taxes as corporate, income profits, or excess profits taxes assessed upon the income of the Landlord (or assignee, sub-tenant, concessionaire, licensee, or other persons conducting business on or from the premises), whether the taxes, rates, duties, assessments, and license fees are charged by municipal, parliamentary, school, or other body. The Tenant will indemnify and keep indemnified the Landlord against payment for all loss, cost, charges, and expenses arising from all the taxes, rates, duties, assessments, and license fees referred to and all taxes which may in future be levied in lieu of those taxes, and any loss, costs, charges, and expenses suffered by the Landlord may be recovered by the Landlord in the same manner as rent hereby reserved and in arrears. Upon request of the Landlord the Tenant will deliver promptly to the Landlord for inspection receipts for payment of all taxes, rates, duties, assessments, and other charges in respect of all improvements, equipment, facilities, and business of the Tenant in the Office Complex which were due and payable up to one (1) month prior to the request, and will deliver to the Landlord if requested by the Landlord evidence that is satisfactory to the Landlord before the 31st day of January in each year of payments for the preceding calendar year.

This lengthy paragraph specifies the scheme by which the tenant will make payment for taxes and licenses on business operations, etc. that are payable by the tenant itself. It also provides a process and a means for the landlord to (a) be indemnified from exposure to those liabilities, and (b) inspect the tenant business for proper tax compliance.

(3) If any of the amounts referred to in Sub-sections (1) and (2) are not paid at the time provided in this Lease, it will be collectible as rent with the next installment of rent falling due, but nothing in this Lease suspends or delays the payment of an amount of money when it becomes due and payable, or limits any other remedy of the Landlord.

3.05 Payment of Additional Rent and Charges

Wherever the Tenant is to pay in a lease year the Tenant's proportionate share of an amount of money referable to a period of time wholly or partly within the lease year the Landlord will estimate the Tenant's proportionate share of the amount before the beginning of the lease year and the Tenant will pay to the Landlord the Tenant's proportionate share of the amount in monthly installments in advance during the lease year with the other rental payment provided for in this Lease. Within ninety (90) days after the end of each lease year the Landlord will make a final determination of the Tenant's proportionate share of the amount for the lease year, and will furnish the Tenant with a statement of operating costs and HVAC costs attributable to the premises for the relevant financial year or years of the Landlord, the municipal realty taxes attributable to the premises for the relevant calendar year or years and all other amounts referred to in Sub-section 3.04(l) and (2) paid or payable for any relevant period and in each case the amount thereof payable by the Tenant relating to the lease year and showing in reasonable detail the information necessary for the determination of the costs and the calculations of the Tenant's proportionate share of the amount. If the Tenant's proportionate share of the amount exceeds the sum of installments paid by the Tenant during the preceding lease year, the Tenant will pay to the Landlord as additional rental within thirty (30) days after the date of delivery of the statement by the Landlord the excess without interest or, if the sum of the monthly installments paid by the Tenant during the preceding lease year exceeds the Tenant's proportionate share of the amount, the Landlord will return to the Tenant within thirty (30) days after the date of delivery of the statement by the Landlord the excess, without interest.

This paragraph notes how the landlord will arrive at an estimated annual additional rent figure, and will then apply that to the tenant in equal installments over the ensuing 12 months of the lease. Within 90 days of the lease-year, the landlord will account for the *actual* costs that comprised additional rent for the previous lease year. If the landlord overcharged during the year, it is to refund the paid overage back to the tenant; if the landlord undercharged, the shortfall must be paid by the tenant within 30 days.

3.06 Interest on Amounts in Default

If the Tenant fails to pay when due and payable an amount of minimum rent or additional rent of the character described in Section 3.05, the unpaid amount will bear interest from the due date to the date of payment at the rate of eighteen (18) percent per year calculated and payable monthly.

This paragraph is self-explanatory. For reference and enlightenment, however, the effective annual interest rate on this compounding basis is actually 19.56%.

ARTICLE IV — TAXES AND QUIET ENJOYMENT

4.01 Taxes

The Landlord will pay all real property taxes (including local improvement rates) that may be assessed by a lawful authority against the Office Complex and against common areas and facilities, subject to Section 3.04.

4.02 Business Transfer Tax

If any business transfer tax, value-added tax, multi-stage sales tax, sales tax, goods and services tax, or any like tax is imposed on the Landlord by any governmental authority on any rent (whether fixed minimum rent, percentage rent, or additional rent) payable by the Tenant under this lease, the Tenant shall reimburse the Landlord for the amount of such tax forthwith upon demand or at any time designated from time to time by the Landlord.

Paragraph 4.01 ensures that the landlord will pay any duly authorized taxing authority the necessary real property taxes (which become part of additional rent anyway) in proper order, so that the tenant will never have its enjoyment of the premises diminished due to problems with tax authorities. The next paragraph (4.02) says, in a roundabout way, that the landlord will not be responsible for any taxes on the rent (except income taxes, of course), and will pass any such taxes on to the tenant. The landlord may make a demand for, and the tenant must comply with, immediate and periodic payment of those taxes.

4.03 Quiet Enjoyment

Subject to the provisions of this Lease the Landlord covenants with the Tenant for quiet enjoyment.

As described in the explanatory section prior to this form, "quiet enjoyment" is the tenant's right not to be bothered by the landlord or any others as a result of its leasehold, and to go about its business unimpeded.

ARTICLE V — REPAIR

5.01 Repair by the Landlord

The Landlord will:

(a) keep in a good and substantial state of repair, to the standards of a first class office complex, but subject to Section 5.03;

    (i) the common areas and facilities including but not limited to foundations, roofs, exterior walls (excluding store fronts and glass in premises set aside by the Landlord for leases to Tenants of the Office Complex) structural sub-floors, bearing walls, columns, beams, and other structural elements thereof, and the systems provided for bringing utilities to the Office Complex; and

    (ii) the structural elements of the premises; and

(b) repair defects in construction performed or installations made by the Landlord in the premises.

Essentially the landlord is responsible to repair common areas and the building's superstructure, structural elements of the premises itself, and any defective construction or installations that it previously made anywhere on the property.

5.02 Repair by the Tenant

The Tenant will:

(a) be responsible for maintenance and repairs, performed by the Landlord to keep in a good and substantial state of repair as would a careful and prudent owner, but subject to Section 5.03 the premises including all leasehold improvements and all trade fixtures therein, the storefront, all glass and utilities and all heating, air-conditioning, and ventilating equipment therein or related thereto, but with the exception of structural elements of the premises and defects in construction performed or installations made by the Landlord in the premises;

The tenant is responsible for maintaining and repairing all fixtures and parts of the premises *except* those repairs to the premises for which the landlord is responsible, specifically not for the structural elements nor defective repairs and constructions initiated by the landlord.

(b) permit the Landlord or its agent to enter and view the state of repair, and will repair upon notice in writing by the Landlord, subject only to the exceptions referred to in Clause (a), and will leave the premises in a good and substantial state of repair to the standards of a first class office complex, subject only to the exceptions referred to in Clause (a); and

This says that the tenant will permit inspections of the premises by the landlord and will make repairs for which it is responsible (see Clause (a) above) as demanded by the landlord.

(c) if part of the Office Complex including the common areas and facilities becomes in disrepair, or is damaged or destroyed through the negligence of the Tenant or its officers, employees, customers, or other invitees, reimburse the Landlord the cost of repairs or replacements promptly upon demand except to the extent that the Landlord is indemnified by insurance.

By this paragraph, the tenant promises to make repairs to or reimburse the landlord for any damage it causes directly, that its agents or employees cause, or that its customers cause to any part of the premises or common areas. The tenant will not be responsible in circumstances in which the landlord's insurance covers the damage.

> We have to read the language of contracts critically and ask hard questions where there is cause for confusion or misinterpretation. For instance, in Section 5 of this lease document, reference is made to "standards of a first class office complex." What, we might ask, are some specific standards of a first-class office complex? Moreover, how do they differ from and what distinguishes them from a second-class office complex? This type of subjective description is the kind of contract language that creates litigation. Then again, perhaps there is a specific definition among property managers; it is worth asking about in advance.

5.03 Abatement of Rent

If there is damage to the premises or damage to the Office Complex which prevents access to the premises or the supply of services essential to the premises and if the damage is such that the premises or a substantial part of the premises is rendered not reasonably capable of use by the Tenant for the conduct of its business for a period of time exceeding ten (10) days,

(a) unless the damage was caused by the negligence of the Tenant or an assignee, sub-tenant, concessionaire, licensee, or other person conducting business on or from the premises or an officer, employee, customer, or other invitee of any of them, the fixed minimum rent payable under Section 3.03 for the period beginning at the end of ten (10) days after the occurrence of the damage and until at least a substantial part of the premises is again reasonably capable of use and occupancy for the purpose aforesaid will abate in the proportion that the area of the part of the premises rendered not reasonably capable of use by the Tenant for the conduct of its business bears to the rentable area of the premises but not exceeding the amount of rental income insurance proceeds payable to the Landlord for the period; and

(b) unless this Lease is terminated under Section 5.04, the Landlord or the Tenant or both, as the case may be (according to the nature of the damage and their respective obligations to repair under Sections 5.01 and 5.02), will repair the damage with all reasonable diligence, but any abatement of minimum rent to which the Tenant is entitled under this section will not extend beyond the date by which in the reasonable opinion of the Landlord the Tenant should have completed its repairs with all reasonable diligence.

This section, 5.03, describes the circumstances that would give rise to and the limitations of rental abatement (reduction or decrease in amount of rent payable). The landlord will abate the tenant's rent proportionally to damage to any part of the premises or office complex in general that makes the premises unuseable for the tenant's purposes for more than 10 days. This, of course, would not apply if the damage was caused by the tenant or one of its guests. Note that the rental abatement would not include those first 10 lost days, only days after the "repair period." Furthermore, the abatement will not be provided beyond when the landlord "reasonably" determines that the tenant should have completed its repairs. Obviously this applies to situations in which the tenant would be responsible for some of the repairs, and does not preclude the abatement continuing if the landlord is responsible for repairs and has not completed them. Or would it? You might want to ask your lawyer.

5.04 Termination in the Event of Damage

1. The Landlord by written notice to the Tenant given within thirty (30) days of the occurrence of damage to the Office Complex may terminate this Lease

   (a) if the Office Complex is damaged by any cause which in the reasonable opinion of the Landlord either cannot be repaired or rebuilt with reasonable diligence within one hundred eighty (180) days after the occurrence of the damage or the cost of repairing or rebuilding it would exceed by more than $100,000.00 the proceeds of the Landlord's insurance available for the purpose; or

   (b) if the premises are damaged by any cause and the damage is such that the premises or a substantial part of the premises is rendered not reasonably capable of use by the Tenant for the conduct of its business and in the reasonable opinion of the Landlord cannot be repaired or rebuilt with reasonable diligence by six (6) months before the end of the term.

In the event that there is damage to any part of the office complex that the landlord believes will cost over $100,000 more than the available insurance, or would not be complete within 180 days (Sub-section (a)), *or* repairs of damage to the tenant's premises is not expected to be completed prior to six months before the end of the lease term (Sub-section (b)), the landlord has the option to terminate the lease for damage on 30 days' notice to the tenant.

2. The Tenant, by written notice to the Landlord given within thirty (30) days of the occurrence of the damage, may terminate this Lease if the premises are damaged by any cause and the damage is such that the premises or a substantial part of the premises is rendered not reasonably capable of use by the Tenant for the conduct of its business and in the reasonable opinion of the Landlord cannot be repaired or rebuilt with reasonable diligence by six (6) months before the end of term.

The tenant has the option to terminate the lease for damage by the same causes as available to the landlord in 5.05(1)(b). The tenant must, however, within 30 days of the damage occurring, give notice to the landlord of its intent to terminate the lease.

3. If this Lease is terminated under either of Sub-sections 1 or 2, neither the Landlord nor the Tenant will be bound to repair as provided in Sections 5.01 and 5.02, and the Tenant will deliver up possession of the premises to the Landlord with reasonable speed but in any event within sixty (60) days after the giving of notice of termination, and all rent will be apportioned and paid to the date upon which possession is delivered up, subject to any abatement to which the Tenant may be entitled under Section 5.03, but otherwise the Landlord or the Tenant or both, as the case may be (according to the nature of the damage and their respective obligations to repair under Sections 5.01 and 5.02), will repair the damage with all reasonable diligence.

The thrust of this paragraph is that either (1) if the lease is terminated for damage, then repairs are not required and the premises must be surrendered within 60 days, with rent apportioned to the day of surrender and net of any abatements due or (2) if the lease is not terminated for damage, the landlord and tenant must promptly make their respective repairs.

5.05 Certificate of Architect

If the premises or the Office Complex is damaged and there is a doubt as to whether the premises or the Office Complex can be repaired or rebuilt within one hundred eighty (180) days or by six (6) months before the end of the term or as to the cost of repairing or rebuilding the Office Complex or as to whether the premises or a substantial part of the premises is rendered not reasonably capable of use by the Tenant for the conduct of its business or once again has become capable of such use, the doubt will be settled by the architect and his certificate will be conclusive.

The bottom line here is that any dispute regarding the feasibility and timing of repairs is ultimately arbitrated by an architect "deemed [read: selected] by the Landlord" (from paragraph 1.01).

ARTICLE VI — UTILITIES AND SERVICES — PREMISES

6.01 Utility and Service Charges

The Tenant is solely responsible for and will promptly pay all charges for water, gas, electricity, janitor service, window cleaning, and any other utility or service used on the premises. It is understood and agreed that in the case of an interruption or failure in the supply of utilities or services to the premises the Landlord shall as soon as reasonably possible restore such utilities or service and the Landlord shall not, having acted with reasonable promptness, be liable to the Tenant or its officers or employees for any indirect or consequential damage, nor damages for personal discomfort nor illness arising by reason of the interruption of such utilities or service, nor shall the Tenant be allowed any abatement of rent as a result thereof.

The tenant is responsible for obtaining, maintaining, and paying for all utilities and services provided on the premises. In the event that utilities are prevented from reaching the premises, the landlord will promptly restore those services. In no event is the landlord liable for damages as a result of utilities and services being cut off for any period of time if it has acted with reasonable promptness.

6.02 Supply of Utilities by Landlord

If the Landlord elects to supply water, electricity, or any other utility or service, the Tenant will purchase its requirements for those utilities from the Landlord, and the Tenant will pay the Landlord therefor as additional rent at the rates current from time to time, within twenty (20) days after the Landlord delivers statements for the services to the Tenant.

Should the tenant receive its utilities and services via the landlord, the tenant will be billed by the landlord for such services by way of additional rent, and the tenant will be responsible for paying the landlord within 20 days of billing.

6.03 Tenant Not to Overload Utility and Service Facilities

The Tenant will not install equipment that will exceed or overload the capacity of utility facilities and agrees that if equipment installed by the Tenant requires additional facilities, these additional facilities will be installed at the Tenant's expense in accordance with plans and specifications approved by the Landlord prior to installation.

ARTICLE VII — SUBORDINATION, ATTORNMENT, STATUS STATEMENT BY TENANT

7.01 Subordination Clause

This Lease is subject and subordinate to all mortgages (including any deed of trust and mortgage securing bonds and all indentures supplemental thereto) which may now or hereafter affect the Office Complex and to all the renewals, modifications, consolidations, replacements, and extensions thereof. The Tenant agrees to execute promptly any certificate in confirmation of such subordination as the Landlord may request and hereby constitutes the Landlord the agent or attorney of the Tenant for the purpose of executing any such certificate and of making application at any time and from time to time to register postponements of this Lease in favour of any such mortgage in order to give effect to the foregoing provisions of this paragraph.

This states that the lease is subject to the landlord's mortgages, etc. on the office complex. It appoints the landlord as the tenant's agent or attorney with power to execute for registration a certificate confirming the subordination of this lease to any mortgage etc. given by the landlord with the complex as security. For the most part, this clause does not and would not affect the tenant under normal circumstances.

7.02 Status Statement

At any time or times at reasonable intervals within fifteen (15) days after a written request by the Landlord, the Tenant will execute, acknowledge, and deliver to the Landlord or such assignee or mortgagee as the Landlord designates, a certificate stating

(a) that this Lease is unmodified and in force and effect in accordance with its terms (or if there have been modifications, that this Lease is in force and effect as modified, and identifying the modification agreements, or if this Lease is not in force and effect, that it is not);

(b) the date to which rental has been paid under this Lease;

(c) whether or not there is an existing default by the Tenant in the payment of rent or any other sum or money under this Lease, and whether or not there is any other existing default by either party under this Lease with respect to which a notice of default has been served, and if there is such a default, specifying its nature and extent; and

(d) whether or not there are any set-offs, defence, or counterclaims against enforcement of the obligations to be performed by the Tenant under this Lease.

This lengthy set of specifications states little more than that the tenant agrees to provide to the landlord, upon request, a certificate of details about the status of the tenant's lease. The certificate would be of use to the landlord with its own financiers, and has little real effect on the tenant except that the tenant has to go to the trouble of preparing and delivering the status report to the landlord.

ARTICLE VIII — USE OF COMMON AREAS AND FACILITIES

The clauses that follow basically allow the tenant and its guests to use the office complex's common areas subject to the landlord's approval and management at all times.

8.01 Non-Exclusive Use

The Tenant, its officers, employees, customers, and other invitees in common with others designated by the Landlord or otherwise entitled, have the use or benefit of the common areas and facilities for the purposes from time to time permitted, approved, or designated by the Landlord, subject to the management and control of the common areas and facilities by the Landlord.

8.02 Management and Control by Landlord

The Landlord has the exclusive right to manage and control the Office Complex and from time to time to establish, modify, and enforce reasonable rules and regulations regarding the use, maintenance, and operation of the common areas and facilities, and the rules and regulations in all respects will be observed and performed by the Tenant, its officers, employees, customers, and other invitees.

ARTICLE IX — ASSIGNMENT AND SUBLETTING

9.01 Assignment and Subletting by Tenant

The Tenant shall not assign or sublet or part with the possession of the premises or any part thereof nor allow any other person other than the Tenant, its servants, and employees to occupy in any manner whatsoever the premises whether by lease, license, or otherwise without first obtaining the written consent of the Landlord, which consent shall not be unreasonably withheld. AND PROVIDED that any assignment of the within Lease shall not relieve the Tenant from the covenants and agreements herein contained.

The tenant may sublet the premises with the landlord's approval, although the sublease does not relieve the tenant of its responsibilities to the landlord for performance of the tenant's obligations by the assignee or the sub-lettor.

9.02 Assignment by Landlord

If the Landlord sells an interest in the Office Complex or in this Lease, to the extent that the purchaser or assignee is responsible for compliance with the covenants and obligations of the Landlord hereunder, the Landlord without further written agreement shall be relieved of liability under the covenants and obligations.

The landlord is permitted to sell or assign either the lease or the property without notice to or approval from the tenant. Once the lease or property has been assigned, the landlord is relieved of all its obligations. The terms and conditions of the lease attorn with the assignee, who must perform the obligations of the landlord.

ARTICLE X — SIGNS, FIXTURES AND ALTERATIONS

10.01 Alterations by Landlord

The Tenant shall permit the Landlord with workmen or others to enter upon the premises for the purpose of repairing, altering, renewing, or adding to the premises or any part thereof, or any part of the building with which they form part or the adjoining premises or the sewer drains or water courses of the said building or the adjoining premises, including without restricting the generality of the foregoing, using all walls of the demised premises for making any such alteration or addition, and the costs of remedying such defects insofar as such defects are included in the Tenant's covenants to repair contained in this Lease shall be a debt due from the Tenant to the Landlord, to be forthwith recoverable by action. In exercising the rights under this clause the Landlord shall not interfere with the Tenant any more than reasonably necessary. All buildings, structures, alterations, additions, installations, furniture, decorations, and all other improvements upon the premises at or prior to the commencement of the term of the lease or at any time thereafter during the term, including all appurtenances thereto, whether now belonging to the Landlord or hereafter built or placed upon the premises by the Tenant, either out of insurance monies or out of its own funds or both, shall immediately become and remain the property of the Landlord.

The tenant must allow the landlord to make alterations or repairs in or adjacent to the premises as necessary. If repairs that the landlord is making are the responsibility of the tenant (see Section 5.02), then the cost of the repairs is a debt due to the landlord from the tenant. The second paragraph states that any additions, fixtures, or alterations immediately attach to the property and become the Landlord's.

10.02 Installations and Changes by Tenant

All fixtures installed by the Tenant will be of first class quality. The Tenant will not make or cause to be made any change, decoration, addition, or improvement or cut or drill into, nail, or otherwise attach, secure, or install any trade fixture, exterior sign, floor covering, interior, or exterior lighting, or mechanical or electrical system or fixture, or plumbing fixture, shade, or awning to any part of the premises or to the exterior of the premises including the storefront or hang from or affix anything to a ceiling without first obtaining the Landlord's written approval. The Tenant will present to the Landlord plans and specifications for the work at the time approval is sought and the work will be done by contractors or other workers or tradesmen approved by the Landlord and in a good and workmanlike manner with first class materials. The Tenant will not make any change to the structural elements of the premises.

Although—or perhaps because—they would become the landlord's property, any changes made by the tenant that would affix to the property must be approved by the landlord. The tenant can, under no circumstances, make changes that alter the structure of the premises.

10.03 Alterations by Tenant

Subject to the provisions of this Lease, if the Tenant requires any further repairs, alterations, additions, or improvements, he will make the same at his own expense provided that they shall not be made without first obtaining the written consent of the Landlord and that they shall become, on affixation, the property of the Landlord. The Tenant agrees that any alterations, additions, improvements, and fixtures made to or installed upon or in the premises at or prior to the commencement of the term of the Lease or at any time thereafter, at the expense of the Tenant pursuant to Sections 10.02 and 10.03 hereof, other than unattached moveable trade fixtures, shall remain upon and be surrendered to the Landlord with the premises as part thereof upon the expiration or earlier termination of this Lease and shall become the absolute property of the Landlord unless the Landlord shall by notice in writing require the Tenant to remove the same, in which event the Tenant covenants and agrees to restore the premises as provided in Section 5.02(b). Every installation, removal, or restoration by the Tenant of its fixtures will be done at the sole expense of the Tenant and the Tenant promptly will make good or reimburse the Landlord the cost of making good all damage to the premises by the installation and removal thereof.

This somewhat repetitive paragraph restates that any changes and alterations made by the tenant must be approved by the landlord and immediately become the landlord's property. However, the landlord may, at its option, ask the tenant to remove the fixtures and restore the property ("make good") at the tenant's cost.

10.04 Not to Overload Floors

The Tenant will not bring upon the premises any machinery, equipment, or thing that by reason of weight, size, or use might damage the premises and will not at any time overload the floors of the premises. If overloading occurs and damage ensues the Tenant forthwith will repair the damage or pay to the Landlord the cost of making it good.

This paragraph is fairly self-explanatory. Note, however, that if the tenant tells the landlord of its intended use of the premises, and certain machinery is reasonably and rightfully expected to be used for that purpose, the tenant may have opportunity and possibility for recourse to simply leave the premises. This circumstance would, however, provide an excellent time to speak to a lawyer.

10.05 Dangerous Articles

The Tenant shall not store or bring on the premises any articles of any flammable or dangerous nature nor permit or suffer anything to be done by reason whereof the present or any future policy of insurance as relates to fire or other casualty may be rendered void or voidable or by which the rate of premium thereon may be increased, without the consent of the Landlord; provided, however, that if the Tenant wishes to do something which will not render any insurance void or voidable but which may be insured against upon paying an additional premium, then the Tenant may do so.

10.06 Inspection by Landlord

The Tenant shall permit the Landlord and all persons employed or utilized by it, to enter upon the demised premises at all reasonable times for the purpose of viewing the state of repair of the premises and for any other reasonable purpose and the Tenant shall forthwith make good any defects found upon the premises and for which the Tenant is liable hereunder.

Simple version: You have to let the landlord enter to inspect the premises—when reasonable—and promptly make repairs to problems the landlord finds.

This brings up the issue of what constitutes a "reasonable" time for the landlord to enter and inspect. Common sense should be the guide on all points: if the landlord would be interfering in something or would be unwittingly compromising sensitive discussions or information, that would not be a good time. On the other hand, the tenant cannot wait for Jupiter to rise in the house of Leo before letting the landlord in to look.

ARTICLE XI — INSURANCE AND INDEMNITY

11.01 Tenant's Insurance

(a) The Tenant shall continuously from the Commencement Date of the Term and during the entire Term hereof, at its sole cost and expense, take out and keep in full force and effect the following insurance (or such other insurance in lieu thereof that the Landlord may reasonably require from time to time):

   (i) upon property of every description and kind owned by the Tenant and located in the Complex or for which the Tenant is legally liable or which is installed by or on behalf of the Tenant, including without limitation furniture, fittings, installations, alterations, additions, partitions, and fixtures, and anything in the nature of a leasehold improvement in an amount not less than ninety (90) percent of the full replacement cost thereof (which shall mean the cost of repairing, replacing, or reinstating any item of property with materials of like kind and quality on the same site without deduction for physical, accounting, or other depreciation), with a minimum of standard all-risk coverage including earthquake and flood. In the event that there shall be a dispute as to the amount which comprises full replacement cost, the decision of the Landlord's insurance broker shall be conclusive; and

   (ii) broad form tenant's legal liability insurance including personal injury liability, contractual liability, tenants' legal liability, non-owned automobile liability, and owners' and contractors' protective insurance coverage with respect to the Tenant's use of any part of the Complex and which coverage shall include the business operations conducted by the Tenant and any sub-tenants on the Leased Premises. Such policies shall be written on a comprehensive basis with limits of not less than $1,000,000.00 for any one occurrence and such higher limits as the Landlord may reasonably require from time to time. All liability policies shall include the Landlord as an additional insured, shall contain provisions for cross-liability and severability of interest and shall be primary and shall not call into contribution any other insurance available to the Landlord;

This section, 11.01(a), basically says that the tenant will maintain reasonable and customary (for the business and industry) amounts of insurance. Specifically, the tenant will maintain all-risk coverage property insurance for 90% of replacement cost of all its properties (sub-paragraph (i)). The asset values are not to be depreciated for calculation, and in the event of a dispute over the replacement value to be insured, the Landlord's insurance broker will have the last word. Also, the tenant will maintain comprehensive liability insurance, with limits of not less than $1 million *per occurrence*, which names the landlord as an additional insured under the policy. This would then cover the landlord for any situation in which the tenant and the landlord were named as co-defendants. The landlord demands certain terms be part of the policy, perhaps the most important of which is that the tenant's insurance will be primary—that is, be the first insurance policy called on in any action in which there may be more than one policy covering the action (see Chapter 8 for more detail about insurance)—and not call the landlord's insurance for contribution.

(b) All property damage insurance policies written on behalf of the Tenant shall contain a waiver of any subrogation rights which the Tenant's insurers may have against the Landlord and against those for whom the Landlord is, in law, responsible whether any such damage is caused by the act, omission, or fault of the Landlord or by those for whom the Landlord is, in law, responsible.

This clause prevents the tenant's insurer from subrogating ("stepping into the shoes of the insured") and making claim against the landlord or anyone or anything the landlord is responsible over. Essentially what this says is that the tenant cannot hold the landlord responsible or liable for damage; nor can the tenant's insurers, after subrogating a claim, go after the landlord for damages—whether or not the landlord was actually responsible.

(c) All policies shall be taken out with insurers reasonably acceptable to the Landlord in form satisfactory from time to time to the Landlord. The Tenant agrees that certificates of insurance or, if required by the Landlord, certified copies of each such insurance policy will be delivered to the Landlord as soon as practicable after the placing of the required insurance. All policies shall contain an undertaking by the insurers to notify the Landlord in writing, not less than thirty (30) days prior to any material change or cancellation thereof;

(d) It is agreed the naming of the Landlord as an additional insured is with respect only to responsibility for liability arising out of the operations of the Tenant or use of the Leased Premises as permitted hereunder or the obligations of the Tenant assumed by the Landlord under this Lease.

This paragraph is in the tenant's favour, inasmuch as it limits the requirement of the tenant's insurance coverage over the landlord to only those causes and situations in which coverage of the landlord is warranted. The tenant does not provide a blanket over the landlord.

(e) The Tenant covenants and agrees that in the event of damage or destruction to any leasehold improvements in the Leased Premises covered by insurance required to be taken out by the Tenant pursuant to Sub-section 11.01 (a)(i), the Tenant will use the proceeds of such insurance for the purpose of repairing or restoring such leasehold improvements unless the Landlord or the Tenant elects to terminate this Lease pursuant to Section 5.04 hereof.

This paragraph demands of the tenant to use its insurance proceeds for damages to leasehold improvements in the premises to repair or replace those leasehold improvements—i.e., unless the lease is terminated due to damage, as provided in Section 5.04. (Remember always to follow the internal references.)

11.02 Landlord's Insurance

The Landlord covenants and agrees that it will insure the Complex (excluding foundations and excavations) and the machinery, boilers, and equipment contained therein owned by the Landlord (excluding any property with respect to which the Tenant is obliged to insure pursuant to the provisions of Section 11.01 hereof) against damage by fire and other standard all-risk coverage in such reasonable amounts as would be carried by a prudent owner of a similar property. The Landlord will also carry third-party liability insurance with respect to the operation of the Complex in such reasonable amounts as would be carried by a prudent owner of a similar property. The Landlord may, but shall not be obliged to, take out and carry any other form or forms of insurance as it or the mortgagees of the Landlord may reasonably determine advisable. Notwithstanding any contribution by the Tenant to the cost of insurance premiums as provided herein, the Tenant acknowledges that it has no right to receive any proceeds from any such insurance policies carried by the Landlord. Upon the request of the Tenant from time to time the Landlord will furnish a statement as to the perils in respect of which and the amount to which it has insured the Complex and the improvements and installations in the Leased Premises, and the Tenant shall be entitled at reasonable times upon reasonable notice to the Landlord to inspect copies of the relevant portions of all policies of insurance in effect and copies of any relevant opinions of the Landlord's insurance advisors.

In this clause the landlord agrees to carry whatever property, liability, and other insurance it deems fitting and necessary. Ironically, even though the tenant may have to pay additional rent for the extended insurance coverage and premiums, the tenant waives all right or claim to any insurance payouts under any policy for which it has paid a portion of the premium.

11.03 Increase in Landlord's Insurance Premiums

1. The Tenant agrees that nothing will be done, omitted to be done, kept, used, sold, or offered for sale on or from the Leased Premises that may contravene any of the Landlord's policies insuring any part of the Complex or which will prevent the Landlord from procuring policies with companies acceptable to the Landlord. The Tenant will pay all increases in premium resulting from the type of merchandise sold on or from the Leased Premises or anything done or kept thereon or use to which they may be put, whether or not the Landlord has consented to them. In determining whether increased premiums are the result of the use of the Leased Premises a Schedule issued by the organization making the insurance rate on the Leased Premises showing the various components of the rate will be conclusive evidence of the several items and charges which make up the fire insurance rate on the Leased Premises.

The tenant agrees that it will not, by any use of the premises, contribute to or itself contravene any terms of the landlord's insurance. Furthermore, any insurance premium increases that are due to the tenant's activities will be borne by the tenant *whether the landlord consented to those activities or not*. The schedule of premium components provided by the landlord's insurer will be the determining factor in assessing whether and how much of the premium is attributable to the tenant.

> 2. If the occupancy or use of the Leased Premises causes an increase of premium for any of the policies insuring the Leased Premises or any part of the Complex above the rate for the least hazardous type of use or occupancy legally permitted in the Leased Premises, the Tenant will pay the amount of the increase. The Tenant also will pay in that event any additional premium for rental income insurance carried by the Landlord for its protection against rent loss through an insured risk. Bills for the increases and additional premiums may be rendered by the Landlord to the Tenant when the Landlord elects, and will be due and payable by the Tenant when rendered, and the amount thereof will be paid as Additional Rent.

Essentially, according to the promise made in this clause, if the tenant's mere presence pushes the landlord's insurance premium rates beyond the "least hazardous use" rate level, the tenant will pay not only for the premium premiums but also for any rental insurance that the landlord may carry. These charges will be levied on the tenant as additional rent.

11.04 Cancellation of Insurance

> If an insurance policy upon part of the Complex is cancelled or threatened by the insurer to be cancelled, or the coverage thereunder reduced or threatened to be reduced by the insurer because of the use and occupation of the Leased Premises, and if the Tenant fails to remedy the condition giving rise to cancellation, threatened cancellation, reduction, or threatened reduction of coverage within forty-eight (48) hours after notice thereof by the Landlord, the Landlord may either:

In the event that any of the landlord's insurance is cancelled or threatened to be cancelled due to the tenant's activities or mere presence, the tenant must remedy the situation within 48 hours. If the tenant does not do so, the landlord may either ((a) below) reenter (i.e., reclaim the leased premises and "evict" the tenant), or ((b) below) enter the tenant's premises and remedy the situation at the tenant's cost. In no event does the landlord bear any liability for its entry upon the premises.

> (a) re-enter the Leased Premises whereupon Section 12.01 will apply; or
>
> (b) enter the Leased Premises and remedy the condition giving rise to the cancellation or reduction or threatened cancellation or reduction, and the Tenant will pay to the Landlord the costs thereof on demand as Additional Rent, and the Landlord will not be liable for damage or injury caused to property of the Tenant or others located on the Leased Premises as a result of the entry.

11.05 Indemnification

> The Tenant and the Landlord shall each indemnify the other against all liabilities, costs, damages, loss, fines, suits, claims, demands, and actions or causes of action of any kind, for injuries to persons or loss of life or damage to property, including loss or damage to the property of the other, and whether for third-party liabilities or direct or indirect loss to the property of the Landlord or the Tenant, for which either may become liable or suffer, by reason of or arising out of or connected with any negligence, non-compliance with, or breach of laws or by-laws or the terms, covenants, and provisos of this Lease, on the part of the other party hereto, or its servants or employees.

This is an example of a fairly rigorous, or at least wordy, mutual indemnification clause. This is good fortune for us, since most of the indemnification clauses provided within the other sample contracts in this book are one-way.

11.06 Loss and Damage

The Landlord shall not be liable for any damage or injury or death to any person or property including the persons and property of the Tenant, its servants, agents, customers, invitees, and licensees, on the Leased Premises from any cause whatsoever, except when such damage, injury, or death is caused by the negligence of the Landlord, or its agents or servants.

Short-form translation: "We are not responsible for . . . unless we were negligent and therefore responsible after all."

ARTICLE XII — DEFAULT OF TENANT

12.01 Right to Re-Enter

If the Tenant fails to pay rent or additional rent that is in arrears, within five (5) days after notice from the Landlord that it is in arrears, or to observe or perform in accordance with proper notice of default under Section 18(2) of the Landlord and Tenant Act any other of the terms, conditions, or covenants of this Lease to be observed or performed by the Tenant, or if the Tenant or an agent of the Tenant falsifies a report required to be furnished to the Landlord pursuant to this Lease, or if re-entry is permitted under other terms of this Lease, the Landlord in addition to any other right or remedy it may have will have the right to immediate re-entry and may remove all persons and property from the premises and the property may be removed and stored in a public warehouse or elsewhere at the cost of and for the account of the Tenant, all without service of notice or resort to legal process and without being considered guilty of trespass or becoming liable for loss or damage occasioned thereby.

Reentry is similar to repossession. If the tenant breaches the lease contract, including being in arrears for rent payment and not rectifying the situation within five days of notice by the landlord, or in this case the tenant is not in compliance with Sec 18(2) of the Landlord and Tenant Act (Manitoba),[8] the landlord may reenter the premises, displace all people therein (boot them out), and move the tenant's property to storage. All this happens at the tenant's cost, and the landlord is neither required to provide notice nor liable for any loss, damage, or trespass resulting from the reentry.

12.02 The Bankruptcy of Tenant

(a) If

    (i) any of the goods and chattels of the Tenant on the premises at any time during the term are seized or taken in execution or attachment by a creditor of the Tenant;

    (ii) the Tenant or a guarantor or indemnifier of this Lease makes an assignment for the benefit of creditors or becomes bankrupt or insolvent and takes the benefit of any act that may be in force for bankrupt or insolvent debtors;

    (iii) a receiver-manager is appointed to control the conduct of the business on or from the premises;

    (iv) an order is made for the winding up of the Tenant;

(b) the then current month's rent and the next ensuing three (3) months' rent immediately will become due and payable as accelerated rent and the Landlord may re-enter and take possession of the premises subject to Section 46(2) of the Landlord and Tenant Act.

The noteworthy part of this otherwise relatively self-evident paragraph is that the assignment for creditors, bankruptcy, or insolvency of a *guarantor* or *indemnifier* (Section 12.02(a)(ii)) will trigger the landlord's rights in sub-paragraph (b). The landlord is immediately entitled to the current month's rent, which it should already have anyway since it is due in advance, plus the next three months' rent. The landlord may also reenter the premises. Presumably if a tenant is making its payments and complying with the lease otherwise, despite having obtained the lease by a guarantor's or indemnifier's agreement in the first place, a landlord would not take such action. But, the landlord would well be within its rights to do so.

12.03 Landlord May Perform Tenant's Obligations

If the Tenant fails to perform an obligation of the Tenant under this Lease the Landlord may perform the obligation and for that purpose may enter upon the premises on not less than five (5) days' prior notice to the Tenant or without notice in the case of an emergency and do such things upon or in respect of the premises as the Landlord considers necessary. The Tenant will pay as additional rent all expenses incurred by or on behalf of the Landlord under this section plus fifteen (15) percent for overhead upon presentation of a bill therefor. The Landlord will not be liable to the Tenant for loss or damage resulting from such action by the Landlord unless caused by the negligence of the Landlord or another person for whose negligence the Landlord is responsible in law.

If the tenant does not perform an obligation, most likely to repair, the landlord may give five days' notice to the tenant and then enter the premises and act in the tenant's stead to perform those obligations. In the event of an emergency, the landlord need not provide notice. If this were to happen, the landlord is then entitled to be repaid, by way of additional rent, the direct cost incurred plus a 15% bump for "overhead." The landlord will have no liability to the tenant except for negligence.

12.04 Right to Re-Let

If the Landlord re-enters, as herein provided, it may either terminate this Lease or it may from time to time without terminating the Tenant's obligations under this Lease, make alterations and repairs considered by the Landlord necessary to facilitate a re-letting, and re-let the premises or any part thereof as agent of the Tenant for such term or terms and at such rental or rentals and upon such other terms and conditions as the Landlord in its reasonable discretion considers advisable. Upon each re-letting all rent and other monies received by the Landlord from the re-letting will be applied, first to the payment of indebtedness other than rent due hereunder from the Tenant to the Landlord, second to the payment of costs and expenses of the re-letting including real estate commissions and solicitor's fees and the costs of all the alterations and repairs, and third to the payment of rent due and unpaid hereunder. The residue, if any, will be held by the Landlord and applied in payment of future rent as it becomes due and payable. If the rent received from the re-letting during the month is less than the rent to be paid during that month by the Tenant, the Tenant will pay the deficiency to the Landlord. The deficiency will be calculated and paid monthly. No re-entry by the Landlord will be construed as an election on its part to terminate this Lease unless a written notice of that intention is given to the Tenant. Instead of re-letting without termination, the Landlord may elect at any time to terminate this Lease for a previous breach. If the Landlord terminates this Lease for any breach, in addition to other remedies it may have, it may recover from the Tenant all damages it incurs by reason of the breach including the cost of recovering the premises, reasonable legal fees, and the worth at the time of termination of the excess, if any, of the amount of rent and charges equivalent to rent reserved in this Lease for the remainder of the term over the then reasonable rental value of the premises for the remainder of the term, all of which amounts immediately will be due and payable by the Tenant to the Landlord. In determining the rent which would be payable by the Tenant after default, the annual rent for each year of the unexpired term will be equal to the average fixed minimum and additional rents paid or payable by the Tenant from the beginning of the term to the time of default. In any of the events referred to in Sections 12.01, 12.02, and 12.03, in addition to all other rights including the rights referred to in this section and Section 12.01, the full amount of the current month's minimum rent, plus additional rent and all other payments required to be made monthly, and the next three (3) months' minimum rent, immediately will become due and payable and the Landlord may immediately distrain for it, together with arrears then unpaid.

Under normal circumstances, if a landlord re-lets premises which the tenant has vacated or which the landlord has reentered, the landlord may be statutorily obliged to terminate the lease under some legislations. In that instance, the tenant would have no further obligation to the landlord beyond that date.

This clause works around that circumstance by the landlord re-letting the premises as *the tenant's agent* (i.e., the *tenant* is actually doing the re-letting of the premises). Thus, the tenant remains obliged in full to the landlord, although the landlord reserves the right to terminate the lease at any time rather than re-let. Note that the landlord's reentry on the premises is not an indication of its terminating the lease.

This paragraph also provides a scheme by which the rent received by the landlord from re-letting the premises is to be applied to debts and obligations owing it by the tenant, and later lists all the costs, damages, and rent amounts which the landlord may claim when it terminates the lease. Among those amounts is the estimated remaining rent, which is calculated by adding the minimum rent per month to the average monthly additional rent paid by the tenant and multiplying by the remaining months in the lease term. Over and above all other rights, the landlord can "distrain" (seize) the tenant's possessions and assets to the extent of the current plus ensuing three months' rent.

12.05 Waiver of Distress—Fraudulent Removal

If the Tenant fraudulently or clandestinely conveys away, or carries off or from the premises his goods or chattels to prevent the Landlord from distraining the same for arrears of rent so reserved, due, or made payable, the Landlord or any person by him for that purpose lawfully empowered, may, within thirty (30) days next ensuing the conveying away or carrying off, take and seize such goods and chattels wherever the same are found, as a distress for the arrears of rent, and the same sell or otherwise dispose of in such manner as if the goods and chattels had actually been distrained by the Landlord upon the premises for the arrears of rent.

The landlord can retrieve for the purpose of distraining and selling or disposing any of the tenant's chattels, which the tenant may have secretly taken off-site to avoid them being seized by the landlord to compensate for rental arrears, from anywhere as if they were on the premises. The landlord has this right on each seized asset for 30 days from the time that asset was taken off the premises. Who would, and how would anybody, know when each chattel was removed—especially if it was done under the cover of darkness? ("Gee, oddly enough, these pieces of equipment have been here for months. Sorry.") Believe it, there are ways.

ARTICLE XIII — ACCESS BY LANDLORD

13.01 Right of Entry

The Landlord and its agents may enter the premises at all reasonable times to examine them and to show them to a prospective purchaser, Tenant, or mortgagee. Without limiting the Landlord's rights to make alterations, additions, and changes of the location under Section 10.01, the Landlord may make alterations, additions, and adjustments to and changes of location of the pipes, conduits, wiring, ducts, and other installations of any kind in the premises where necessary to serve another part of the Office Complex, and the Landlord may take all material required therefor onto the premises without constituting an eviction of the Tenant in whole or in part, and the rent reserved will not abate while the alterations, additions, or changes of location are being made by reason of loss or interruption of the business of the Tenant, or otherwise, and the Landlord will not be liable for damage to property of the Tenant or of others located on the premises as a result of an entry unless caused by the negligence of the Landlord or another person for whose negligence the Landlord is responsible in law. During the six (6) months prior to the expiration of the term, the Landlord may place upon the premises the usual notice for rent, which the Tenant will permit to remain without interference. If the Tenant is not present to open and permit entry into the premises when for a proper reason entry is necessary or permissible, the Landlord or its agents may enter by a master key or may forcibly enter without rendering the Landlord or its agents liable therefor and without affecting this Lease. Nothing in this section however, imposes upon the Landlord an obligation, responsibility, or liability for the care, maintenance, or repair of the premises or any part thereof except as specifically provided in this Lease.

The most important feature of this section is that the landlord has the right to enter and repair within the tenant's premises without any liability or responsibility for the tenant's business operations being impaired or for damage unless it is due to the landlord's negligence. Technically, the landlord could enter the premises to make a repair and bring work by the tenant to an effective standstill for days, then indirectly cause damage to the tenant's property or work-in-process. The landlord could do this without any responsibility and the tenant can do nothing about it. Of course, a landlord with business habits like that might find it increasingly difficult to find and keep tenants.

ARTICLE XIV — OVERHOLDING AND RENEWAL

14.01 No Tacit Renewal

If the Tenant remains in possession of the premises after the end of the term and without the execution and delivery of a new Lease or a written renewal or extension of this Lease, there is no tacit or other renewal of this Lease, and the Tenant will be considered to be occupying the premises as a tenant from month to month at a monthly rental payable in advance on the first day of each month equal to the sum of:

(a) twice the monthly installment of fixed minimum rent payable for the last month of the term; and

(b) one-sixth (1/6) of the amount of additional rent and charges payable by the Tenant for the year immediately preceding the last lease year of this Lease, and otherwise upon the terms and conditions set forth in this Lease so far as applicable.

The long and the short of this paragraph is that the tenant can remain on the premises as an overholding tenant beyond the term of the lease, but the tenancy becomes month-to-month at double the minimum rent and double the average monthly additional rent for the final year of the lease. Ouch! Do you suppose there is a subtle hint here?

14.02 Renewal of Lease

(a) Provided that the Tenant shall not be in default in any of the covenants or conditions of this Lease, the Landlord hereby grants to the Tenant a right of renewal, exercisable by the Tenant giving written notice to the Landlord not less than six (6) months and not more than twelve (12) months prior to the expiration of the Term, to renew the Term of this Lease for a further period of five (5) years.

(b) The renewal lease shall contain the same covenants, conditions, and agreements as are contained in this Lease, except:

  (i) the right of renewal already exercised shall be omitted;

  (ii) any article or clause of this Lease which requires revision to state correctly the manner in which it is to be applied during the Renewal Term shall be so revised; and

  (iii) Minimum Rent and Parking for the Renewal Term shall be determined as provided in Article 14.02 (c).

(c) The Minimum Rent payable and Parking payable with respect to the Renewal Term shall be the greater of:

  (i) the Minimum Rent payable and Parking payable during the final year of the Term; or

  (ii) the fair market Minimum Rent and fair market Parking for the Leased Premises as at the commencement date of the Renewal Term.

(d) The parties shall make bona fide efforts to agree as to the fair market Minimum Rent and Parking with respect to the Leased Premises as at the commencement date of the Renewal Term. For that purpose the parties may refer to the Minimum Rent and Parking payable for similar accommodation for a similar commercial operation. If, however, the parties have not agreed as to the amount of rent by the sixtieth (60th) day prior to the commencement of the Renewal Term, then such Minimum Rent and Parking shall be determined either:

  (i) by an arbitrator mutually agreed upon by the parties who shall be a person currently active in the Province of Manitoba as an Accredited Real Estate Appraiser having not less than five (5) years experience as an appraiser; or

  (ii) if the parties are unable to agree as to an arbitrator pursuant to Clause (i) of this article, then such rental shall be determined by a single arbitrator in accordance with the provisions of the Arbitration Act of Manitoba and amendments thereto or legislation in substitution therefor.

This clause, regarding renewal of the lease, sets a lot of rules for renewing the lease agreement. The basics are that: (1) the renewal option must be exercised within a six-month window commencing one year prior to the expiration of the lease; (2) the lease will renew for five years on the same terms and conditions except for the renewal clause (only once can the tenant renew); and (3) update to dates, times, and rent amounts, etc., will be made so that the renewal agreement is "current."

Renewal rent is determined by the higher of the last rental price and the fair market value of the premises. If the fair market value is not agreed upon between landlord and tenant by 60 days prior to the end of the original lease term, an arbitrator sets the fair market value of the premises. (My question about the logic of the renewal rent being the higher of current rate or fair market value is: If the fair market value is substantially lower than the current rental rate, why would the tenant not let the agreement lapse and re-rent the premises at a fair market value rental rate?)

ARTICLE XV — USE OF PREMISES

15.01 Purpose of Use

The premises will not be used for any purpose other than the purpose of conducting the business of <state business purpose> and the Tenant will not use the premises or permit them to be used for any other purpose whatsoever except with the consent of the Landlord first obtained in writing.

15.02 Solicitation of Business

Neither the Tenant nor the Tenant's employees or agents will solicit business in any area of the common areas and facilities or display merchandise outside the premises without the prior written consent of the Landlord.

I think we can liberally interpret this to mean actively advertising, promoting, or setting up displays in the common areas. (Subjective language observation: What about those common areas that the tenant is paying for because they are "untenable" [Section 3.01] and thus are part of the leased square-footage?) One has to assume a reasonable interpretation of soliciting business as well. If I meet you in the lobby or mail room of the office complex and try to sell you on my product/service, I do not think that would constitute grounds for breach of contract.

ARTICLE XVI — WASTE AND GOVERNMENTAL REGULATIONS

16.01 Waste or Nuisance

The Tenant will not commit or permit to be committed waste upon the premises or a nuisance or other thing that may disturb the quiet enjoyment of any other tenant in the Office Complex or the owners and occupiers of the adjoining premises, whether or not the nuisance arises out of the use of the premises by the Tenant for a purpose permitted by this Lease.

Here's the fairly reasonable logic of this provision. You get "quiet enjoyment" of your premises, and so does everyone else. You cannot be the cause of other tenants' lack of that "quiet enjoyment." Note that waste, noise, nuisance, etc. can be created and applies even if it arises out of your normal use of the premises as specified in Section 15.01.

16.02 Compliance with Laws

(a) The Tenant, at the Tenant's costs, will comply with the applicable requirements of all municipal, provincial, federal, and other government authorities now in force or which may hereafter be in force pertaining to the Tenant's occupancy or use of the premises and will observe in the occupancy and use of the premises all municipal by-laws and provincial and federal statutes and regulations now in force or which may hereafter be in force, and will comply with all regulations and requirements of the Canadian Underwriters Association, with respect to insurance.

(b) Without limiting the generality of the foregoing, it is understood and agreed by the parties hereto that the Tenant shall be responsible for any expense incurred with respect to business tax and licensing fees, with respect to the premises.

16.03 Compliance with Condominium Act

The Tenant shall comply and shall require its employees, customers, and others doing business with it from time to time, to comply with the Condominium Act and the Declaration, By-laws, Rules, and Regulations passed pursuant thereto of Winnipeg Condominium Corporation #82.

This clause pertains to Winnipeg in general, and to the Winnipeg Condominium Corporation's rules specifically. Since the effect of this rule probably is of no concern to anybody outside Winnipeg, we'll ignore it except to say that where there are provisions for compliance with specific legislation, rules, bylaws, etc., it is usually a good idea to become familiar with them, at least in passing.

ARTICLE XVII — ACCEPTANCE OF PREMISES

17.01 The Tenant acknowledges that he has examined and knows the condition of the said premises and has received the same in good order and repair, except as herein otherwise specified, and no representations as to the condition or repair thereof have been made to the Landlord or his agents prior to or at the execution of this Lease, that are not herein expressed or endorsed thereon.

Signing the lease with this paragraph included removes all recourse for the tenant to have the landlord correct a deficiency in the premises that is discovered one second or more after signing the agreement. As with reading over the final draft of a contract carefully before signing it, make sure that you have completely and fully inspected the premises. Moreover, make sure that any problems or concerns with the premises are raised and documented in writing as part of the lease.

ARTICLE XVIII — REMEDIES OF LANDLORD AND WAIVER

18.01 Remedies of Landlord Accumulative

No exercise of a specific right or remedy by the Landlord or by the Tenant precludes it from or prejudices it in exercising another right or pursuing another remedy or maintaining an option to which it may otherwise be entitled either at law or in equity.

We saw this clause in the chattel lease sample. It is fairly self-explanatory here.

18.02 Waiver

The waiver by the Landlord or the Tenant of a breach of a term, covenant, or condition of this Lease will not be considered to be a waiver of a subsequent breach of the term, covenant, or condition, or another term, covenant, or condition. The subsequent acceptance of rent by the Landlord will not be considered to be a waiver of a preceding breach by the Tenant of a term, covenant, or condition of this Lease, regardless of the Landlord's knowledge of the preceding breach at the time of acceptance of the rent. No covenant, term, or condition of this Lease will be considered to have been waived by the Landlord or by the Tenant unless the waiver is in writing, signed by the Landlord or by the Tenant, as the case may be.

ARTICLE XIX — MISCELLANEOUS

19.01 Accord and Satisfaction

No payment by the Tenant or receipt by the Landlord of a lesser amount than rent herein stipulated will be considered to be other than on account of the earliest stipulated rent, nor will an endorsement or statement on a cheque or in a letter accompanying a cheque or payment of rent be considered to be an accord or satisfaction, and the Landlord may accept the cheque or payment without prejudice to the Landlord's right to recover the balance of the rent or to pursue any other remedy.

Here is a trick some crafty (read: unscrupulous) folk will use from time to time: they incur a financial obligation which they cannot pay, so they send a partial payment with a note on or attached to the cheque that says something to the effect of "By accepting and tendering this cheque you agree to accept this amount as full settlement of my debt."

Sometimes they get away with it, because the recipient of that note either does not cash it for fear of accepting the offer and having no recourse to collect the remaining debt (not knowing that the law is on her side), or does cash it and writes off the balance as a lesson learned. In either case, the debtor wins. This paragraph prevents such a game from getting started, let alone being played.

19.02 Unavoidable Delay

If there is an unavoidable delay in the performance of an act or compliance with a covenant or condition, performance or compliance during the period of the unavoidable delay will be excused and the period for the performance or compliance will be extended for a period equal to the period of the unavoidable delay.

19.03 Partial Invalidity

If a term, covenant, or condition of this Lease or the application thereof to any person or circumstances is held to any extent invalid or unenforceable, the remainder of this Lease or the application of the term, covenant, or condition to persons or circumstances other than those as to which it is held invalid or unenforceable will not be affected.

19.04 Notice

Notice, demand, request, or statement of other evidence required or permitted to be given under this Lease must be written and will be sufficiently given if delivered in person to the Landlord or the Tenant, or to an officer of the Landlord or of the Tenant, as the case may be, or mailed in the Province of Manitoba, by registered mail, addressed

  (a) if to the Landlord, as follows:

    <insert address>

  (b) if to the Tenant, as follows:

    <insert address>

A notice, demand, request, statement, or other instrument mailed as aforesaid will be considered to have been given to the party to which it is addressed on the third business day following the date of mailing.

The party at any time may give notice to the other party of a change of its address, and after the giving of the notice the address therein specified will be considered to be the address of the party which gave the notice.

19.05 Amendment to Be in Writing

No alteration, amendment, change, or addition to this Lease will bind the Landlord or the Tenant unless in writing and signed by them.

19.06 Rules and Regulations

The Landlord from time to time may establish, modify, and enforce reasonable rules and regulations regarding the use and occupancy of the premises set aside by the Landlord for leasing to tenants of the Office Complex. All rules and regulations and modifications whether made under this section or Section 8.02 become a part of this Lease and bind the Tenant and the Tenant's default in complying with any such rule or regulation shall be deemed to be a default under this Lease. Notice of the rules and regulations and modifications, if any, will be given to the Tenant by the Landlord. No rule or regulation or modification will contradict a provision of this Lease.

In short-form English: the landlord makes the rules for occupancy on its property and in its building, and the tenant must abide by those rules. Sort of takes one back to childhood and hearing dad say "My house, my rules," doesn't it?

19.07 Rental Net to Landlord

It is the purpose and intent of the Landlord and the Tenant that the rent shall be absolute net to the Landlord so that this Lease shall yield net to the Landlord the annual rent specified in Section 3.03 hereof in each year during the term, without notice or demand, free of any charge, assessment, imposition, or deduction of any kind and without abatement, deduction, or set-off, and under no circumstances or conditions whether now existing or hereinafter arising, or whether beyond the present contemplation of the parties, is the Landlord to be expected or required to make payment of any kind whatsoever or to be under other obligation or liability hereunder except as herein otherwise expressly set forth and all expenses and obligations of every kind and nature whatsoever relating to the premises which may arise or may become due during or out of the term of this Lease shall be paid by the Tenant and the Landlord shall be indemnified and saved harmless by the Tenant from all the costs of same.

Only a lawyer (especially the late John Diefenbaker) would feel satisfied that a 174-word sentence is intelligible. The upshot of this ramble is that the landlord receives the minimum rent each month, no ifs, ands, or buts. The landlord is also protected from paying any other costs attributable to the premises, which are the exclusive responsibility of the tenant, unless specifically noted within the lease (which would be, generally speaking, the landlord's obligations for certain repairs or improvements to the premises).

19.08 Successors and Assigns

This Lease binds and benefits the parties and their respective heirs, executors, administrators, successors, and assigns. No rights, however, benefit an assignee of the Tenant unless under Article 9.01 the assignment was consented to by the Landlord.

19.09 Rider

A rider consisting of 2 pages with paragraphs numbered 20.01 to 20.04 is attached hereto and constitutes an integral part hereof.

IN WITNESS WHEREOF the parties hereto have caused these presents to be executed as of the 16th day of May, A.D., 1999.

COMMERCIAL PROPERTY CORPORATION

_____   Per: _____
Witness   Landlord
                                   c/s

NEW TENANT COMPANY INC.

_____   Per: _____
Witness   Tenant
                                   c/s

Referred to in the attached Lease dated the 16th day of May, 1999, between Commercial Property Corporation, as Landlord, and New Tenant Company Inc., as Tenant.

(To be initialled by both parties for identification purposes.)

The terms that are put into the Rider are specific terms of the deal between the landlord and the tenant that do not generally apply to the overall lease agreement and would not apply to a renewal. They are, however, integral and likely conditional to the tenant's overall "deal" with the landlord and are therefore attached to the lease document.

20.01 Rent Abatement

Notwithstanding anything to the contrary herein contained, a portion of paragraph 3.03 rent in the amount of three thousand three hundred ninety-seven dollars and fifty cents ($3,397.50) per month, shall be abated during and in respect of that period commencing on the 1st day of June, 1999 and ending on the 30th day of November, 1999, for a total rent abatement of twenty thousand three hundred eighty-five dollars and zero cents ($20,385.00). Paragraph 3.03 rent reserved herein shall, during the aforesaid six (6) Months of the Term of this Lease and in respect thereof only, be reduced accordingly.

Not infrequently a landlord will agree to a rent abatement—perhaps as an incentive or to compensate for something—in negotiation of the lease. It is one-time and does not change the actual lease term, rent, or conditions. So it is properly part of the rider to the lease. This same logic applies to leasehold improvements as indicated in 20.02, below.

20.02 Leasehold Improvements

It is hereby agreed and understood by both parties that the Landlord shall contribute a one time only allowance toward Leasehold improvements in the demised premises. The Leasehold improvements as detailed in drawings submitted by the Tenant will be completed by a contractor mutually agreed to by the Tenant and the Landlord and under the supervision of the Landlord.

20.03 Parking

The Landlord hereby gives and grants to the Tenant the exclusive right to use 4 parking stalls at the rate of seventy-five dollars ($75.00) per stall, per month, PROVIDED THAT the Landlord shall have the right to adjust the monthly rental rate and relocate any or all of these stalls upon thirty (30) days' written notice to the tenant.

Again, the permission to use or rent parking spaces at a predetermined and periodically amended rate is part of the lease deal but not the actual leasehold itself.

20.04 Relocation Allowance

It is hereby agreed and understood by both parties that the Landlord shall contribute a one time only allowance of eighteen thousand dollars and zero cents ($18,000.00). Payment of this relocation allowance shall be made by the Landlord to the Tenant by way of abated minimum rent. The Landlord and Tenant therefor agree that inclusive of and together with the rental abatement provided for in paragraph 20.01 hereof, the Tenant's obligation to pay basic rent to the Landlord in accordance with paragraph 3.03 hereof shall not commence until December lst, 1999, and shall be in the amount of six thousand three hundred ninety-seven dollars and fifty cents ($6,397.50).

This paragraph is very similar to 20.01 except that it is explicitly for the purpose of providing an incentive for the tenant to relocate. Its form—abatement or otherwise—and timing can be anything the landlord and tenant agree upon to make the lease deal.

<Schedule "A">
<Schedule "B">

As mentioned earlier, under paragraph 2.01, two Schedules would normally be attached to the lease, and they would appear here. They are specific descriptions and drawings for a property being leased, and have not been included. For your purposes, however, you would want to make sure that the Schedules are accurate and complete.

Chapter 9
Insurance Contracts

Commercial Building, Equipment and Stock, and General Liability

Almost everybody, by the time he or she has completed high school, has a rudimentary understanding of what insurance is all about. If nothing else, we understand that if we enroll and pay a small price, for a certain period we will be compensated financially for any loss that is insured, be it for health or life loss, or property loss.

The details of how insurance works are not much more difficult to grasp. In fact, as most of us know after dealing with an insurer once or twice, the basics of how the insurance business operates can be boiled down to one sentence. Pooled money collected from relatively small insurance premiums paid in by the many participants (insureds) provides a capital base to pay out the loss claims of the unfortunate few who suffer during the period of insurance coverage. How the insurance company makes money is by the magic of mathematics and investment. In other words, they mathematically calculate the likelihood and dollar value of claims being paid out in a given period, and offset it against insurance premiums to be paid in. Investment of those incoming premiums in the capital markets generates additional income. If they have guessed correctly and pay out less than they have taken in, a surplus builds to cover those times when the insurance company has guessed badly. It is not completely unlike playing the odds at a roulette wheel or craps table.

We should be careful to distinguish between the concept of insurance and the *business* of insurance as carried out by companies acting as intermediaries in the process.

For instance, one can *self-insure*, a process by which a pool of capital is set aside by a business to cover its potential losses or costs for some given purpose. Assume that we installed a very expensive computer system in a highly volatile location—like Bosnia—and could not obtain insurance coverage at an even remotely reasonable price because of the high probability of loss or damage. We would be obliged, if we were thinking, to set aside a pool of capital to effectively "insure" ourselves that we were prepared and could replace the computer system immediately. With each ensuing period of our own contribution to and no payout by our insurance fund, the internal "liability" cost obviously (1) decreases and (2) accrues to us as a gain on our insurance program.

We could get together with others and set up our own insurance program. Each of us that belonged to the "Self-Insuring Consultants of Canada" could contribute to a fund that would be available to cover any liability claims made upon any one of us. The trouble with this program is that because we basically (I suspect) have no clue as to how such an insurance program could best be run, we encounter the dual risks of (1) requiring of each participant an onerous premium and (2) having our fund wiped out by one claim and not having enough to cover further claims by other participants.

The upshot of these preceding descriptions is that the process of insurance and insuring does not require the participation of a proper insurance company any more than a blackjack game requires a casino. On the other hand, the insurance company is an intermediary that makes insurance more affordable by doing several things.

1. It brings a larger number of policyholders to the program, diversifying risks and costs further.
2. It amasses larger dollar volumes from premiums that are professionally invested to further offset risk payouts.
3. It more accurately and scientifically calculates the risk/reward probabilities and can lower premiums by better "working the odds."

I am sure insurance companies provide more benefit to the insurance process, but this seems like a good argument in their favour already.

If my example in the previous paragraphs seemed oversimplified, it was so by design, because the proper operation of an insurance company, given a fairly competitive environment, is much too complicated to get into here. Insurers must operate close to the margin for the most part; otherwise, premiums grow out of line and the insurer is quickly out of business. A more significant and readily controllable part of the insurer's business is establishing what constitutes valid claims (what will be paid on), what is excluded (what will not be paid on), limits of insurance, and the likelihood of having to pay on claims (actuarial science). It stands to reason that the older and more experienced the insurance business (individually or as an industry), the better its "guessing" ability.

Generally speaking, although an insurance policy is between the insurer (the insurance company) and the insured (you), one usually has to work through or with other parties in obtaining and collecting on an insurance policy. The *insurance agent* is the entity from whom one obtains insurance. The agent acts on behalf of the insurer and has agency authority to bind the insurer to the policy. An *insurance broker*, on the other hand, has traditionally worked on behalf of the party seeking insurance to advise on matters such as coverage requirements and then to seek the best insurer to meet those needs. In practice, the agent and broker are often one and the same.

Eventually, if you "win" the insurance lottery and have to make a claim, you will have to deal with an *insurance adjuster*. This person is either an employee of or contracted by the insurance company to determine if the claimed loss is covered by the insurance, and, if so, to what extent. As a matter of course, the insurance adjuster is usually the face associated with the worst part of insurance, because more often than not his or her job is perceived to limit the payout by denying claims.

COMMON AND PARTICULAR FEATURES OF INSURANCE CONTRACTS

Before going any further, you need to know that insurance policy contracts were written in the late 18th century by legal gnomes. Their primary purpose in writing the contract was to make it completely unintelligible to the lay person. That tradition has been carried forward to the present and will likely continue forever. Nobody—not the lawyers, the insurers, the agents, the courts—really knows what an insurance document says. In point of fact, nobody has the patience to follow the trail of exclusions and exceptions to exclusions, and even exceptions to the exceptions to the exclusions, long enough to finally arrive at the final contractual word on any matter. I would expect that the vast majority of claims and settlements are the result of one of two scenarios. Imagine the two following scenes.

1. General Douglas McArthur, aboard the *Missouri*, with the Japanese. You guess who represents whom in an insurance claim.
2. Rocky Balboa and Apollo Creed settling at the end of the original *Rocky* movie.

Seriously, insurance contracts are exceptionally hard for anyone to follow, because of their continual references to other parts of the document and the "nested" nature of the exceptions and exclusions. My advice to you is that you become basically familiar with the document *in principle* and then have specific interpretations provided by experts. Had I not included this type of contract in this book, I would never have read my own insurance contracts twice (at least until I made a claim that was disputed). Assuming that you do want to understand it better, and want to have an insurance contract interpreted into common terms, I have done what I can. What follows, before getting into the examples, is an overview of what generally constitutes an insurance document.

FUNDAMENTALS OF INSURANCE CONTRACTS

There are five fundamental parts to any insurance contract. They are:

1. *Risk covered*
The insurance contract specifies those risks that are covered for loss, but more so those that are excluded from coverage.

2. *Value of coverage*

The contract will stipulate a maximum payout value for any one-time, possibly aggregate, and various other claim payouts.

3. *Term of coverage*

An insurance contract has a fixed and specified duration, usually a year, during which the insurer takes the risk of paying out on a valid claim for loss.

4. *Premium for coverage*

The premium is the fixed payment (consideration) required for the insured party to obtain the benefits and obligations provided/undertaken by the insurer.

5. *Payee*

Every contract of insurance provides for the *beneficiary* of a loss payment. This may be the insured, or as we have seen with other contracts in this book (lease and loan), another party altogether. For instance, it is a little impractical to make the insured party under a life insurance contract the payee. (The payout would go to the estate, but my point stands.)

In addition to these fundamentals, insurance contracts have some special features unique to the industry. Most of these are provided for in the applicable legislation(s) for each province. Nevertheless, we will consider them briefly now.

SPECIAL FEATURES OF INSURANCE CONTRACTS

Offer and Acceptance

The operative rule here is that an insurance company rarely if ever makes an offer, even if it prepares and sends a policy proposal or renewal to you. These documents are generally—inference from past practice between the parties notwithstanding—*invitations to treat* (see Chapter 1) and turn into offers when the prospective insured makes an offer to purchase the insurance from the insurance company on the terms and conditions of the proposal. The offer is accepted by the insurer at different times depending on the type of insurance in question:

- Life insurance is usually accepted when the policy is delivered *and* the first premium is paid.
- Property insurance (including liability and other property insurance) can be accepted by the insurer's agent upon signing and providing the policy. The premium may be paid after the insurance kicks in. The agent can provide a *binder* which will give the insured protection from the time the insurance request was made and agreed to orally.

Legality

There are two parts to the issue of "legality" of the insurance. First, the insured act cannot be contrary to law or public policy. For example, deliberately creating a situation where insurance is to be paid out is not legal (e.g., "planned lightning"). Nor, for that matter, is murdering a person on whom one has an insurance policy and then claiming on it. That is not to say this type of *insurance fraud* does not happen. Rather, the insurer is not obliged under such circumstances.

Second, the beneficiary of the insurance policy must have an *insurable interest* in the property or life (the *"object"*) being insured. In other words, there must be a definable element of loss on the part of the insured if the object of the insurance were to be damaged, die, etc. Insurable interest is complex and hard to generalize about, but for the most part we can say that the insurable interest must exist at the time the insurance contract is formed. In the case of property insurance, the insurable interest must also exist when the claim (and therefore loss) arises. After all, if there is no loss there is no reason for payout to compensate for loss. For life insurance, however, there need not be an insurable interest in the person when that insured person dies. (Consider when a company takes out life insurance on its key managers; or if a husband insures his spouse who dies after they have been separated. In both instances, if the insurance contract is still in force the payout would likely be made.)

Terms of Contract

Life insurance contracts, as mentioned above, are governed by and subject to rigorously and fully developed statutes in each province. Beyond this, the courts tend to interpret insurance contract disputes in opposition to the insurer, because the insurance policy is a standard-form contract (see Chapter 1) and skewed in favour of the insurer. In effect, the court attempts to even out application of the terms so as to be more "reasonable."

Two other factors generally arise in the terms of the contract that, while not exclusive to insurance, are more important than they might be in other contracts. First, the insurance contract demands as much or more than any other contractual relationship that both parties show *utmost good faith* in their dealings. The essence of this term is to ensure that information between the parties—information upon which decisions are based—is accurate; it tries to ferret out the "technical accuracies" that could alter the insurance decision. Second, the insurance contract requires immediate and prompt notice by the insured of any new factors or circumstances that would materially alter the insurance risk situation. The insurer is bound to provide prompt notice to the insured of changes to the policy and coverage.

Assignment

In principle, as it relates to the insured, property insurance may not be assigned without the insurer's consent. Most often the contract will be brought to an end and a new contract created to replace it, a process called novation. The *benefit* from an existing claim on a property insurance policy may, however, be assigned by the insured without the insurer's consent. Similarly, the benefit of a life insurance policy—particularly one with a cash value—may be assigned by the insured without the insurer's consent. For instance, a company may pledge the life insurance it holds on a key manager as collateral for a loan credit.

Subrogation

Subrogation, as we've noted elsewhere in this book, is the right of the insurer to "step into the shoes" of the insured. Its purpose is to allow the insurer to make a claim against a liable party on losses for which it has already paid out an insurance claim. The purpose of this clause is to override the insured's lack of interest in prosecuting a liable party after it has been compensated by an insurance payout. For instance, say your neighbour smashes your neon sign. You make a claim to the insurance company, which pays out the damage. Chances are you won't pursue the liable party—your neighbour—too far. Your insurer will be glad to do so, though.

As a general principle of insurance law, the insurer that has made a payment on a claim can subrogate the claim and sue the liable party (your neighbour in the example above) for compensation. By this method, the insurer can place the financial burden where it properly should rest, and reconstitute its funds for the payment of future claims.

Co-Insurance

Intuitively, this could refer to two or more insurers providing insurance on an insured object, and in practice, if one stretches the imagination, this is exactly what co-insurance is. The important thing to remember is that, generally speaking, the co-insurer is the *insured*. Basically a co-insurance clause will set out a minimum value (often as a percentage of property value) for which a property must be insured; otherwise, the insured will share with the insurer any losses that occur. The idea behind this term is to make those obtaining a policy insure for total value rather than scrimping on premiums by only insuring part of the property's value. Absence of this clause would have particular effect in the case of fire insurance, since often only part of the total property is damaged by fire and there is strong economic incentive to insure for only a portion of the property's overall value.

COMMERCIAL PROPERTY (Building, Equipment, and Stock) INSURANCE

Most business people, when they are asked about commercial insurance, will think of property insurance. It is the hard, visible assets of the business that are being insured by this type of insurance. Optically, at least, property insurance appears to be more common and necessary. Other kinds of insurance, as mentioned earlier or addressed specifically later in this chapter, are equally common. Yet, regardless of whether businesses maintain liability insurance, directors and officers insurance, or any other type, odds are property insurance of one form or another is in their risk-reduction mix.

The first insurance contract we will examine is a typical commercial building, equipment, and stock broad form as provided by the Insurance Council of Canada. This form, along with the liability insurance form that follows, is prepared by the Council as a guideline for its members and for insurers in general. Most insurance forms, regardless of the insurer, will have the bulk of the components included here. Bear in mind, as you read through the form and the comments attached to it, that the content of a specific contract may be different from that presented here. If you have any doubts about the meaning of your own policy contract, consult the agent or attorney.

Commercial Building, Equipment, and Stock Broad Form

Indemnity Agreement

1. In the event that any of the property insured be lost or damaged by the perils insured against, the Insurer will indemnify the Insured against the direct loss so caused to an amount not exceeding whichever is the least of:
    (a) the actual cash value of the property at the time of loss or damage;
    (b) the interest of the Insured in the property;
    (c) the amount of insurance specified on the "Declarations Page" in respect of the property lost or damaged.
    Provided, however, that where the insurance applies to the property of more than one person or interest, the Insurer's total liability for loss sustained by all such persons and interests shall be limited in the aggregate to the amount or amounts of insurance specified on the "Declarations Page."

The primary (perhaps, only) obligation of the insurer is to *indemnify* (i.e., save harmless) the insured within the limits of the insurance during the period that the insurance is in effect for specific losses or damages. This paragraph provides that covenant, including the nature and value of the indemnity. Notably, the insurer will always pay, for any proper claim, the least of the values indicated in this paragraph. The insured will never recover more than the actual cash value of the property insured (point (a)), the insured's interest—worth—in the property (point (b)), or the limit of the insurance purchased by the insured from the insurer (point (c)). Also, the last part of the paragraph provides the caveat that the insurer will pay out a maximum value equal to that listed on the declarations page for any property jointly owned. See the box on this page for a discussion of the declarations page.

For property insurance, this makes eminent sense, because, unlike life insurance, there would be too great an incentive to defraud if one could be paid out more than the total value of, or the value of the insured's interest in, the insured property. In the case of life insurance, there is no set, definable value on a life ("Well, sir, we've seen people of similar make and quality to the deceased available at retail—marked down, mind you—for only $350,000, so I'm sorry, we can't pay out insurance in a sum greater than that"), so the payment of the premium is the key determining factor of how much will be paid out on a valid claim. Fortunately, we are not examining life insurance here.

The Declarations Page: Heart of the Policy

Every insurance policy has a cover page known as the "Declarations," which, not surprisingly, is where everything is declared. It contains all the pertinent information about the insurance policy being contracted. Moreover, it comprises the information you have provided to the insurer's agent for the purpose of their calculating the premium and providing the policy. Because this information is the basis upon which the insurance is provided, its accuracy is warranted by you and is a condition of the contract. At various points in an insurance contract you will find language to that effect. Thus, if the information is inaccurate, or plainly false, there is cause for the insurer to not provide complete coverage as contemplated by the policy. Let's assume that you always provide to the insurer complete and accurate information to the best of your knowledge.

Generally speaking, the information required to complete the declarations page includes the following:

1. The name of the insurer and its authorized agent/broker.
2. The policy number and the number of the policy it is replacing, if any, for reference.
3. The name and address of the insured.
4. The start and end period of the policy contract.
5. Details about the nature of the building property(ies) being insured (e.g., construction, etc.) plus the commercial and other use of those premises.
6. Details of any additional loss payees for some or all of the insurance coverage. (Remember, lessors and lenders often insist upon being a named loss payee for insurance on leased/mortgaged properties.)
7. A list of riders and the coverage being provided for various types of insurance being contracted, including property, burglary, liability, and other miscellaneous insurance. In this section are specified the deductibles, co-insurance percentages, insured amounts (the maximum payable "limit"), and the premium applicable to each coverage separately or in aggregate.

Property Insured

2.A. This form insures the following property but only those items for which an amount of insurance is specified on the "Declarations Page":

> "BUILDING"
> "EQUIPMENT"
> "STOCK"

> The insurance in this Clause 2.A. applies only while at the location(s) specified on the "Declarations Page."

Generally, property insurance is always purchased for *equipment* (see the definition of the term at Section 19(c)), and then depending on the type of business being insured and the circumstances of the insurance required, the *building* and *stock* may be also insured. For example, a tenant will obtain tenant's insurance as required for the leased premises but likely not property insurance on the actual building. In any event, note that this paragraph is the general description of the coverage, and it pertains to (1) only those properties listed on the declarations page, and (2) only at the locations specified on the declarations page.

The "Floater"

"So it says in the paragraph(s) that list the coverage provided that only those items listed on the declarations page will be covered to the limit of the insurance attached to them on that page. Surely one is not expected to list every stapler and cell phone battery." Quite right. Not only would it be Pythonesquely absurd, but completely impractical for all parties. Insurers understand that not everything can be listed, and that all those unlisted properties are intended to be insured within the context of the policy. The solution is the "floater" rider, which is, for lack of better description, a catchall equipment or stock insurance coverage that implies something to the effect of "You have a variety of miscellaneous properties, the listing of which would kill all of us in administration time and expense. So, you tell us how many dollars of that kind of property you have and wish to insure, and we will put it into the 'floater' bucket and attach a premium for that maximum insurable value."

Thus, everything is insured without extensive listing. The catch is that the deductible applies to all claims, and in order to collect on the loss or damage of unlisted properties there would have to be an "occurrence" of an insured peril. Furthermore, you would have to then list the miscellaneous properties (with values) that were lost or damaged. The adjuster would then determine in his or her infinite wisdom whether your listed properties were (1) valid equipment, and (2) worth what you say.

The same sort of principle applies to various classes of property. For example, an office computer package may be affixed as a rider to property insurance. It provides specific coverage and conditions applicable to computer and data processing equipment being insured.

In short, all properties, even if they are not specifically listed, are usually covered.

2.B. This form also insures "equipment" and "stock" but only those items for which an amount of insurance is specified on the "Declarations Page":

TEMPORARY LOCATIONS: "Equipment" and "stock" other than at a specified location except while in transit, but there shall be no liability under this item at any location owned, rented, or controlled in whole or in part by the Insured.

NEWLY ACQUIRED LOCATION: "Equipment" and "stock" at any acquired location that is owned, rented, or controlled by the Insured in whole or in part or in or on vehicles within 100 metres of such location. This limit of insurance attaches at the time of the acquisition and extends for a period of thirty (30) days or to the date of endorsement of this form adding such location, whichever first occurs.

PARCEL POST: "Equipment" and "stock" in any one package in course of transit by parcel post.

OTHER TRANSIT: "Equipment" and "Stock," in transit other than by parcel post.

SALES REPRESENTATIVE: "Equipment" and "Stock," whether in transit or otherwise, in the custody of a sales representative of the Insured.

The insurance in this Clause 2.B. applies only while the described property is within Canada and the continental United States of America (excluding Alaska).

Although the first line of this paragraph appears redundant behind the preceding paragraph, 2.A., except for the notable omission of building insurance, paragraph 2.B has a specific important difference. This paragraph applies to insured properties being covered at a location other than that/those listed on the declarations page. Paragraph 2.A applies only where the insured properties are on-site. The global limitation in this sample, after the specific off-site locations are described, is that the insurance coverage is geographically limited to Canada and the continental United States excluding Alaska. Overseas travellers would require a different rider or endorsement to ensure that the property was covered at their destination. The extents of coverage, as listed, may or may not be included depending on the insurance coverage being purchased.

The specific off-site coverage and exclusionary circumstances noted above are as understandable as any other part of the contract. Presumably if one or more of these clauses were to appear in your policy it/they would be accompanied by insurance limits as well. Be aware of the following nonetheless:

- The coverage under "temporary locations" applies at any location other than those specified on the declarations page *except* if the location is controlled by the insured. Essentially, this means that if you move your goods to another location of your own that is not listed and insured, the "equipment" and "stock" property is not insured either. The phrase "except while in transit" may have more meaning if the coverage of "parcel post" and "other transit," below, are omitted.
- The insurer provides a coverage grace period of 30 days over a new property, within which time the insured must obtain an endorsement that adds the new location to the coverage. Otherwise, equipment and stock at the new location is not covered.
- "Equipment" and "stock" are covered while in transit either by parcel post (PARCEL POST paragraph) or by any other form of transit (OTHER TRANSIT paragraph), which presumably includes common and private carriers.
- The insurance policy could be purchased to cover the insured property when it is off-site in the possession of a sales representative on business.

Deductible

3. The Insurer is liable for the amount by which the loss or damaged caused by any of the perils insured against exceeds the amount of the deductible specified on the "Declarations Page" in any one occurrence.

The deductible payable on any loss claim is listed for each rider on the declarations page. This clause provides that the insurer is obliged to pay the excess of the loss over the deductible value. This is the legal language for the well-known "deductible" requirement on insurance claims.

Co-Insurance

4. This clause applies separately to each item for which a co-insurance percentage is specified on the "Declarations Page" and only where the total loss exceeds the lesser of 2% of the applicable amount of insurance or $5,000.

Recall from the earlier discussion of co-insurance that the insurer stipulates a level of insurance required to be in place on any property; otherwise, the insured shares the loss burden with the insurer. The co-insurance level is derived as a percentage of the actual cash value of the insured property. This part of the paragraph deals with the threshold value that triggers the co-insurance clause. On properties where co-insurance would otherwise be applicable according to this clause, if the loss is less than *the lesser of* 2% of the property's value or $5,000, the co-insurance clause does not apply. For example, say there is a co-insurance clause of 80% applicable to a property, the actual value of which is $200,000, which sustains a loss valued at $3,500. Where ordinarily there may be a co-insurance requirement of the insured for loss on this property, because the loss is less than $4,000 (the lesser of $5,000 and 2% of $200,000), the co-insurance clause does not apply.

> The Insured shall maintain insurance concurrent with this form on the property insured to the extent of at least the amount produced by multiplying the actual cash value of the property by the co-insurance percentage specified on the "Declarations Page," and failing so to do, shall only be entitled to recover that portion of any loss that the amount of insurance in force at the time of loss bears to the amount of insurance required to be maintained by this clause.

This second part of the co-insurance clause specifies the requirement for the insured to maintain insurance on individual properties to a minimum level as established by the co-insurance rate and the cash value of the property. The paragraph goes on further to specify the co-insurance consequences that will befall the insured that does not insure to such a level for each property.

To continue the earlier example, if the property in question had a $200,000 value and the co-insurance coefficient is 80%, the insured *must* insure that property for at least $160,000. If not, the insured will be exposed to the co-insurance requirement. Assume the insurance on the property was $140,000, triggering a co-insurance requirement from the insured. If there is damage to the property in excess of the threshold amounts above (say $100,000 in damage occurred), the insurer would be obliged to pay only the portion of the $100,000 cost equal to the proportion of the *insurance in force* to the *minimum insurance required* (i.e., the insurer would be liable for only the fraction equal to $140,000 of $160,000, or 87.5% of the claim's cost—$87,500 in this example). The balance would be the responsibility of the insured.

Perils Insured

5. This form, except as herein provided, insures against all risks of direct physical loss of or damage to the property insured.

What we have here is known, in the vernacular, as "the big print." Notice how, on first blush, this clause would seem to indicate that all risks of direct physical loss of or damage to the property are insured. Whatever you do when going over your insurance policy contract, do not stop reading here because the next things to come are the . . .

Exclusions

"What the big print giveth, the small print here taketh away." Although every insurance contract is different, notice how in this particular sample the broad coverage description contains (by the most generous calculation) 874 words but the exclusions run to 1,700 words. Insurance is an exclusionary process, probably the result of learning by costly experience.[1] Different exclusions apply depending on the nature of the insurance being provided. Generally, exclusions are made because the occurrence of each such type of property loss or peril is possibly (1) not suitably predictable mathematically, (2) very expensive, or (3) prohibitively expensive and would drive overall premiums up unless separated into its own coverage type and purchased only by those who need that kind of coverage. (What we are talking about in the last case is really product customization and marketing.) Bear in mind that to stay in business an insurance company must consistently receive more premium revenue than it pays out in claim expense, and that when premiums get out of line the company loses business to the competition.

Property Excluded

6.A. This form does not insure loss of or damage to:

(a) sewers, drains, or watermains located beyond the outside bearing walls or foundations of the property insured, outside communication towers, antennae (including satellite receivers) and equipment attached thereto, street clocks, exterior signs, exterior glass or vitrolite and lettering or ornamentation thereon, but this exclusion does not apply to loss or damage caused directly by "Named Perils";

The consistency here is that the properties are either outside the bounds of the premises being insured or are exterior fixtures and appurtenances. The last phrase is the first significant instance of an exception to an exclusion, which should mean an "inclusion." Essentially, all those items noted in this paragraph should be covered if the loss or damage is the direct result of a "Named Peril." In order to establish what that might be, we need to follow the bouncing ball to Section 19(i).

(b) property at locations which to the knowledge of the Insured, are vacant, unoccupied, or shut down for more than thirty (30) consecutive days;

Obviously you cannot "abandon" property and still expect to have it covered by insurance.

(c) electrical devices, appliances, or wiring caused by artificially generated electrical currents, including arcing, unless fire or explosion as described in Clause 19(i) ensues and then only for such ensuing loss or damage;

That means, as I understand it, that an electrical short caused by overloading or other mechanical problem is not covered unless it results in a fire or explosion (of the specific kind permitted under Section 19(i)). Lightning and the effect of lightning on electrical systems is not artificially generated, and is therefore presumably included.

(d) growing plants, trees, shrubs, or flowers, all while in the open except as provided in the Extensions of Coverage Clause 7(e);

Interestingly, this clause *ex*cludes while the referred-to clause 7(e) *in*cludes. Clause 7(e), however, puts a limit on the insurance payable with regard to these growing plants.

(e) animals, fish, or birds, but this exclusion does not apply to loss or damage caused directly by "Named Perils" or from theft or attempt threat;

Once the language is distilled, this paragraph means "we will cover the animals if they are killed [or damaged?] by fire, lightning, an allowable explosion, or an attempt, successful or not, to steal them. If the animals are killed by a cause that is anything else, such as natural causes or industrial accidents, we will not cover it."

(f) bullion, platinum, and other precious metals and alloys, securities, stamps, tickets and tokens, evidence of debt or title;

Negotiable securities, legal tender, and precious metals are not insurable in most instances. (Perhaps because of the ease with which they can be converted: "Oh sure…uh, we actually had 58,000 twenties in the filing cabinet. Er . . . well, we always keep a good float on Tuesdays.")

(g) automobiles, watercraft, amphibious or air cushion vehicles, aircraft, spacecraft, trailers, motors, or other accessories attached to or mounted on such property, but this exclusion shall not apply to watercraft, amphibious or air cushion vehicles held for sale, unlicensed automobiles, or unlicensed trailers used in the business of the Insured when on the "premises" of the Insured;

So you need to have a special rider for the space shuttle you keep in the inventory warehouse. (All of these excluded properties could probably be insured under a separate policy, if required. Notice, however, that if the otherwise excluded motor vehicles are unlicensed and part of your asset base, they are covered, and if the watercraft etc. are inventory for sale they are covered.)

(h) furs, fur garments, jewels, jewellery, costume jewellery, watches, pearls, precious and semi-precious stones, and pre-recorded video tapes but this exclusion does not apply to:
  (i) first one thousand dollars ($1,000) of any loss insured herein;
  (ii) any loss or damage caused directly by "Named Perils";

Similarly to the situation with the animals, the insurer is only insuring these items for damage from those Named Perils, and not from damage as created by attempt at theft or vandalism. But sub-paragraph (i) would seem to permit you to claim $1,000 of any loss of any items otherwise excluded by this paragraph.

(i) property insured under the terms of any Marine Insurance, and property while waterborne, except while on a regular ferry or railway car transfer in connection with land transportation;

Marine insurance is an entirely different animal from property insurance, and it is required for any transit overseas. The property insurance contemplated here applies to transit over water as part of a land route (e.g., in a container car on the Victoria-Vancouver ferry en route to Edmonton).

(j) property on loan or on rental or sold by the Insured under conditional sale, installment payment, or other deferred payment plan, from the time of leaving the Insured's custody, but this exclusion does not apply while such property is in the custody of a carrier for hire for the purpose of delivery at the risk of the Insured;

This particular paragraph returns us to the contract of sale and the matter of ownership and responsibility. When a sale is made, or the property is put into another's possession for rent, the property is not insured because it is effectively the other's (purchaser or lessee) responsibility. If the goods remain the responsibility of the insured while being transported, the insurance is in force.

(k) property in the custody of a sales representative outside the "premises" of the Insured, unless an amount of insurance is shown on the "Declarations Page" pertaining to "Sales Representative";

The important word in this paragraph is "unless." If there is a specified amount of insurance attributable to "Sales Representative" on the declarations page (see clause 2.B.), this clause is inoperative.

(l) property illegally acquired, kept, stored, or transported; property seized or confiscated for breach of any law or by order of any public authority;

We have seen this before in other situations. Enough said.

(m) (i) any pressure vessel having normal internal working pressure greater than 103 kilopascals (15 pounds per square inch) above atmospheric pressure;

    (ii) any boiler, including the piping and equipment connected thereto, which contains steam or water under steam pressure (except tanks having an internal diameter of 610 millimetres (24 inches) or less used for the storage of hot water for domestic use);

caused directly or indirectly by explosion, rupture, bursting, cracking, burning out or bulging of such property while connected ready for use, but this exclusion does not apply to:

    (1) manually portable gas cylinders;

    (2) explosion of natural, coal, or manufactured gas;

    (3) explosion of gas or unconsumed fuel within a furnace or within the gas passages therefrom to the atmosphere.

This exclusion, which would appear to apply to larger, say "industrial-quality," pressurized containers that in most cases would constitute larger natural gas fittings and boilers or such, could be important if such equipment were integral to your business or property. Because it is not "normal" for basic business coverage, one would obtain a rider or endorsement for such properties that could be added to the policy, along with an increased premium, if such coverage were required. Note that the exclusion excepts portable gas canisters (point (1)), and explosions that are actually Named Perils (point (2)), and for other specific explosions (point (3)).

Perils Excluded

6.B. This form does not insure against loss or damage caused directly or indirectly:

(a) by earthquake, except for ensuing loss or damage which results directly from fire, explosion, smoke, or leakage from fire protective equipment, all as described in Clause 19(i);

Consider yourself not covered in the event of an earthquake, but be happily rewarded if, after an earthquake, the loss or damage is actually caused by those things noted after the word "except" above.

(b) by flood, including waves, tides, tidal waves, tsunamis, or the rising, the breaking out, or the overflow of, any body of water, whether natural or man-made, but this exclusion does not apply to ensuing loss or damage which results directly from fire, explosion, smoke, leakage from fire protective equipment, all as described in Clause 19(i) or leakage from a watermain;

See my comments to the immediately preceding paragraph, but the hope should apply to everything following the word "but" above. Additionally, damage caused by leakage from a water main is covered.

Exclusions (a) and (b) do not apply to property in transit;

This is most interesting, because it essentially says that if you are covered for property in transit, then would be the best time to be the subject of earthquake or tidal/water-caused loss because the properties are covered when they are moving.

(c) (i) by seepage, leakage, or influx of water derived from natural sources through basement walls, doors, windows, or other openings therein, foundations, basement floors, sidewalks, sidewalk lights, or by the backing up of sewers, sumps, septic tanks, or drains, unless concurrently and directly caused by a peril not otherwise excluded in Clause 6.B. hereof;

Figuring out what might be permissible in this instance, looking for a peril not otherwise excluded that might lend itself to the creation of damage by water "derived from natural sources," could keep us awake for a while. On the other hand, if a water main were to break, flooding one part of the property and causing sewers and sumps to back up into another part of the insured property, that damage should be covered.

> (ii) by the entrance of rain, sleet, or snow through doors, windows, skylights, or other similar wall or roof openings unless through an aperture concurrently and directly caused by a peril not otherwise excluded in Clause 6.B. hereof;

Precipitation that comes inside because of your negligence in keeping it out is not covered. On the other hand, if it comes in through a hole created by some other peril that is included—say lightning—then the damage is claimable.

> (d) by centrifugal force, mechanical or electrical breakdown, or derangement in or on the "premises," unless fire ensues and then only for the loss or damage caused directly by such ensuing fire;

Ignoring the matter of centrifugal force, the operative issue here is that mechanical breakdowns or "blowouts" (e.g., the lathe caught on something and sent hunks of metal spinning out of control around the room) are not covered unless, of course, fire ensues. Then one would have to argue about whether the damaged property was fire-damaged (as it may very well be) or if it was damaged *first* by the excluded peril, which one would guess then renders it no longer covered by insurance.[2]

> (e) dampness or dryness of atmosphere, changes of temperature, contamination, freezing, heating, shrinkage, evaporation, loss of weight, leakage of contents, exposure to light, change in colour or texture or finish, rust or corrosion, marring, scratching, or crushing, but this exclusion does not apply to loss or damage caused directly by "Named Perils," rupture of pipes or breakage of apparatus not excluded under paragraph (m) of Clause 6.A hereof, theft or attempt thereat, or accident to transporting conveyance. Damage to pipes caused by freezing is insured provided such pipes are not excluded in paragraph (m) of Clause 6.A hereof;

The first part of this paragraph says that the insurer will not indemnify for *common*, normal business risks to holding inventory and stock, or using property. The latter part, in its own convoluted way, says that if the damage as contemplated in the first part of the paragraph is the result of a Named Peril the exclusion does not apply. Furthermore, damage to and caused by pipes and piping perils that are not specifically excluded in Section 6.A(m)—regarding pressurized vessels—including freezing of pipes is included. The mention of theft and accident to transporting conveyance (how about just "vehicle"?) would likely refer to the last few perils listed in the first part of the paragraph (i.e., "marring," etc.).

> (f) by smoke from agricultural smudging or industrial operations;
> (g) by rodents, insects, or vermin, but this exclusion does not apply to loss or damage caused directly by a peril not otherwise excluded in Clause 6.B. hereof;

If a bunch of rats got under the hood of your truck and ate away the wiring, the damage would not be covered. But consider this: Lightning strikes your truck sitting at the end of the lot late one Friday night. The force of the lightning throws the truck's doors open. During the ensuing weekend, rats and mice and other "vermin" pile into the vehicle, and chew away the wiring, seat covers, and the chocolate bar in the glove compartment. This might be covered, because it was a result of a peril not excluded. Then again, would the damage *really* be "caused directly by [that] peril not otherwise excluded"? Tough call.

> (h) by delay, loss of market, or loss of use or occupancy;

Business decisions and common risks cannot be indemnified. Say you own a bunch of inventory of your product, whatever that might be, which is really a fashion or fad item. If very suddenly the market disappears for your product, that's not an insurance problem.

    (i) by war, invasion, act of foreign enemy, hostilities (whether war be declared or not), civil war, rebellion, revolution, insurrection, or military power;

    (j) (i) by any nuclear incident as defined in the Nuclear Liability Act or any other nuclear liability act, law, or statute, or any law amendatory thereof or nuclear explosion, except for ensuing loss or damage which results directly from fire, lightning, or explosion of natural, coal, or manufactured gas;

I am going to guess here that in the event that your business (assuming it is not a nuclear facility) is near or subject to a nuclear incident or explosion, that determining whether damage was caused by the ensuing fire (and there would be one, oh yeah) or by the incident or explosion would be a pointless expedition, since there would be a low practical likelihood of finding an answer that went beyond theory. Suffice it to say that if there were a nuclear explosion or incident around which your property is damaged, you should write the whole thing off, because it will result in a lifelong legal wrangle with the insurer. Besides, it's probably not the biggest concern for all those and sundry near the incident or explosion. Which leads us to . . .

    (ii) by contamination of radioactive material;

This is more of a liability issue for the company involved in the explosion or incident than a property insurance matter. Again, suffice it to say that contamination by radioactive material, which is fairly easy to detect, is not covered. You would need a nuclear accident policy. Move on.

    (k) by any dishonest or criminal act on the part of the Insured or any other party or interest, employees or agents of the Insured, or any person to whom the property may be entrusted (bailees for hire excepted), but this exclusion does not apply to physical damage, caused directly by employees of the Insured, which results from a peril otherwise insured and not otherwise excluded under this form;

Think up your own possible situation in which the exclusion might be excepted. Extra points if you can establish how the damage could be caused "*directly* by employees" which results from a peril otherwise insured and not excluded.

    (l) to "buildings" by:

        (i) snowslide, landslide, subsidence, or other earth movement, except for ensuing loss or damage which results directly from fire, explosion, smoke, or leakage from fire protective equipment, all as described in Clause 19(i);

        (ii) explosion (except with respect to explosion of natural, coal, or manufactured gas), collapse, bursting, cracking, burning out, or bulging of the following property owned, operated, or controlled by the Insured, unless fire ensues and then only for the loss or damage caused directly by such ensuing fire:

           a) the portions containing steam or water under steam pressure of all boilers generating steam, and piping or other equipment connected to said boilers and containing steam or water under steam pressure;

           b) piping and apparatus or parts thereof normally containing steam or water under steam pressure from an external source and while under such pressure;

           c) other vessels and apparatus and pipes connected therewith while under pressure, or while in use or in operation provided their maximum normal internal working pressure exceeds 103 kilopascals (15 pounds per square inch) above atmospheric pressure but this exclusion does not apply to loss or damage resulting from the explosion of manually portable gas cylinders or of tanks having an internal diameter of 610 millimetres (24 inches) or less used for the heating and storage of hot water for domestic use;

d) moving or rotating machinery or parts thereof;

e) any vessels and apparatus and pipes connected therewith while undergoing pressure tests but this exclusion does not apply to other property insured hereunder that has been damaged by such explosion;

f) gas turbines;

The entire tedious recitation of exclusions and exceptions in 6.B(l) to this point can all be read similarly to the exclusions we have covered earlier inasmuch as certain perils are excluded as they relate to specifically "building" properties. These exclusions are then modified to except damage or loss caused directly by a Named Peril (Section 19(i)) or some derivative of them. In every instance, possibility for reinclusion is extremely limited.

(iii) settling, expansion, contraction, moving, shifting, or cracking unless concurrently and directly caused by a peril not otherwise excluded in Clause 6.B. hereof;

Fair enough.

(m) proximately or remotely, arising in consequence of or contributed to by the enforcement of any by-law, regulation, ordinance, or law regulating zoning or the demolition, repair, or construction of buildings or structures, which by-law, regulation, ordinance, or law makes it impossible to repair or reinstate the property as it was immediately prior to the loss.

The short-form translation of this text is that the insurance does not cover loss of use or inability to reinstate to the type and form of use and status immediately prior to a change in bylaw, regulation, ordinance, or law. If your area is rezoned and your property has been grandfathered, but after some damage to the property the rezoning prohibits you from repairing the property for the same use (which is now no longer permitted by the zoning change), too bad. Insurance does not cover that loss.

NOR DOES THIS FORM INSURE:

Just in case you had forgotten what was happening. It is, after all, a long ways back to establish that the opening to the list was: "This form does not insure against loss or damage caused directly or indirectly." Besides, the grammatical construction of the ensuing list needed alteration for readability.

(n) wear and tear, gradual deterioration, latent defect, inherent vice, or the cost of making good faulty or improper material, faulty or improper workmanship, faulty or improper design, provided, however, to the extent otherwise insured and not otherwise excluded under this form, resultant damage to the property is insured;

Property that depreciates from normal wear and tear or that is inherently improper is not covered. But damage to that or presumably other property as a result of these defects and such, would be covered—unless otherwise excluded (of course).

(o) mysterious disappearance or shortage of "equipment" or "stock" disclosed on taking inventory;

The operative word here is "mysterious." If equipment or stock is missing following a break-in or move, that would be unfortunate but obvious. When suddenly tracts of inventory are just "missing" ("What happened to them?" "Who knows? They're just gone.") that would be mysterious, and the cynical among us would include fraud as an optional explanation.

(p) loss or damage sustained to "equipment" or "stock" while actually being worked upon and directly resulting therefrom or caused by any repairing, adjusting, or servicing of "equipment" or "stock," unless fire or explosion as described in Clause 19(i) ensues and then only for such ensuing loss or damage;

(q) disturbance or erasure of electronic recordings by electric or magnetic injury except by lightning.

These two paragraphs, (p) and (q), relate to incompetence or accident of stupidity, inability, or negligence. Most insurers have trouble paying to repair committed damage.

Pollution Excluded

6.C. This form does not insure against:

(i.) loss or damage caused directly or indirectly by any actual or alleged spill, discharge, emission, dispersal, seepage, leakage, migration, release, or escape of "pollutants," nor the cost or expense or any resulting "clean up," but this exclusion does not apply:

(i) if the spill, discharge, emission, dispersal, seepage, leakage, migration, release, or escape of "pollutants" is the direct result of a peril not otherwise excluded under this form;

(ii) to loss or damage caused directly by a peril not otherwise excluded under this form;

The effect of this paragraph (6.C(i.) with its sub-clauses) is to set up a broad exclusion from liability arising out of pollutant spills, and then to except that exclusion *if* the pollutant spill is the direct result of, effectively, a Named Peril. A pollution coverage policy would be required to cover these liabilities. All that is taken care of in 6.C(i.)(i). Frankly, to my untrained and obviously ignorant legal eye, 6.C(i.)(ii) does not add anything that is not covered by the sub-paragraph (i).

(ii.) cost or expense for any testing, monitoring, evaluating, or assessing of an actual, alleged, potential, or threatened spill, discharge, emission, dispersal, seepage, leakage, migration, release, or escape of "pollutants."

Pollution testing and monitoring, either before or after a spill, is not a cost covered by the insurance; it is a cost of doing business and avoiding liability. Such costs might be covered under a pollution liability policy.

Extensions of Coverage

7. The following extensions of coverage shall not increase the amounts of insurance applying under this form and are subject to all conditions of this form.

(i.) Removal: If any of the insured property is necessarily removed from the location(s) specified herein to prevent loss or damage or further loss or damage thereto, that part of the insurance under this form that exceeds the amount of the Insurer's liability for any loss already incurred shall, for seven (7) days only, or for the unexpired term of the policy if less than seven (7) days, insure the property removed and any property remaining in the location(s) specified herein in the proportions which the value of the property in each of the respective location(s) bears to the value of the property in them all.

Believe it or not, for me this was the most confusing paragraph in the policy. My read of it, however, is that if you move insured property from the location(s) listed on the declarations page *to protect it from further damage*, the insurer will cover it for a fixed grace period in the following manner.

(1) The Insurer will insure the moved property to a value equal to the limit of insurance less damage already incurred. (See "A.")

(2) The remaining property will have limits set for each uninsured location that are equal to the proportion of remaining insured property (value) at each location relative to all remaining insured property. (See "B.")

A

Limit of insurance	$100,000
Loss already incurred	(20,000)
Remaining limit of insurance	$80,000

B

Uninsured Location	Moved Property Value by Location	Proportion of All Moved Property	Location $ Value Limit
Location A	$60,000	60%	$48,000
Location B	30,000	30%	24,000
Location C	10,000	10%	8,000
Totals	**$100,000**	**100%**	**$80,000**

The grace period for this extension of coverage is seven days or to the end of the policy period, whichever comes sooner, after which time the property must be otherwise insured if it is staying at the "temporary" location or it must be moved back to the listed locations.

(b) (i) Debris Removal: The Insurer will indemnify the Insured for expenses incurred in the removal from the "premises" of debris of the property insured, occasioned by loss or damage to such property, for which loss or damage insurance is afforded under this form.
The amount payable under this extension shall not exceed 25% of the total amount payable for the direct physical loss to property insured plus the amount of the applicable deductible.

If the insurance-covered damage or loss on a property has resulted in debris from that property requiring removal from the premises, the insurer will pay up to an additional 25% of the loss coverage payable toward the removal of that debris. The applicable deductible is required of the insured first.

(ii) Removal of Windstorm Debris: The Insurer will indemnify the Insured for expenses incurred in the removal of debris or other property which is not insured by this form but which has been blown by windstorm upon a location specified on the "Declaration Page."

Cleanup or removal of any other debris a windstorm has blown onto a listed location will be paid for by the insurer. Of course, the general extensions noted in this and the previous sub-clause are modified by what comes next.

Extensions of coverage b(i) and b(ii) do not apply to costs or expenses:
(a) to "clean up" pollutants from land or water; or
(b) for testing, monitoring, evaluating, or assessing of an actual, alleged, potential, or threatened spill, discharge, emission, dispersal, seepage, leakage, migration, release, or escape of "pollutants."
Debris removal expense shall not be considered in the determination of actual cash value for the purpose of applying the Co-insurance Clause.

In the event that the property in question regarding this debris removal matter is a property for which co-insurance is specified, the cost of the debris removal afforded to the Insured by these clauses will not be used in the calculation of the actual cash value of the property (loss). Co-insurance payment will be required from the Insured—if applicable—only on the direct property loss sustained.

(c) Personal Property of Officers and Employees: At the option of the Insured, "equipment" also includes personal property of officers and employees of the Insured. The insurance on such property:
(i) not attach if it is insured by the owner unless the Insured is obliged to insure it or is liable for its loss or damage;
(ii) in any event, limited to a maximum recovery of $250 in respect of any one officer or employee;
(iii) shall apply only to loss or damage occurring at a location specifically described on the "Declarations Page" or included in "Newly Acquired Location."

This policy will cover the equipment of employees and officers to a maximum of $250 payable per person. However, the insurance will only apply if the employer (insured) *must* insure the employee's property or if the properties are not otherwise insured by the employee. Also, it only covers employees' and officers' property while on a listed location.

> (d) "Building" Damage by Theft: This form is extended to insure damage (except by fire) to that part of a "building" occupied by the Insured directly resulting from theft or any attempt thereat and from vandalism or malicious acts committed on the same occasion, provided the Insured is the owner of such "building" or is liable for such damage and the "building" is not otherwise insured hereunder. This extension of cover shall be limited to a maximum recovery of twenty-five hundred dollars ($2,500) in respect of any one loss. Glass and lettering or ornamentation thereon is excluded from this extension.

This particular clause only has effect if the building that has been damaged in a theft attempt, or by vandalism during a theft or theft attempt, is owned by the insured and is not insured under this policy.

> (e) Growing Plants, Trees, Shrubs or Flowers in the Open: This form is extended to insure loss or damage to growing plants, trees, shrubs, or flowers in the open caused directly by "Named Perils" (with the exception of windstorm or hail as described in clause 19 (g)) or from theft or attempt thereat. This extension of coverage shall be limited to a maximum recovery of five hundred dollars ($500) for each growing plant, tree, shrub, or flower in the open including debris removal expense.

This extension is provided in the same way a rider is attached to a contract. It is easier to exclude it (see Section 6.A (d)) and then provide certain limited coverage in an extension.

Permission

8. Permission is hereby granted:
   (a) for other insurance concurrent with this form;
   (b) to make additions, alterations, or repairs;
   (c) to do such work and to keep and use such articles, materials, and supplies in such quantities as are usual or necessary to the Insured's business.

Sometimes an insurance policy will prevent the insured from purchasing other insurance (point (a)). But other insurance may be required to fully insure the property and this policy permits such purchases without effect on this policy. Additionally, an insurance policy is written on properties as they exist; additions, alteration, etc. would change the value of the property (point (b)). Because the insurer usually covers stock and materials by way of an estimated volume or under a floater, it will not know exactly how much of this stock is actually subject to peril. And, as we have seen, most insurers very much like to know in advance what's what and how much of it there is (point (c)). This clause gives the insured a waiver from any inferred or actual prohibition from undertaking any of these acts.

Breach of Condition

9. Where a loss occurs and there has been a breach of condition relating to a matter before the happening of the loss, which breach would otherwise disentitle the Insured from recovery under this form, the breach shall not disentitle the Insured from recovery if the Insured establishes that the loss was not caused or contributed to by the breach of condition or if the breach of condition occurred in any portion of the premises over which the Insured has no control.

Generally speaking, breaching a condition in a contract can be cause for the other party to terminate the contract. In this instance, the insurer allows the breach of a condition on the part of the insured to not affect the indemnity and coverage of a loss. This allowance is subject to the breach being either (1) not material to the loss's occurrence or (2) in a part of the premises over which the insured has no control—perhaps because it is being used by another party.

Reinstatement

10. Loss under any item of this form shall not reduce the applicable amount of insurance.

A loss, and presumably the coverage of that loss by the insurer, will not change the overall coverage provided during the policy period. So, if you were to make a $100,000 claim on a $1,000,000 policy, the next time you had to make a claim during this period the full million dollars would be in effect, *not* just $900,000. The examples and the actual "applicable amounts of insurance" are, of course, subject to the various limits imposed within the policy: each of the occurrence limits, aggregate limits, etc., which are provided on the declarations page.

Subrogation

11. The Insurer, upon making any payment or assuming liability therefore under this form, shall be subrogated to all rights of recovery of the Insured against others and may bring action to enforce such rights. Notwithstanding the foregoing, all rights of subrogation are hereby waived against any corporation, firm, individual, or other interest with respect to which insurance is provided by this policy.

    Where the net amount recovered, after deducting the costs of recovery, is not sufficient to provide a complete indemnity for the loss or damage suffered, that amount shall be divided between the Insurer and the Insured in the proportion in which the loss or damage has been borne by them respectively.

    Any release from liability entered into by the Insured prior to loss shall not affect the right of the Insured to recover.

We understand subrogation, and therefore the first paragraph is relatively easy to follow. The second paragraph above, however, makes no sense unless the indemnity under the property at issue is subject to co-insurance. The paragraph essentially means that if the insurer subrogates and litigates, and recovers some money, *and* the net recovered amount is less than the insurer paid out on the claim, the insured shares the excess it paid over the recovered amount with the insurer (i.e., gives some of it back). Unless this is a co-insurance situation, it hardly makes any sense to get the policy.

Property Protection Systems

12. It is agreed that the Insured shall notify forthwith the Insurer of any interruption to, or flaw or defect coming to the knowledge of the Insured in any:
    (a) sprinkler or other fire extinguishing system; or
    (b) fire detection system; or
    (c) intrusion detection system;
    and shall also notify forthwith the Insurer of the cancellation or non-renewal of any contract which provides monitoring or maintenance services to any of these systems or of the notification of the suspension of police service in response to any of these systems.

The availability, use, and monitoring of property protection systems, such as fire alarms, sprinklers, and burglar systems, has an impact upon an insurer's decision to insure the property and upon the applicable premium. (The presence or absence of such devices alters the risk.) It is only fair and just that the insurer is advised if those systems become inoperative, thereby increasing the risk of loss or damage to the property. Under this clause, the insured must advise the insurer of such changes.

Premium Adjustment

13. This clause is applicable if a specific amount of insurance is shown on the "Declarations Page" for "stock."
    If within 6 (six) months after the expiry or anniversary date of each period of insurance, the Insured shall file with the Insurer a Premium Adjustment Application Form showing, for the said period, the actual cash value of the "stock" insured on the last day of each month at each location as commented upon by the Insured's Accountant, the actual premium for the said period shall then be calculated at the rate applying to each location for the average amount of the total values declared. If the premium paid by the Insured for such "stock" exceeds the actual premium thus calculated, the Insurer shall refund to the Insured any excess paid, subject to a maximum refund of 50% of the

premium paid. In the event of any monthly declared values being in excess of the amount of insurance, the amount of the excess shall not be included in the premium adjustment calculations.

As you probably know, and may recall from our earlier discussion of the "floater" arrangement of coverage for miscellaneous equipment, sometimes insurance is based on an estimated average or existing value of some kind of property. In this case, the "stock," which can be inventory of parts or required materials of any sort, is the insured property. As it would be impractical to keep track of inventories on a daily or even monthly basis for continual adjustment of the insurance coverage, most policies are written on an estimated value of "stock" on hand at any given time. So the natural question would be: What if I've insured my "stock" for $1,000,000 but actually only had about $800,000 of inventory that needed to be insured at any given time? Why should I be overinsuring? The glib, but perhaps practical, answer is: Better safe than sorry. In other words, overinsure the "stock" if you do not know what the average value will be during the insurance period.

On the other hand, when you can tell exactly what the risk level (actual insurance requirement) was—usually after the fact—shouldn't you be able to amend the insurance cost to properly reflect the insurer's risk? The answer, provided in this paragraph, is yes. How that is done is explained in this clause 13. Within six months of the end of the insurance period, you can provide to the insurer an accounting of the month-end "stock" values for the previous policy period. If the average balance is lower, the insurer will adjust and refund to you the premium difference, to a maximum of 50% of the premium paid. In calculating the actual average, each month's balance will be the lower of the insured or actual value.

Verification of Values

14. The Insurer or its duly appointed representative shall be permitted at all reasonable times during the term of this policy, or within a year after termination or expiration, to inspect the property insured and to examine the Insured's books, records, and such policies as relate to any property insured hereunder. Such inspection or examination shall not waive nor in any manner affect any of the terms or conditions of this form.

I am not really sure what the purpose of having this right might be to the insurer, except to assess the actual or booked values of the insured properties to satisfy itself that the listed and aggregated properties' values are valid. In and of itself this is a good reason for the insurer to have this right. After all, if the insurer could only take the insured's word on the number, type, and value of assets, what would prevent that insured from "insuring" nonexistent or previously damaged assets, then claiming them as lost, stolen, broken, etc.?

Valuations

15. For the purposes of calculating the total value of the property for the application of Co-Insurance, value reporting and for loss adjustment, the following valuation basis applies:
    (a) on unsold "stock"—the actual cash value of the property at the time any loss occurs, but in no event to exceed what it would cost to repair or replace with material of like kind and quality;
    (b) on sold "stock"—the selling price after allowance for discounts;
    (c) on property of others in the custody or control of the Insured for the purpose of performing work thereon—the amount for which the Insured is liable but in no event to exceed the actual cash value at the time and place of loss plus allowance for labour and materials expended to such time;
    (d) on tenant's improvements and records—as defined in paragraphs (a) and (b) of Clause 16;
    (e) on all other property insured under this form and for which no more specific conditions have been set out—the actual cash value at the time the loss or damage occurs but in no event to exceed what it would then cost to repair or replace with material of like kind and quality.

This section is easy enough to read and understand. The only point to obtain clarification on from the insurer, its agent, or a lawyer is: in sub-section (b), what "discounts" would or might be applied to the selling price in determining the value of sold "stock." Also, you will want to follow the trail from sub-clause (d) to the referenced sections below if tenancy improvements are an issue to you and your insurance.

Special Basis of Settlement

16.(a) Tenant's Improvements: The liability of the Insurer shall be determined as follows:

    (i) if repaired or replaced with due diligence and dispatch, the amount actually and necessarily expended but in no event exceeding the actual cash value of the tenant's improvements immediately prior to the time of destruction or damage;

    (ii) if not repaired or replaced with due diligence and dispatch after such loss, that portion of the original cost of the damaged or destroyed tenant's improvements which the unexpired term of the lease at the time of loss bears to the period(s) from the date(s) such tenant's improvements were made to the expiration date of the lease.

This clause is relatively clear, although disputes about value might arise around a claim. Basically, if leasehold improvements are damaged or lost, and subsequently repaired or replaced, they are insured for the cost of repair or replacement up to the actual value of those improvements immediately prior to their damage or loss (Section 16(a)(i)). If you do not repair or replace those improvements quickly, the insurer will pay out the prorated remaining value to the tenant for the remainder of the lease.

    (b) Records: The liability of the Insurer for loss or damage to:

    (i) books of accounts, drawings, card index systems, and other records, other than as described in (ii) below, shall not exceed the cost of labour for actually transcribing or copying said records;

    (ii) media, data storage devices, and program devices for electronic and electro-mechanical data processing or for electronically controlled equipment, shall not exceed the cost of reproducing such media, data storage devices, and program devices from duplicates or from originals of the previous generation of the media, but no liability is assumed hereunder for the cost of gathering or assembling information or data for such reproduction.

    Whichever of the above is applicable shall be the basis to be adopted for the purpose of applying Co-Insurance.

The first part of this paragraph (i) is, I suppose, easier to quantify for cost and value than the latter. In the case of electronic media—computer disks, etc.—the real issue will likely not be the cost of the duplication of tapes and disks, but the recreation of damaged data. In both cases, actually, the recreation and rebuilding of files and accounts will be the costly and time-consuming part of the job. And that part is not covered. The moral of the story is to make sure that your file archives—particularly financial data—are safely stored or currently backed up and kept off-site.

Property of Others

17. At the option of the Insurer, any loss may be paid to the Insured or adjusted with and paid to the customer or the owner of the property.

Locked Vehicle Warranty

18. This clause does not apply to property which is under the control of a common carrier.

Warranted by the Insured that any vehicle in which the property insured is carried is equipped with a fully enclosed metal body or compartment, and the Insurer shall be liable in case of loss by theft from an unattended vehicle only as a direct result of forcible entry (of which there shall be visible evidence) into such body or compartment the doors and windows of which shall have been securely locked.

This clause would not apply to property in the possession and control of a common carrier, because the property is, at that point, the responsibility of the third party. The insurance coverage on theft of property in a vehicle (presumably in transit or in the possession of a sales rep, etc.), in this instance, is limited by the protection afforded to that property. The insurer will not pay if the vehicle from which the property was stolen was not locked. The implicit assumption here is that the property and the vehicle are unattended. One should presume that if, while stopped at a traffic light or in a parkade, one is carjacked and the property is stolen while the car is attended, the insurance will pay despite there being no visible signs of forced entry. (Would there be telltale signs of a gun pointed through the window, behind which a burly man is requesting that the doors be opened? Would you force that man to create visible signs of forced entry? I wouldn't either.)

Definitions

19. Wherever used in this form:

(a) *"Declarations Page"* means the "Declarations Page" applicable to this form.

(b) *"Building"* means the building(s) described on the "Declarations Page" and includes:

 (i) fixed structures pertaining to the building(s) and located on the "premises";

 (ii) additions and extensions communicating and in contact with the building(s);

 (iii) permanent fittings and fixtures attached to and forming part of the building(s);

 (iv) materials, equipment, and supplies on the "premises" for maintenance of, and normal repairs and minor alterations to, the "building" or for building services;

 (v) growing plants, trees, shrubs, or flowers inside the "building" used for decorative purposes when the Insured is the owner of the "building."

(c) *"Equipment"* means:

 (i) generally all contents usual to the Insured's business including furniture, furnishings, fittings, fixtures, machinery, tools, utensils, and appliances other than "building" or "stock" as herein defined;

 (ii) similar property belonging to others which the Insured is under obligation to keep insured or for which he is legally liable;

 (iii) tenant's improvements which are defined as building improvements, alterations, and betterments made at the expense of the Insured to a "building" occupied by the Insured and which are not otherwise insured, provided the Insured is not the owner of such "building." If the Insured purchased the use interest in tenant's improvements made by a predecessor tenant, this form applies as though such tenant's improvements had been made at the expense of the Insured;

(d) *"Stock"* means:

 (i) merchandise of every description usual to the Insured's business;

 (ii) packing, wrapping, and advertising materials; and

 (iii) similar property belonging to others which the Insured is under obligation to keep insured or for which he is legally liable;

(e) *"Premises"* means the entire area within the property lines and areas under adjoining sidewalks and driveways at the locations described on the "Declarations Page" and in or on vehicles within 100 metres (328 feet) of such locations.

(f) *"Fire Protective Equipment"* includes tanks, watermains, hydrants, valves, and any other equipment whether used solely for fire protection or for fire protection and for other purposes, but does not include:

 (i) branch piping from a joint system where such branches are used entirely for purposes other than fire protection;

 (ii) any watermains or appurtenances located outside of the described "premises" and forming a part of the public water distribution system;

 (iii) any pond or reservoir in which the water is impounded by dam.

(g) *"Pollutants"* means any solid, liquid, gaseous, or thermal irritant or contaminant, including odour, vapour, fumes, acids, alkalis, chemicals, and waste. Waste includes materials to be recycled, reconditioned, or reclaimed.

(h) *"Clean Up"* means the removal, containment, treatment, decontamination, detoxification, stabilization, neutralization, or remediation of "pollutants," including testing which is integral to the aforementioned processes.

(i) *"Named Perils"* means:

This section of the definitions is important to review. Apart from the information on the declarations page, it is probably the most-referred-to part of the document, and certainly the basis from which all coverage and exclusions are made. Obviously, as you read through it, you will see that "theft" is not a Named Peril. Theft, as we have seen, is either implied in the loss of "equipment" or "stock" or specifically named as an insured loss. Rarely in this insurance policy does theft come up as an exclusion or an exception to an exclusion, whereas the Named Perils noted in this section are constantly addressed.

(A) Fire or Lightning

(B) Explosion: Except with respect to explosion of natural, coal, or manufactured gas, there shall in no event be any liability hereunder for loss or damage caused by explosion, rupture, or bursting in or of the following property owned, operated, or controlled by the Insured:

  (i) (a) the portions containing steam or water under steam pressure of all boilers generating steam, and piping or other equipment connected to said boilers and containing steam or water under steam pressure;

    (b) piping and apparatus or parts thereof normally containing steam or water under steam pressure from an external source and while under such pressure;

    (c) the combustion chambers or fire boxes of steam generating boilers of the chemical recovery type and the flues or passages which conduct the gases of combustion therefrom;

    (d) smelt dissolving tanks;

  (ii) other vessels and apparatus, and pipes connected therewith, while under pressure, or while in use or in operation, provided their maximum normal internal working pressure, or while in use or in operation, provided their maximum kilopascals (15 pounds per square inch) above atmospheric pressure except that liability is specifically assumed for loss or damage resulting from the explosion of manually portable gas cylinders;

  (iii) moving or rotating machinery or parts of same when such loss or damage is caused by centrifugal force or mechanical breakdown;

  (iv) any vessels and apparatus and pipes connected therewith while undergoing pressure tests, but this exclusion shall not apply to other property insured hereunder that has been damaged by such explosion;

  (v) gas turbines;

The basic awareness to work from is that explosions of pressurized tanks, pipes, fittings, etc., and the damage they do to other property, are generally not covered by this insurance policy. Anything better would be a pleasant surprise. If such accidents are a concern, you could purchase the right policy extension for that coverage.

The following are not explosions within the intent or meaning of this section:

  (a) electric arcing or any coincident rupture of electrical equipment due to such arcing;

  (b) bursting or rupture caused by hydrostatic pressure or freezing;

  (c) bursting or rupture of any safety disc, rupture diaphragm or fusible plug.

(C) Impact by Aircraft, Spacecraft or Land Vehicle: The terms "Aircraft" and "Spacecraft" include articles dropped therefrom.

There shall in no event be any liability hereunder due to cumulative damage or for loss or damage:

  (i) caused by land vehicles belonging to or under the control of the Insured or any of his employees;

  (ii) to aircraft, spacecraft, or land vehicles causing the loss;

  (iii) caused by any aircraft or spacecraft when being taxied or moved inside or outside of "buildings."

(D) Riot, Vandalism or Malicious Acts: The term Riot includes open assemblies of strikers inside or outside the "premises" who have quitted work and of locked-out employees.

There shall in no event be any liability hereunder for loss or damage:

  (i) due to cessation of work or by interruption to process or business operations or by change(s) in temperature;

  (ii) due to flood or release of water impounded by a dam, or due to any explosion other than an explosion in respect of which there is insurance under Clause 19(g)(B);

  (iii) due to theft or attempt threat.

(E) Smoke: The term "Smoke" means smoke due to a sudden, unusual, and faulty operation of any stationary furnace. There shall in no event be any liability hereunder for any cumulative damage.

Be particularly mindful of this and the other definitions. "Smoke" as used in this document means nothing but that smoke that comes from a stationary furnace. Smoke that is generated by a machine that overheats or from a fire would apply to damage from such incidents only and not "smoke" damage generally. Cumulative damage would imply that you should have fixed the furnace earlier so that any damage that did occur was a one-time issue.

(F) Leakage from Fire Protection Equipment: The term Leakage from Fire Protective Equipment means the leakage or discharge of water or other substance from within the equipment used for fire protection purposes for the "premises" described on the "Declarations Page" or for adjoining premises and loss or damage caused by the fall or breakage or freezing of such equipment.
(G) Windstorm or Hail: There shall in no event be any liability hereunder for loss or damage:
  (i) to the interior of "buildings" insured or their contents unless damage occurs concurrently with and results from an aperture caused by windstorm or hail;
  (ii) directly or indirectly caused by any of the following, whether driven by wind or due to windstorm or not: snow-load, ice-load, tidal wave, high water, overflow, flood, waterborne objects, waves, ice, land subsidence, landslip.

GENERAL LIABILITY

Liability insurance in general, whether professional liability (malpractice) or product liability (think "Tylenol"), is an important form of insurance for any business. If it isn't the second or third most common kind of insurance purchased by commercial entities, it should be. We, in Canada, tend to be less litigious than our southern neighbours; yet liability actions are not uncommon here either. While nobody sets out to cause anyone harm by their actions or with their products, sometimes it happens. And the damages that can be awarded by a court can be prohibitive to ongoing business survival.

Liability insurance covers the costs and damages of tort liabilities such as negligence, libel, etc. Liabilities arising out of contractual damages and costs are generally not covered by liability insurance unless special provision has been made for such coverage in a policy. As we will see in the following typical, broad sample form (no part of which has been deleted here), this insurance usually covers costs and awards for bodily injury, property damage, personal injury, medical payments, and tenant's liability. Any of the several forms of coverage can be deleted from the broad form to eliminate that type of coverage and reduce the premium.

The following form was provided by the Insurance Council of Canada, and, similarly to the property insurance form examined earlier in the chapter, it is a standard that forms the basis of most insurers' own liability policy forms. Deviations from the content of this form are possible, and I hasten to remind you that the form and comments that follow are for general understanding only. It would be imprudent to rely on my commentary for anything more than basic understanding; consult your lawyer for detailed explanation of your specific contract's terms.

Commercial General Liability Policy

Various provisions in this policy restrict coverage. Read the entire policy carefully to determine rights, duties, and what is and is not covered.

This is good advice and fair warning.

Throughout this policy the words "you" and "your" refer to the Named Insured shown in the Declarations. The words "we," "us," and "our" refer to the Company providing this insurance.
The word "insured" means any person or organization qualifying as such under SECTION II—WHO IS AN INSURED.
Other words and phrases that appear in quotation marks have special meaning.

1. Insuring Agreement

　　a. We will pay those sums that the insured becomes legally obligated to pay as compensatory damages because of "bodily injury" or "property damage" to which this insurance applies. No other obligations or liability to pay sums or perform acts or services is covered unless explicitly provided for under SUPPLEMENTARY PAYMENTS—COVERAGES A, B, AND D. This insurance applies only to "bodily injury" and "property damage" which occurs during the policy period. The "bodily injury" or "property damage" must be caused by an "occurrence." The "occurrence" must take place in the "coverage territory." We will have the right and duty to defend any "action" seeking those compensatory damages but:

　　　　1) The amount we will pay for compensatory damages is limited as described in SECTION III—LIMITS OF INSURANCE.

　　　　2) We may investigate and settle any claim or "action" at our discretion; and

　　　　3) Our right and duty to defend end when we have used up the applicable limit of insurance in the payment of judgements or settlements under Coverages A, B, or D or medical expenses under Coverage C.

This first part of the sweeping coverage statement, which regards bodily injury and property damage only—other types of coverage are addressed in separate (and separable) sections—plainly states that the insurer is obliged only to pay damages of money. The insurer is not obliged to perform any acts or services, which are possible court awards. The insurer states its right to act on the insured's behalf to defend against actions for compensation. The three sub-sections are limiters and provide detail as to what kind and how much of a defense the insurer may mount. Sub-section 2 effectively removes from the insured the right to defend or to settle any action. Essentially, the insurer's position is "If we are paying, we make the economic decisions."

　　b. Compensatory damages because of "bodily injury" include compensatory damages claimed by any person or organization for care, loss of services, or death resulting at any time from the "bodily injury."

　　c. "Property damage" that is loss of use of tangible property that is not physically injured shall be deemed to occur at the time of the "occurrence" that caused it.

The obvious difference between these two sub-sections is the time limitation on when a claim may be made that will be paid out. The implication is that injuries that directly result from an "occurrence" may arise or conclude some time after the "occurrence." Property damage, specifically property damage that is "loss of use of a tangible property that is *not* physically injured," is expected to arise immediately with the occurrence. Such losses are referred to as "consequential damages." These paragraphs would, I suspect, limit the valid claim and coverage period for such consequential damages.

2. Exclusions

This insurance does not apply to:

　　a. "Bodily injury" or "property damage" expected or intended from the standpoint of the insured. This exclusion does not apply to "bodily injury" resulting from the use of reasonable force to protect persons or property.

If you intend to injure someone or somebody's property, or expect it to happen for reasons you may control, insurance for "bodily injury" and "property damage" will not be in force. The only exception is self-defense of yourself or your property.

　　b. "Bodily injury" or "property damage" for which the insured is obligated to pay compensatory damages by reason of the assumption of liability in a contract or agreement. This exclusion does not apply to liability for compensatory damages:

　　　　1) Assumed in a contract or agreement that is an "insured" contract; or

　　　　2) That the insured would have in the absence of the contract or agreement.

Contractual liabilities are not the same as tort liabilities. That is, contractual liabilities arise from obligations voluntarily taken on for consideration; tort liabilities arise from "accidents." This liability insurance will not be in force for contracted liabilities, unless the contract is insured (go to the definitions to familiarize yourself with an "insured contract") or if the liability would have existed if the contract were not in place.

> c. Any obligation of the insured under a workers' compensation, disability benefits, or unemployment compensation law or any similar law.

Interestingly enough, each of these laws would have a different requirement of the insured and payout to the beneficiary, for different purposes. However, they are all legislated situations created to indemnify the insured and/or beneficiary (object) in certain industrial circumstances. This liability insurance policy would not be in effect as described in this paragraph, because the legislated benefits are "primary" and the payout of this insurance would be double indemnity. (For those who don't know: it is not considered fair pool or legally acceptable to double-insure and double-collect on any insurable "event.")

> d. "Bodily injury" to an employee of the insured arising out of and in the course of employment by the insured. This exclusion applies:
> a) Whether the insured may be liable as an employer or in any other capacity; and
> b) To any obligation to share compensatory damages with or repay someone else who must pay compensatory damages because of the injury.
> This exclusion does not apply:
> i) To liability assumed by the insured under an "insured contract"; or
> ii) To employees on whose behalf contributions are made by or required to be made by the insured under the provisions of any workers' compensation law.

Presumably there are different types of insurance available to protect an employer for employee injury liability, although I would hazard a guess that this crosses into the territory of labour standards and the employer's obligations to provide safe working conditions. Workers' compensation and other such programs are designed to deal with such situations, and employers cannot opt out of these government programs. Thus, to some degree anyway, this clause is perfectly understandable.

> e. 1) "Bodily injury" or "property damage" arising out of the ownership, use, or operation by or on behalf of any insured of:
> a) Any "automobile";
> b) Any motorized snow vehicle or its trailers;
> c) Any vehicle while being used in any speed or demolition contest or in any stunting activity or in practice or preparation for any such contest or activity; or
> d) Any vehicle which if it were to be insured would be required by law to be insured under a contract evidenced by a motor vehicle liability policy, or any vehicle insured under such a contract, but this exclusion does not apply to the ownership, use, or operation of machinery, apparatus, or equipment mounted on or attached to any vehicle while at the site of the use or operation of such equipment.

I cannot speak to the automotive insurance situation in other provinces; but in Manitoba this clause makes perfect sense, because every driver and automobile license/insurance registrant must purchase liability insurance (government-run insurance). In provinces where the situation is different, a different policy is probably available that is specific to automotive third-party liability. I presume the same applies to other licensed vehicles such as snowmobiles, boats, etc. It is almost comical that the sub-clause about demolition-derby activities has to be included. I think that falls into the same category as life insurance for freefall skydivers partaking of their preferred hobby.

e) "Bodily injury" or "property damage" with respect to which any motor vehicle liability policy is in effect or would be in effect but for its termination upon exhaustion of its limit of liability or is required by law to be in effect.

This Exclusion e. does not apply to "bodily injury" to an employee of the insured on whose behalf contributions are made by or required to be made by the insured under the provisions of any workers' compensation law.

This is one of those common and frequent points in an insurance policy where the "does not apply" refers to an exclusion, which according to mathematical properties is an inclusion.[3]

f. "Bodily injury" or "property damage" arising out of the ownership, maintenance, use, operation, loading or unloading, or entrustment to others, by or on behalf of any insured of any watercraft.
This exclusion does not apply to:
  1) A watercraft while ashore on premises you own or rent;
  2) A watercraft you do not own that is:
    a) Less than 8 metres long; and
    b) Not being used to carry persons or property for a charge.
  3) "Bodily injury" to an employee of the insured on whose behalf contributions are made by or required to be made by the insured under the provisions of any workers' compensation law.

To start, boats are not covered, which is immediately followed by exceptions to the effect that liability resulting from your boat, not on the water but on your property, and a relatively small boat used for pleasure (i.e., not to make money from passengers or cargo) are covered.

With special regard to sub-clause 3, do you think the insurer is trying to make a point? This is about the tenth time this text has appeared, and it comes up again later.

> As a general rule, when reading contracts you will likely find repetitive phrases, sentences, or clauses. It is important not to skim past them too quickly. First, these repetitions must be put into the proper context. A repetition later in a contract document could be going the opposite direction to those of previous instances. Second, read them thoroughly for the small differences; you may encounter lists of words or specific phrases that are ever-so-slightly different. Chances are there is a good reason—find out.

g. 1) "Bodily injury" or "property damage" arising out of the ownership, maintenance, use, operation, loading or unloading, or the entrustment to others, by or on behalf of any insured of:
    a) Any aircraft; or
    b) Any air cushion vehicle.
  2) "Bodily injury" or "property damage" arising out of the ownership, existence, use, or operation by or on behalf of any insured of any premises for the purpose of an airport or aircraft landing area and all operations necessary or incidental thereto.

If your business does not maintain an airport or aircraft landing strip, this clause will hardly affect you. Very few businesses have hovercraft, but the exclusion is there. It should be noted. If your business does have a plane, hangar, airport, airstrip, or any combination of those, you would probably have the proper insurance to cover those special circumstances.

h. "Property damage" to:
  1) Property you own, rent, or occupy;
  2) Premises you sell, give away or abandon, if the "property damage" arises out of any part of those premises;
  3) Property loaned to you;
  4) Personal property in your care, custody, or control;

5) That particular part of real property on which you, or any contractor or subcontractor working directly or indirectly on your behalf is performing operations, if the "property damage" arises out of those operations; or

6) That particular part of any property that must be restored, repaired, or replaced because "your work" was incorrectly performed on it.

The issue at hand in this clause, generally speaking, has to do with the difference between "product damage" as a liability and product damage as a matter for property insurance. If you own it, lend it, lease it, take custody of it, or operate on/in it, or you damaged it because you were working on it, then it's not really a liability issue. Although somebody may sue you to obtain damages in such an event, there was no "third-party," tort-type accident involved. So it is excluded. Your property insurance coverage should take care of most of the losses and claims though, except in the instance of sub-clauses 5 and 6, in which circumstance you will probably have to go it alone—at least under this policy.

Paragraph 2 of this exclusion does not apply if the premises are "your work" and were never occupied, rented, or held for rental by you.

Referring back to the previous comment, the caveat attached to this exception is that the "premises" are effectively your product and not your property, so the liability insurance would be effective.

Paragraphs 3, 4, 5, and 6 of this exclusion do not apply to liability assumed under a sidetrack agreement.

The big unknown here is, what exactly is a sidetrack agreement? If you guessed, as I did originally, that it is an insurance industry variation of a "side agreement," you would also be wrong. Fortunately, I have found out what a sidetrack agreement is, and am pleased to report that it probably has no effect on you or your business operation.

A sidetrack agreement is usually one related to a railway siding. Although rail traffic has declined, in the past it was common for businesses to have their own railway sidings on which to receive raw materials and to ship its finished product. Freight cars would be detached from trains and shunted onto the side track (hence the name) allowing the business access as required, and later they would be picked up and taken to the railway marshalling point. The railways usually attached conditions to this facility, such as an indemnity. These agreements often resulted in a contractual assumption of any and all of the railway company's liability that might arise out of the existence and use of the side track.

Chances are you have no such worries or concerns. In any event, the effect of this paragraph is to make the exclusions 3 through 6, which generally relate to property damage to properties in your care, invalid (i.e., included within the parameters of this policy's coverage).

Paragraph 6 of this exclusion does not apply to "property damage" included in the "products-completed operations hazard."

Refer to Section V(9) to establish what constitutes a "products-completed operations hazard" and how this affects paragraph 6. Just this once, I will save you the time. Basically, if paragraph 6 involves a situation that is off your premises, complete, and of "work" no longer in your possession, the liability insurance is in force.

i. "Property damage" to "your product" arising out of it or any part of it.
j. "Property damage" to "your work" arising out of it or any part of it and included in the "products-completed operations hazard."
This exclusion does not apply if the damaged work or the work out of which the damage arises was performed on your behalf by a subcontractor.

Again, the circumstances in the two points above are not general liability. Your product or work is defective and you have to deal with it in some way. (If there is insurance to cover bad workmanship, it must cost a fortune.) Notice that if somebody else (a subcontractor) did the work for which you are liable, then this insurance should be in force.

> k. "Property damage" to "impaired property" or property that has not been physically injured, arising out of:
>> 1) A defect, deficiency, inadequacy, or dangerous condition in "your product" or "your work"; or
>> 2) A delay or failure by you or anyone acting on your behalf to perform a contract or agreement in accordance with its terms.
>> This exclusion does not apply to the loss of use of other property arising out of a sudden and accidental physical injury to "your product" or "your work" after it has been put to its intended use.

This particular clause is a little harder to comprehend or rationalize. The first part says that liability for property damage to "impaired property" (other property rendered useless, etc. by your work or product—see Section V(5)), or other property *that has not been physically injured* due to your product/work or your not fulfilling a contractual obligation, is not covered by this insurance. Within these parameters, I can think of liability under a contract (the contract of the company for whom you are an original equipment manufacturer (OEM) or contractor), or even product liability (same situation), but I have some trouble with a reasonable example of property damaged to that "impaired property," etc.

In any event, the second part of the clause excepts loss of use of other property (almost "impaired") by virtue of a "sudden and accidental physical injury" to your OEM product/work *after* it has been put to its intended use. That makes sense, because the situation has now truly become an accidental product liability circumstance.

> l. Any loss, cost, or expense incurred by you or others for the loss of use, withdrawal, recall, inspection, repair, replacement, adjustment, removal, or disposal of:
>> 1) "Your product";
>> 2) "Your work"; or
>> 3) "Impaired property";
>> if such product, work, or property is withdrawn or recalled from the market or from use by any person or organization because of a known or suspected defect, deficiency, inadequacy, or dangerous condition in it.

This paragraph refers to product recall for defect. To repeat what has been stated earlier, this is not something I would think is typically insurable. And, if it is insurable under a different policy, the premiums must be quite significant. I would suspect this is a cost that has to be borne by the business as penance for its mistake and profit therefrom.

> m. Pollution Liability—See COMMON EXCLUSIONS
> n. Nuclear Liability—See COMMON EXCLUSIONS
> o. War Risks—See COMMON EXCLUSIONS

Regarding sub-clauses m., n., and o., do what they suggest. COMMON EXCLUSIONS are found near the back of the contract.

COVERAGE B. PERSONAL INJURY LIABILITY
1. Insuring Agreement
> a. We will pay those sums that the insured becomes legally obligated to pay as compensatory damages because of "personal injury" to which this insurance applies. No other obligation or liability to pay sums or perform acts or services is covered unless explicitly provided for under SUPPLEMENTARY PAYMENTS—COVERAGES A, B, AND D. We will have the right and duty to defend any action seeking those compensatory damages but:
>> 1) The amount we will pay for compensatory damages is limited as described in SECTION III—LIMITS OF INSURANCE;

    2) We may investigate and settle any claim or "action" at our discretion; and

    3) Our right and duty to defend end when we have used up the applicable limit of insurance in the payment of judgements or settlements under Coverages A, B, or D or medical expenses under Coverage C.

b. This insurance applies to "personal injury" only if caused by an offence:

    1) Committed in the "coverage territory" during the policy period; and

    2) Arising out of the conduct of your business, excluding advertising, publishing, broadcasting, or telecasting done by or for you.

Although it refers to personal injury now, the preceding is strikingly similar to the "Insuring Agreement" for Coverage A. "Bodily injury" is a punch in the nose or a wheel coming off a car and crushing a pedestrian. "Personal injury," on the other hand, is convincing a person's employer that the person is a war criminal without definite proof, or one of any number of other non-physical ways of making a person's or business's life a little more miserable. You should refer to the definitions of these terms for fuller explanation.

Perhaps the most interesting pre-exclusion exclusion is paragraph b.2, which states that this personal injury coverage does not apply if it arises out of anything advertised, published, broadcast, or telecast by or for you. The distinction to be aware of is that if you have paid for these distribution and dissemination services the liability coverage is not in force; if the same thing is disseminated by a member of the news media or information distributor, without payment from you, the insurance should be in full force. Not that I would suggest how to libel someone and have this particular insurance policy sample cover it.

2. Exclusions

This insurance does not apply to:

"Personal injury":

    1) Arising out of oral or written publication of material, if done by or at the direction of the insured with knowledge of its falsity;

Very simple. If you willfully slander or libel, the insurer will not assist you.

    2) Arising out of oral or written publication of material whose first publication took place before the beginning of the policy period;

This one, unfortunately, is a little dicier for anyone who tends to walk on the edge of inflicting personal injury on others—whether for fun or profit. The insurer will only cover those incidents which arise during its period of coverage. If a defamation incident occurs before the insurance period but the action is commenced during the insurance period, the incident is not covered. This is not to your advantage, but it is fair. At the other end, should a slander occur during the policy period but not be acted upon until after the insurance period, there appears to be no indication that the insurer will cover the liability. This is fair, perhaps, but definitely not equal.

    3) Arising out of the willful violation of a penal statute or ordinance committed by or with the consent of the insured; or

Crime doesn't pay. It's not insurable either.

    4) For which the insured has assumed liability in a contract or agreement. This exclusion does not apply to liability for compensatory damages that the insured would have in the absence of the contract or agreement.

We have seen this before. Contractual liabilities are not covered unless the liability would have arisen in the absence of the contract.

COVERAGE C. MEDICAL PAYMENTS

1. Insuring Agreement

    a. We will pay medical expenses as described below for "bodily injury" caused by an accident:

        1) On premises you own or rent;

        2) On ways next to premises you own or rent; or

        3) Because of your operations;

    Provided that:

        a) The accident takes place in the "coverage territory" and during the policy period;

        b) The expenses are incurred and reported to us within one (1) year of the date of the accident; and

        c) The injured person submits to examination, at our expense, by physicians of our choice as often as we reasonably require.

    b. We will make these payments regardless of fault. These payments will not exceed the applicable limit of insurance. We will pay reasonable expenses for:

        1) First aid at the time of an accident;

        2) Necessary medical, surgical, x-ray and dental services, including prosthetic devices; and

        3) Necessary ambulance, hospital, professional nursing, and funeral services.

As usual, the insurance agreement, which comes before the exclusions, sounds pretty good. Notice that the insurer time-limits the claim period in Section 1(b). The insurance payment does not come without conditions, and that should be expected. However, the policy is "no-fault."

2. Exclusions

    We will not pay expenses for "bodily injury":

    a. To any insured.

    b. To a person hired to do work for or on behalf of any insured or a tenant of any insured.

    c. To a person injured on that part of premises you own or rent that the person normally occupies.

    d. To a person, whether or not an employee or any insured, who at the time of injury is entitled to benefits under any workers' compensation or disability benefits law or a similar law.

    e. To a person injured while taking part in athletics.

    f. The payment of which is prohibited by law.

    g. Included within the "products-completed operations hazard."

    h. Excluded under Coverage A.

As you may have noticed, this is the most concise and simple set of exclusions in the whole document. For the most part, these exclusions refer to situations that are not properly liability coverage, but some other form of extended health and disability insurance (a., b. as it refers to employees, and c.), would/should not be covered (b. as it refers to tenants, d., e., and f.), or are otherwise excluded (g.—refer to the definition of "products-completed operations hazard," and h.[4]). To see what else has been excluded, it would be wise to refer to what is excluded from "bodily injury coverage" under Coverage A.

COVERAGE D. TENANTS' LEGAL LIABILITY

1. Insuring Agreement.

    We will pay those sums that the insured becomes legally obligated to pay as compensatory damages because of "property damage" to which this insurance applies. No other obligations or liability to pay sums or perform acts or services is covered unless explicitly provided for under SUPPLEMENTARY PAYMENTS—COVERAGES A, B, AND D. This insurance applies only to "property damage" caused by fire, explosion, smoke, or leakage from fire protective equipment to premises rented to you or occupied by you. This insurance applies only to "property damage" which occurs during the policy period. The "property damage" must be caused by an "occurrence." The "occurrence" must take place in the "coverage territory."

We will have the right and duty to defend any "action" seeking those compensatory damages but:

   a. The amount we will pay for compensatory damages is limited as described in SECTION III—LIMITS OF INSURANCE;
   b. We may investigate and settle any claim or "action" at our discretion; and
   c. Our right and duty to defend end when we have used up the applicable limit of insurance in the payment of judgements or settlements under Coverages A, B, or D or medical expenses under Coverage C.

This is a similar insurance coverage covenant as provided for in the previous coverage types. Be mindful that this insurance is "liability" insurance for accidents of the type specifically listed that cause property damage to premises rented or occupied by you. Damage to this rented property that does not arise from the accidents specifically listed would likely be covered by a tenant's property policy with terms similar to those we examined in the example provided earlier on in the chapter.

2. Exclusions

   This insurance does not apply to:

   a. "Property damage" expected or intended from the standpoint of the insured.
   b. "Property damage" for which the insured is obligated to pay by reason of the assumption of liability in a contract or agreement. This exclusion does not apply to liability for compensatory damages that the insured would have in the absence of the contract or agreement.
   c. Pollution liability—See COMMON EXCLUSIONS.
   d. Nuclear Energy Liability—See COMMON EXCLUSIONS.
   e. War Risks—See COMMON EXCLUSIONS.

Again, similarly to the coverage exclusions we have encountered in the previous coverage-type sections, this particular tenant's property liability coverage does not cover damage that is not an "accident." That is, if you knew it would happen or expected it to happen, your allowing it to happen would be willful negligence. And insurance is designed to cover problems that are beyond the control of the insured party. Furthermore, a liability undertaken in a contractual obligation is a known risk, which, if it is insurable at all, would probably require a separate policy or endorsement.

The Common Exclusions follow immediately below, and have probably been separated in this sample document to save on repeating the exact same text and language three times. Remember, this is a "broad form" example, and an insurance policy for any one of the coverage types included in this sample would probably not separate the exclusions at all.

COMMON EXCLUSIONS — COVERAGES A, C, AND D

This insurance does not apply to:

1. Pollution Liability

   a. "Bodily injury," "property damage," and "clean up costs" arising out of the actual, alleged, or threatened discharge, dispersal, seepage, release, or escape of pollutants:

      1) At or from any premises, site, or location which is or was at any time, owned or occupied by, or rented or loaned to, an Insured;
      2) At or from any premises, site, or location which is or was at any time, used by or for any Insured or others for the handling, storage, disposal, processing, or treatment of waste;
      3) Which are or were at any time transported, handled, stored, treated, disposed of, or processed as waste by or for any Insured or any person or organization for whom the Insured may be legally responsible; or
      4) At or from any premises, site, or location on which any Insured or any contractors or subcontractors working directly or indirectly on any Insured's behalf are performing operations:
         a) if the pollutants are brought on or to the premises, site, or location in connection with such operations by such Insured, contractor, or subcontractor; or
         b) if the operations are to test for, monitor, clean up, remove, contain, treat, detoxify, or neutralize, or in any way respond to, or assess the effect of pollutants.

b. Sub-paragraphs 1 and 4(a) of paragraph A of this exclusion do not apply to "bodily injury" or "property damage" caused by:

   1) heat, smoke, or fumes from a hostile fire. As used in this exclusion, a "hostile fire" means one which becomes uncontrollable or breaks out from where it was intended to be.

   2) any loss, cost, or expense arising out of any:

      a) request, demand, or order that any Insured or others test for, monitor, clean up, remove, contain, treat, detoxify, or neutralize or in any way respond to, or assess the effect of, pollutants; or

      b) claim or suit by or on behalf of a government authority for damages because of testing for, monitoring, cleaning up, removing, containing, treating, detoxifying, or neutralizing or in any way responding to or assessing the effects of pollutants.

"Pollutants" means any solid, liquid, gaseous, or thermal irritant or contaminant, including smoke, vapour, soot, fumes, acids, alkalis, chemicals, and waste. Waste includes materials to be recycled, reconditioned, or reclaimed.

In examining the previous insurance contract sample (property insurance), we ran across a similar "pollutant" exclusion. More costly "pollution liability" insurance can be purchased. My suspicion is that "pollution" is an exclusion here because (1) polluting, as defined, is not an accidental circumstance and (2) it is more costly to defend and/or pay out losses. It is a condition that the business must be aware is happening, or know the potential for its occurrence. As with other types of exclusions we have discussed above, willful negligence is generally not insurable. Taunting the fates so that the risk of liability is more probable or the outcome more costly, if insurable at all, usually comes as a separate policy or endorsement and at a higher price.

   2. Nuclear Energy Liability (revised May 1989)

   a. Liability imposed by or arising from any nuclear liability act, law, or statute, or any law amendatory thereof;

   b. "Bodily injury" or "property damage" with respect to which an insured under this policy is also insured under a contract of nuclear energy liability insurance (whether the insurance is unnamed in such contract and whether or not it is legally enforceable by the insured) issued by the Nuclear Insurance Association of Canada or any other Insurer or group or pool of Insurers or would be an insured under any such policy but for its termination upon exhaustion of its limit of liability;

   c. "Bodily injury" or "property damage" resulting directly or indirectly from the nuclear energy hazard arising from:

      1) The ownership, maintenance, operation, or use of a nuclear facility by or on behalf of an insured;

      2) The furnishing by an insured of services, materials, parts, or equipment in connection with the planning, construction, maintenance, operation, or use of any nuclear facility;

      3) The possession, consumption, use, handling, disposal, or transportation of fissionable substances, or of other radioactive material (except radioactive isotopes, away from a nuclear facility, which have reached the final stage of fabrication so as to be useable for any scientific, medical, agricultural, commercial, or industrial purpose) used, distributed, handled, or sold by an insured.

As used in this policy:

   1) The term "nuclear energy hazard" means the radioactive, toxic, explosive, or other hazardous properties of radioactive material;

   2) The term "radioactive material" means uranium, thorium, plutonium, neptunium, their respective derivatives and compounds, radioactive isotopes or other elements, and any other substances which may be designated by any nuclear liability act, law, or statute, or any law amendatory thereof, as being prescribed substances capable of releasing atomic energy, or as being requisite for the production, use, or application of atomic energy;

   3) The term "nuclear facility" means:

      a) any apparatus designed or used to sustain nuclear fission in a self-supporting chain reaction or to contain a critical mass of plutonium, thorium, and uranium or any one or more of them;

      b) any equipment or device designated or used for (i) separating the isotopes of plutonium, thorium, and uranium or any one or more of them, (ii) processing or packaging waste;

      c) any equipment or device used for the processing, fabricating, or alloying of plutonium, thorium, or uranium enriched in isotope uranium 233 or in the isotope uranium 235, or any one or more of them if at any time the total amount of such material in the custody of the insured at the premises where such equipment or device is located consists of or contains more than 25 grams of plutonium or uranium 233 or any combination thereof, or more than 250 grams of uranium 235;

    d) any structure, basin, excavation, premises, or place prepared or used for the storage or disposal of waste radioactive material;

and includes the site on which any of the foregoing is located, together with all operations conducted thereon and all premises used for such operations.

4) The term "fissionable substance" means any prescribed substance that is, or from which can be obtained, a substance capable of releasing atomic energy by nuclear fission.

If you do not own, manage, or otherwise operate a nuclear facility, or supply the nuclear industry in some manner, this section is completely inapplicable. If you are in this somewhat small and closed industry, chances are you will already have nuclear energy liability insurance provided by the Nuclear Insurance Association of Canada or some other body. I would hope that those relatively few people who would have requirement to deal with nuclear energy liability insurance are prepared and trained for what they might encounter, so that anything I contribute here would be moot. Suffice it to say that most of us should simply ignore entirely this exclusion (which may never even appear on a liability policy you purchase, anyway).

3. War Risks

"Bodily injury" or "property damage" due to war, invasion, act of foreign enemy, hostilities (whether war be declared or not), civil war, rebellion, revolution, insurrection, or military power.

As I have said in every other place that this exclusion has been encountered, it makes some sense. After all, if you are doing business in and where hostilities break out, chances are it was not a complete surprise, and therefore it is a business risk you are prepared to take. My question in this instance, however, is: What freaky circumstance would cause a typical Canadian commercial endeavour to be liable for "bodily injury" or "property damage" due to war, with the exception of employees that might get caught and hurt in one while carrying out their jobs? And who would go to a war zone or hot spot without specific insurance?

SUPPLEMENTARY PAYMENTS — COVERAGES A, B, AND D

We will pay, with respect to any claim or "action" we defend:

    a. All expenses we incur.

    b. The cost of bonds to release attachments, but only for bond amounts within the applicable limit of insurance. We do not have to furnish these bonds.

    c. All reasonable expenses incurred by the insured at our request to assist us in the investigation or defense of the claim or "action," including actual loss of earnings up to $100 a day because of time off work.

    d. All costs taxed against the insured in the "action" and any interest accruing after entry of judgement upon that part of the judgement which is within the applicable limit of insurance.

These payments will not reduce the limits of insurance.

Under this Supplementary Payments clause, the insurance company will pay the costs for several other expenses that may arise in the defense of a lawsuit filed or otherwise threatened against you that would fall under the terms of this insurance policy. The expenses listed and their limitations are readily understandable with the possible exception of item b. That payment would be for the "cost" associated with a bond to release a property or establish bail. The insurer is not required to provide (i.e., underwrite) the surety bond itself, but will pay the required costs for bonds obtained in connection with an action or claim that is covered by this policy.

As usual within the insurance policy, the payment of bond premiums and expenses, and the payment of costs awarded by judgement, are payable only to the limit of the insurance. These expense payments do not reduce the limits of insurance, meaning that even if expenses such as surety bond premiums or bail are taken to the maximum limit of insurance, the available insurance coverage for actual damages, etc. (which is what is primarily covered by this liability policy) are not reduced.

SECTION II—WHO IS AN INSURED

1. If you are designated in the Declarations as:
   a. An individual, you and your spouse are Insureds, but only with respect to the conduct of a business of which you are the sole owner.
   b. A partnership or joint venture, you are an insured. Your members, your partners, and their spouses are also Insureds, but only with respect to the conduct of your business.
   c. An organization other than a partnership or joint venture, you are an insured. Your executive officers and directors are Insureds, but only with respect to their duties as your officers or directors. Your stockholders are also Insureds, but only with respect to their liability as stockholders.

In commercial liability coverage, the nature and extent of the people being covered for their actions depends on the nature of the business entity, as described in the preceding list. The operative assumption, until you read conclusively that the allowed "insured" parties are different, should be that the principal or key people within the business are insured. But they are only insured under a commercial liability policy for their acts and words in conducting or operating the commercial entity being insured.

2. Each of the following is also an insured:
   a. Your employees, other than your executive officers, but only for acts within the scope of their employment by you. However, none of these employees is insured for:
      1) "Bodily injury" or "personal injury" to you or to a co-employee while in the course of his or her employment; or
      2) "Bodily injury" or "personal injury" to any person who at the time of injury is entitled to benefits under any workers' compensation or disability benefits law or a similar law; or
      3) "Bodily injury" or "personal injury" arising out of his or her providing or failing to provide professional health care services; or
      4) "Property damage" to property owned or occupied by or rented or loaned to that employee, any of your other employees, or any of your partners or members (if you are a partner or joint venture).

This paragraph, a, with its four exclusions, first extends this policy's liability coverage over the business' employees *in the context of their employment*, then limits that coverage. The thrust of the exclusions is that if an employee does "bodily injury" or "personal injury" to anyone within the company, or anyone entitled to worker's compensation benefits, those injuries are not covered by this "liability" insurance. Presumably they would be covered by worker's compensation, extended health, or other coverage. Considering the first exclusion, (1), if an employee on the job defames the business or its executives, this policy would not cover the employee. This makes sense; otherwise, an unscrupulous business could have its employees slandering it, sue them, settle, and have the insurer pay the civil settlement.

The property exclusion, (4), makes some sense, because the damage would be done to property in one form or another in the custody of the insured. As such, insurance for damage to that property would properly fall under a property insurance policy.

The only really interesting exclusion is the third one regarding professional medical attention. Having a passing knowledge of people being sued and found liable after unsuccessfully attempting to assist an injured party, I understand why the coverage might not extend over a nonprofessional attempting to provide professional health care. Not providing professional health care would obviously apply to doctors and nurses on staff. The exclusion is reasonable because such professionals are held to a higher standard within their field of expertise and should (must) have professional liability errors and omissions coverage.

b. Any person (other than an employee), or any organization while acting as your real estate manager.

c. Any person or organization having proper temporary custody of your property if you die, but only:
   1) With respect to liability arising out of the maintenance or use of that property; and
   2) Until your legal representative has been appointed.

This is obviously only temporary coverage, since the presumable first step of the legal representative (executor or administrator) would be to reclaim the estate's properties. This extension of coverage would pertain only to coverage of an individual (proprietorship or partnership), since a corporate body cannot really "die."

d. Your legal representative if you die, but only with respect to duties as such. That representative will have all your rights and duties under this policy.

Very simply, the liability coverage that you enjoyed while you were still able to be liable for anything, extends to the executor, administrator, or trustee of your estate with respect to any liabilities to which she might be exposed in dealing with your estate.

3. Any organization you newly acquire or form, other than a partnership or joint venture, and over which you maintain ownership or majority interest, will be deemed to be a Named Insured if there is no other similar insurance available to that organization. However:
   a. Coverage under this provision is afforded only until the 90th day after you acquire or form the organization or the end of the policy period, whichever is earlier;
   b. Coverages A and D do not apply to "bodily injury" or "property damage" that occurred before you acquired or formed the organization; and
   c. Coverage B does not apply to "personal injury" arising out of an offense committed before you acquired or formed the organization.

No person or organization is an insured with respect to the conduct of any current or past partnership or joint venture that is not shown as a Named Insured in the Declarations.

This extension is a grace-period extension over your proprietorship or corporate-entity (majority-owned) business expansions that lasts for 90 days from the date of formation or acquisition. It is, naturally, limited to various liabilities that arise only once you have acquired or formed the business expansion organization. The last sentence of the clause limits the insured parties of existing or past *partnerships* and *joint ventures* to people and entities that have been named as insured parties in the Declarations. (Obviously this does not apply if the principle insured party under this policy is a partnership itself, the insured for which are described above in Section II(1)b.)

SECTION III—LIMITS OF INSURANCE

1. The Limits of Insurance stated in the Declarations and the rules below fix the most we will pay regardless of the number of:
   a. Insureds;
   b. Claims made or "actions" brought; or
   c. Persons or organizations making claims or bringing "actions."

Here are the often-referred-to limits of insurance. This clause seems straightforward and definitive, but the "rules" provided in the remainder of this section institute various limits such as the "Aggregate Limit," an "Each Occurrence Limit," and limits on the maximum payouts under each type of coverage.

2. The Aggregate Limit is the most we will pay for the sum of:
   a. Medical expenses under Coverage C; and
   b. Compensatory damages under Coverage A, Coverage B, and Coverage D.

This is the complete, total, final, no-more-left-anyway-you-slice-it limit of insurance. Once you reach the dollar number associated with this limit, that is it for the insurance, period. You are now on your own. If you have reached the Aggregate Limit, it will either have been due to one massive liability claim payout (assuming the Each Occurrence Limit permits) or a lot of small ones. In the former case, that is why you have insurance and it's too bad that you were not insured for a greater limit. In the latter case, you might consider rethinking your business practices.

> 3. Subject to 2. above, Each Occurrence Limit is the most we will pay for the sum of:
>   a. Compensatory damages under Coverage A and Coverage D; and
>   b. Medical expenses under Coverage C
> because of all "bodily injury" and "property damage" arising out of any one "occurrence."

Never to exceed the Aggregate Limit, the Each Occurrence Limit is the maximum payable for all coverage-type damages arising out of any single *non*-personal-injury claim. So, the insurer would pay out the Each Occurrence limit on each "occurrence" as applicable during any given year, to the extent that the sum of the payouts reaches the Aggregate Limit. Then paragraph 2 takes effect.

> 4. Subject to 2. above, the Personal Injury Limit is the most we will pay under Coverage B for the sum of all compensatory damages because of all "personal injury" sustained by any one person or organization.

Slightly different from the previous Each Occurrence Limit, the Personal Injury Limit is the maximum amount of money the insurer will pay out for Personal Injury damages arising during the insurance period.

> 5. Subject to 3. above, the Tenants' Legal Liability Limit is the most we will pay under Coverage D for compensatory damages because of "property damage" to any one premises.

The Tenant's Legal Liability Limit is a limit complementary to the Each Occurrence Limit in the sense that the dollar limit for tenants' liability is bounded by Each Occurrence Limit dollar value (which would include the other coverage). For the purpose of Tenant's Liability insurance, this paragraph equates an "occurrence" to a "premises."

> 6. Subject to 3. above, the Medical Expenses Limit is the most we will pay under Coverage C for all medical expenses because of "bodily injury" sustained by any one person.

This limitation is very easy to understand. The maximum dollar value of medical expenses that the insurance covers for any single occurrence is bounded by the Each Occurrence Limit (which would include the other coverage). For the purpose of Medical Expenses coverage, this paragraph equates an "occurrence" to a "person."

> The limits of this policy apply separately to each consecutive annual period and to any remaining period of less than twelve (12) months, starting with the beginning of the policy period shown in the declarations, unless the policy period is extended after issuance for an additional period of less than twelve (12) months. In that case, the additional period will be deemed part of the last preceding period for purposes of determining the Limits of Insurance.

In case there was any doubt, these limits refresh themselves with each annual insurance period, using the beginning of the first policy period (initial effective) date as an anniversary for purposes of calculating the annual periods. The significance of the first sentence's statement, "and to any remaining period of less than 12 months," is that the value and limit of insurance does not prorate downward through the annual period simply as a function of the passage of time (i.e., six months into the policy, the limits are the same, not half the original amounts). In the event that the insurance coverage is extended for less than a full 12-month period (i.e., not an annual renewal), that extension will be part of the preceding "normal" 12-month period of insurance. While the limits will not change, the availability of payout will not have been replenished by the turn of the anniversary. In other words, if you used up some of the insurance toward the Aggregate Limit or Tenants' Liability Limit on a premises, those erosions of available insurance will also apply in the extended period.

Section IV—Commercial General Liability Conditions

This section comprises the general terms by which this contract is interpreted, as well as some conditions agreed to by the parties that do not pertain specifically to the heart of the contract itself but are nevertheless important. They are generally quite easy to follow, so comments are provided only where the text is heavy or the meaning is not quite as explicit as it may appear.

1. **Bankruptcy**

   Bankruptcy or insolvency of the insured or of the Insured's estate will not relieve us of our obligations under this policy.

2. **Canadian Currency Clause**

   All limits of insurance, premiums, and other amounts as expressed in this policy are in Canadian currency.

3. **Cancellation**

   a. The first Named Insured shown in the Declarations may cancel this policy by mailing or delivering to us advance written notice of cancellation.

   b. We may cancel this policy by mailing or delivering to the first Named Insured written notice of cancellation at least:

      1) Fifteen (15) days before the effective date of cancellation if we cancel for nonpayment of premium; or

      2) Twenty (20) days before the effective date of cancellation if we cancel for any other reason.

   Except in Quebec, if notice is mailed, cancellation takes effect fifteen (15) or thirty (30) days after receipt of the letter by the post office to which it is addressed, depending upon the reason for cancellation. Proof of mailing will be sufficient proof of notice.

   In Quebec, cancellation takes effect either 15 or 30 days after receipt of the notice at the last known address of the first Named Insured, depending upon the reason for cancellation.

The distinction between Quebec and the rest of Canada is due to different statutory requirements between Quebec and the other jurisdictions of Canada. My suspicion is that this has something to do with the fact that Quebec is a civil code jurisdiction, as compared to the common law consistent through the remaining jurisdictions of Canada. In any case, the time the clock starts ticking toward a cancellation's (by the insurer) effective date is more generous toward the insured party in Quebec.

   c. We will mail or deliver our notice to the first Named Insured's last mailing address known to us.

   d. The policy period will end on the date cancellation takes effect.

   e. If this policy is cancelled, we will send the first Named Insured any premium refund due. If we cancel, the refund will be pro rata. If the first Named Insured cancels, the refund may be less than pro rata. The cancellation will be effective even if we have not made or offered a refund.

There is a possible penalty applicable to a premium refund—if any—when the insured party cancels the contract. Perhaps even more interesting than that is the fact that if you do give notice to cancel this policy, you do so even if the premium refund you expected does not come from the insurer. If the premium refund is a decision factor for cancellation, it would be wise to make sure that the insurer will, in fact, provide that refund prior to giving notice.

4. **Changes**

   This policy contains all the agreements between you and us concerning the insurance afforded. The first Named Insured shown in the Declarations is authorized to make changes in the terms of this policy with our consent. This policy's terms can be amended or waived only by endorsement issued by us and made a part of this policy.

5. **Duties in the Event of Occurrence, Claim, or Action**

   a. You must see to it that we are notified promptly of an "occurrence" which may result in a claim. Notice should include:

1) How, when, and where the "occurrence" took place; and

2) The names and addresses of any injured persons and of witnesses.

b. If a claim is made or "action" is brought against any insured, you must see to it that we receive prompt written notice of the claim or "action."

c. You and any other involved insured must:

1) Immediately send us copies of any demands, notices, summonses, or legal papers received in connection with the claim or "action";

2) Authorize us to obtain records and other information;

3) Cooperate with us in the investigation, settlement, or defense of the claim or "action"; and

4) Assist us, upon our request, in the enforcement of any right against any person or organization which may be liable to the insured because of injury or damage to which this insurance may also apply.

d. No insureds will, except at their own cost, voluntarily make a payment, assume any obligation, or incur any expense, other than for first aid, without our consent.

Paragraph 5 very clearly lists your obligations in the event that you are in a circumstance that may be insurable under this policy, *if you expect to make a claim*. It is all reasonable, given that the insurer is indemnifying you from financial harm. You ignore these requirements at your own peril: failure to comply with these obligations may give the insurer the opportunity to avoid some or all of its obligations to indemnify.

6. **Examination of Your Books and Records**

We may examine and audit your books and records as they relate to this policy at any time during the policy period and up to 3 (three) years afterward.

7. **Inspection and Surveys**

We have the right but are not obligated to:

a. Make inspections and surveys at any time;

b. Give you reports on the conditions we find; and

c. Recommend any changes.

Any inspections, surveys, reports, or recommendations relate only to insurability and the premiums to be charged. We do not make safety inspections. We do not undertake to perform the duty of any person or organization to provide for the health or safety of workers or the public. And we do not warrant that conditions:

a. Are safe or healthful; or

b. Comply with laws, regulations, codes, or standards.

This condition applies not only to us, but also to any rating, advisory, rate service, or similar organization which makes insurance inspections surveys, reports, or recommendations.

The most important part of this paragraph is that any inspections or reports generated by the insurance company have no other purpose than for their own internal requirements. Additionally, you are obliged to find out and be assured on your own that (1) your insurance needs for potential liabilities are being adequately covered, (2) you are in compliance with laws and applicable regulations, etc., and (3) you are not generally out of bounds with regard to liability exposure and the insurer's requirements of you.

8. **Legal Action Against Us**

No person or organization has a right under this policy:

a. To join us as a party or otherwise bring us into an "action" asking for compensatory damages from an insured; or

b. To sue us on this policy unless all of its terms have been fully complied with.

A person or organization may sue us to recover on an agreed settlement or on a final judgement against an insured obtained after an actual trial; but we will not be liable for compensatory damages that are not payable under the terms of this policy or that are in excess of the applicable limit of insurance. An agreed settlement means a settlement and release of liability signed by us, the insured, and the claimant or the claimant's legal representative. Every "action" or proceeding against us shall be commenced within 1 (one) year next after the date of such judgement or agreed settlement and not afterwards. If this policy is governed by the law of Quebec every action or proceeding against us shall be commenced within 3 (three) years from the time the right of action arises.

Know this: this contract does not create any other relationship between the parties other than that between an insured and an insurer. The insurer and the insured remain at arm's length, and therefore nobody can join the insurer to a claim against the insured party. After a claim or action under this policy has been settled by agreement or by court order/judgement in another party's favour, that party may sue the insurer for payment to the extent of its obligations (limit of insurance). The insurer has put a limitation on the length of time within which any lawsuit against it may be filed (three years in Quebec; one year in the rest of Canada).[5] Sub-clause 8(b) is interesting because it is so very unclear. One interpretation is that you or your legal representative forgo the right to sue the insurer under this policy unless and until all your obligations under the contract have been completed, or until all the terms and obligations under the contract in general have been completed. Alternatively, it could mean that nobody else can sue the insurer under this policy until such time as all the terms of the policy have been complied with. The trouble with this second, fairly reasonable interpretation of the sentence is that it makes no practical sense.

9. Other Insurance

If other valid and collectible insurance is available to the insured for a loss we cover under Coverages A, B, or D of this policy our obligations are limited as follows:

a. Primary Insurance

This insurance is primary except when b. below applies. If this insurance is primary, our obligations are not affected unless any of the other insurance is also primary. Then, we will share with all that other insurance by the method described in c. below.

b. Excess Insurance

This insurance is excess over any of the other insurance, whether primary, excess, contingent, or on any other basis:

1) That is Property Insurance such as, but not limited to, Fire, Extended Coverage, Builder's Risk, Installation Risk, or similar coverage for "your work" or for premises rented to you; or

2) If the loss arises out of the maintenance or use of watercraft to the extent not subject to Exclusion f. of Coverage A (Section 1).

When this insurance is excess, we will have no duty under Coverage A, B, or D to defend any claim or "action" that any other Insurer has a duty to defend. If no other Insurer defends, we will undertake to do so, but we will be entitled to all the Insured's rights against all those other Insurers.

When this insurance is excess over other insurance, we will pay only our share of the amount of the loss, if any, that exceeds the sum of:

1) The total amount that all such other insurance would pay for the loss in the absence of this insurance; and

2) The total of all deductible and self-insured amounts under all that other insurance.

We will share the remaining loss, if any, with any other insurance that is not described in this Excess Insurance provision and was not bought specifically to apply in excess of the Limits of Insurance shown in the Declarations of this policy.

c. Method of Sharing

If all other insurance permits contribution by equal shares, we will follow this method also. Under this approach each Insurer contributes equal amounts until it has paid its applicable limit of insurance or none of the loss remains, whichever comes first.

If any of the other insurance does not permit contribution by equal shares, we will contribute by limits. Under this method, each Insurer's share is based on the ratio of its applicable limit of insurance to the total applicable limits of insurance of all Insurers.

Nothing in this agreement prohibits the insured party from purchasing other insurance that indemnifies for essentially the same liabilities. Perhaps this insurer would or could not underwrite the total limit of insurance desired, so you would turn to additional insurers. In any event, this clause spells out this insurer's obligations relative to other insurers covering these same liabilities.

Primary insurance: The primary Insurer is responsible to its limit of insurance before any other Insurer enters the scene. It is the "lead" and would defend any actions. This insurance policy is primary except where it is specifically classified as "excess" insurance.

Excess insurance: Excess insurance is the insurance that pays after the primary Insurer has fulfilled its indemnity obligations to the limit of its insurance. In this case, the policy is "excess" to property insurance.

Sharing: Where there is more than one primary Insurer, the insurance companies share the cost of the loss. Under this policy, the burden is shared either by equal payments to each Insurer's limit of liability, or by paying the portion of the loss equal to the Insurer's proportion of the Insured's total limit of insurance (i.e., the total limit of insurance of all the Insurers' policies).

10. **Premium Audit**
    a. We will compute all premiums for this policy in accordance with our rules and rates.
    b. Premium shown in this policy as advance premium is a deposit premium only. At the close of each audit period we will compute the earned premium for that period. Audit premiums are due and payable on notice to the first Named Insured. If the sum of the advance and audit premiums paid for this policy term is greater than the earned premium, we will return the excess to the first Named Insured subject to the retention of the minimum premium shown in the Declarations of this policy.
    c. The first Named Insured must keep records of the information we need for premium computation, and send us copies at such times as we may request.

We saw how, under the property insurance policy, it was possible to have premiums rebated after the end of an insurance period for excess coverage of stocks. This clause operates similarly, inasmuch as the declarations page will provide for a premium to be paid in advance (on some interval basis) for the policy as well as a minimum premium for the insurance period. According to the language above, the advance premiums you pay during any period are deposit premiums that must be reconciled against the audit premiums that are earned by the insurer. (After an audit period has elapsed, the insurer will calculate the actual premium owed on the policy, according to their rates and rules, and compare it with what you have paid.) If you have underpaid, you owe the insurer immediately; if you have overpaid, the insurer will rebate the overage to you *but only to the extent that you will still have paid the minimum premium in full.*

11. **Premiums**
    The first Named Insured shown in the Declarations:
    a. Is responsible for the payment of all premiums; and
    b. Will be the payee for any return premiums we pay.

12. **Representations**
    By accepting this policy, you agree:
    a. The statements in the Declarations are accurate and complete;
    b. Those statements are based upon representations you made to us; and
    c. We have issued this policy in reliance upon your representations.

13. **Separation of Insureds, Cross Liability**
    Except with respect to the Limits of Insurance, and any rights or duties specifically assigned to the first Named Insured, this insurance applies:
    a. As if each Named Insured were the only Named Insured; and
    b. Separately to each insured against whom claim is made or "action" is brought.

Basically this clause states that each Named Insured will be treated as though the policy was for that one person only should a claim arise against him or her.

14. Transfer of Rights of Recovery Against Others to Us

If the insured has rights to recover all or part of any payment we have made under this policy, those rights are transferred to us. The insured must do nothing after loss to impair them. At our request, the insured will bring "action" or transfer those rights to us and help us enforce them.

The best example of this would be having a previous decision against you overturned on appeal after the insurer had paid out to the other party. (Yes, I will also believe that pigs can fly in order to make a point.) You would then presumably have a right to recover from the other party part or all of the payment made under this policy. It is your obligation to immediately turn that right over to the insurer.

15. Transfer of your Rights and Duties Under this Policy

Your rights and duties under this policy may not be transferred without our written consent except in the case of death of an individual Named Insured.

If you die, your rights and duties will be transferred to your legal representative but only while acting within the scope of duties as your legal representative. Until your legal representative is appointed, anyone having proper temporary custody of your property will have your rights and duties but only with respect to that property.

This clause, particularly the last part of it, is actually a repetition of something we have encountered in Section II(2)(c) and (d).

Section V—Definitions

1. *"Action"* means a civil proceeding in which compensatory damages because of "bodily injury," "property damage," or "personal injury" to which this insurance applies are alleged. "Action" includes an arbitration proceeding alleging such damages to which you must submit or submit with our consent.
2. *"Automobile"* means any self-propelled land motor vehicle, trailer, or semi-trailer (including machinery, apparatus, or equipment attached thereto) which is principally designed and is being used for transportation or persons or property on public roads.
3. *"Bodily injury"* means bodily injury, sickness, or disease sustained by a person, including death resulting from any of these at any time.
4. *"Coverage territory"* means:
    a. Canada and the United States of America (including its territories and possessions);
    b. International waters or airspace, provided the injury or damage does not occur in the course of travel or transportation to or from any place not included in a. above; or
    c. All parts of the world if:
        1) The injury or damage arises out of:
            a) Goods or products made or sold by you in the territory described in a. above; or
            b) The activities of a person whose home is in the territory described in a. above, but is away for a short time on your business; and
        2) The Insured's responsibility to pay compensatory damages is determined in an "action" on the merits, in the territory described in a. above or in a settlement we agree to in writing.
5. *"Impaired property"* means tangible property, other than "your product" or "your work," that cannot be used or is less useful because:
    a. It incorporates "your product" or "your work" that is known or thought to be defective, deficient, inadequate, or dangerous; or
    b. You have failed to fulfill the terms of a contract or agreement;
    If such property can be restored to use by:
    a. The repair, replacement, adjustment, or removal of "your product" or "your work"; or
    b. Your fulfilling the terms of the contract or agreement.

6. *"Insured contract"* means:
   a. A lease of premises;
   b. A sidetrack agreement;

A sidetrack agreement, as we learned in Section I.A.2(h), relates to an agreement with a railway company for the provision and use of a siding track for loading/unloading of railcars on the insured's property.

   c. An easement or license agreement in connection with vehicle or pedestrian private railroad crossings at grade;
   d. Any other easement agreement;
   e. An indemnification of a municipality as required by ordinance, except in connection with work for a municipality;
   f. An elevator maintenance agreement; or
   g. That part of any other contract or agreement pertaining to your business under which you assume the tort liability of another to pay compensatory damages because of "bodily injury" or "property damage" to a third person or organization, if the contract or agreement is made prior to the "bodily injury" or "property damage." Tort liability means a liability that would be imposed by law in the absence of any contract or agreement.
   An "insured contract" does not include that part of any contract or agreement that indemnifies an architect, engineer, or surveyor for injury or damage arising out of:
   1) Preparing, approving, or failing to prepare or approve maps, drawings, opinions, reports, surveys, change orders, designs, or specifications; or
   2) Giving directions or instructions, or failing to give them, if that is the primary cause of the injury or damage.

7. *"Occurrence"* means an accident, including continuous or repeated exposure to substantially the same general harmful conditions.
8. *"Personal injury"* means injury, other than "bodily injury," arising out of one or more of the following offences:
   a. False arrest, detention, or imprisonment;
   b. Malicious prosecution;
   c. Wrongful entry into, or eviction of a person from, a room, dwelling, or premises that the person occupies;
   d. Oral or written publication of material that slanders or libels a person or organization or disparages a person's or organization's goods, products, or services; or
   e. Oral or written publication of material that violates a person's right of privacy.
9. a. *"Products-completed operations hazard"* includes all "bodily injury" and "property damage" occurring away from premises you own or rent and arising out of "your product" or "your work" except:
   1) Products that are still in your physical possession; or
   2) Work that has not yet been competed or abandoned.
   b. "Your work" will be deemed completed at the earliest of the following times:
   1) When all of the work called for in your contract has been completed.
   2) When all of the work to be done at the site has been completed if your contract calls for work at more than one site.
   3) When that part of work done at a job site has been put to its intended use by any person or organization other than another contractor or subcontractor working on the same project.
   Work that may need service, maintenance, correction, repair, or replacement, but which is otherwise complete, will be treated as completed.
   c. This hazard does not include "bodily injury" or "property damage" arising out of the existence of tools, uninstalled equipment or abandoned or unused materials.
10. *"Property damage"* means:
   a. Physical injury to tangible property, including all resulting loss of use of that property; or
   b. Loss of use of tangible property that is not physically injured.
11. *"Your product"* means:
   a. Any goods or products, other than real property, manufactured, sold, handled, distributed, or disposed of by:

      1) You;

      2) Others trading under your name; or

      3) A person or organization whose business or assets you have acquired; and

   b. Containers (other than vehicles), materials, parts, or equipment furnished in connection with such goods or products.

"Your product" includes warranties or representations made at any time with respect to the fitness, quality, durability, or performance of any of the items included in a. and b. above.

"Your product" does not include vending machines or other property rented to or located for the use of others but not sold.

12. *"Your work"* means:

   a. Work or operations performed by you or on your behalf; and

   b. Materials, parts, or equipment furnished in connection with such work or operations.

"Your work" includes warranties or representations made at any time with respect to the fitness, quality, durability, or performance of any of the items included in a. or b. above.

Chapter 10
Partnerships

General Partnership Agreement, Partnership Dissolution Agreement, Limited Partnership Agreement

Besides the sole proprietorship and the limited company is another common form of business association between two or more parties that seek to make a profit: the partnership. Professional practices, such as legal or accounting firms, are most often partnerships, although other kinds of business can be formed to run as partnerships as well. Unlike sole proprietorships, which are merely a commercial extension of the person in business, and unlike corporations, which are unique "persons" under the law, partnerships are separate entities from their principals but are nonetheless business extensions of those partners.

To clarify a bit, consider the situation in terms of liability. A corporation is a unique and distinct entity from all its shareholder owners, and those shareholders have their liability limited to only the amount of money they have invested in the company. Not to put too fine a point on it, regardless of what else happens to the company, the shareholders are not responsible.[1] At the other end of the spectrum is the sole proprietorship, which is little more than a person conducting business in her own right. The business does not exist apart from that person, and she is fully responsible and liable in every respect without limitation. A partnership is recognized as an entity in its own right, owning assets and engaging business in the name of the partnership. In this sense it is like a corporation. But that is where the similarity ends, because each partner is fully liable for the debts and responsibilities of the partnership jointly and severally.

> The phrase "jointly and severally" comes up in contracts quite frequently, particularly in regard to issues of responsibility and liability. Its meaning is in the roots of the two words it comprises: "join" and "sever." In other words, as a group and as individuals. Thus, when this phrase occurs, it will mean that the responsibility or liability will fall fully upon the parties named both as a group and as separate individuals. So if partners are responsible for the debts of the partnership jointly and severally, it means either as a group sharing the liability or as any severed part of that group individually liable.

Partnerships are governed by the *Partnership Act* of Britain as adopted and enacted in each province. These codified laws of partnership have stood the tests that time and circumstance have imposed on them, and remain the essence of partnerships today. And, for the most part, the legal responsibilities of the partners are those set out in the *Act*. That said, the regulation of individual partnerships is most often the domain of the respective partnership agreements, which spell out the terms of the relationship among the partners. Only if there is no written agreement (not good policy, in general) and terms must be implied do the *Act's* provisions have greater effect on partnership activities.

Recently, joint ventures have become a more common form of association between companies that wish to share the costs and/or responsibilities of a specific project that neither would care to undertake alone. These ventures are sometimes pursued by way of jointly owned subsidiary companies. However, as often as not, they are pursued in a form that amounts to nothing more than a partnership between corporate entities. Just because the partners are corporations does not change the application of the *Partnership Act* nor the respective company-partners' responsibilities and liabilities.

The following partnership agreement precedent is a good example in which we can see common relationships and operating characteristics as created by a written partnership agreement. Where applicable, we will see how the *Act* is incorporated into that agreement. Explanations of the terms are provided in which the language or the meaning of the words is not readily understandable.[2]

GENERAL PARTNERSHIP AGREEMENT
General Partnership Agreement

THIS AGREEMENT is made at Winnipeg, in the Province of Manitoba, between Christian Richardson, Richard Christianson, and Bobby Jones, <*et al.*> all of Winnipeg, Manitoba (the parties being collectively referred to as the "Partners" and each individually referred to as a "Partner").

WHEREAS the parties have agreed to enter into a partnership to carry on business as management consultants.

IN CONSIDERATION of the premises and the valuable covenants contained in this Agreement, and other good and valuable consideration (the receipt and sufficiency of which is acknowledged by each of the parties), the parties agree as follows:

1. **Effective Date**

    The parties agree and enter into a partnership effective the 1st day of February, 1999, on and subject to the terms and conditions and stipulations set forth in this Agreement.

2. **Partnership Name**

    The name of the partnership shall be Richardson, Christianson + Jones Consultants and the business of the partnership (the "Business") shall be that of management consulting and commercial advisory service and, in addition, all other incidental activities which may be carried on in connection with the Business.

This section should be similar to the information provided in the Recitals, above, if the agreement's recitals contain language regarding the name and intent of the partnership, as does this example.

3. **Head Office**

    The head office of the Business shall be at Suite 3500, 360 Main Street, Winnipeg, Manitoba, or at such other place or places as the parties shall from time to time agree on.

4. **Term**

    (1) Subject to the provisions contained in this Agreement, the partnership shall commence as of the date of this Agreement and shall continue for a term ending on the earlier of:

Note the "subject to" provision of this paragraph, which in this example specifically refers to clause 1, above. In essence, this paragraph provides a default commencement date for the agreement.

    (a) the date on which the partnership is voluntarily dissolved by agreement of the Partners; or

    (b) the date on which the partnership is dissolved by operation of law.

    (2) The partnership may be terminated without notice and on such date as may be specified in such notice.

In this agreement example, the written text is badly drafted despite the fact that we generally know what is meant. The word "notice" in the first instance means "notice period" in the sense of advance warning; in the second instance it must mean a communication, as in written or orally presented advance warning. The last half of the sentence also assumes notice (a communication indicating advance warning) is given.

5. **Percentage of Partnership Interest**

    Each of the Partners shall have a partnership interest (the "Partnership Interest") equal to the percentage set out below, namely: one third ownership interest each, and the net profits of the partnership shall be divided in accordance with each Partner's Partnership Interest. The expenses and losses of the partnership in any one partnership year shall first be paid out of the earnings of the partnership for that year, and if such earnings shall be insufficient to pay all expenses and losses as mentioned, the deficiency shall, unless otherwise agreed, be made up by the Partners in proportion to each Partner's Partnership Interest.

This clause is true boilerplate that sets out the proportional responsibilities and benefits for each partner. Of special note is the use of the "unless otherwise agreed" clause near the end of the paragraph. In a customized document the only "unless otherwise agreed" terms would be those agreements that happen among the partners at the time of a particular provision would become effective. In this example, the language seems to indicate that there might be some other, preexisting agreement on how financial deficiencies would be covered in an unequal-contribution scenario. (For example, one or more partners may have no responsibility for further financial contribution, so shortfalls would have to be made up in different proportions; or alternative forms of financing may be the way capital shortfalls are shored up. This language is very loose.)

6. Partnership Assets — Owned by Partners

The parties agree that all assets listed in Schedule "A" attached to this Agreement under the names of the partners are assets of the partnership, but that title to each asset shall remain vested with the Partner under whose name it is listed. All expenses of insuring, maintaining, repairing, and replacing these assets shall be borne by the partnership out of its general revenue.

This type of clause is common, in which established businesses or proprietors come together as partners, each bringing assets (equipment, etc.) for the use of the partnership. The partners that brought the assets retain title to them, although those assets become "assets of the partnership." This is not as illogical a leap as it may sound, since the partnership entity is, generally speaking, the collective of the partner entities. If this clause appeared in the unanimous shareholders' agreement of a corporate body, it would be dodgy both logically and legally, because the corporation is a body independent of its owners. It would be kind of like saying your car is your property in all right and title but is an asset belonging to your sister-in-law.

7. Draws

Each Partner may draw on account of his profit such amount or amounts as may be agreed on by the Partners from time to time but if at the periodical taking of accounts referred to in this Agreement, any Partner has drawn out during the past year a sum exceeding the profits to which he is entitled, he shall repay the excess to the partnership.

Partners are not entitled to salaries. Any regular pay packet a partner receives is a draw against her portion of partnership earnings. Thus, this paragraph provides a clear understanding about what happens if a partner withdraws more from the partnership in one period than is available to him.

8. Capital Contributions

(1) If at any time and from time to time capital or further capital is required for carrying on the Business, the capital shall be advanced by the Partners in proportion of each Partner's Partnership Interest provided that if any Partner shall, with the consent of the other Partners, bring in additional capital or leave any part of his profits in the business, it shall be considered a debt due from the partnership and shall bear interest at the rate per annum of the prime rate of the Canadian Imperial Bank of Commerce, provided further that it shall not be drawn out of the partnership except on giving forty-five (45) days' written notice and, in addition, he shall be required to draw out such monies on a like notice given by any other Partner; at the expiration of such period, interest shall cease to be payable on it. Subject to the foregoing, any capital of the partnership belongs to the Partners in proportion to each Partner's Partnership Interest.

To keep the partnership constant and equitable, all partners must contribute in equal proportions (or in proportions according to a formula that takes into account each respective partner's role, status, and claim on earnings/losses) with the first capitalization and again with any ensuing capital injections. In the event that one or more partners cannot ante up with the necessary portion should capital be needed at a later date, to keep the split constant, the partners that can contribute do so as a loan to the partnership. The loan can then only be drawn out, or pushed out, on thirty (30) days' notice with interest stopping at the end of the notice period. Alternatively, as provided for in paragraph 8(2) below, the partners could agree to novate the agreement, altering the partnership split, by having the capital injection come from one or more new or old partners as "equity."

(2) At such time as the net assets of the Partnership fall below the value of $50,000, or at such time as the parties shall deem it necessary, the parties shall contribute such further amounts of capital as shall be deemed necessary in proportion to their Partnership Interests. In the event that not all of the parties are able to make such further contribution, those parties able to advance monies may either contribute to capital, if all Partners consent to such contribution, in which event the interest of each Partner shall be reapportioned to reflect his total capital contribution, or may lend such monies to the partnership, at such interest rate as may be agreed on, without affecting the interest of any Partner.

This paragraph sets a floor level for the partnership capital that triggers a requirement for further capitalization. Note that this paragraph allows for unequal capital contributions from the partners, which would alter the partnership split. The commentary for the previous sub-paragraph addresses this issue. Alternatively, the financing could come from partners' loans, which would not alter the partnership split at all.

9. **Banking Arrangements**

The parties agree that the partnership shall enter into banking arrangements with any bank or banks or other financial institutions as the Partners shall agree on. All cheques, drafts, and other instruments and documents on behalf of the partnership may be signed by any one of the Partners alone, unless otherwise agreed between the parties. All partnership money shall, when received, be paid and deposited with the bankers of the partnership to the credit of the partnership account.

In practice, to both control partnership finances and make that control manageable, expenditures must be authorized (cheques signed) with the consent of all partners under some type of escalating authority program. The managing partner will often have authority to act alone up to a certain level (see paragraph 16, below), outside of which specific authority the managing partner and any other partner must sign for cheques, and so on up to a level where all partners must actually vote on an issue. These levels of authority and control are usually spelled out in a partnership agreement. After all, each partner is fully responsible for the partnership's obligations, regardless of which partner obliges the partnership. Thus, it makes sense to have controls that keep all the partners aware of what is going on financially. (In this agreement sample, the control is provided in paragraph 12, below.)

10. **Fiscal Year**

The fiscal year end of the partnership shall be the last day of the month of March in each year or such other date as the Partners may agree on.

11. **Financial Statements**

Proper accounts shall be kept of all transactions of the Business and at the end of each year or so soon thereafter as possible, a statement shall be prepared showing the income and expenses of the Business for the past year and what belongs and is due to each of the Partners as his share of the profits. If required by any Partner, the partnership accounts shall be audited by an accountant at the expense of the Business, and in addition, each of the Partners may at any time have the accounts audited by an accountant at his own expense. All books of account and related documents including all information stored electronically by means of a computer or other data storage or data processing device shall be accessible to each of the Partners and his agent at all times.

12. **Borrowing or Encumbrance of Partnership Interest**

No Partner shall, without the previous consent in writing of the others except the Managing Partner as herein provided, sign or encumber his share or interest in the partnership, borrow money on behalf of the Business, or hire any employee or subcontractor.

This clause addresses the issue of all partners knowing what is happening with partnership obligations, as mentioned earlier. It also prevents any partner from encumbering her own interest in the partnership, which is effectively the same as encumbering the partnership itself.

13. Payment of Obligations

Each of the Partners shall punctually pay and discharge his separate debts, liabilities, obligations, duties, and agreements whether at present or future and keep indemnified the partnership property and the other Partners and their estates and effects from all actions, proceedings, costs, claims, and demands of every nature.

This clause prohibits partners from becoming personally insolvent and thereby encumbering their partnership interests. Moreover, the partners must keep listed assets that are partnership assets clear and safe. Each partner hereby promises to protect and hold harmless (indemnify) the partnership and other partners for his or her own personal financial problems. In practice, this clause's effect may be somewhat limited and ineffective.

14. Indemnification

If at any time any of the Partners is required to pay or become liable for more than his proportion of the partnership debts as provided for in this Agreement, that Partner shall have as against the other Partners a right of recovery of the appropriate proportion of the payment or indemnification against such liability, and the Partner shall have, on becoming liable for such debt, the first lien or charge on the capital and all other interest or interests of the offending Partner(s) in the partnership business.

In a partnership, by law all partners are jointly and individually responsible to fully extinguish the partnership's obligations, not merely their respective proportional shares of those obligations. In the event that one or more partners must bail out the partnership when others of the partners cannot, those partners that have paid up over and above their respective shares have the first claim on the other partners' assets and interests in the partnership.

15. No Sale of Partnership Interest

No Partner shall assign or agree to assign his interest in the partnership to any other person, firm, or corporation without the prior written consent of the other Partner(s).

16. Management

(1) The Partners shall meet within thirty (30) days of the date of this Agreement, and every two (2) years thereafter, for the purpose of electing a Managing Partner. The election of the Managing Partner shall be approved by a majority in number of the Partners present at such meetings.

(2) The Managing Partner shall and is authorized to manage the day-to-day business affairs of the partnership.

(3) The Managing Partner has full authority to bind the partnership, however, with respect to the entering into of leases, contracts, mortgages, and other agreements involving greater than $10,000, the Managing Partner shall only enter into such agreements once the approval of fifty-one percent (51%) of the Partners has been obtained.

(4) The Managing Partner shall have such other duties and authority as the Partners may decide.

(5) The Managing Partner may be removed at any time on the request of the majority in number of the Partners.

(6) The term of the position of Managing Partner shall be two (2) years.

(7) The quorum for all meetings of Partners shall be seventy-five percent (75%) in number of the Partners.

(8) A Partner who cannot attend a partnership meeting may appoint, in writing, another Partner as his proxy for the purpose of voting at such meetings.

A partnership, particularly as it grows larger, cannot be effectively run by committee. Therefore a managing partner is elected to manage the partnership's day-to-day affairs. For the purpose of putting some controls in place so that the managing partner does not take the partnership in a direction that the other partners are unaware or unprepared to go, a variety of restrictions are placed on the managing partner. This paragraph provides a sampling of some such partnership controls, which may not be precise for the three initial and existing partners, but can be worked within and will allow for growth in the number of partners.

17. Valuation of Partnership Interest

The value of each Partner's interest in the Business shall be determined as follows and such value shall be the "purchase price" for the purposes of paragraphs 17, 18 and 19 of this Agreement:

(a) the sum of the values of:

(i) the fixed assets of the Business at their book value as set out in Schedule "B" to this Agreement, as amended from time to time by the parties by their annexation of additional parts to Schedule "B," initialled by each of the Partners for identification. If there is any disagreement between the Partners or their respective heirs, administrators, successors, and assigns as to the book value of such fixed assets then that value shall be determined by reference to the partnership's accountant who in his sole and absolute discretion may determine the value and this determination shall be final and binding on the parties to this Agreement;

This sub-paragraph fairly clearly spells out the asset valuation to be used in evaluating the partnership. It is important to be aware that the assets being evaluated here are true partnership assets and not those whose titles rest with the partners that brought them to the partnership (listed in Schedule "A"). Those listed assets would not be included in this calculation, as they presumably belong to their respective owner(s).

(ii) the accounts receivable of the Business less an allowance of five percent (5%) for doubtful accounts;

(iii) an amount equal to the work in progress, as agreed by the Partners or their respective heirs, executors, administrators, successors, and assigns, failing such agreement as determined by reference to the partnership's accountant who in his sole and absolute discretion may determine such value and such determination shall be final and binding on the parties; and

Work-in-process is "accounts receivable" prior to billing, and this type of clause would generally be found in a professional partnership agreement. Oddly, there is no provision for a 5% bad debts reserve, as there is for actual accounts receivable.

(iv) the sum of $1.00 in respect of goodwill;

Goodwill is an ephemeral thing and often quite hard to quantify. In this instance, it is essentially the "premium" on the intangible value of the partnership's name, reputation, business, ability to attract customers, and so forth. This example arbitrarily shows $1.00, but in practice the goodwill in a longstanding partnership's name may be quite significant.

(b) less the liabilities of the Business (excluding any realized but undistributed profits of the Business).

"Realized but undistributed profits" should really be considered as not belonging to the partnership anymore, but rather as money merely being held for the partners pending payout or distribution in the appropriate proportions. For purposes of a valuation and distribution, however, their inclusion or exclusion is material only inasmuch as the evaluator recognizes and notes that undistributed profits have been included in establishing the value of the partnership or have been excluded from such valuation because the money is to be distributed to the existing partners. Undistributed profits are certainly not liabilities of the partnership.

18. Withdrawal from Partnership

(1) Subject to dissolution of the partnership as provided for, any Partner may withdraw from the partnership on not less than three (3) months' written notice to the other Partners to be effective at the year end of the partnership, unless the date of withdrawal is otherwise mutually agreed on by the remaining Partners.

This clause demands 90 days' notice of withdrawal from the partnership, which must usually be made 90 days prior to a partnership year-end unless otherwise agreed among the partners. This timing issue (withdrawals happening at a year-end) exists probably more for convenience than any other reason.

(2) Unless a majority of the remaining Partners agree within thirty (30) days of what would otherwise be the effective withdrawal date or date of the death of a Partner, that the partnership shall be dissolved, the withdrawal or death of a Partner shall not dissolve the partnership, but the partnership shall continue in existence, in which event the interest of the withdrawing or deceased Partner shall be acquired by the remaining Partners. In such event, the purchase price shall be that set out in paragraph 17. The transaction of purchase and sale shall take place not more than ninety (90) days from the date of withdrawal or death of a Partner.

If a partner withdraws, by desire or by dying, the other partners must decide within 30 days whether to dissolve the partnership. If they do not, the remaining partners must buy up the withdrawing partner's interest at the value established by the rules set out in paragraph 17. The purchase would presumably be made in accordance with paragraph 8, which provides for new capital and changes to the partnership interest balances. Nothing specific is noted here, so it is possible that one partner could purchase the interest of the withdrawing partner in its entirety.

19. Dissolution

The partnership shall be dissolved only if all the Partners agree. The Partners shall cause the assets of the partnership to be realized and the liabilities of the partnership to be paid. The net amount realized therefrom, after deducting all reasonable expenses incurred in disposition and realization of the assets, shall be divided among the Partners in accordance with their Partnership Interests as such sums are received.

20. Marriage Contracts

Each of the Partners covenants that he will enter into a marriage contract within the meaning of The Marital Property Act (Manitoba) (the "Act") with his spouse which contract shall be in the form set out in Schedule "C" to this Agreement.

Schedule "C" would likely contain a form of prenuptial agreement that protects the partnership interest from the partner's new spouse in the event of a marital breakdown or the partner's death.

21. Full Time and Attention

The Partners agree to devote their full time, attention, and energy to the Business.

Right! The purpose of this clause is not to preclude a partner from giving of herself to charitable causes and other networking forms of extracurricular activity. Its purpose is to prevent a partner from using the partnership as a launching pad for other moneymaking activities that do not pass through the partnership. It would not really be fair to the other partners if one were to occupy partnership office space and use partnership overheads, and ultimately share in the partnership's profits, if one were not contributing to the partnership. Instead, one might be running or representing a different type of business, creating personal income that does not come to the partnership for sharing with the partners. (Don't laugh; it happens more often than you might think.)

22. Amendment of Agreement

If at any time during the continuation of this Agreement the Partners shall deem it necessary or expedient to make any alteration in any clause contained in this Agreement, they may do so by a writing signed by them and endorsed on these articles, and all of these alterations shall be adhered to and have the same effect as if they had been originally embodied in and formed part of this Agreement.

23. Notice

Any notice required or permitted to be given or delivered hereunder by any Partner shall be in writing and shall be given by prepaid registered mail addressed to the other Partners at their last known residence address and any notice so given or delivered shall be deemed to have been received three (3) days after mailing.

24. Governing Law

This Agreement and the application or interpretation of it shall be governed exclusively by the terms and by the laws of the Province of Manitoba and each partner irrevocably attorns to the jurisdiction of the courts of Manitoba.

25. **Time**

    Time shall be of the essence of this Agreement.

26. **Headings**

    The headings appearing throughout this Agreement shall not form part of this Agreement. The parties desire that this Agreement be given a broad and liberal interpretation.

Remember that a court may interpret a contract either strictly or liberally; either according to the precise meaning of the words or according to the obvious overall intent of the agreement. The manner of interpretation could have dramatically different results in a court proceeding. This contract specifies internally that the contract is to be interpreted by its intended meaning.

27. **Severability**

    Each provision of this Agreement shall be severable. If any provision of it is illegal or invalid, the illegality or invalidity shall not affect the validity of the remainder of this Agreement.

28. **Number and Gender**

    This Agreement is to be read with all changes in gender or number as required by the context.

29. **Agreement Binding**

    This Agreement shall enure to the benefit of and be binding on the respective heirs, executors, administrators, and permitted assigns of each of the parties to it.

    IN WITNESS WHEREOF this Agreement has been executed by the parties as of the 1st day of February, 1999.

    SIGNED, SEALED AND DELIVERED

    in the presence of: <*etc.*>

    <*add Schedules "A," "B," "C," etc.*>

PARTNERSHIP DISSOLUTION

Partnerships can be dissolved by an act of or the working of the law, in which instance a formal dissolution of the partnership is not required. To be doubly sure, and more importantly, to properly dissolve a partnership when the working of the law is not a factor in the partnership's dissolution, a dissolution agreement should be executed. By doing so, the partners properly limit or reallocate the liabilities of the former partners and the partnership. A brief example with explanations where necessary follows.

Partnership Dissolution Agreement

THIS AGREEMENT is made at the City of Winnipeg, in the Province of Manitoba, between Bobby Jones, of the City of Winnipeg, in the Province of Manitoba (the "Departing Partner"), and Christian Richardson, of the City of Winnipeg in the Province of Manitoba, and Richard Christianson, of the City of Winnipeg in the Province of Manitoba (collectively the "Continuing Partners").

WHEREAS:

1. The Departing Partner and the Continuing Partner have since the 1st day of February, 1999, carried on as a partnership the business of management consulting under the name Richardson, Christianson + Jones Consultants (the "Business");

2. Pursuant to the provisions of The Partnership Act (Manitoba) all partners are liable for the debts of the Business to the full extent of the law;

3. The Departing Partner and the Continuing Partners have decided to dissolve the partnership.

IN CONSIDERATION of the premises and the mutual covenants in this Agreement and other good and valuable consideration (the receipt and sufficiency of which is acknowledged by each of the parties) the parties agree as follows:

1. Dissolution

The partnership existing between the parties is dissolved as of the 31st day of October, 2001.

Technically, this clause dissolves the partnership not only for the departing partner but for all of them. The remaining partners would create a new partnership agreement, essentially on the same terms and conditions, without the exiting partner and with revised interest portions.

2. Purchase of Partnership Interest

In consideration for the purchase of his partnership interest, the Departing Partner shall be paid the sum of $25,000 by the Continuing Partners and the Continuing Partners will assume any and all obligations and liabilities which the Departing Partner had under the partnership agreement, specifically *<list obligations>*.

The continuing partners agree to purchase the exiting partner's share of the partnership and relieve that exiting partner of any further liability for partnership activities and obligations.

3. Indemnification

Notwithstanding any of the Departing Partner's liabilities associated with the Business, the Continuing Partners assume all of the debts and obligations of the Business, and will indemnify and save harmless the Departing Partner from all claims, demands, and liabilities of every nature and kind whatsoever the Departing Partner may have as a partner in connection with the Business.

4. Binding Effect

This Agreement shall enure to the benefit of and be binding on the heirs, executors, successors, legal representatives, and assigns of each of the parties respectively.

5. Governing Law

This Agreement shall be governed by and construed in accordance with the laws of the Province of Manitoba.

6. Entire Agreement

The foregoing contains the entire agreement between the parties in connection with the subject-matter of this Agreement and no modification shall be binding on the parties unless it is in writing and signed by the respective parties. IN WITNESS WHEREOF this Agreement has been executed by the parties as of the 31st day of October, 2001. SIGNED, SEALED AND DELIVERED
in the presence of: *<etc.>*

LIMITED PARTNERSHIP

The limited partnership is a special kind of partnership that operates more similarly to a limited liability company than a normal partnership. It has a personality separate from those of most of the partners. A limited partnership is created by law and requires not only registration in the province in which it is being created, but also both a subscription agreement and a limited partnership agreement.

In a limited partnership there are "general partners" and "limited partners." The key difference between the normal partnership situation and the limited partnership is that the maximum liability of the "limited partner" is the value of the investment made by purchase of a partnership share. The general partner(s) remain fully liable as they would in a regular partnership.

An important matter to the limited partner is the restriction placed on his contribution to the partnership, beyond the subscription to and payment for the partnership share. In order to retain the limited liability status, a limited partner must not participate in the management of the partnership. If a limited partner becomes active in the partnership's management, he risks being deemed a general partner and losing his limited liability standing.

The following precedent is provided and annotated to better understand the nature of the limited partnership. Where the legal language is readily understandable, explanation is omitted.[3]

Limited Partnership Agreement

THIS AGREEMENT made the 15th day of June, 1999, between New Ventures Limited, a company incorporated under the laws of Manitoba (the "General Partner") and those persons signing this Agreement as limited partners (the "Limited Partners").

WHEREAS the parties desire to form a limited partnership to carry on the business of hospitality and food service. It is mutually agreed as follows:

1. Partners and Partnership

(1) The parties agree to form a limited partnership (the "Partnership") in accordance with and pursuant to the provisions of The Partnership Act (Manitoba).

Limited partnerships, more like limited liability companies than true partnerships, are creatures of the law. Thus they are regulated more closely than run-of-the-mill partnerships in most respects.

(2) The name of the Partnership shall be Food on the Run. The principal office of the Partnership shall be 22nd Floor, 400 St. Mary Avenue, Winnipeg, Manitoba.

(3) The business of the Partnership (the "Partnership Business") shall be hospitality and food service.

(4) The property of the Partnership may be registered in the name of the Partnership.

(5) The term of the Partnership shall commence on the date of the filing of a Declaration of Limited Partnership under The Partnership Act (Manitoba).

The filing of the appropriate document(s) is required in order to create a limited partnership. This document demands disclosure in a manner not unlike a prospectus or offering memorandum for share capital.

2. Capital

(1) The General Partner shall contribute to the capital of the Partnership the sum of $50,000.

(2) Each person who agrees to become a Limited Partner shall execute a written limited partnership subscription agreement (the "subscription agreement") in the form annexed as Schedule "A," setting forth, among other things, the total amount of cash agreed to be contributed by him to the capital of the Partnership (his "agreed contribution"), which shall be paid by him to the Partnership as provided in and in accordance with the provisions of the subscription agreement. The aggregate maximum amount of agreed contributions in subscription agreements accepted by the General Partner shall not exceed $300,000.

Limited partners must subscribe for their partnership shares (again, like share capital in a corporation), and there is a limit placed on the amount of capital to be generated by the offering of limited partnerships.

(3) No actual business activities of the Partnership shall be initiated or commenced until the General Partner shall have received and accepted subscription agreements representing agreed contributions of $200,000 in the aggregate. In the event subscription agreements for such amount of agreed contributions are not received and accepted by the General Partner prior to the 30th day of September, 2001, the Partnership shall be terminated and all contributions received from subscribers shall be returned to them by the General Partner, without interest.

Essentially, like a share offering, the limited partnership offering must "close" by the general partners obtaining subscriptions for a specified or acceptable number of limited partnership units. Until that time, neither the limited partnership nor the underlying business exists or may legally be carried on. Subscription money is held in escrow until the offering closes.

(4) An individual capital account shall be maintained for each partner and shall initially be credited with the amount of his cash contribution to the capital of the Partnership. No partner shall be entitled to withdraw any part of his capital account or to receive any distribution from the Partnership except as provided in paragraphs 4(7) and (8) and 5(1).

What this states is that the limited partnership books must contain separate capital accounts for each limited partner's investment in order to properly record and maintain correct accounts of investment, accumulation, and so forth.

> (5) No interest shall be paid on any capital contributed to the Partnership.

A limited partner is an "equity" holder in the partnership, and as such is not entitled to interest on her capital investment. The following paragraph expands on that premise and further specifies that the "limited" part of the "limited partnership" is that the bottom limit of the partner's loss is his initial capital contribution. Unlike regular partnerships, the limited partner is not liable for the limited partnership's obligations.

> (6) No Limited Partner, as such, shall be obliged to make any contribution to the capital of the Partnership in excess of his agreed contribution, nor shall any Limited Partner have any personal liability as such for any of the debts of the Partnership or for any of the losses thereof beyond the amount of his agreed contribution.

3. Management

> (1) The business and affairs of the Partnership shall be managed by the General Partner. The General Partner shall have all necessary powers to carry on the Partnership business, provided, however, that the General Partner shall have no authority:
>
>> (a) to sell, exchange, pledge, mortgage, or otherwise encumber or dispose of all or a substantial part of the assets of the Partnership without the prior written consent of at least two-thirds in interest of the Limited Partners, or
>>
>> (b) to borrow money on behalf of the Partnership, other than for the purpose of discharging obligations of the Partnership not voluntarily incurred by the General Partner, without the prior written consent of at least two-thirds in interest of the Limited Partners.

This section provides the general partner with full authority over the business of the partnership except for certain specified circumstances, such as borrowing, encumbering the partnership, and disposing of assets. All of these acts cut to the heart of the partnership and may not have a great deal to do with the operation of the business.

> (2) No person dealing with the General Partner shall be required to determine its authority to make or execute any instrument or undertaking on behalf of or take any other action binding on the Partnership, or to determine any fact or circumstance bearing on the existence of such authority, or to see to the application and distribution of any revenues or proceeds paid to the Partnership in connection herewith.

The general partner is effectively the business to any and all outsiders, who are under no obligation to establish the breadth of the general partner's authority. Coupled with paragraph 3(1) above, this section essentially gives the general partner full authority to run the business, but puts a leash on him. But that leash is a private, internal matter, and has no effect on parties outside the partnership.

> (3) The General Partner may, in its discretion, employ other persons interested in or companies owned by, associated with, or affiliated with the General Partner to render, on behalf of the Partnership, part of all of such specialized and general administrative services as are reasonably required to accomplish the purposes of the Partnership.

This paragraph was probably created and added to boilerplate because it allows the general partner, who can be in the same business as the limited partnership, to use its own resources to manage and run the limited partnership's business without conflict of interest. In some cases this is probably a reasonable and good thing. It does, however, make it possible for the general partner to cream out, by way of expenses, more money directly into her pocket.

(4) The General Partner shall not be liable, responsible, or accountable in damages or otherwise to the Partnership or to any of the other partners for acts performed by it in good faith and without gross negligence.

The key words in this paragraph are "in good faith" and "without *gross* negligence." I would expect the limited partners would all hope that the general partner acted in such manner. Yet this clause does not provide for the general partner's liability toward the partnership in the case of mere good intentions and bad judgement.

(5) No Limited Partner, as such, shall take any part in the management of the business or affairs of or transact any business for the Partnership and shall have no right to and shall not sign for or bind the Partnership in any way.

Give the money and watch from the sidelines. Remember that the limited partner can lose the protection of limited liability status by becoming involved in the operation of the business. This paragraph probably exists to address that fact.

(6) From the funds contributed to the capital of the Partnership, the Partnership shall pay or reimburse the General Partner all expenses incurred in connection with the organization of the Partnership, the acquisition and financing of <*assets*> and the sale of the interests of the Limited Partners including, without limitation, printing costs and fees and disbursements.

(7) The General Partner shall be reimbursed by the Partnership, as and when the Partnership receives funds available therefor, for all reasonable out-of-pocket expenses incurred by it on behalf of the Partnership provided that such expenses were not incurred during the term of the agreement referred to in paragraph (6) in respect of matters covered thereby.

What the previous two paragraphs indicate is that the general partner is never out of pocket except for its contribution as provided in paragraph 2(1). The limited partners actually pay for the promotion and sale of those limited partnerships to them.

(8) The General Partner shall be paid an annual fee of $<*fee*> as compensation for its management of the business and affairs of the Partnership, provided that if the General Partner shall hire any person to perform all or part of its management functions, the remuneration of such person shall be paid by the General Partner out of its annual fee.

In this example, it is questionable just what other services will or will not be paid out of management fees (see paragraph 3(3)) and what will come out of general expenses. The extent of "Management" of business affairs is not spelled out, which leaves the door open to some interesting creative possibilities.

(9) Any partner may engage in or possess an interest in other business ventures of every nature including, without limitation, hospitality and food service establishments; neither the Partnership nor the other partners shall by virtue of this Agreement have any rights in or to such other ventures.

I always find it interesting how the general partner has no prohibition from competitive ventures, because my encounters with limited partnerships have been in the area of golf courses, restaurant ventures, and such. Perhaps in the traditional areas in which limited partnerships were/are used, such as resource exploration, this clause makes much more sense. Nevertheless, I find it ironic that the general partner, the mind of the business, can actually open and operate any number of competitive ventures. Again, to my cynical mind, it opens the door to some interesting possibilities.

4. Accounts

(1) The General Partner shall maintain full and accurate books of the Partnership at the Partnership's principal place of business, showing all receipts and expenditures, assets and liabilities, profits and losses, and all other records necessary for recording the Partnership Business and its affairs, including those sufficient to record the allocations and distributions provided for in paragraphs (6), (7), and (8). The books of the Partnership will be kept on

an accrual basis. The books and records shall be open to the inspection and examination of all partners in person or by their duly authorized representatives at reasonable times.

(2) The fiscal year of the Partnership shall be the calendar year.

(3) The General Partner shall cause to be prepared for the Partnership an annual statement showing the income and expenses of the Partnership and the balance sheet thereof at the end of the year. The Partnership shall have an annual review of its income and expense by a firm of Canadian chartered accountants of national recognized standing selected by the General Partner and shall furnish to each partner copies of such balance sheet and a statement of such partner's share of the Partnership's profit or loss, together with a report of such accountants covering such balance sheet and statement, within sixty (60) days after the end of each fiscal year. The Partnership shall also furnish to any Limited Partner such other reports on the Partnership's operations and condition as may be reasonably requested.

(4) All funds of the Partnership shall be deposited in its name in such chequing and savings accounts or time certificates as shall be designated by the General Partner. Withdrawals therefrom shall be made on such signature or signatures as the General Partner may designate.

(5) All decisions as to accounting principles, except as specifically provided to the contrary in this Agreement, shall be made by the General Partner and shall be acceptable to the firm of chartered accountants referred to in paragraph (3).

Most chartered accountants will render their opinions and audits on the basis of generally accepted accounting principles (GAAP), and their report (see paragraph 4(3)) will state fairly clearly the accountant's understanding of the partnership's financial reporting practices.

(6) The profits and losses of the Partnership shall be determined each year in accordance with accounting principles and methods followed for Canadian income tax purposes and shall be allocated among the partners and credited (or charged) to their capital accounts in proportion to their respective capital contributions to the Partnership.

Bear in mind when reading this paragraph that this is a partnership, and as such the portion of profits and losses that are applicable to each partner are to be the tax responsibility of that partner. Therefore, the profits and losses are recorded directly to each partner's capital account. Paragraph 4(9), farther below, provides the procedure by which the partnership will provide the appropriate information to the partners.

(7) On or before December 31st in each of the years <first applicable year> through <last applicable year>, after providing for the satisfaction of the obligations to which Partnership properties are subject and which have accrued at the time the distributions referred to in this sentence are made, there shall be distributed to partners, in proportion to their respective capital contributions to the Partnership, cash in an aggregate amount equal to twenty-five percent (25%) of the available profit (as defined) of the Partnership during such year. As used in this Agreement, the term "available profit" means all revenue received by the Partnership from operations less all expenses required to operate the partnership, plus a contingency reserve, as set by the General Partner, in its sole discretion, each year. The obligation to make such distributions shall be cumulative, but unpaid amounts shall not bear interest.

During certain periods in the life of the limited partnership, this clause provides for a guaranteed distribution of certain profits. The distributed sum in the paragraph is similar to a dividend in some senses. That is, the paragraph does not provide for full profit distribution (see paragraph 4(8) for that), but rather the guaranteed distribution of some smaller amount of the net profits. This particular distribution may only be for the first few years of the limited partnership, the last few years, a set number of years in the middle, or for all the years of the partnership's life. And, even though it may leave behind a fair amount of cash, (1) these distributions are required and cumulative and (2) any additional money left behind in the limited partnership in any year is dealt with in paragraph 4(8).

(8) After providing for the satisfaction of the debts and obligations of the Partnership or to which Partnership properties are subject, providing a reasonable reserve for expenses expected to be incurred by the Partnership, and providing for the payment of the distribution required by paragraph (7) for the then current calendar year, any remaining funds shall be distributed to the partners at such time or times as the General Partner shall, in its sole discretion, determine, in proportion to their respective capital contributions to the Partnership.

In this agreement, a reserve for unexpected expenses is held back in the partnership but all other profits are distributed to the partners each year at time or times chosen by the general partner.

(9) The Partnership shall furnish each Limited Partner, not later than the sixty (60) days following the end of each fiscal year, with such information with respect to the activities of the Partnership and the interests of the Limited Partners therein as may be required in order to effect any filing required of the limited partners pursuant to the laws of Canada or any province thereof including filings under the Income Tax Act, R.S.C. 1952, c. 148.

Various laws and authorities, not the least of which is the *Income Tax Act* and Revenue Canada, require reporting of holdings and interests not only of the partnership entity, but of the partners as well. Because it is still a partnership—albeit of the limited variety—the profits and/or other changes to the partnership are pushed out to the partners every year for income tax purposes. This agreement provides internally for the procedures and timing of how such information will be properly and accurately distributed to all the partners.

5. Dissolution

(1) The Partnership shall be dissolved on the first to occur of the following:

(a) the dissolution, bankruptcy, or assignment for the benefit of creditors of the General Partner; or

(b) December 31, 2005.

This section is relatively self-explanatory, but one should note that the general partner's bankruptcy is effectively the bankruptcy of the limited partnership entity. Also note that the limited partnership has a finite life.

Subject where applicable to compliance with the provisions of The Partnership Act (Manitoba) for the renewal thereof, the Partnership shall not dissolve or terminate on the death, bankruptcy, assignment of property in trust for the benefit of creditors, or adjudication of incompetency or insanity, legal incapacity, withdrawal, or attempted withdrawal, of or by any Limited Partner, or the admission of any additional or substituted Limited Partners.

(2) On the dissolution of the Partnership, the properties of the Partnership shall be sold by the General Partner (or if dissolution is pursuant to paragraph (1)(a), by the nominee of two-thirds in interest of the Limited Partners) who shall have full power to sell, assign, or encumber any or all of the Partnership assets, as liquidating trustee, and the proceeds remaining after the payment of or provision for the debts of the Partnership shall be distributed to the partners in proportion to their respective capital contributions to the Partnership.

The bankruptcy of the general partner forces the limited partners to elect a nominee to liquidate the assets of the partnership and distribute the proceeds in the proper proportions.

(3) The General Partner may not, nor may any Limited Partner without the written consent of the General Partner, withdraw from the Partnership.

(4) No Limited Partner, without the written consent of the General Partner, shall sell, assign, transfer, pledge, hypothecate, or encumber his interest in the Partnership except that a Limited Partner may assign not less than his entire interest in the Partnership to a member of his immediate family or a corporation or partnership controlled by him or a charitable organization exempt from income taxes under the Income Tax Act. On any assignment in conformity with the preceding sentence, the assignee shall have the right to become substituted as a Limited Partner in place of his assignor.

Of note here is that a limited partnership interest cannot be negotiated as an asset in any way, nor can it be assigned except in its entirety under specific conditions, at least within this sample agreement.

(5) On the death or legal incapacity of a Limited Partner, his interest shall descend to and vest in his legal representatives with full power in them or his heirs or legatees to become substituted as Limited Partners in his place.

(6) As conditions to the admission of a permitted assignee, transferee, or successor of a Limited Partner as a substituted Limited Partner, any such person shall

(a) execute and acknowledge such instruments, in form and substance satisfactory to the General Partner, as the General Partner shall deem necessary or desirable to effect such admission and to confirm the agreement of the person being admitted as a substituted Limited Partner to be bound by all of the terms and provisions of this Agreement and to continue the Partnership without its dissolution or termination or its becoming a general partnership under the laws of the Province of Manitoba or of any other relevant jurisdiction, or for any other reason; and

For a person to be admitted as a substitute limited partner to the limited partnership, and to prevent the limited partnership from becoming a general partnership, the new partner must be bound to the terms of the original limited partner, and various filings may need to be made. Apparently an assignee is obliged to initiate and undertake such necessary actions, and to assume all costs associated with the filings.

(b) pay all reasonable expenses in connection with such admission including, but not limited to, the cost of preparation and filing of all necessary amending certificates in such jurisdictions.

(7) A General Partner may assign all or any part of its interest in the profits and losses of the Partnership but no assignee of a General Partner shall have the right to become substituted as a General Partner in place of his assignor.

This clause gives the general partner the right to assign or "pledge" its share of the (anticipated) partnership profits to anyone, in whole or in part. The assignee of those rights does not assume the duties associated with the general partner, and those duties and obligations remain attached to the general partner regardless of whether it assigns its profit/loss interest. For all intents and purposes, this clause should have little impact on the limited partners.

(8) Each partner represents and warrants that he is acquiring his interest in the Partnership for his own account for investment and not with a view to the distribution thereof.

6. Miscellaneous

(1) Each Limited Partner irrevocably constitutes and appoints the General Partner with full power of substitution, his true and lawful attorney, in his name, place, and stead, to make, execute, consent to, swear to, acknowledge, record, and file:

(a) a Declaration of Limited Partnership under the laws of the Province of Manitoba;

(b) every other certificate or other instrument which may be required to be filed by the Partnership to the partners under the laws of the Province of Manitoba to the extent that the General Partner deems such filing to be necessary or desirable;

(c) all other instruments as the General Partner may deem necessary or desirable fully to carry out the provisions of this agreement in accordance with its terms.

(2) It is expressly understood and intended by each Limited Partner that the grant of the foregoing power of attorney is coupled with an interest and such grant shall be irrevocable.

(3) The foregoing power of attorney shall, in respect of any Limited Partner who shall have died or shall have assigned his interest, or any part thereof, in the Partnership, survive such death or the assignment of such interest, as the case may be. In the event of any conflict between this Agreement and any instruments filed by such attorney-in-fact pursuant to such powers of attorney, this Agreement shall prevail.

In sub-sections (1), (2), and (3), the limited partners give a power of attorney to the general partner for the purpose of executing documents necessary for filings and reports. The interesting feature of this language is that the power of attorney being given is irrevocable and absolute over any other power of attorney that the limited partner may make (at least as regards the scope and extent of the powers afforded by this power of attorney).

(4) The General Partner, or Limited Partners representing twenty-five percent (25%) of interest of the Limited Partners, may by ten (10) days' notice in writing to all other partners (including the date for which notice is given but exclusive of the date on which notice is given) call a meeting in *<blank>* of the partners. Such notice shall specify the time, date, and place of the meeting and shall particularize the business to be transacted at the meeting. The partner or partners calling any such meeting shall appoint a chairman therefor.

This paragraph provides the formula for calling a meeting of the partners to discuss or otherwise transact partnership business. The notice period of 10 days means on the 10th day *after* mailing, but you have to add another three days to account for the effective receipt of the notice by the limited partners, as per paragraph 6(5)(b), below. All told, notice should be effective on the 13th day after mailing.

(5) All notices under this Agreement shall be in writing, duly signed by the party giving such notice, and transmitted by registered or certified mail addressed as follows:
(a) if given to the Partnership, or to the General Partner, at the principal place of business of the Partnership; and
(b) if given to any Limited Partner, at the address set forth below his signature at the end of this Agreement, or at such other address as he may hereafter designate by notice to the Partnership. Any notice so given shall be deemed to have been received on the third business day following the date of mailing.
(6) This Agreement may not be modified or amended except with the written consent of all the partners.
(7) This Agreement may be executed in any number of counterparts and all of such counterparts shall for all purposes constitute one agreement, binding on the parties, notwithstanding that all parties are not signatory to the same counterpart.
(8) This Agreement shall be governed by and construed in accordance with the laws of the Province of Manitoba and all parties irrevocably attorn to the jurisdiction of the courts of the province.
(9) Each of the parties represents and warrants that he is over the age of eighteen (18) years.
(10) Except as otherwise provided to the contrary, this Agreement shall be binding on and enure to the benefit of the parties, their legal representatives, successors, heirs, and assigns.

IN WITNESS WHEREOF this Agreement has been executed by the parties as of the 15th day of June, 1999.
SIGNED, SEALED AND DELIVERED
in the presence of: *<etc.>*
<attach Schedule "A">

Chapter 11
Licenses and Franchise Agreements

Licensing, Franchising, Franchise Agreement

Licensing and franchising are a significant part of the commercial landscape in Canada. A license is essentially the right to use another's property (trademark, name, process, etc.) for a fee. Franchises are an extended form of product licensing. Together licenses and franchises are such a common part of commerce today that we hardly stop to think about it. When you read or hear that some brand of cola is "bottled under license" does it trigger a synapse? Does the amazing and rapid propagation of popular brand clothing or sports-logo-emblazoned merchandise all around the world not make one wonder, "How are they in so many places so fast?" Could McDonald's possibly manage and control as many corporate-owned stores as it maintains franchised operations? It all happens through the magic of licensing and franchising.

LICENSING

A business creates something of value, say for instance a process, a formula, and a brand name (think of Coca-Cola or Kentucky Fried Chicken—KFC, if you prefer), and develops it into a strong business in its own right. In order to grow rapidly, that small business will create relationships with arm's-length partners to expand the business model to different areas. The partner is interested because by using the proven product rather than trailblazing its own product, it has a greater certainty of sales and profits. Thus the partner will, through its business, license the right to use, produce, manufacture, market, and sell the product that results from that process, formula, and brand name in (usually) a certain geographic area.

Nothing, not even a license, is free. The licensor (the party offering the right to the product) will generally provide the license to the licensee (the party obtaining the right) for a fee. In the simplest of circumstances, the licensee will pay to the licensor a fixed dollar amount or percentage of revenue (the "royalty") from each item sold under license. In practice, the licensor will usually demand minimum volume royalty payment guarantees, and other payment concessions. Depending on the value of the license, the costs can become onerous for the licensee.

So, why does the licensee choose to license a product? In a perfect world the answer is relatively simple: the licensed product provides higher probability for success. Even if the licensee has a higher cost structure, all the developmental work of the product and the brand is done. So, the licensee needs only to manufacture and market the product properly and aggressively in order to create a business.

The licensor, on the other hand, benefits by obtaining a smaller, but relatively more certain cash flow and revenue from the licensed product. That is, despite forgoing some revenue by giving up a right to the product to the licensee, the licensor does not have to capitalize or manage the human resource, production, and marketing required to develop new markets. The goal is, of course, to create ever-higher volumes of sales by reaching more markets with greater resources. The cost to the licensor is a lack of complete control.

I would not want to suggest by my examples and style in the preceding paragraphs that licenses are only on garments, merchandise, and other consumer goods. Resource companies often license mineral and oil rights in order to create their products. And, arguably the most misunderstood, fastest-growing, and generally ubiquitous license used in business today is the software license.

For those who are still not aware of the facts, computer software is never purchased, except by software vendors or businesses that commission the development of a special custom application. Software as we know it, the boxes of disks and books that come from Microsoft, Lotus, Aldus, and others, is provided under license. (This fact probably goes a long way to explain the "License Agreement" printed on the sealed envelope that contains the program disks.) The software vendor could not sell its product to you for a variety of reasons, not the least of which is if you purchased the software, you would actually own the source code that they spent millions of dollars writing. So, what you get for your one-time license fee of $495 (or whatever) is the right to use that software under the terms and conditions set forth in the License Agreement.

Arguably, there are a few key parts to a solid license agreement. They are explained briefly in the following points.

• *Property licensed*

This is a key term of the license agreement, inasmuch as it is the reason for the agreement in the first place. The licensed property could be a trademark, copyright, patent, process, design, formula, or the right to use or produce and sell any such properties.

• *Term of license*

Most licenses, like many other contracts, have fixed periods during which they are in effect. Some are quite short, a year or two, while others are much longer—10 or 20 years, or in perpetuity. During the term of the license, the licensor warrants that the licensee will have use of the licensed property under the conditions specified in the contract. Shorter-term contracts will often have renewal and renegotiation options built in.

• *Territory of license*

All licenses contain, in addition to a fixed term, a fixed territory. Most often this territory will be geographic such as a particular city, province, country, or continent. Not very frequently are valuable licenses provided for the globe, although this would constitute a fixed territory. In some cases in which the licensee wanted to overreach, the licensor would protect herself by writing a license on one market and offering the right of first refusal on other markets.

• *License fees, royalties, and payment structure*

The consideration or cost of the license is another key part of the agreement. In some cases there might be a license fee: a one-time or periodic charge to obtain and keep the license. Franchises, as we will see below, are commonly obtained only after first paying just such an up-front fee. In addition, the licensee is required to pay an ongoing fee based on sales success. This revenue percentage or per-unit charge is generally referred to as a *royalty*. License agreements stipulate periodic calculation and payment of royalties to the licensor on some basis such as on actual sales units, sales revenue, gross profits, or occasionally on direct cost of manufacture. As an incentive to the licensee, and an assurance to the licensor, licenses will almost always contain minimum royalty guarantees for fixed periods, such as per year, and these minimums usually escalate with each successive period.

• *Conditions of license*

The conditions of the license vary from agreement to agreement. Some conditions crop up with tremendous consistency. Among them are:

  • The licensor's right to inspect the books and records of the licensee.
  • The licensee's requirement to operate within fixed guidelines set for the use and marketing of the licensed properties.
  • The licensee's requirement to produce or manufacture within moral guidelines set by the licensor.
  • The licensee's requirement to uphold certain quality, pricing, and image standards for the licensed product.

We will see these and other terms of license within the sample franchise contract. As a franchise agreement comprehends a license, and often contains many of the same terms as regards the grant of the license to use marks, processes, etc., I have included only a franchise agreement in this edition.

Franchising

Franchising is licensing with attitude. That is, the heart of a franchise agreement is the license to market a (usually) strongly branded product or service, including the use of trademarks, within a particular geographic market. Where the franchise develops the "attitude" that takes it beyond a common license agreement is in the operation of the franchised business. Unlike a pure licensed situation, in which the licensee will abide by some quality, pricing, and broad marketing guidelines as contractually set out by the licensor, the franchisee (the person buying and operating a franchise outlet) must operate her business *exactly* as the franchisor (the owner of the franchise business) specifies. This includes systems, procedures, purchasing, exact pricing, and marketing. Rarely in a franchise agreement is the franchisee allowed to operate the business in a manner independent of or inconsistent with the franchisor's rules. In short, the franchisor continues to exert a significant amount of control over the franchisee's *independent* business.

Although this is not a book about the benefits or drawbacks of the commercial choices represented by these agreements, in all fairness, the franchise route is not necessarily as oppressive as I may have suggested in the previous paragraph. There are benefits to the franchise that offset the restrictions upon and operating costs added to a franchisee's business by being a franchisee. These benefits all add up in the following question: How much faster will your business establish, grow, and prosper because your market already knows and recognizes the name "McDonald's" but doesn't know "Jack's Great Burgers"?

Franchising is, in some senses, the easy way to establish a business. Easy because the business model has been created; easy because the systems and procedures are in place; easy because the brand is recognized and advertised; easy because the franchisor often provides the assistance and training necessary (at some cost to the franchisee) to succeed in your business. It does not have a long ramp-up period while you try to convince your market to buy your service/product. You do not have to experiment with suppliers. All of which goes a long way to explain why franchising now represents $100 billion per year in sales and has grown 22% in the past four years.[1]

Oddly, despite the size and growth of franchising in Canada, there is very little legislation to govern it. Only one or two provinces have enacted laws, and a few others are giving consideration to creating laws or amending existing statutes to embrace franchise law. So the relations between the franchisor and franchisee are primarily governed, as it were, by the common law of contracts.

In addition to the usual terms within a license agreement, which we examined earlier, the franchise agreement typically contains some unique features, as we will see in the sample below. Above all, we should be aware that in contrast to many licenses, which are created specifically for and between the two parties to that particular license, a franchise agreement is created by the franchisor for use with every franchisee that comes down the pike. In other words, the franchise agreement is a standard form agreement. (You might want to refer back to the section on standard form agreements in Chapter 1 to refresh your memory.)

The following franchise agreement fairly represents the nature of the major terms in most franchise agreements. It is very important to be aware that the terms and conditions of individual franchise agreements vary according to the franchisor's needs and requirements. The up-front fee may be large or small (relatively speaking); the ongoing royalties may be all-inclusive or may be a minimum amount onto which will be added a variety of other fees such as training and education, marketing and advertising contributions, etc. In addition, the franchisor may provide or insist upon being the exclusive supplier of product, in which case some further—some might say "hidden"—compensation will accrue to the franchisor. What is provided below represents a long and broad example.[2]

FRANCHISE AGREEMENT

Franchise Agreement

> THIS AGREEMENT made the 18th day of September, 1997, among Ribs Restaurants Inc., a corporation incorporated under the laws of Canada (the "Franchisor") and New Guy on the Block Ltd., a corporation incorporated under the laws of Manitoba (the "Franchisee"), and Big Brother Corporation, a corporation incorporated under the laws of Canada (the "Guarantor").

Note the requirement for a guarantor to be part of the agreement. Although it may be possible to have a franchise without a guarantor in other instances, later parts of this agreement suggest that a guarantor is not only required for but integral to the agreement and the franchised business.

WHEREAS:

1. The Franchisor has developed a unique marketing plan and system (the "system") for the development, opening, and operating of distinctive fast food restaurants for the production, merchandising, and sale of barbecue styled foods and other related products;

2. The distinguishing features of the System include, but are not limited to, food presentation, formulae, secret recipes, unique methods and procedures, specially designed premises with distinctive equipment, equipment layouts, interior and exterior accessories, identification schemes, products, management programs, standards, specifications, and proprietary marks and information;

3. The Franchisor carries on its business under the trade name "Barbi Q's" and other proprietary identifying characteristics used in relation to and in connection with its business and is the owner of the trade mark "Barbi Q's";

4. By reason of a uniform business format or system and high standards of quality and service, the Franchisor has established an excellent business reputation, created a substantial demand for its products, and built up valuable goodwill;

5. The Franchisee is desirous of acquiring from the Franchisor the right and license to operate a "Barbi Q's" restaurant utilizing the Franchisor's business format, methods, specifications, standards, operating procedures, trade marks and upon the terms and conditions hereinafter set forth:

NOW THEREFORE this agreement witnesses that in consideration of the mutual covenants and agreements herein contained the parties do hereby covenant and agree with each other as follows:

Be aware of the premise and the foundation for the agreement, that is the context for the agreement, and how it is set up in the above recitals.

1. Definitions

Where used herein or in any schedules or amendments attached hereto, the following terms shall have the following meanings:

(1) "Franchised Business" means the fast food restaurant to be operated by the Franchisee under the trade name "Barbi Q's" at the Premises pursuant to the provisions of this agreement;

(2) "Franchise Year" means, in respect of any year, thirteen (13) consecutive periods of four (4) weeks each, as the Franchisor may in its discretion from time to time determine, provided that any change shall not increase the Franchisee's liability for any amounts payable under this agreement;

Do the math for yourself. This is 52 weeks, or one full year. The franchise periods are divided into 13 so that they are exactly equal in size, unlike calendar months.

(3) "Gross Sales" means the entire amount of the actual sales price of all sales of Products and all other receipts or receivables whatsoever from any and all business conducted upon or originating from the Premises, including telephone order sales, whether such sales or other receipts be by cheque, for cash, credit, charge accounts, exchange, or otherwise and whether such sales be made by means of mechanical or other vending devices in the Premises. There shall be no deduction allowed for uncollected or uncollectable credit accounts and no allowances shall be made for bad debts. Gross Sales shall include the amount of all sales assumed to have been lost by the interruption of business at the Premises, to be determined on the basis upon which proceeds of any business interruption insurance are paid or are payable to the Franchisee or other occupiers of the Premises. Gross Sales shall not include:

• the amount of any tax imposed by any federal, provincial, municipal, or governmental authority directly on sales and collected from customers if such tax is added to the selling price and actually paid by the Franchisee to such governmental authority;

- the amount of the refund or credit given in respect of any products returned or exchanged by a customer for which a refund of the whole or a part of the purchase price is made or for which a credit is given, provided that the selling price thereof was included in Gross Sales; and
- the amount of any credit granted by the Franchisor to the Franchisee under any national coupon redemption or similar promotion program. Each charge or sale upon installment or credit shall be treated as a sale for the full price in the week during which such charge or sale shall be made, irrespective of the time when the Franchisee shall receive payment (whether full or partial) therefor;

This is a tough paragraph on the franchisee in a commercial sense. First, gross sales includes everything and anything, including vending machine revenues. Second, uncollectable accounts and bad debts are of no consequence to the franchisor, and hence the franchisee owes a royalty on those sales as well. Returns and refunds are, however, deducted (paragraph 3(b)) from gross sales. Third, the franchisee must pay on a deemed sales volume if there is a business interruption, although we have to presume this would be of/on any monies recovered through business interruption insurance. Fourth, according to paragraph 3(c), credit sales are recognized for royalty payment in the period in which they are made, not in the period in which they are collected.

(4) "Initial Term" means the ten (10) year term provided for in paragraph 3(1);

(5) "Interest Rate" means a rate of interest equal to the lesser of two percent (2%) per month (24% per annum) or the maximum rate of interest permitted by law;

The effective rate of interest by this calculation method is actually 26.82% per annum. More important, however, is the very last part, which could increase that amount considerably depending on the prevailing legal maximum rate of interest. That is, if you were to calculate the compounding of interest on $100 on a monthly basis at 2% per month, the total principal plus interest at the end of the year would be $126.82. Thus, the effective annual interest rate is 26.82%, not 24% (the nominal rate).

(6) "Manual" means, collectively, all books, recipes, pamphlets, bulletins, memoranda, letters, notices, or other publications or documents prepared by or on behalf of the Franchisor for use by franchisees generally or for the Franchisee in particular, setting forth information, advice, standards, requirements, operating procedures, instructions, or policies relating to the operation of "Barbi Q's" restaurants, as may be amended from time to time;

(7) "Marks" means the trade marks, trade names, and other commercial symbols and related logos as set forth in Schedule "A" hereto, including the trade name "Barbi Q's," together with such other trade names, trade marks, symbols, logos, distinctive names, service mark, certification mark, logo design, insignia, or otherwise which may be designated by the Franchisor as part of the System from time to time, and not thereafter withdrawn;

(8) "Monthly Period" means each four (4) week period into which a Franchise Year is divided;

Refer to the comment after paragraph 1(2), and bear in mind that these will not coincide with calendar month-end except at the end of the franchise year.

(9) "Premises" means the Premises at which the Franchised Business is to be located, as described in Schedule "B" hereto;

(10) "Products" means all foods, beverages, wares, merchandise, supplies, accessories, and items sold, dispensed, handled, or otherwise dealt in, and all services performed at or from the Premises.

2. Grant

Subject to the provisions of this agreement and for the term hereinafter specified, the Franchisor hereby grants to the Franchisee a non-exclusive right to operate a "Barbi Q's" restaurant at and only at the Premises, and a non-exclusive license to use the System and Marks solely and exclusively in the operation thereof. Termination or expiration of this agreement shall constitute a termination or expiration of the rights and license granted herein.

This is what the franchise is all about: the grant by the franchisor to the franchisee of the license to use the system and marks, etc. Be aware that the grant of license is nonexclusive because there are other franchisees. Although I have no intent to provide commercial advice, it seems to me that a prospective franchisee facing this term would be well advised to make the license grant exclusive within a fixed territory. Otherwise, the franchisor could grant (there is nothing in this agreement to prevent it) a franchise or open a corporate location across the street and this franchisee would have no recourse or right to prevent it from happening.

3. Term

(1) *Initial term.* The term of this agreement shall commence on the date hereof, and shall expire either at midnight on the day preceding the tenth anniversary thereof or on the expiration of the Franchisee's lease or sublease of the Premises, whichever date shall be the earlier, unless terminated sooner in accordance with the provisions of this agreement.

The interesting thing about this clause is the issue of the lease/sublease term and the effect of its expiry on the franchise agreement. Ideally, one would attempt to have the terms of the lease and the franchise grant coincide.

(2) *Renewal.* If throughout the Initial Term the Franchisee shall have fully complied with all of the terms and conditions of this agreement and any other agreement entered into between the Franchisor and the Franchisee and shall have complied with the operating standards and criteria established for the Franchised Business including, without limitation, the System, the Franchisee shall have the option to renew this agreement for only one renewal term. Such renewal term shall commence on the expiry of the Initial Term of this agreement and end on the earlier of the fifth anniversary thereof, or on the expiry of the Franchisee's lease or sublease of the Premises, unless terminated sooner in accordance with the terms and conditions of this agreement. Such renewal shall not require any payment of an initial or renewal franchise fee, but shall be subject to the following terms and conditions being complied with in full prior to the expiration of the Initial Term:

The franchisee has the right to only one five-year renewal term on this agreement without a fee for a maximum franchised Business life of fifteen (15) years. To renew the agreement after the initial term, the listed conditions that follow must be met.

(a) the Franchisee shall give the Franchisor written notice of his desire to exercise the renewal option herein provided for not less than six (6) months prior to the expiration of the Initial Term, provided that such notice shall not be given before the commencement of the last year of the Initial Term;

There is a six-month window in which to exercise the renewal option which begins on the commencement of the 10th year of the initial franchise term.

(b) the Franchisee shall do or cause to be done all such things as the Franchisor may require to ensure that the Franchised Business satisfies the then current image, standards, and specifications established by the Franchisor for new franchises in the System whether or not such image, standards, or specifications reflect a material change in the System in effect during the Initial Term. Without limiting the generality of the foregoing, the Franchisee shall make such capital expenditures as the Franchisor shall determine as being reasonably required in connection with the foregoing for the modernization and refurbishing of the Premises and all fixtures, furnishings, equipment, and signs therein or thereon;

A capital investment to update and refurbish the franchised business may be required to renew the agreement.

(c) the Franchisee is not in default of any provision of the lease or sublease for the Premises and satisfies the Franchisor that it has the right to remain in possession of the Premises for such renewal term;

This lease/sublease issue keeps coming up throughout this agreement. Most likely it is because the franchisor would not want to have the potential for image or goodwill problems created by the franchised business being "ejected" from its location due to lease problems.

> (d) the Franchisee shall reimburse the Franchisor for all reasonable legal fees and other costs and expenses incurred by it incident to the exercise of the renewal option herein provided for; and

Any legal fees incurred in the renewal process are to be paid by the franchisee. How such legal fees might be generated is provided in paragraph 3(2)(e) below.

> (e) at the commencement of the renewal term, the Franchisee shall, at the option of the Franchisor, execute a new franchise agreement in the form then being used by the Franchisor, which may contain different royalty rates and advertising contributions than contained in this agreement, and shall execute such other documents and agreements as are then customarily used by the Franchisor in the granting of franchises and licenses. If the Franchisor shall elect not to execute such a new franchise agreement, all of the provisions contained in the franchise agreement in effect immediately prior to the commencement of such renewal term shall remain in force during such renewal term (except for any further right of renewal).

Notice how by virtue of this paragraph the franchisor can use the renewal to trigger a wholesale change in the franchise agreement. Thus, it may not be much of a "renewal" at all, but rather a whole new deal. A franchisee considering renewal would be well advised to determine whether these changes would come into effect before committing to the renewal.

4. Initial Fee and Royalty

> (1) *Initial fee.* In consideration of the Franchisee receiving the opportunity to establish the Franchised Business, the Franchisee shall pay to the Franchisor, forthwith upon the execution of this agreement, an initial non-recurring, non-refundable franchise fee in the amount of one hundred thousand dollars ($100,000.00). This initial franchise fee shall be deemed to be fully earned by the Franchisor when paid and in consideration of the grant by it to the Franchisee of the opportunity to establish the Franchised Business as herein provided, and the Franchisee shall not be entitled to a refund of any part thereof, regardless of the date of termination of this agreement.

The up-front fee is nonrefundable and is the franchisee's "consideration" in the contract for the grant of license. These fees vary in magnitude depending on the value of the franchise's name and trademarks.

> (2) *Continuing royalty.* In return for the ongoing rights and privileges granted to the Franchisee hereunder, the Franchisee shall pay to the Franchisor throughout the term of this agreement a royalty of seven percent (7%) of Gross Sales for each Monthly Period, such royalties to be payable in arrears on or before the tenth (10th) day of the month immediately following the expiry of the Monthly Period for which payment is being made, including the tenth (10th) day following the final Monthly Period of the term.

Each four-week period's gross sales, as defined in paragraph 1(3), generates a 7% royalty payable to the franchisor throughout the agreement's life. Interestingly, this payment formula's timing relaxes as the year progresses, until the very end of the year. As the table below shows, in month one there will be 13 days' grace to file and remit but by the 11th month there are 39 days.

Monthly Period	Payment Date	Days to Remit
Jan. 1–Jan. 28	Feb. 10	13
Jan. 29–Feb. 25	Mar. 10	13
Feb. 26–Mar. 25	Apr. 10	16
Mar. 26–Apr. 22	May 10	18
Apr. 23–May 20	June 10	21

May 21–June 17	July 10	23
June 18–July 15	Aug. 10	26
July 16–Aug. 12	Sep. 10	29
Aug. 13–Sep. 9	Oct. 10	31
Sep. 10–Oct. 7	Nov. 10	34
Oct. 8–Nov. 4	Dec. 10	36
Nov. 5–Dec. 2	Jan. 10	39
Dec. 3–Dec. 30	Jan. 10	11

5. Advertising

(1) *Local Advertising.*

   (a) The Franchisee agrees, during the Initial Term or any renewal thereof, to expend annually on advertising and promotions not less than an amount equal to two percent (2%) of Gross Sales each Franchise Year and such amount as may be required to be expended for such purposes by the lease or sublease for the Premises;

This paragraph provides for a minimum level of promotional spending based on a portion of gross sales volume. The very last part of the paragraph ("and such amount") primarily refers to leases in malls or within other stores or locations where the landlord or sub-lettor demands some specific amount of advertising spending or contribution per year as part of the leasehold.

   (b) The Franchisee shall have the right to conduct such advertising and promotions in respect of the Franchised Business as the Franchisee shall, in its reasonable discretion desire, provided that:

   (i) the Franchisee shall advertise and promote only in a manner that will reflect favourably on the Franchisor, the Franchisee, and the Products and good name, goodwill, and reputation thereof;

   (ii) the Franchisee shall submit to the Franchisor for its approval, which approval shall not be unreasonably withheld or unduly delayed, all advertising and promotions to be utilized by the Franchisee and until such time as the Franchisor shall give its prior written approval to the use of such advertising and promotions, the Franchisee shall not utilize same in any advertising or promotion;

   (iii) the Franchisee shall prominently display, at its expense, in and upon the Premises signs of such nature, form, colour, number, location, and size and containing such matter as the Franchisor may direct or approve in writing from time to time and such signs shall be purchased from <*supplier name*> or, at the Franchisee's option, from suppliers approved by the Franchisor.

Still on the topic of advertising and promotion, the franchisor must approve all advertising and promotions before they are run. The signage used in and on/around the franchised business must be as specified and approved by the franchisor, and purchased from or manufactured by a franchisor-authorized supplier.

   (2) *General advertising fund.* Recognizing the value of uniform advertising and promotion to the goodwill and public image of the System, the Franchisee agrees that the Franchisor may maintain and administer a general advertising fund (the "Fund") for such national, regional, and other advertising programs as the Franchisor may deem necessary or appropriate, in its sole discretion. The Franchisor shall direct all such advertising programs in its sole discretion with respect to the creative concepts, materials, endorsement, and media used therein, and the placement and allocation thereof.

   Upon receiving notice of the establishment of the Fund, the Franchisee shall contribute to the Fund in each Franchise Year an amount equal to up to three percent (3%), as determined by the Franchisor, of the Gross Sales for such franchise Year. Any amounts payable hereunder to the Fund shall be paid together with the royalty fees hereunder and shall be based upon Gross Sales for the preceding Monthly Period.

   The Fund shall be used and expended for media costs, commissions, market research costs, creative, and production costs including, without limitation, the costs of creating promotions and artwork, printing costs, and other

costs relating to advertising and promotional programs undertaken by the Franchisor. The Franchisor reserves the right to place and develop such advertisements and promotions and to market same as agent for and on behalf of the Franchisee, either directly or through an advertising agency retained or formed for such purpose. The Fund shall be accounted for separately from the other funds of the Franchisor and shall not be used to defray any of the Franchisor's general operating expenses, except for such reasonable salaries, administrative costs and overhead (calculated on a fully allocated basis), if any, as the Franchisor may incur in activities reasonably related to the administration or direction of the Fund and its advertising programs (including, without limitation, conducting market research). A statement of the operations of the Fund shall be prepared annually and shall be made available to the Franchisee upon request, the cost of such statement to be paid by the Fund.

The Franchisee acknowledges and agrees that the Fund is intended to maximize general public recognition and patronage of "Barbi Q's" restaurants for the benefit of all Franchisees in the System and that the Franchisor undertakes no obligation in administering the Fund to ensure that any particular franchisee, including the Franchisee, benefits directly or pro rata from the placement or conduct of such advertising and promotion. Except as expressly provided in this paragraph, the Franchisor assumes no direct or indirect liability or obligation to the Franchisee with respect to the maintenance, direction, or administration of the Fund.

The long and the short of this lengthy paragraph is that the franchisor can charge an additional fee of up to 3% of gross sales for a general advertising fund. The use, administration, and benefits from that fund are solely the franchisor's with no obligation or liability (or responsibility, for that matter) to any particular franchisee. It is conceivable that the franchisor could take the contributions from the franchisees, including this one, and spend the money on development and on media buys in the big three metropolitan markets (which does not include Winnipeg), in which it will get the best value for its media placement money. This franchisee's benefit from the "national" campaign would be questionable, but there would be nothing the franchisee could do about it.

6. Accounting, Records, Reports, Audits

(1) *Bookkeeping, accounting, and records.* The Franchisee shall establish a bookkeeping, accounting, and record-keeping system conforming to the requirements prescribed from time to time by the Franchisor including, without limitation, the use and retention of cash registers, tapes, invoices, cash receipts, inventory records, purchase orders, payroll records, cheque stubs, bank deposit receipts, sales tax records and returns, cash disbursement journals, and general ledgers together with such further and other records and documents as may from time to time be required by the Franchisor, and including computerized bookkeeping systems established from time to time. The Franchisee and all personnel employed by the Franchisee shall record, at the time of sale, in the presence of customers, all receipts from sales or other transactions, whether for cash or credit, on cash registers approved by the Franchisor.

This paragraph prescribes bookkeeping and record-keeping systems for the franchisee by the franchisor. It also specifically states that the franchisee must use an approved cash register, and that it must be rung up for every sale at the time of sale.

(2) *Reports and financial information.* The Franchisee shall furnish to the Franchisor such reports as the Franchisor may require from time to time. Without limiting the generality of the foregoing, the Franchisee shall furnish to the Franchisor in the form from time to time prescribed by the Franchisor and together with such detail and breakdown and copies of supporting records as the Franchisor may from time to time require:

(a) by the tenth day following the end of the preceding Monthly Period, a report of the Gross Sales for such Monthly Period, signed and verified by the Franchisee;

(b) within sixty (60) days after the end of each three (3) consecutive Monthly Periods, a profit and loss statement for the Franchised Business for such Monthly Periods;

(c) within sixty (60) days after the end of each fiscal year of the Franchised Business, financial statements for the Franchised Business, including a balance sheet, a profit and loss statement, and a statement of retained earnings for such period, which statements shall be signed and verified by the Franchisee; and

(d) within sixty (60) days of the end of each fiscal year of the Franchised Business, a statement of Gross Sales for such fiscal year determined in accordance with generally accepted accounting principles applied on a consistent basis, and audited by a firm of independent chartered accountants acceptable to the Franchisor.

The specific reports that are required from the franchisee by the franchisor are as follows.

- Paragraph (a) is a royalty statement due 10 days following the end of a monthly period.
- Paragraph (b) is a quarterly profit and loss statement due within 60 days of the end of a quarter (of monthly periods, not calendar months).
- Paragraph (c) is a set of unaudited annual financial statements, due within 60 days of year-end.
- Paragraph (d) is an audited annual statement of gross sales, which should, all things being equal, reconcile the monthly gross sales reports previously submitted.

(3) *Inspection and audit.* The Franchisor shall have the right, during normal business hours and without prior notice to the Franchisee, to inspect or audit, or cause to be inspected or audited, the financial books, records, bookkeeping and accounting records, documents, or other materials in respect of the Franchised Business, including the right, without limitation, to have a person on the Premises to check, verify, and tabulate Gross Sales, and/or to examine accounting records and procedures affecting the determination of Gross Sales.

In the event that any such audit or inspection shall disclose an understatement of Gross Sales, the Franchisee shall pay to the Franchisor, within fifteen (15) days after receipt by the Franchisee of the inspection or audit report, the royalty and other sums due on account of such understatement. Further, if such audit or inspection is made necessary by the failure of the Franchisee to furnish reports, financial statements, or any other documentation as herein required, or if it is determined by any such audit or inspection that the Franchisee's records and procedures were insufficient to permit a proper determination of Gross Sales for any Franchise Year or part thereof to be made, or that Gross Sales for the period in question were understated by three percent (3%) or more of the Gross Sales actually received, or that the Franchisee was not complying with each of the provisions of this paragraph, the Franchisee shall immediately take such steps as may be necessary to remedy such default in accordance with the recommendations of such auditor and the Franchisee shall promptly pay to the Franchisor all costs incurred in connection with such audit or inspection including, without limitation, charges of an accountant and the travel expenses, room, board, and compensation of employees of the Franchisor.

If the Franchisee's records and procedures were insufficient to permit a proper determination of Gross Sales, the Franchisor shall have the right to deliver to the Franchisee an estimate, made by the Franchisor, of Gross Sales for the period under consideration and the Franchisee shall immediately pay to the Franchisor any amount shown thereby to be owing on account of the royalty fees and other sums due on account of any understatement. Any such estimate shall be final and binding upon the Franchisee.

This long paragraph provides for the following:

- Surprise spot audits that require no notice and can be during normal business hours.[3]
- If there is a shortfall of royalties owing vs. royalties reported and paid, it is due immediately.
- If the audit is a result of missing reports or if it turns up irregularities or substantial shortages on royalties, or noncompliance with record-keeping conditions, the franchisee must remedy all such problems immediately *and* pay all costs.
- If gross sales could not be determined due to record-keeping problems, the franchisor can estimate the gross sales for such period, and that estimate will be the basis for royalty and other payments to the franchisor.

(4) *Auditors report to be final.* Any report of the Franchisor's auditor rendered from time to time pursuant to this paragraph shall be final and binding upon all of the parties, provided that, in making any such report, the Franchisor's auditor shall make such report pursuant to generally accepted accounting principles.

This paragraph is fair in its intent, and simply by being said up front. That said, GAAP rules allow for choices in accounting methods in various areas, not the least of which are inventory valuation and asset amortization. Thus, the statement in this paragraph in not as definitively reassuring in its impartial integrity as it may at first seem.

7. Training and Operating Assistance

(1) *Training by Franchisor.* The Franchisor shall provide to the Franchisee, prior to the opening of the Franchised Business, for itself and one other key employee designated by the Franchisee, a training course of such duration and at such location as the Franchisor may deem necessary, covering all phases of the System. The Franchisee shall be responsible for all travel and living expenses and all wages payable to any trainees, and no wages shall be payable by the Franchisor to any such trainee for any service rendered at any "Barbi Q's" outlet during the course of such training. The Franchisor further agrees to furnish one person, experienced in the System, to assist the Franchisee at the Premises for such period immediately preceding or following the opening as the Franchisor in its sole discretion deems reasonable. Additional start-up assistance or retraining or refresher courses may be provided by the Franchisor, at its discretion, and at a cost to the Franchisee based on the Franchisor's then current daily fee for the Franchisor's personnel performing such assistance, plus other reasonable expenses, including all travel, meal, and accommodation expenses.

The paragraph says that the franchisee and one other employee of the franchisee will be trained by the franchisor. It also says that the franchisor will put someone it designates on-site, at the franchisee's cost, prior to or during the opening to train and supervise. Additional training, at the franchisee's request or the franchisor's discretion, will be available at the franchisee's expense.

(2) *Operating assistance.* During the term of this agreement, the Franchisor shall furnish to the Franchisee such continuing advice and guidance as is from time to time reasonably required by the Franchisee with respect to the planning, opening, and operation of the Franchised Business, including consultation and advice regarding:

(a) selection, purchasing, stocking, and display of food products and supplies;

(b) hiring and training of employees;

(c) design and layout of menus;

(d) provisions from time to time of results of research on market trends of new products and menu items, where practicable;

(e) formulation and implementation of advertising and promotional programs;

(f) provision of merchandising and operating aids and services as are developed by the Franchisor from time to time. The price for such aids and services shall be the same as that charged by the Franchisor to its franchisees generally;

(g) establishment and maintenance of administrative, bookkeeping, accounting, inventory control, and general operating procedures;

(h) consultation and advice by the Franchisor's field supervisors, either by personal visit, telephone, mail, or otherwise, as the Franchisor deems reasonably necessary from time to time;

(i) provision of special recipes, food preparation techniques and instructions, and other operational developments as may from time to time be developed by the Franchisor for use in connection with the System;

(j) improvements to the System, including new product development; and

(k) financial advice and consultation.

(3) *Additional assistance.* Upon a reasonable written request from the Franchisee, as determined by the Franchisor, the Franchisor shall endeavour to furnish services to the Franchisee to aid in the solution of specific problems encountered by the Franchisee which are beyond the scope of the Franchisor's obligations in paragraph 7(2) hereof. The Franchisee shall reimburse the Franchisor promptly for its actual time expended and its actual expenses incurred in aiding the Franchisee with such problems, and the Franchisor shall, upon written request from the Franchisee, provide the Franchisee with reasonable evidence of its actual expenses so incurred.

(4) *Expand the franchise System.* The Franchisor agrees to use its reasonable best efforts to seek out prospective franchisees to operate other restaurants in the province in which the Premises are located and elsewhere in Canada and to promote and enhance the reputation and goodwill associated with the Marks.

(5) *Right to inspect.* The Franchisor and/or its representatives shall have the right at all times to inspect the Premises and the furnishings, equipment, and fixtures thereon and the Products, to take inventory of such Products, and otherwise to examine the manner in which the Franchisee is conducting its business; in the event of any such inspection, the Franchisee and its staff shall co-operate fully.

The first several paragraphs of this section provide the general to specific actions that the franchisor will take to assist the franchisee directly or indirectly. Only the last paragraph, 7(5), diverges somewhat to provide an inspection right to the franchisor. It may be necessary, but in this context not really of great assistance to the franchisee.

8. Operation of Franchised Business

(1) *Duties and obligations.* The Franchisee acknowledges that the Franchisor has invested and is investing time and capital in the advertising and promotion of "Barbi Q's" Franchises as a regional network of fast food restaurants serving barbecued cuisine and conducting business in a uniform and high-quality manner. The Franchisee understands and acknowledges that such advertising and promotion by the Franchisor has created and is creating goodwill and customer association in the trade mark, which benefit the Franchisor, the Franchisee and all other "Barbi Q's" franchisees. The Franchisee acknowledges that, to foster and preserve such goodwill, it is necessary for the Franchisee to operate the Franchised Business in a manner and to a quality consistent with the System and the fast food restaurants heretofore operated by the Franchisor and/or its franchisees. The Franchisee acknowledges that, in order to maintain such uniformity and quality consistency, it is necessary for the Franchisor to exercise a degree of control over the operation of each and every "Barbi Q's" franchisee. Therefore, the Franchisee agrees to operate the Franchised Business strictly in accordance with the System, whether contained in the Manual or otherwise. Without limiting the generality of the foregoing, the Franchisee agrees as follows:

(a) to operate the Franchised Business with due diligence and efficiency in an up-to-date, quality, and reputable manner during such days, nights, and hours as may be designated by the landlord for the Premises or by the Franchisor;

(b) the Franchisee shall ensure that at all times prompt, courteous, and efficient service is accorded to its customers. The Franchisee shall in all dealings with its customers, suppliers, and the public adhere to the highest standards of honesty, integrity, fair dealings, and ethical conduct;

(c) the Franchisee shall sell only such products and menu items as meet the Franchisor's uniform standards of quality and quantity, as have been expressly approved for sale in writing by the Franchisor and have been prepared in accordance with the Franchisor's methods and techniques for product preparation. The Franchisee shall sell all approved items pursuant to a menu approved by the Franchisor and the Franchisee shall not offer for sale any other products or services from the Premises. The Franchisee shall discontinue the sale of any food or drink items or any other merchandise of any kind whatsoever as the Franchisor, in its sole discretion, prohibits in writing;

(d) the Franchisee agrees that all food and drink items will be served in containers bearing accurate reproductions of the Marks, which reproductions shall be submitted to the Franchisor for prior written approval before usage. All napkins, straws, bags, cups, matches, menus, and other paper goods and like articles used in connection with the Franchised Business shall be of a quality and style and bear such reproductions of the Marks as the Franchisor shall specify and all art work and reproductions used in connection therewith shall conform to specifications established by the Franchisor and be submitted to the Franchisor for prior written approval before usage. Such imprinted items shall be purchased by the Franchisee only from the Franchisor or from suppliers or manufacturers approved in writing by the Franchisor;

(e) the Franchisee agrees to maintain the condition and appearance of the Franchised Business and the equipment used therein consistent with the then image, as it may be from time to time, of the Franchisor's franchised fast food restaurants serving barbecue cuisine as an attractive, modern, clean, convenient, and efficiently operated fast food restaurant offering high-quality products prepared under the highest degree of sanitary conditions, served promptly and courteously. The Franchisee agrees to effect such maintenance of and repairs to the Premises and the equipment installed therein as is reasonably required on a regular and frequent basis and maintain such condition, appearance, and efficient operation, including without limiting the generality of the foregoing, replacement of worn-out or obsolete fixtures, furnishings, equipment, and signs, repair of the interior and exterior of the Premises, and periodic cleaning, painting, and decorating. The Franchisor specifically retains the right, to be exercised no more than once every five (5) years during the term of this agreement, to require the Franchisee to completely refurbish, remodel, redecorate, and effect such necessary structural changes to the Premises and the signs installed at the Premises, all at the Franchisee's sole expense, to conform to the building design, colour schemes, signs, and presentation of the Marks consistent with the Franchisor's then current public image within sixty (60) days of receipt by the Franchisee of demand therefor. In the event that the Franchisee fails to take such action within the said sixty-day period, the Franchisor may, without prejudice to any other rights or remedies it may have, cause such repairs or maintenance, remodelling, or redecorating to be done at the sole cost and expense of the Franchisee. The Franchisee shall reimburse the Franchisor for the amount of such cost and expenses forthwith upon receipt of a written demand from the Franchisor;

(f) the Franchisee shall not make or cause to be made any alterations to the interior or exterior of the Premises so as to modify the appearance thereof or any alterations or replacements of any of the leasehold improvements, fixtures, or equipment at the Premises without first having obtained the written approval of the Franchisor, which approval may be given or withheld in the sole discretion of the Franchisor;

(g) the Franchisee shall participate fully in all national, regional, and local promotions initiated by the Franchisor;

(h) the Franchisee shall, upon request by the Franchisor, once during the Initial Term, and thereafter, at the option of the Franchisor, no more frequently than once each calendar year, make available for a reasonable period of time each of his staff and manager for training or retraining by the Franchisor, at the Franchisor's head office or other locality designated by the Franchisor. Such training or retraining shall be conducted at no cost to the Franchisee provided, however, that the Franchisee shall be responsible for all travel, food, and lodging costs;

(i) the Franchisee shall comply with all municipal, provincial, and federal laws and regulations and shall obtain and at all times maintain any and all permits, certificates, or licenses necessary for the proper conduct of the Franchised Business pursuant to the terms of this franchise agreement; and

(j) the Franchisee and the Guarantor shall devote their full time and attention to the establishment, development, and operation of the Franchised Business.

The important thing to be aware of here is that the franchise manual is a key part of the agreement, with which the franchisee must comply. Most of the operating conditions listed above are self-explanatory. Consider the following, however.

• In paragraph 8(1)(c) the franchisee can only sell approved product and must discontinue using or selling prohibited products.

• Paragraph 8(1)(d) is somewhat repetitive of other parts of the agreement, but note that the franchisee must use only the franchisor's specified paper and other products, as manufactured by approved suppliers.

• Paragraph 8(1)(e) is significant, because once the nondescript language at the top is out of the way, it goes on to allow the franchisor the right to demand once during the agreement term that the entire business premises be retrofitted to comply with new image/design standards. If exercised, this could be a very costly, contingent, mid-contract upgrade for which the franchisee is responsible. And, if the franchisee has not specifically planned for it (or even if it has, actually), the upgrade may be prejudicial to the franchisee's cash flow.

• Paragraph 8(1)(j) is a time and attention clause that is interesting in two respects. First, the franchisee, it could be argued by this paragraph, cannot have any other business interests besides the franchised business. Second, the guarantor must devote full time and attention to the franchise, which is unusual inasmuch as guarantors are not commonly involved operationally. It could have several implications, such as the franchisee incorporating the business entity and then providing a personal guarantee, or there effectively being a franchisee partnership between two suitable (read: financially strong) people/entities for each franchised Business.

(2) *Purchase and sale of Products.*

(a) The Franchisee acknowledges that the reputation and goodwill of the System is based upon, and can be maintained and enhanced only by, the sale of high-quality Products and the satisfaction of customers who rely upon the uniformly high quality of Products that are sold under the System and such continued uniformity is essential to the goodwill, success, and continued public acceptance of the System. Accordingly, the Franchisee agrees to sell or otherwise deal in only such Products as the Franchisor shall first approve of in writing, which approval may be given or withheld in the sole discretion of the Franchisor;

The key to this paragraph is the last sentence, which begins "Accordingly."

(b) Recognizing that the Products, accessories, and supplies to be used in the Franchised Business must conform to the Franchisor's standards and specifications, the Franchisee hereby agrees to purchase all such products, accessories, and supplies from the Franchisor, or suppliers approved or designated by the Franchisor (which may include affiliates of the Franchisor) or from any other source or supplier, provided that the Franchisor shall have first approved in writing such other source or supplier, which approval shall not be unreasonably withheld so long as the Franchisee can demonstrate to the Franchisor's reasonable satisfaction that its source or supplier is able to supply on a reliable basis a product or service meeting the Franchisor's standards and specifications and approved product list. The Franchisee shall submit to the Franchisor samples of any such products, accessories, or supplies, which the Franchisee wishes to acquire from any other source or supplier and the Franchisor shall be entitled to submit such samples, at the Franchisee's expense, to an independent testing laboratory to determine whether the standards of the System are met;

This paragraph directs the franchisee to purchase supplies from the franchisor or one of its designated suppliers. If the franchisee needs/wants to obtain supplies from elsewhere, the franchisor must first approve the supplier and the product, which could include testing etc., the costs for which must be borne by the franchisee.

(c) Wherever reasonably possible, the Franchisee shall sell or dispose of all Products at such prices as the Franchisor may reasonably suggest from time to time, provided it is hereby agreed that notwithstanding the foregoing, the Franchisee is under no obligation to accept such suggested resale price and the Franchisee may sell the Products, at any reasonable price it chooses, having regard to its concern to develop and continually increase sales and to make a profit. If the Franchisee does not sell or dispose of the Products at the prices suggested by the Franchisor, the Franchisee will not suffer in any way in its business relations with the Franchisor or any other person over whom the Franchisor has otherwise influence or control;

This paragraph essentially says, stick to the pricing scheme. But, if the economics of growth and profits prevent the franchisee from sticking to the price schedule, the franchisee does not have to do so. It is curious that the contract would even bring up the issue of business relations (not) being hurt if the franchisee chooses not to price according to the franchisor's schedule, is it not?

(d) So long as the Franchisee is not in default hereunder, the Franchisor will endeavour to use its reasonable best efforts to fill all orders placed by the Franchisee as promptly as possible. However, the Franchisor will not be liable for loss or damage due to delay in delivery resulting from any cause beyond its reasonable control, including, but not limited to, compliance with any regulations, orders, or instructions of any federal, provincial, or municipal government or any department or agency thereof, acts or omissions of the Franchisee, acts of civil or military authority, fires, strikes, lock-outs, embargoes, delays in transportation, and inability due to causes beyond the Franchisor's control to obtain the necessary products or ingredients. In no event shall the Franchisor be liable for financial loss, including consequential or special damages on account of delay due to any cause.

This paragraph is relevant when the franchisor is the supplier of products, materials, training, and so forth. The franchisor warrants that it will act quickly in all instances. It will not, however, be responsible if it cannot or does not act quickly enough.

(3) *Discounts, rebates, bonuses.* In the event that any volume discounts, rebate fees or discount bonuses (whether by way of cash, kind, or credit) are received by the Franchisor from any manufacturer or supplier designated by the Franchisor, whether or not on account of purchases made by the Franchisor for its own account or for the account of the Franchisee or by the Franchisee directly for its own account, the Franchisor shall be entitled to retain the whole of the amount of such volume discounts, rebate fees, or discount bonuses.

This clause is quite unilaterally in the franchisor's favour—almost reprehensibly. The first part of the paragraph says that if the franchisor buys on account of the franchisee (supplies, renovation, or services, etc.) and receives a discount, rebate, or bonus of some sort, that benefit accrues to the franchisor. In other words, the franchisee always pays full price while the franchisor gets the incentives. The next part of the paragraph says that any such benefits received by the franchisee buying directly on its own account revert to the franchisor as well. This is an excellent deal for at least one of the parties.

Not that this book's intent is to make comment on the commercial value of the contract from either party's perspective, but this clause goes a long way to locking the franchisee into an intractable cost structure. After all, it is essentially impossible for the franchisee to benefit from any cost savings or reductions except labour. If I understand it correctly, it could be argued that the implication of this clause borders on unjust enrichment to the franchisor. The franchisee is essentially deprived of benefits it deserves, while the franchisor unjustly benefits. Something that the law would not allow to happen save for this clause.

(4) *System modifications.* The Franchisee acknowledges and agrees that the Franchisor may from time to time hereafter add to, subtract from, modify, or otherwise change the System including, without limitation, the adoption and use of new or modified trade marks or trade names, new products or services, and new techniques in connection therewith, and the Franchisee agrees, at its own cost, to promptly accept, implement, use, and display all such alterations, modifications, and changes.

This paragraph is repetitious. It, again, expresses that the franchisee must implement all system changes promptly and at its own cost.

9. Premises

(1) *Use of Premises.* The right and license granted to the Franchisee pursuant to paragraph 2 has been granted to the Franchisee solely for use by him at the Premises. The Franchisee shall use the Premises for the operation of the Franchised Business only and for no other purpose.

(2) *Sublease by Franchisee.* The Franchisee will, simultaneously with or immediately following the execution of this agreement, enter into a sublease for the Premises substantially in the form attached hereto as Schedule "C" or in such other form as may otherwise be required by the Franchisor or any lessor of the Premises. The Franchisee further agrees that, if requested to do so either by the Franchisor or any lessor of the Premises, the Franchisee shall execute a covenant and/or agreement directly in favour of such lessor, covenanting and agreeing to be bound by, and to perform and observe all of the terms and conditions of, the lease or any other instruments under which the right to occupy the Premises has been obtained.

If the Franchisor is, for any reason whatsoever, unable to obtain the written consent of any lessor of the Premises whose consent may be required to the subletting of the Premises by the Franchisor to the Franchisee, then this agreement shall be terminated and of no further force or effect and the Franchisor shall not be responsible for any losses, costs, or expenses whatsoever incurred by the Franchisee as a result of such inability to obtain the consent.

This paragraph assumes that the premises have been selected. It also presumes, because nothing is otherwise expressly stated, that the franchisor has leased the premises, which it will sublet to the franchisee. If this is so, then the franchisor is also the franchisee's landlord. One has to presume in this case that the standard form is being broadened to include every possible variation, because this assumption we have made about the preceding paragraph is not really consistent with the following paragraph. Obviously, the best way to do away with the entire matter of leases and subleases is for the franchisee to purchase and own the property on which the premises are to be built.

(3) *Early termination of lease.* If prior to the termination of this agreement, the lease of the Premises expires or terminates without fault of the Franchisee, or if the Premises are destroyed or otherwise rendered unusable, the Franchisee shall, provided it has not otherwise breached or violated any of the provisions of this agreement, have a period of six (6) months from the date of the termination of the lease within which to relocate the Franchised Business to a location reasonably satisfactory to the Franchisor. If the Franchisee is unable to relocate and recommence the operation of the Franchised Business within the aforesaid period, this agreement shall terminate and be of no further force or effect and the Franchisor shall not be responsible for any losses, costs, or expenses whatsoever incurred by the Franchisee as a result of such early termination, it being hereby acknowledged that the term of this agreement will not necessarily coincide with the term of the lease or other instrument under which the right to occupy the Premises was held. In the event the Franchisee is able to relocate, the Franchisee shall be required to obtain all prior consents and approvals of the Franchisor, as provided in this agreement, and to otherwise comply with all terms and conditions of this agreement. All costs and expenses incurred with respect to any such relocation and recommencement of the Franchised Business shall be borne solely by the Franchisee.

If the lease terminates through no fault of the franchisee, the franchisee has six months to relocate the franchised business. The franchisor must approve all changes and selections, and is not responsible for any costs, losses, etc. incurred by the move.

10. Design and Construction

(1) *Development of Premises—By the Franchisee.* The Franchisee shall construct and equip the Premises in conformity with the System standard layout plans, specifications, and drawings provided by the Franchisor. The Franchisor shall have the right to inspect the construction and development of the Premises at reasonable times. The cost of plans and specifications and all costs and expenses pertaining to the construction and equipping of the Premises shall be borne exclusively by the Franchisee. The Franchisor shall provide such advice and assistance to the Franchisee in constructing and equipping the Premises as may reasonably be required. The Franchisee agrees to do or cause to be done the following at its sole cost and expense:

(a) ensure that all applicable by-laws, building codes, permit requirements and lease requirements and restrictions are complied with in connection with such construction;

(b) obtain all required building, utility, sign, health, sanitation, and business permits and licenses and any other required permits and licenses;

(c) construct all required improvements to the Premises and decorate the Premises in compliance with plans and specifications approved by the Franchisor acting reasonably;

(d) subject to the provisions hereof, purchase, or lease and install all fixtures, equipment, and signs required for the Premises by the Franchisor; and

(e) present chosen contractor and contractor's tender for approval by the Franchisor and retain and compensate all contractors, subcontractors, or other professionals required in connection with the construction and development of the Premises.

With regard to design and construction of the premises to be occupied, the franchisor, as usual, sets the rules and calls the tune, but the franchisee pays the piper. Specific responsibilities of the franchisee are provided in the alphabetical list.

Did anyone else notice the strange inconsistency, probably for the express purpose of bleeding more money out of the franchisee, in the opening paragraph of this, 10(1)? The first sentence says that the franchisee must construct and equip the premises according to the plans, specifications, and drawings "provided by the Franchisor." Yet two sentences later, the franchisor makes the cost of those allegedly standard (meaning complete and available) plans and specifications the exclusive cost of the franchisee. Would it not seem to you, the potential franchisee, that the up-front fee would include that?

> (2) *Development of Premises—By the Franchisor.*
>> (a) Notwithstanding the foregoing provisions of paragraph 10(1) and in lieu thereof, the Franchisor may, at its option, undertake, on an independent consultant basis, the development and fixturing of the Premises on the same basis as contemplated in paragraph 10(1), by giving written notice thereof to the Franchisee. In the event that the Franchisor so exercises such option, the Franchisee hereby authorizes and directs the Franchisor to undertake the development of the Premises as aforesaid and to do or cause to be done all such things as may be necessary to complete the Premises for use by the Franchisee. The Franchisee acknowledges that all or any part of such work may be performed by a person or persons as the Franchisor will nominate including persons affiliated with the Franchisor. Said work will be performed on a basis deemed commercially reasonable by the Franchisor having regard to the estimate previously furnished to the Franchisee provided, however, the Franchisor shall not be obligated to solicit competitive bids for any work performed or merchandise supplied in connection with such development;

This paragraph gives the franchisor the option to develop the premises for the franchisee *as an independent consultant* (read: for a fee). The franchisor may subcontract all the work to others, even—or especially—affiliates, and is *not required* to obtain competitive bids. Sounds like the type of independent consultant I would want spending my money.

>> (b) The Franchisor, at its sole option, may require the Franchisee to deposit with the Franchisor the amount or any part thereof of the estimated costs for the development as determined by the Franchisor. In arriving at the said estimate of costs, the Franchisor will have regard to the prices generally charged by suppliers and tradespeople in the area in which the Premises are situated, as well as to its general experience in developing restaurant premises for other Franchisees, provided that such estimate in no way be construed as a guarantee of the costs of such development. To the extent that the costs and expenses from time to time incurred by the Franchisor in respect of such development exceed the amount or amounts previously paid by the Franchisee to the Franchisor under this paragraph, the Franchisee shall pay to the Franchisor an amount equal to such excess forthwith upon receipt from the Franchisor of a statement setting forth in reasonable detail the costs and expenses for which such additional funds are required.

The franchisee agrees to pay to the franchisor—in advance—an amount of money demanded by the franchisor as its estimate of the total development costs of the premises. There is no guarantee that the costs will not be higher, and this paragraph provides that the franchisee will immediately pay to the franchisor any costs actually incurred over the deposit it initially made. Note that there is no provision for payback to the franchisee if the estimate was too high. (Maybe Section 8(3) would apply? Your guess is as good as mine.)

>> (c) For the services to be performed hereunder by the Franchisor, the Franchisee covenants and agrees to pay to the Franchisor the sum of ten percent (10%) of the total cost of construction, to be payable pro rata with the payments to be made under this paragraph. "Total cost of construction," without limiting the generality of the foregoing, shall include all costs of the Franchisee's leasehold improvements, whether performed by the landlord or by the Franchisor's contractor, on behalf of the Franchisee, of equipment and smallwares, of

signs and logos, of permits and fees and whatever else the Franchisor encounters in the way of costs in bringing about the completion of the Franchisee's location so as to be presentable to the Franchisee as a turnkey operation. The Franchisee acknowledges that any guarantees or warranties with respect to the performance and function of any of the equipment selected for use in the Franchised Business will be limited to those provided by the manufacturer of such equipment.

The franchisor gets paid a 10% commission on all costs to develop the premises, including license fees and costs for work, things that it had nothing to do with at all. The franchisor gets paid its proportion, as an independent consultant, as the bills are paid, not at the end of its job. The franchisor takes no responsibility for its equipment selection.

(3) *Fixtures, equipment, and signs.* The Franchisee agrees to use in the operation of the Franchised Business only those brands or types of display cases and other fixtures, cash registers, equipment, and signs that the Franchisor has approved, in its sole discretion, as meeting its specifications and standards for design, appearance, function, performance, and serviceability. The Franchisee may purchase approved brands or types of fixtures, equipment, and signs from any supplier approved by the Franchisor, which may include the Franchisor or its affiliates. If the Franchisee proposes to purchase any brand or type of fixture, equipment, or sign which is not then approved or from a supplier that is not then approved, the Franchisee shall first notify the Franchisor and shall submit to the Franchisor upon its request sufficient specifications, photographs, drawings, and/or other information or samples for a determination by the Franchisor of whether or not such brand, type, or supplier complies with the Franchisor's specifications and standards, which determination shall be made and communicated to the Franchisee within a reasonable time. The Franchisee further agrees to place or display at the Premises (interior and exterior) only such signs, emblems, lettering, logos, and display materials as are from time to time approved in writing by the Franchisor, which approval may be given or withheld in the sole discretion of the Franchisor.

This paragraph seems to be more repetition of things we have read earlier, and so it is. But it is specific to equipment and sign usage and purchases. The short form of the paragraph is: the franchisee can only buy and use franchisor-approved equipment and signage. Other equipment/signage must be presented to the franchisor for written approval before being purchased or used.

11. Marks

(1) *No permanent interest.* Neither this agreement nor the operation of the Franchised Business shall in any way give or be deemed to give to the Franchisee any interest in the Marks except for the right to use the Marks solely at and on the Premises and in accordance with the terms and conditions of this agreement. The Franchisee shall not use the Marks in any manner calculated to represent that it is the owner of the Marks. Neither during the term of this agreement nor at any time after termination hereof shall the Franchisee, either directly or indirectly, dispute or contest the validity or enforceability of the Marks, attempt any registration thereof, or attempt to dilute the value of any goodwill attaching to the Marks. Any goodwill associated with the Marks shall enure exclusively to the benefit of the Franchisor.

This paragraph provides protection for the franchisor's proprietary property. Remember, this is in effect a "license," so there is no ownership right transferred.

(2) *Franchisee's obligations with respect to Marks.* Without in any way restricting or limiting paragraph 11(1), the Franchisee covenants and agrees as follows:
  (a) that contemporaneously with the execution of this agreement or forthwith upon any request by the Franchisor, the Franchisee will at its expense (including, without limitation, paying all disbursements) execute and file such applications or agreements or such other instruments in such form and with such parties, as the Franchisor in its sole discretion shall specify, for the purpose of protecting the interests and rights of the Franchisor in such Marks, or complying with any applicable trade name, trade mark or other similar legislation;

The franchisee agrees to execute and file any other documents or forms necessary to protect the franchisor's marks for the exclusive benefit of the franchisor. It could conceivably include business name registration in the franchisee's jurisdiction, and other such filings. And, all at the franchisee's cost as well. Would it not seem reasonable that the franchisor take care of all these little legal snags before offering a franchise in the territory? Technically, if these filings could not be made (so that the franchisee has no right to use the marks or name in its province), the franchisor has nothing to sell to the franchisee and has committed a fraud.

> (b) that the Franchisee will not use either the Marks or any variations thereof as any part of its corporate, firm, or business name or for any other purposes, save and except in accordance with the terms and conditions of this agreement or as may otherwise be specifically authorized by the Franchisor in writing;

This paragraph would probably serve to prevent the franchisee from naming its company "Barbi Q's (Manitoba) Ltd.," or some such thing, unless the franchisor were to authorize it.

> (c) that if the business, partnership, or corporate statutes of any jurisdiction require that the Franchisee make application to use the Marks within such jurisdiction, such application of the Franchisee shall specify that the Franchisee's use of such Marks is subject to and limited by the terms and conditions of this agreement; and

Again, this paragraph provides nothing more than proper protection to the franchisor's property.

> (d) forthwith upon the termination for any reason whatsoever of this agreement, the Franchisee shall cease all use of the Marks for any purposes whatsoever and the Franchisee shall not make known, either directly or indirectly, following such termination, that the Franchisee previously conducted business under the Marks.

Upon termination of this agreement, the former franchisee must pretend that it was never in the business as a franchisee operation.

> (3) *Affixing of notice.* The Franchisee hereby covenants and agrees that it will affix in a conspicuous location in or upon the Premises, a sign containing the following notice:
> "this restaurant is owned and operated independently by New Guy on the Block Ltd., who is an authorized licensed user of the trade mark 'Barbi Q's,' which trade mark is owned by Ribs Restaurants Inc."

This is a common notice I have personally seen in almost every franchised operation I have ever entered. It is all about disclosure.

> (4) *Infringement or change of Marks.* The Franchisee shall immediately notify the Franchisor of any infringement of or challenge to the Franchisee's use of any of the Marks and the Franchisor shall have the sole discretion to take such action as it deems appropriate. The Franchisor agrees to indemnify the Franchisee against and to reimburse the Franchisee for all damages for which it is held liable in any proceeding arising out of the use of any of the Marks in compliance with this agreement and for all costs reasonably incurred by the Franchisee in the defense of any such claim brought against him or in any such proceeding in which he is named as a party, to a maximum aggregate amount of the initial franchise fee paid by the Franchisee pursuant to paragraph 4. If it becomes advisable at any time in the sole discretion of the Franchisor for the Franchisee to modify or discontinue the use of any of the Marks or use one or more additional or substitute trade names or trade marks, the Franchisee agrees to do so and the sole obligation of the Franchisor in any such event shall be to reimburse the Franchisee for the actual out-of-pocket expenses reasonably incurred by the Franchisee in replacing signs or other printed material then being used by the Franchisee in the conduct of the Franchised Business and bearing the Marks to be modified or discontinued.

In this paragraph, the franchisor indemnifies the franchisee against claims and damages for its proper use of the marks as set out in the agreement. Such troubles could arise if someone in the franchisee's jurisdiction previously registered a business name that Barbi Q's was deemed to infringe upon. The total protection the franchisee will receive from the franchisor in this regard is limited to the initial franchise fee of $100,000. If the franchisor decides that, rather than fight, it will discontinue or replace the disputed marks, the franchisee must go along with the change. The franchisor will be responsible only for the franchisee's actual out-of-pocket expenses to effect the change.

12. Operating Manual and Confidentiality

(1) *Compliance with Manual.* The Franchisee shall conduct the Franchised Business strictly in accordance with all of the provisions set out in the Manual as amended from time to time.

For the franchisee: Deviate from the franchise manual's rules (without special dispensation from the franchisor) at your peril.

(2) *Nondisclosure.* The Franchisee acknowledges that it has had no part in the creation or development of, nor does it have any property or other rights or claims of any kind in or to any element of, the System, the Marks, or any matters dealt with in the Manual and that all disclosures made to the Franchisee relating to the System and including, without limitation, the specifications, standards, procedures, and the entire contents of the Manual, are communicated to the Franchisee solely on a confidential basis and as trade secrets, in which the Franchisor has a substantial investment and a legitimate right to protect against unlawful disclosure. Accordingly, the Franchisee agrees to maintain the confidentiality of all such information during the currency of this agreement or at any time thereafter and shall not disclose any of the contents of the Manual or any information whatsoever with respect to the Franchisee's or the Franchisor's business affairs or the System other than as may be required to enable the Franchisee to conduct its business from the Premises, and the Franchisee further agrees not to use any such information in any other business or in any manner not specifically approved in writing by the Franchisor. This paragraph shall survive the termination of this agreement for any reason whatsoever.

Lawyers sometimes get carried away with the minutiae of things legal (which is arguably why they exist), so what might otherwise be a simple paragraph gets turned into a marathon jumble of confusing words. The paragraph really says that the franchise manual, representing the system, is proprietary and confidential to the franchisor, and that the franchisee must maintain the knowledge in it in confidence forever.

(3) *Manual is property of the Franchisor.* The Franchisee hereby acknowledges that the Manual is loaned to the Franchisee and shall at all times remain the sole and exclusive property of the Franchisor, and upon the termination of this agreement for any reason whatsoever, the Franchisee shall forthwith return the Manual together with all copies of any portion of the Manual which the Franchisee may have made, to the Franchisor.

Just as we saw in reference to the trademarks in Section 10, the franchisor owns and retains all rights to the property, which in this case is the written text of the franchise manual. The franchisee must surrender the properties to the franchisor when the license terminates.

The section on insurance that follows is quite similar to the insurance requirements stipulated by landlords, chattel lessors, and lenders. Essentially, in this case, the franchisee is obliged to maintain various forms of insurance as specified by the franchisor (Sections 13(1) and (2)). Those policies must name both the franchisee and the franchisor as insureds (see Chapter 8 for more details), with both copies and notice of all documents and changes going to the franchisor as well as the franchisee (Sections 13(2) and (3)). If the franchisee does not maintain insurance as required, the franchisor may do so and the franchisee must reimburse the franchisor immediately (Section 13(4)).

13. Insurance

(1) *Types of insurance.* The Franchisee shall, at its sole cost and expense, take out and keep in full force and effect throughout the term of this agreement and any renewal thereof, such insurance coverage as may be required, pursuant to the lease or sublease for the Premises and as the Franchisor may from time to time require (including, without limitation, product liability insurance, fire and extended coverage insurance on the equipment, leasehold improvements and stock of the Franchised Business, business interruption insurance, and public liability and indemnity insurance), and in such amounts as the Franchisor may from time to time require, fully protecting as named insureds the Franchisor and the Franchisee against loss or damage occurring in connection with the operation of the Franchised Business. All costs in connection with the placing and maintaining of such insurance shall be borne solely by the Franchisee.

(2) *Policies of insurance.* All policies of insurance obtained pursuant to this paragraph shall:

    (a) be placed only with insurers reasonably acceptable to the Franchisor;

    (b) be in such form and amounts as is reasonably acceptable to the Franchisor;

    (c) contain a clause that the insurer will not cancel or change or refuse to renew the insurance without first giving to the Franchisor thirty (30) days' prior written notice; and

    (d) name the Franchisor as an additional named insured, as its interest appears.

(3) *Copies.* Copies of all policies or certificates of insurance and any renewals thereof, shall be delivered promptly to the Franchisor by the Franchisee from time to time throughout the term of this agreement and any renewal thereof.

(4) *Placement of insurance by the Franchisor.* If the Franchisee fails to take out or keep in force any insurance referred to in paragraph 13(1), or should any such insurance not be as provided in paragraph 13(2), and should the Franchisee not rectify such failure within forty-eight (48) hours after written notice is given to the Franchisee by the Franchisor, the Franchisor has the right, without assuming any obligation in connection therewith, to effect such insurance at the sole cost of the Franchisee and all outlays by the Franchisor shall be immediately paid by the Franchisee to the Franchisor on the first (1st) day of the next month following such payment by the Franchisor without prejudice to any other rights and remedies of the Franchisor under this agreement.

14. Restrictive Covenants and Trade Secrets

(1) *Competition during term of agreement.* The Franchisee and the Guarantor (in consideration of the Franchisor entering into this agreement) covenant and agree that, during the term of this agreement and any renewal period thereof, the Franchisee shall not, without the prior written consent of the Franchisor, either individually or in partnership or jointly or in conjunction with any person, firm, association, syndicate, or corporation, as principal, agent, shareholder, or in any manner whatsoever, carry on or be engaged in or be concerned with or interested in or advise, lend money to, guarantee the debts or obligations of or permit their names or any part thereof to be used or employed in any business operating in competition with or similar to the Franchised Business.

This is a decidedly one-way noncompetition clause that goes hand-in-hand with clause 8(1)(j) which demands the franchisee's and guarantor's full time and attention. This paragraph is not, nor is there anywhere else in the agreement, a reciprocal clause preventing the franchisor from granting another franchise or opening a corporate location that would directly compete with this franchised Business.

(2) *Competition after termination.* In the event of termination of this agreement for any reason whatsoever, each of the Franchisee and the Guarantor (in consideration of the Franchisor entering into this agreement) shall not, without the prior written consent of the Franchisor, at any time during the period of two (2) years from the date of such termination either individually or in partnership or jointly or in conjunction with any person or persons, firm, association, syndicate, company, or syndication as principal, agent, shareholder, or in any other manner whatsoever carry on, be engaged in, or be concerned with or interested in or advise, lend money to, guarantee the debts or obligations of, or permit its name or any part thereof to be used or employed by any person or persons, firm, association, syndicate, company, or corporation engaged in or concerned with or interested in, any business

competitive with or similar to the Franchised Business or franchising businesses similar to the Franchised Business, at the Premises or within a two (2) mile radius of the Premises.

This paragraph extends the noncompetition clause beyond the termination of the agreement. It also puts a relevant geographic limitation on the noncompetition area around the franchised business, outside of which the franchisee and guarantor are free to set up shop again after this agreement has terminated.

> (3) *Acknowledgement of corporate Franchisee.* In the event the Franchisee is a corporation, the Franchisee covenants and agrees to deliver to the Franchisor at any time the Franchisor may request, the written acknowledgement of such directors, officers, shareholders, or employees of the Franchisee, as the Franchisor shall in its discretion determine, acknowledging that they have reviewed the provisions of section 14, and that they agree to abide by and be bound by all such provisions.

By this paragraph's meaning, at the franchisor's discretion, it is practically impossible for any shareholder or partner (even the silent "money guy") to become involved in another competitive restaurant. And, although its practical application would be very difficult to control, no employee of the franchised business can become involved in a competitive business. (I say difficult to control because many a minimum-wage "assistant manager" moves on, and turnover is relatively high in the fast food business. To follow up on every employee's post-franchise business or work endeavours is futile and not economically worthwhile.)

15. Termination

> (1) *Events of termination.* The Franchisor shall have the right to terminate this agreement and the rights granted hereunder (provided, however, that paragraphs 12 and 14 shall continue in full force and effect for the periods therein specified), without prejudice to the enforcement of any other legal right or remedy, immediately upon giving written notice of such termination upon the happening of any of the following events:

There are two things to notice and keep in mind as you read the list of events that give rise to termination. First, certain of these covenants live on after termination. Second, the termination is effective *immediately* upon notice by the franchisor, to the franchisee, of one of the listed breaches.

> (a) if in the Franchisor's opinion, acting reasonably, the Franchisee's participation in the Franchisor's initial training program pursuant to paragraph 7(1) discloses the Franchisee's or the Franchisee's key employees' inability to adequately manage and operate a "Barbi Q's" restaurant. In the event of such termination, the Franchisor shall refund to the Franchisee, within seven (7) days after the effective date of termination, all money received by it from the Franchisee, less the Franchisor's reasonable costs;

Perhaps the franchisee is simply not cut out for the franchise business. But one would think that would be flushed out long before getting past the payment and setup and on to this stage.

> (b) if default shall be made in the due and punctual payment of any amount payable under this agreement, when and as same shall become due and payable, and such default shall continue for a period of two (2) days after written notice thereof has been given to the Franchisee;

This paragraph provides the franchisee with two days, after notice, in which to remedy any late payment breach, *or else*. At least in paragraphs 15(1)(c) and (d), below, there is a 10-day remedy period.

> (c) if the Franchisee shall breach any other of the terms or conditions of this agreement or any other agreement or undertaking entered into between the Franchisor and Franchisee and such breach shall continue for a period of ten (10) days after written notice thereof has been given to the Franchisee;

(d) if the Franchisee shall fail to observe or perform any of the rules, bulletins, directives, or other notices set forth in the Manual and any such failure to observe or perform same shall continue for a period of ten (10) days after written notice thereof has been given to the Franchisee;

(e) if the Franchisee shall fail to observe or perform any of the terms and conditions of any lease, sublease, or other instruments under which the Franchisee has acquired the right to occupy the Premises;

We saw this noted as a breach in paragraph 3(2)(c) as well as in the various provisions of Section 9. But I suppose it never hurts to repeat a good thing.

(f) if the Franchisee fails to conduct business in, at, or from the Premises for a period of five (5) consecutive business days without the prior written consent of the Franchisor or if the Premises are used by any party other than such as are properly entitled to use same;

(g) if the Franchisee ceases or threatens to cease to carry on business, or takes or threatens to take any action to liquidate its assets, or stops making payments in the usual course of business;

(h) if either the Franchisee or the Guarantor makes or purports to make a general assignment for the benefit of creditors;

(i) if either the Franchisee or the Guarantor makes or purports to make a bulk sale of their assets;

(j) if either the Franchisee or the Guarantor shall institute any proceeding under any statute or otherwise relating to insolvency or bankruptcy, or should any proceeding under any such statute or otherwise be instituted against the Franchisee or the Guarantor;

(k) if a custodian, receiver, manager, or any other person with like powers shall be appointed to take charge of all or any part of the Franchisee's or Guarantor's undertaking, business, property, or assets;

(l) if any lessor or encumbrancer, or any other person, corporation, or entity lawfully entitled, shall take possession of any of the undertaking, business, property, or assets of either the Franchisee or the Guarantor;

(m) if either the Franchisee or the Guarantor shall commit or suffer any default under any contract of conditional sale, mortgage, or other security instrument;

(n) in the event the Franchisee or the Guarantor is a corporation,

(i) if an order shall be made or a resolution passed for the winding up or liquidation of either the Franchisee or the Guarantor;

(ii) if either the Franchisee or the Guarantor passes or purports to pass, or takes or purports to take any corporate proceedings to enable them to take proceedings for their dissolution, liquidation, or amalgamation;

(iii) if either the Franchisee or the Guarantor shall lose their charter by expiration, forfeiture, or otherwise; or

(iv) if any proceedings with respect to either the Franchisee or the Guarantor are commenced under the *Companies' Creditors Arrangement Act*, R.S.C. 1985, c. C-36.

Sub-paragraphs (f) through (n), above, deal primarily with the actual or potential end of the franchisee as a going concern in some way. It is only reasonable that under such circumstances that the franchisor might want to take some action.

(o) if a distress or execution against any of the undertaking, business, property, or assets of either the Franchisee or the Guarantor shall not be discharged, varied, or stayed within twenty (20) days after the entry thereof or within such time period as action must be taken in order to discharge, vary, or stay the distress or execution, whichever shall be the earlier;

A distress or execution is an order to seize assets, generally for debts owed. This paragraph differs from the previous only in that the franchisee has some time to have the problem rectified in some way. Paragraph 15(1)(p), below, is similar, but it specifically pertains to damages awarded against the franchisee by a court.

(p) if final judgement for the payment of money in any amount in excess of $2,500 (twenty-five hundred dollars) shall be rendered by any court of competent jurisdiction against either the Franchisee or the Guarantor and such judgement shall not be discharged, varied, or execution thereof stayed within twenty (20) days after entry thereof or within such time period as action must be taken in order to discharge, vary, or stay execution of the judgement, whichever shall be the earlier;

(q) if the Franchisee or any agent or representative of the Franchisee:

    (i) fails to submit any report required to be furnished to the Franchisor pursuant hereto within three (3) days of the date such report is due; or

    (ii) understates Gross Sales by more than three percent (3%) on such report; or

    (iii) if the Franchisee materially distorts any material information pertaining to the Franchised Business, or fails to maintain its records in a manner which permits a determination of Gross Sales, unless the Franchisee proves to the satisfaction of the Franchisor that it had no knowledge of such distortion; and

This paragraph and the sub-paragraphs deal specifically with the timing and accuracy of the franchisee's records and of reports to the franchisor. The timing and permissible variances or errors are specified within this text.

(r) subject to the provisions of paragraph 17, if the Franchisee shall die or otherwise become permanently incapacitated and the Franchisee's or the Guarantor's spouse or an adult child does not desire or is not capable to continue to operate the Franchised Business as provided in accordance with the provisions of paragraph 17 or if the Franchisee shall not have a spouse or adult child.

This paragraph ties to the provisions of paragraph 17, and makes the event of the franchisee's death—under certain conditions—a cause for immediate termination of the agreement.

At the outset of this section on franchise agreements, we noted that the franchise agreement is a standard form. From Chapter 1, we recall that standard forms typically favour the contract's writer. Notice how this section of this agreement in particular typifies that general rule: there is no provision for the immediate termination of the agreement by the franchisee under any circumstances—even if the franchisor goes bankrupt or such.

(2) *Effect of termination.* Upon the expiration and non-renewal or termination of this agreement for any reason whatsoever, the following shall apply:

(a) the Franchisee shall, immediately upon the Franchisor's request (in order that the Franchisor may protect its proprietary marks and other proprietary rights and the Franchisor's other Franchisees), permit the Franchisor or the Franchisor's representative to enter the Premises and, at the Franchisor's option, to cure any default by the Franchisee, to operate the Premises for the Franchisor's account or to secure the Franchisee's complete and timely compliance with the other obligations set forth in this paragraph;

The gist of this paragraph is that the franchisor can take over the franchised business upon termination, if it so chooses.

(b) the Franchisee shall pay to the Franchisor, within seven (7) days after the effective date of termination or non-renewal, all royalties, advertising fees, and other charges then due and unpaid by Franchisee including, but not limited to, the Franchisor's costs and expenses in re-entering the Premises and in completing the acts specified in this paragraph;

Although paragraph 6, regarding reporting and royalties, says that royalties are due on the 10th day of the month following the month in which the monthly period ended, the final payment of royalties and advertising fees, etc., is due seven days after the contract is terminated. Refer to the comment following paragraph 19(17) if you wonder how the franchisor could enforce this timing obligation given that the contract is terminated and there is little leverage left in the agreement.

(c) the Franchisee shall immediately discontinue the operation of the Franchised Business, the System, and the use of the Franchisor's proprietary marks and other proprietary rights licensed under this agreement, and similar names and marks, or any other designations or marks associating the Franchisee with the Franchisor or the System. The Franchisee shall cease displaying and using all signs, stationery, letterheads, packaging, forms, marks, manuals, bulletins, instruction sheets, printed matter, advertising, and other physical objects used from time to time in connection with the System or containing or bearing any of the Franchisor's proprietary marks or other names, marks, or designations, and shall not thereafter operate to do business under any name or in any manner in violation of paragraph 11(2) or that might tend to give the general public the impression that it is associated with the Franchisor or the System or that it is operating a restaurant similar to a "Barbi Q's" restaurant or that it previously conducted its business under the Marks;

We have seen this term, generally, in other parts of the agreement related to trademark usage. But it is repeated and expanded upon as part of the termination procedure on the franchisee's part.

(d) if the Franchisee retains possession of the Premises, the Franchisee shall promptly and, at its expense, make such modifications to the interior and/or exterior decor of the Premises as the Franchisor shall require to remove all identification as a "Barbi Q's" restaurant;

It is possible that the franchisee owns the building in which the franchised business is operated. Alternatively, the franchisee may still hold the lease on the property. In either case, the franchisee must alter the look of the building's interior and exterior so that the public does not think the location is still in operation as the franchised business.

Sub-paragraphs 15(2)(e) and (f) that follow are fairly straightforward. Paragraph (e) especially is designed to distance the franchisee from the franchised business, as well as to provide continuity to the ongoing operations of the franchised business by the franchisor or its nominee.

(e) the Franchisee shall promptly execute such documents or take such actions as may be necessary to abandon the Franchisee's use of any fictitious business name containing any of the Franchisor's proprietary marks adopted by the Franchisee and to remove (in respect of the next publication) at the Franchisor's request, the Franchisee's listing as a "Barbi Q's" from the Yellow Pages, all other telephone directories, and all other trade or business directories and to assign (if the business of the Franchisee is being continued by the Franchisor or its nominee) to the Franchisor or any other party designated by the Franchisor all of the Franchisee's telephone numbers and listings in connection with the Franchised Business; and

(f) within seven (7) days after the effective date of expiration or termination, the Franchisee shall return to the Franchisor all copies of the Manual, all other confidential material provided to the Franchisee by the Franchisor and all other materials required to be returned in accordance with this agreement or the Manual.

(3) *Rights of the Franchisor.*

- Upon the termination of this agreement for any reason whatsoever, save and except in the event of a purchase pursuant to the provisions of paragraph 17 of this agreement, the Franchisor shall have the right, but not the obligation, such right to be exercised by notice in writing delivered to the Franchisee within thirty (30) days of the date of termination of this agreement for any reason whatsoever, to purchase from the Franchisee all or any portion of the Products located on the Premises or otherwise held by the Franchisee for the purposes of sale or distribution at the Premises, and/or all or any part of the fixtures, equipment, furniture, or other assets located on, in, or at the Premises or otherwise used in connection with the Franchised Business.

The franchisor has the right to purchase inventory, supplies, and assets from the franchisee after termination of this agreement. The franchisor must notify the franchisee, in writing, within 30 days of termination to exercise that right.

- The purchase price payable by the Franchisor to the Franchisee for any assets purchased by the Franchisor under this paragraph shall be determined as follows:

- for each of the Products so purchased, the Franchisor shall pay an amount equal to the cost (less freight or other shipping charges) thereof to the Franchisee less twenty-five percent (25%); and
- for each fixture, or item of equipment or furniture or other asset so purchased, the Franchisor shall pay an amount equal to the net depreciated book value of each such fixture, item of equipment or furniture, or other asset. In calculating "net depreciated book value," all fixtures, equipment, furniture, or other assets shall be deemed to have been depreciated at the maximum amount of depreciation allowed in accordance with the provisions of the *Income Tax Act*, R.S.C. 1952, c. 148. In no event shall any amount be payable under this paragraph for "goodwill" or "going concern value."

This paragraph definitely provides a distress sale, sweetheart arrangement for the franchisor. For inventory, it can purchase from the franchisee at cost *less* freight and shipping *less* 25%. For assets, it can purchase at the fully depreciated value (i.e., the value of the asset not yet fully written off for tax purposes) calculated at the *maximum* allowable capital cost allowance (depreciation) rate. The intrinsic market value of the asset has no bearing on the price for the franchisor under this arrangement.

- The Franchisor shall deliver to the Franchisee a statement prepared by the Franchisor's auditors setting forth the basis upon which the purchase price has been calculated. Such statement shall be conclusive and binding upon the parties. The purchase price shall be paid in cash at the closing of the purchase transaction, which shall take place no later than thirty (30) days after receipt by the Franchisee of the Franchisor's notice pursuant to paragraph 15(3)(a), at which time the Franchisee shall:
  (i) deliver all documents and instruments necessary to transfer good and merchantable title to the assets purchased to the Franchisor or its nominee, free and clear of all liens and encumbrances; and
  (ii) transfer or assign to the Franchisor all licenses or permits utilized by the Franchisee in the conduct of the Franchised Business which may be assigned or transferred. The Franchisee shall, prior to closing, comply with the *Bulk Sales Act*, R.S.O. 1990, c. B.14. The Franchisor shall have the right to set off against and reduce the purchase price by any and all amounts owed by the Franchisee to the Franchisor or any of its affiliates.

Basically, the franchisor will pay cash within 30 days for the purchase at the price calculated by the franchisor's auditors in accordance with the preceding formulas. The franchisee will deliver it all up clear and will turn over all assignable licenses and permits, etc., to the franchisor. The franchisee must also comply with any bulk sale legislation requirements. (Refer to Chapter 4 for more detail about bulk sales.)

(4) *Additional remedies.* The Franchisee expressly consents and agrees that, in addition to any other remedies the Franchisor may have at law, the Franchisor may obtain an injunction and/or appointment of a receiver of the Franchised Business to terminate or prevent the continuation of any existing default, or to prevent the occurrence of any threatened default by the Franchisee of this agreement.

This paragraph builds in a few more options for the franchisor's protection.

(5) *Survival of covenants.* Notwithstanding the termination of this agreement for any reason whatsoever, all covenants and agreements to be performed and/or observed by the Franchisee and/or the Guarantor under this agreement or which by their nature survive the expiration or termination of this agreement, including without limitation, those set out in paragraphs 12, 14(2), 15(2), (3) and (4), 17 and 18 shall survive any termination.

(6) *Failure to act not to affect rights.* The failure of the Franchisor to exercise any rights or remedies to which it is entitled upon the happening of any of the events referred to in paragraph 15(1) shall not be deemed to be a waiver of or otherwise affect, impair, or prevent the Franchisor from exercising any rights or remedies to which it may be entitled, arising either from the happening of any such event, or as a result of the subsequent happening of the same or any other event or events provided for in paragraph 15(1). The acceptance by the Franchisor of any

amount payable by or for the account of the Franchisee under this agreement after the happening of any event provided for in paragraph 15(1) shall not be deemed to be a waiver by the Franchisor of any rights and remedies to which it may be entitled, regardless of the Franchisor's knowledge of the happening of such preceding event at the time of acceptance of such payment. No waiver of the happening of any event under paragraph 15(1) shall be deemed to be waived by the Franchisor unless such waiver shall be in writing.

This paragraph starts out like a standard "no waiver" clause, which usually says that one party's failure to act on a single breach by the other party is not a waiver of the covenant itself (i.e., "You got away with it this time, but don't make a habit of it"). It also includes a sort of "no waiver by remedy" clause that says even if the franchisee pays up what may be outstanding—and giving rise to some form of recourse to the franchisor—the franchisor's acceptance of that money is not a waiver of its rights in that instance.

The odd aspect of this paragraph—and if you were to encounter one similar to it you might want to ask your lawyer—is that the franchisor seems to have an ongoing right to remedy any "event" regardless of how long in the past it may have arisen. That is: the franchisee breaches the agreement, which the franchisor is aware of and ignores. The franchisee later remedies that default event. According to this paragraph, it would appear that the franchisor has the right to act on that particular breach—never mind later breaches of the same condition—next year or later. Only a waiver in writing does the job of ending that right, an action which is more commonly used to waive the condition in perpetuity.

16. Sale, Assignment, Transfer

(1) *Assignment by the Franchisee.*

(a) The Franchisee acknowledges that the Franchisor, in granting this franchise and the rights and interests under this agreement, has relied upon, among other things, the character, background, qualifications, and financial ability of the Franchisee and, where applicable, its partners, officers, directors, shareholders, managers, and the Guarantor. Accordingly, this agreement, the Franchisee's rights and interests hereunder, the lease or sublease of the Premises and the property and assets owned and used by the Franchisee in connection with the Franchised Business shall not be sold, assigned, transferred, shared, or encumbered in whole or in part in any manner whatsoever without the prior written consent of the Franchisor with a right of first refusal as set forth in paragraph 16(2). Any actual or purported assignment occurring by operation of law or otherwise without the Franchisor's prior written consent shall be a material default of this agreement and shall be null and void.

The short version of this paragraph's text is that the franchisee may not assign the agreement without the franchisor's consent, excepting other provisions in this agreement such as paragraph 17(1)(a). Note the use of the word "purported," which in this context would mean "deemed." Its significance is that if the franchisor deems an assignment has effectively been made it would have the same effect as an actual transfer of ownership.

This paragraph raises an interesting question or point that, were you to encounter something similar, you should refer to your lawyer. It seems that the franchisor is attempting to put itself ahead of the law. In the last sentence, the words, "by operation of law" are important, because this paragraph basically says that the "operation of law" must have "the Franchisor's prior written consent." Good luck! The sentence, as it relates to the issue of default and void of the agreement, is on slippery ground, and is probably neither legal nor enforceable. The issue of the contract being breached if the franchisee goes bankrupt or into receivership etc. is dealt with in paragraphs 15(1)(f) through (n), however, so removing the questionable "operation of law" reference in this paragraph would not appreciably change the contract's overall effect.

(b) In considering the request for sale, assignment, transfer, or encumbrance (all of which are included within the word "transfer") pursuant to paragraph 16(1)(a), the Franchisor may consider, among other things, the information set out in the Franchisee's application, the qualifications, good character, requisite general business experience, apparent ability to operate the Franchised Business and credit standing of the proposed transferee, and its partners, managers, principal shareholders, directors, and officers, as appropriate. In addition, the Franchisor shall be entitled to require as a condition precedent to the granting of its consent that:

(i) as of the date of the Franchisee's request for consent and as of the effective date of transfer there shall be no default in the performance or observance of any of the Franchisee's obligations under this agreement or any other agreement between the Franchisee and the Franchisor or any affiliate or supplier thereof, and if the Franchisee intends to transfer its rights of possession of the Premises, that the Franchisee has obtained the consent of all necessary parties to the assignment of the lease or sublease to the proposed transferee;

(ii) the Franchisee shall have settled all outstanding accounts with the Franchisor, its affiliates, and all other trade creditors of the Franchised Business up to the date of closing of the proposed transfer;

(iii) the Franchisee shall have delivered to the Franchisor a complete release of the Franchisor, its directors and officers, its affiliates, and the directors and officers thereof, from all obligations under this agreement of any such persons, in a form satisfactory to the Franchisor;

(iv) the proposed transferee shall have entered into a written assignment under seal, in a form prescribed by the Franchisor, or, at the option of the Franchisor, shall have executed a new franchise agreement in the form then being used by the Franchisor, which may provide for a higher royalty and for greater expenditures for advertising and promotion than are provided hereunder, and shall have executed such other documents and agreements as are then customarily used by the Franchisor in the granting of franchises;

(v) the proposed transferee providing guarantees from anyone whom the Franchisor may request, guaranteeing the proposed transferee's performance of its obligations under the agreements to be entered into;

"[F]rom anyone whom the Franchisee may request" strains the limits of credulity to the breaking point. It could, in the extreme, mean anyone from the franchisor's widowed aunt to Elizabeth Regina. In any event, it is not good contract language from the franchisee's perspective.

(vi) the proposed transferee taking such training in the operations of the Franchised Business, at the proposed transferee's or the Franchisee's sole expense, as the Franchisor may require; and

(vii) the Franchisee paying to the Franchisor any fees and/or expenses which may be incurred by the Franchisor in dealing with the Franchisee's said application for approval up to a maximum of two thousand dollars ($2,000.00) whether or not such approval is given or the transfer is completed.

The refusal of the Franchisor to consent to the proposed transfer based upon the non-compliance with any of the foregoing conditions shall not be deemed to be an unreasonable withholding of consent. The Franchisor's consent to a transfer shall not operate to release the Franchisee from any liability under this agreement.

This paragraph essentially says that the franchisor will examine the proposed transferee and determine whether it will consent to the transfer by the franchisee. Furthermore, the franchisor insists upon a number of conditions (the list of roman numerals) being met before it will consent. The franchisor may "reasonably" choose not to consent because it is not comfortable with the transferee or because the conditions are not met. Even if the franchisor does accept and consent to the transfer, the franchisee is still not relieved of its liabilities that have been created under the agreement.

(2) *Right of first refusal.*

(a) Without in any way derogating from the Franchisor's right to reject a proposed transfer pursuant to paragraph 16(1)(b) if at any time or times during the term of this agreement, including any renewal thereof, the Franchisee obtains a *bona fide* offer (the "Offer") to acquire the whole or any part of its interest in the Franchised Business, which the Franchisee wishes to accept, the Franchisee shall promptly give written notice to the Franchisor together with a true copy of the Offer. Upon receipt of such notice and Offer, the Franchisor shall have the option of purchasing the property forming the subject-matter thereof upon the same terms and conditions as those set out in the Offer except that:

(i) there shall be deducted from the purchase price the amount of any commissions or fee that would otherwise have been payable to any broker, agent, or other intermediary in connection with the sale of such property to the offeror; and

Interestingly, the implication is either that (1) the franchisee really only could realize the net value of the sale price, so that is the valid market price for the franchisor to pay or (2) the franchisor is effectively paying itself a brokerage fee. Either way, it is a clause that seriously favours the franchisor.

> (ii) the Franchisor shall have the right to substitute cash for any other form of consideration specified in the Offer and to pay in full the entire purchase price at the time of closing.
>
> The Franchisor may exercise its option at any time within twenty (20) days after receipt of said notice by giving written notice to the Franchisee. If the Franchisor declines to exercise such option and if such transfer is approved by the Franchisor, the Franchisee shall be at liberty to complete the transfer to such third party transferee in accordance with the Offer, provided that, notwithstanding the terms of the Offer, such transaction must be completed within thirty (30) days of the date on which the Franchisor notifies the Franchisee of its approval of such transaction. If the transaction is not completed within thirty (30) days, the foregoing provisions of this paragraph shall apply again in respect of the proposed transfer and so on from time to time.

The franchisor retains the right to be informed of and match any genuine offer to purchase all or part of the franchisee's interest in the franchised business. If the franchisor does choose to exercise the "sweetheart" option, it must do so within 20 days of its being notified. If the franchisor passes on the option and approves the transfer, the franchisee must conclude the sale within 30 days, or the "right of first refusal" procedure starts all over again.

> (b) In addition to the Offer to be given by the Franchisee to the Franchisor together with the notice described in paragraph 16(2)(a), the Franchisee shall provide the Franchisor with:
>> (i) information relating to the business reputation and qualifications to carry on the Franchised Business of the proposed transferee;
>> (ii) any credit information the Franchisee may have as to the financial ability and stability of the proposed transferee, including, if the proposed transferee is an individual, his personal net worth statement and if the proposed transferee is a corporation, partnership, or other entity, its latest financial statements.

This paragraph, with sub-clauses, simply requires the franchisee to provide information about any proposed transferee (commercial and financial abilities, etc.) to the franchisor along with the offer and other required items to fulfill or prove the conditions of a transfer.

> (3) *Sale of shares or other interest in the Franchisee.* In the event the Franchisee is a corporation or partnership:
>> (a) then the respective transfer, sale, assignment, pledge, mortgage, or hypothecation of any shares or interest, or any change in the composition of partners or any amalgamation which results or could result in the change of control, within the meaning of the Income Tax Act, of the franchisee, as applicable, shall be deemed to be an assignment of this agreement and shall be subject to all of the provisions, terms, and conditions precedent specified in this paragraph which shall apply *mutatis mutandis*;

Mutatis mutandis is Latin and means "the necessary changes having been made."

> (b) the Franchisee will, upon the Franchisor's request from time to time, deliver to the Franchisor a certificate certifying as to then current shareholders, directors, officers, members, or partners, as the case may be, of the Franchisee;

The previous two paragraphs, 16(3)(a) and (b), relate to the franchisee being required to fully and regularly inform the franchisor of the nature and composition of the franchisee *if the franchisee is a corporation or partnership*. Note that in 16(3)(a) any change in partnership interest or share structure that would change control of the franchisee is deemed to be a transfer and would thus be subject to the earlier conditions precedent and provisions of this section 16.

(c) the Franchisee will cause the share certificates representing share ownership in the case of a corporation or the documents of title representing an ownership interest in the case of a partnership or other entity, to have typed or written a legend stating that such shares or documents of title are subject to this franchise agreement among the Franchisor, the Franchisee, and the Guarantor, that the said franchise agreement contains restrictions on the sale, assignment, transfer, mortgage, pledge, hypothecation, donation, encumbrancing, or other dealings with the said shares or documents of title, and that notice of the said agreement is thereby given.

This paragraph requires the franchisee corporation or partnership to notify its shareholders or partners of the franchise agreement and its ownership transfer restrictions *right on the share certificates or partnership documents.*

(4) *Assignment to bank.* Notwithstanding the foregoing provisions of this paragraph, the franchisee may assign the franchised Business, this agreement, and if the franchisee is a corporation or partnership, the shareholders or partners may assign their respective shares or interests in the franchisee to a Canadian chartered bank as security for monies advanced by such bank to the franchisee for use in the franchised Business, provided that the franchisor shall have given its prior written consent to such assignment, such approval not to be unreasonably withheld or unduly delayed.

So long as the franchisor approves and consents, the franchisee may pledge the franchised business or the agreement to a *Canadian chartered bank* (no credit unions or trust companies) as loan security for the business.

17. Death or Incapacitation

(1) *Death or incapacitation.* Upon the death or permanent disability of the Franchisee or the controlling shareholder or partner or partners of the Franchisee as the case may be, if such person has at the date of such death or permanent disability a spouse or any adult children surviving, the following shall apply:

(a) if the surviving spouse and/or adult child desire and are, in the reasonable opinion of the Franchisor, capable of carrying on the Franchised Business, the said spouse and/or adult child shall have the right to continue to operate the Franchised Business provided that they shall directly covenant and agree with the Franchisor to be bound by the terms and conditions of this agreement and any other agreements made between the Franchisor and the Franchisee, and that the fee set out in paragraph 16(1)(b)(vii) is paid;

(b) if the surviving spouse and/or an adult child do not desire or are not, in the reasonable opinion of the Franchisor, capable of carrying on the Franchised Business, or cannot devote their full time and attention to the Franchised Business or if the Franchisee does not have a spouse or adult child surviving, the Franchisor shall have the right, such right to be exercised by the Franchisor giving written notice to the Franchisee or to the Franchisee's estate within ninety (90) days of the date of the Franchisee's death or death of the controlling shareholder(s) or partner(s) of the Franchisee or the date upon which the Franchisee's permanent disability arises or the permanent disability of the controlling shareholder(s) or partner(s) of the Franchisee arises, to purchase all or any part of the assets of the Franchisee used in the operation of the Franchised Business for a purchase price equal to the "asset value" of the Franchisee's assets calculated in accordance with the provisions of paragraph 17(2), less all proper business liabilities assumed by the Franchisor as at the date the said purchase is completed. To satisfy the aforesaid purchase price, the Franchisor shall pay the difference between the said "asset value" and the amount of the liabilities assumed by it, on the date of the completion of the purchase by way of cash or certified cheque.

Paragraph 17(1) sets forth two scenarios for the franchised business in the event the franchisee should die or become incapacitated. Note that this paragraph also specifically refers to controlling partner(s) and shareholder(s) of the franchised business. First, the surviving spouse or adult child(ren) may take over the franchised business, subject to the consent of the franchisor and payment of transfer costs. Second, the franchisor may exercise a right to purchase the franchised business within 90 days. The value and price of the business is set by the terms of paragraph 17(2), and must be paid in cash on closing.

(2) *Valuation.* For the purposes of this paragraph, "asset value" shall be determined as follows:
   (a) "inventory" shall be valued at the Franchisee's actual cost; provided that, in its sole opinion, the Franchisor believes any portion of the inventory is not edible, or is otherwise shopworn, damaged, or not saleable, the Franchisor shall not be required to purchase such portion;

If the franchisor buys up the franchised Business on the franchisee's death or incapacity, it would buy supplies and inventory at cost, but need only purchase what it wants and feels it can use.

   (b) "fixtures, equipment, and furniture" shall be valued at an amount equal to the "net depreciated book value" of each such item as such term is defined in paragraph 15(3)(b);
   (c) "goodwill" shall be valued at an amount equal to the average of the Franchisee's annual after-tax earnings for the three fully completed fiscal years immediately preceding the date of death or permanent disability of the Franchisee or the controlling shareholder(s) or partner(s) of the Franchisee; provided that, if the Franchisee shall have conducted business for less than the said three (3) year period but for at least one fully competed fiscal period, goodwill shall be valued at an amount equal to the Franchisee's average annual after-tax earnings for such lesser period. If the Franchisee has conducted business for less than one fully completed fiscal period, no value shall be attributed to goodwill. In calculating such after-tax earnings, appropriate adjustments shall be made for reasonable management salaries.

Any other assets (except for any leasehold interest) purchased by the Franchisor hereunder shall be valued at the lesser of their depreciated value as shown in the financial records of the Franchisee, or the actual cost to the Franchisee. No value shall be attributed to any interest in the lease or other instruments pursuant to which the Franchisee occupied the Premises. Any purchase pursuant to the provisions of this paragraph shall be completed within ninety (90) days of the date of death or permanent disability of the Franchisee or its controlling shareholder(s) or partner(s), or at such other time as may be mutually agreed upon by the Franchisor and the Franchisee or the appropriate estate representatives.

The formula for establishing the goodwill value of the franchised business (i.e., the built-up equity value) if the franchisor buys the business on the franchisee's death or incapacity is provided in this paragraph. It would seem that the franchisee (or the estate) is entitled to less than one year's post-tax net income as goodwill *less* an adjustment (read: nonsensical reduction) for reasonable management salaries. Again, without getting into the commercial realities of franchise operation, adding "reasonable management salaries," if none were previously taken by the franchisee, defeats and dissolves the economic value otherwise accruing to the franchisee. On the other hand, if the franchisee already removed a salary, there should be no requirement for a management salary deduction.[4] The remainder of the paragraph sets the price of assets to be purchased and timing for the sale to close.

(3) *Deemed permanently disabled.* For the purposes of this paragraph, the Franchisee or any controlling shareholder(s) or partner(s) as the case may be shall be deemed to have a "permanent disability" if the usual participation of the Franchisee or any controlling shareholder(s) or partner(s), as the case may be, in the franchised Business is for any reason curtailed for a cumulative period of ninety (90) days in any twelve (12) month period during the term of this agreement, including renewals.

Obviously the franchisor will not stand for absentee ownership and management of the franchised business.

18. Guarantor's Covenants

(1) *Guarantee and indemnity.* In consideration of the Franchisor entering into this agreement with the Franchisee and in consideration of the sum of one dollar ($1.00) and other good and valuable consideration (the receipt and sufficiency whereof is hereby acknowledged by the Guarantor), the Guarantor hereby unconditionally guarantees to the Franchisor that the Franchisee will pay all amounts to be paid and otherwise observe and perform all terms and conditions to be so observed and performed, either in this agreement and/or in any agreement, and/or any lease, sublease, or other instrument under which the right to occupy the Premises has been obtained (the said lease, sublease, and any other said instrument to be hereinafter referred to individually and collectively as the "Lease Instrument"). If the Franchisee shall default in making any such payments or in the observance or performance of any such obligations, the Guarantor hereby covenants and agrees to pay to the Franchisor forthwith upon demand all amounts not so paid by the Franchisee and all damages that may arise in consequence of any such non-observance or non-performance.

Without in any way restricting or limiting the guarantee given by the Guarantor as set out above or any other rights and remedies to which the Franchisor may be entitled, the Guarantor hereby covenants and agrees to indemnify and save the Franchisor harmless against any and all liabilities, losses, suits, claims, demands, costs, fines, and actions of any kind or nature whatsoever to which the Franchisor shall or may become liable for, or suffer, by reason of any breach, violation, or non-performance by the Franchisee of any term or condition of this agreement, the Lease Instrument or any other agreement made between the Franchisee and the Franchisor. With respect to the guarantee and indemnification provided for by the Guarantor, the Guarantor covenants and agrees to execute and deliver under separate instrument, at such time or times as the Franchisor may request, such form of guarantee and/or indemnity evidencing its obligations under the provisions of this paragraph as the Franchisor shall in its discretion determine.

This paragraph is a guarantee such as we have encountered in other contract types. The guarantor essentially agrees to ensure that the franchisee performs all of its obligations under the contract. If not, the guarantor will do so itself. The guarantor also provides an indemnity to the franchisor for any harm that may arise from the franchisee's actions or inactions.

(2) *Waiver of right to proceed.* In the enforcement of any of its rights against the Guarantor, the Franchisor may in its discretion proceed as if the Guarantor was the primary obligator under this agreement, the Lease Instrument, or any other agreement made between the Franchisee and the Franchisor. The Guarantor hereby waives any right to require the Franchisor to proceed against the Franchisee or to proceed against or to exhaust any security (if any) held from the Franchisee, or to pursue any other remedy whatsoever which may be available to the Franchisor before proceeding against the Guarantor.

This paragraph repeats and specifies, for greater certainty no doubt, that the guarantor is equally responsible with the franchisee. The franchisor need not come to a dead end with the franchisee before going to the guarantor. Rather, the franchisor may effectively interchange these parties at its discretion.

(3) *Any dealings binding on Guarantor.* No dealings of whatsoever kind between the Franchisor and the Franchisee and/or any party from whom the right to occupy the Premises has been obtained and/or any other persons as the Franchisor may see fit, whether with or without notice to the Guarantor, shall exonerate, release, discharge, or in any way reduce the obligations of the Guarantor in whole or in part, and in particular, and without limiting the generality of the foregoing, the Franchisor may modify or amend this agreement or the Lease Instrument, grant any indulgence, release, postponement, or extension of time, waive any term or condition of this agreement or the Lease Instrument or any obligation of the Franchisee, take or release any securities or other guarantees for the performance by the Franchisee of its obligations, and otherwise deal with the Franchisee and/or any party from whom the right to occupy the Premises has been obtained and/or any other persons as the Franchisor may see fit without affecting, lessening, or limiting in any way the liability of the Guarantor. The Guarantor hereby expressly waives notice of all or any default of the Franchisee.

Sometimes when one makes a deal and then the circumstances and conditions are radically changed by one of the other parties, the deal is no longer valid because, plainly, "That's not what I agreed to." This paragraph does not permit the guarantor that luxury. What it says is that the guarantor's obligation to act in the place and stead of the franchisee and to indemnify the franchisor remains in full force regardless of what changes or arrangements may be made between the franchisor and franchisee or landlord or any other party affecting the relationship and the agreement. The paragraph explicitly says that the guarantor need not even be notified of such changes.

(4) *Settlement binding on Guarantor.* Any settlement made between the Franchisor and/or the Franchisee and/or any party from whom the right to occupy the Premises has been obtained and/or any other persons as the Franchisor may see fit to deal with, or any determination made pursuant to this agreement or the Lease Instrument which is expressed to be binding upon the Franchisee, shall be binding upon the Guarantor.

The guarantor, similarly to being fully obliged even if the deal changes without notice to the guarantor, is in this paragraph bound to any deals or settlements between the franchisee and the franchisor or other parties. The remaining sub-clauses (5) through (7), below, similarly serve to bind the guarantor in any and every circumstance.

(5) *Bankruptcy of the Franchisee.* Notwithstanding any assignment for the general benefit of creditors or any bankruptcy or any other act of insolvency by the Franchisee and notwithstanding any rejection, disaffirmation, or disclaimer of this agreement (including its agreement and covenant under this paragraph and/or the Lease Instrument), the Guarantor shall continue to be fully liable hereunder.

(6) *Guarantor's covenants binding.* Without in any way limiting the generality of any other paragraph of this agreement, the covenants and agreement of the Guarantor contained in this paragraph shall enure to the benefit of and be binding upon the Guarantor and the heirs, executors, administrators, successors, and assigns of the Guarantor.

(7) *Guarantor to be bound.* The Guarantor acknowledges reviewing all of the provisions of this agreement and agrees to be bound by all of the provisions hereof in so far as applicable to him, including without limitation, the provisions of paragraphs 12 and 14 which, by his execution of this agreement, he covenants and agrees to abide and be bound by.

19. General Provisions

(1) *Security to the Franchisor.* To secure payment and performance of any and all obligations from time to time owing by the Franchisee to the Franchisor, including payment of any amount owing by the Franchisee to the Franchisor in respect of goods from time to time purchased by the Franchisee, the Franchisee covenants and agrees to provide from time to time, on request by the Franchisor, a security interest or interests by a security agreement, in a form satisfactory to the Franchisor, in such of the inventory, equipment, leasehold improvements, and other assets of the Franchised Business and in such amount or amounts and upon such terms as the Franchisor, in its absolute discretion, determines advisable. Failure to provide such security within ten (10) days following the receipt by the Franchisee of a written request therefor, specifying the nature and extent of the security required, shall be deemed to be a material default under this agreement.

The franchisee must provide a security interest in the property or business to the franchisor for money owing or to be owed to it (purchases, royalties, etc.) just as it would provide security to a bank.

(2) *Overdue amounts.* All royalty and advertising contributions, all amounts due for goods purchased by the Franchisee from time to time from the Franchisor or its affiliates by the Franchisee pursuant to this agreement or otherwise, shall bear interest after the due date at the Interest Rate, calculated and payable weekly, not in advance, both before and after default, with interest on overdue interest at the aforesaid rate. The acceptance of any interest payment shall not be construed as a waiver by the Franchisor of its rights in respect of the default giving rise to such payment and shall be without prejudice to the Franchisor's right to terminate this agreement in respect of such default.

Overdue payments to the franchisor are a breach that triggers a notice of termination. The franchisor may choose not to do so, in which case interest will accrue on the outstanding amounts. The charge, payment, and acceptance of interest does not waive the franchisor's right to make notice and terminate the agreement should it so choose at any time.

> (3) *Indemnification of the Franchisor.* The Franchisee hereby agrees, during and after the term of this agreement, to indemnify and save the Franchisor harmless from any and all liabilities, losses, suits, claims, demands, costs, fines, and actions of any kind or nature whatsoever to which the Franchisor shall or may become liable for, or suffer by reason of any breach, violation, or non-performance on the part of the Franchisee or any of its agents, servants, or employees of any term or condition of this agreement or the lease, sublease, or other instrument by which the right to occupy the Premises is held and from all claims, damages, suits, costs, or rights of any persons, firms, or corporations arising from the operation of the Franchised Business.

> (4) *Legal fees.* In the event the Franchisor shall be made a party to any litigation commenced by or against the Franchisee, then the Franchisee shall indemnify and save the Franchisor harmless against any losses, damages, or claims whatsoever arising therefrom and shall pay all costs and expenses including reasonable legal fees, accountants, and expert witness fees, costs of investigation, and travel and living expenses incurred or paid by the Franchisor in connection with such litigation. Further, if it is established that the Franchisee has breached any of the terms and conditions of the agreement, the Franchisee hereby agrees to pay all costs and expenses including legal fees that may be incurred or paid by the Franchisor in enforcing the Franchisor's rights and remedies under this agreement.

In both paragraphs 19(3) and (4), the franchisee is providing indemnity to the franchisor. Oddly, unlike the indemnity provided by the franchisor to the franchisee with regard to the trademarks (section 11(4)), the franchisee's obligation appears to be unlimited in both time and money. The last part of paragraph 19(4) makes the franchisee responsible for the franchisor's costs if it is established that the franchisee is in breach of any part of the agreement. (So, if the franchisee is late with a payment or report—or has been in the past—there is a very good likelihood that the franchisor's costs in this circumstance will accrue to the franchisee.)

> (5) *No liability.* The Franchisor shall not be responsible or otherwise liable for any injury, loss, or damage resulting from, occasioned to, or suffered by any person or persons or to any property because of any Products sold or otherwise provided by it to the Franchisee.

So, let's assume that the franchisor has specified and "managed" the setup of the franchised business, including design, construction, and equipment installation. Further, let's assume that it has been selling product inventory and supplies to the franchisee (because it is the approved supplier). Now, say a liability situation arises: somebody gets burned by a faultily installed machine or a customer is poisoned by tainted product. The franchisor, despite supplying—forcing such purchases even—and being compensated for those goods and services, is not liable in any event according to this paragraph.

> (6) *Legal relationship.* The parties hereby acknowledge and agree that, subject to paragraph 19(17), each is an independent contractor, that no party shall be considered to be the agent, representative, master, or servant of any other party for any purpose whatsoever, and that no party has any authority to enter into any contract, assume any obligations, or to give any warranties or representations on behalf of any other party. Nothing in this agreement shall be construed to create a relationship of partners, joint venturers, fiduciaries, or any other similar relationship between the parties.

This common clause is important in this instance because of the easy and likely possibility for such misunderstanding or mistakes to be made by others.

(7) *Joint and severable.* If two or more individuals, corporations, partnerships, or other entities (or any combination of two or more thereof) shall sign or be subject to the terms and conditions of this agreement as the Franchisee or Guarantor, the liability of each of them under this agreement shall be deemed to be joint and several.

(8) *Severability.* If for any reason whatsoever, any term or condition of this agreement or the application thereof to any party or circumstance shall to any extent be invalid or unenforceable, all other terms and conditions of this agreement and/or the application of such terms and conditions to parties or circumstances, other than those as to which it is held invalid or unenforceable, shall not be affected thereby and each term and condition of this agreement shall be separately valid and enforceable to the fullest extent permitted by law.

(9) *Franchisee may not withhold payments due the Franchisor.* The Franchisee agrees that he will not, on grounds of the alleged non-performance by the Franchisor of any of its obligations hereunder, withhold payment of any royalty or other amounts due to the Franchisor or its affiliates, whether on account of goods purchased by the Franchisee or otherwise.

This clause is like the "no set-offs" against rent clause in a lease. Basically the franchisee agrees to pay the money due to the franchisor regardless of what other issues may have the franchisor owing to the franchisee.

(10) *Notice.* All notices, consents, approvals, statements, authorizations, documents, or other communications (collectively "notices") required or permitted to be given hereunder shall be in writing, and shall be delivered by facsimile or personally, or mailed by registered mail, postage prepaid, to the said parties at their respective addresses set forth hereunder, namely:

To the Franchisor at:	Ribs Restaurant
	10-A The North Mall
	Mississauga, ON L5M 2T7
To the Franchisee at:	New Guy on the Block Ltd.
	1234 Richmond Street
	Winnipeg, MB R3C 3P2
To the Guarantor at:	Big Brother Corporation
	Suite 3200
	200 Portage Avenue
	Winnipeg, MB R3C 2L5

or at any such other address or addresses as may be given by any of them to the other in writing from time to time. Such notices, if mailed, shall be deemed to have been given on the second (2nd) business day (except Saturdays and Sundays) following such mailing, or, if delivered personally, shall be deemed to have been given on the day of delivery, if a business day, or if not a business day, on the business day next following the day of delivery; provided that if such notice shall have been mailed and if regular mail service shall be interrupted by strike or other irregularity before the deemed receipt of such notice as aforesaid, then such notice shall not be effective unless delivered.

(11) *Headings, paragraph numbers.* The headings and paragraph numbers appearing in this agreement or any schedule hereto are inserted for convenience of reference only and shall not in any way affect the construction or interpretation of this agreement.

(12) *Applicable law.* This agreement shall be construed in accordance with and governed by the laws of the Province of Ontario.

(13) *Time of the essence.* Time shall be of the essence of this agreement and of each and every part hereof.

(14) *Waiver of obligations.* The Franchisor may, by written instrument, unilaterally waive any obligation of or restriction upon the Franchisee under this agreement. No acceptance by the Franchisor of any payment by the Franchisee and no failure, refusal, or neglect of the Franchisor to exercise any right under this agreement or to insist upon full compliance by the Franchisee with his obligations hereunder, including without limitation, any mandatory specification, standard, or operating procedure, shall constitute a waiver of any provision of this agreement.

We have seen this text and sentiment in other parts of the agreement in different forms. The franchisor does not prejudice its rights by not taking action to enforce such rights. The only valid waiver of a right under the contract must be made in writing.

(15) *Franchisee and Guarantor defined, use of pronoun.* The words "Franchisee" and "Guarantor" whenever used in this agreement shall be deemed and taken to mean each and every person or party mentioned as a Franchisee or Guarantor herein, be the same one or more; and if there shall be more than one Franchisee or Guarantor, any notice, consent, approval, statement, authorization, document, or other communication required or permitted to be given by the terms or conditions of this agreement may be given by or to any one thereof, and shall have the same force and effect as if given by or to all thereof. The use of the neuter or male or female pronoun to refer to the Franchisor and/or the Guarantor may be an individual (male or female), a partnership, a corporation, corporations, or other entities. The necessary grammatical changes required to make the provisions of this agreement apply in the plural sense, where there is more than one Franchisee or Guarantor and to either individuals (male or female) partnerships, corporations, or other entities, shall in all instances be assumed in each case. The words "hereof," "herein," "hereunder" and similar expressions used in any paragraph of this agreement relate to the whole of this agreement (including any Schedules attached hereto) and not to that paragraph only, unless otherwise expressly provided for or the context clearly indicates to the contrary.

(16) *Assignment by the Franchisor.* In the event of a sale, transfer, or assignment by the Franchisor of its interest in the System or the Marks or any parts thereof, or in the event of any sale, transfer, or assignment by the Franchisor of this agreement or any interest therein, to the extent that the purchaser or assignee shall assume the covenants and obligations of the Franchisor under this agreement, the Franchisor shall thereupon and without further agreement be freed and relieved of all liability with respect to such covenants and obligations.

The franchisor may assign or sell its interest in the agreement. The assignee assumes all rights and obligations of the franchisor, and the franchisor is then relieved of all liability under the contract. Of course, as we have seen, no such luxury is afforded to the franchisee who continues to be bound by this agreement even after a sale or assignment.

(17) *Lawful attorney.* Notwithstanding anything herein contained, if the Franchisee does not execute and deliver to the Franchisor any documents or other instruments which it is so required to execute and deliver pursuant to this agreement within the time period or periods so specified herein, including without limitation the documents required to be delivered pursuant to paragraph 15(2) hereof, the Franchisee does hereby irrevocably appoint the Franchisor as the Franchisee's lawful attorney with full power and authority to execute and deliver in the name of the Franchisee any such document or instruments and to do all the things as may be required from time to time to comply with the provisions pursuant to which the power of attorney is being utilized, and the Franchisee hereby agrees to ratify and confirm all such acts of the Franchisor as its lawful attorney and to indemnify and save the Franchisor harmless from all claims, losses, or damages in so doing. In accordance with the Powers of Attorney Act the Franchisee hereby declares that the powers of attorney hereby granted may be exercised during any subsequent legal incapacity on his part.

This is a significant clause, because it gives the franchisor the right to act on the franchisee's behalf *at any time.* So, if the franchisee attempts to *not* do something—or, in fact, to *do* something—that the franchisor or the agreement itself say must be done, the franchisor can unilaterally act on behalf of the franchisee as its attorney and do or undo such acts anyway. (But still there exists the pure fantasy that there is no relationship between the two parties, as per paragraph 19(6).)

(18) *Default cumulative.* In the event the Franchisee acquires the right and license to operate another or other retail sales outlets using the System and the Marks, any default by the Franchisee in the performance or observance of any of the terms and conditions under any one agreement governing the aforesaid right and license shall be deemed to be an event of default under all other agreements pursuant to which the Franchisee operates such a retail sales outlet or outlets.

For those franchisees who operate multiple franchised businesses, this clause packs a wallop. A default at any one of those individual franchised operations, each one presumably existing under a separate franchise agreement, is a default at all of them. That gives the franchisor considerable leverage.

(19) *Set-off by the Franchisor.* Notwithstanding anything contained in this agreement, upon the failure of the Franchisee to pay to the Franchisor as and when due, any amounts of money provided for herein, the Franchisor shall have the right at its election, to deduct any and all such amounts remaining unpaid from any monies or credits held by the Franchisor for the account of the Franchisee.

This is another one-sided and not mutually beneficial term in this agreement. Why should the franchisor be allowed to set off while the franchisee is specifically denied the same right? Contrast it to paragraph 19(9).

(20) *Further assurances.* Each of the parties hereby covenants and agrees to execute and deliver such further and other agreements, assurances, undertakings, acknowledgements, or documents, cause such meetings to be held, resolutions passed, and by-laws enacted, exercise their vote and influence, and do and perform and cause to be done and performed any further and other acts and things as may be necessary or desirable in order to give full effect to this agreement and every part hereof.

(21) *Entire agreement.* This agreement constitutes the entire agreement between the parties and supercedes all previous agreements and understandings between the parties in any way relating to the subject-matter hereof. It is expressly understood and agreed that the Franchisor has made no representations, inducements, warranties, or promises, whether direct, indirect, or collateral, express, or implied, oral or otherwise, concerning this agreement, the matters herein, the business franchised hereunder or concerning any other matter, which are not embodied herein. Franchisee acknowledges that it has entered into this agreement as a result of its own independent investigation and not as the result of any representations of the Franchisor, its agents, officers, or employees. Franchisee specifically acknowledges that no representation, promise, guarantee, or warranty concerning the result or profits to be derived from the Franchised Business has been made to induce Franchisee to execute this agreement.

Yeah, right. The purpose of this paragraph is to eliminate the possibility that the franchisee will file against the franchisor for misrepresentation when the franchisor exercises its full rights under the agreement, or the franchise does not live up to the glossy promo material and the sales pitch made to the franchisee before the agreement was signed.

(22) *Binding agreement.* Subject to the restrictions on assignment herein contained, this agreement shall enure to the benefit of and be binding upon the parties hereto and their respective heirs, executors, administrators, successors, and assigns.

(23) *Arbitration.* If, at any time during the continuance of this agreement or after the termination thereof, any dispute, difference, or question shall arise between or among any of the parties hereto or their heirs, executors, administrators, successors, or assigns touching or concerning the construction, meaning, or effect of this agreement or any agreement or covenant entered into pursuant to this agreement or the termination of this agreement or the termination of any such agreements or covenants (other than a matter dealt with in this agreement or any agreement or covenant entered into pursuant thereto whereby such agreement or covenant specifically states that a certain determination shall be final and binding), or the rights or obligations of the parties hereto and of their heirs, executors, administrators, successors, or assigns, then subject to the exceptions referred to hereinbefore, every such dispute, difference, or question shall be submitted to and settled by arbitration, and the decision of the arbitrator, appointed as hereinafter provided, to deal with such matter shall be accepted by all the parties to such dispute, difference, or question and their heirs, executors, administrators, successors, and assigns. The arbitration shall be conducted by a single arbitrator agreed upon by the parties to the matter. If, within five (5) days after notice of the matter has been given by one of such parties to the other or others, such parties cannot agree upon a single arbitrator, then in such event, the arbitration shall be conducted by a single arbitrator appointed by a judge of the Supreme Court of Ontario on the application of any such party with notice to the other or

others. The arbitration shall be conducted in accordance with the provisions of the *Arbitration Act, 1991*, S.O. 1991, c. 17 and of any amendment thereto, or of any successor statute thereof, in force at the time of such dispute, difference, or question. The decision of the arbitrator shall be binding upon all the parties to such dispute, difference, or question, and there shall be no appeal therefrom. The prevailing party shall be entitled to an award of arbitration costs.

Refer to Chapter 3 for another discussion of arbitration clauses. This paragraph exists to provide a dispute resolution mechanism and procedure under the applicable legislation, and would go a fair distance to preventing court action.

(24) *Rights of the Franchisor are cumulative.* The rights of the Franchisor hereunder are cumulative and no exercise or enforcement by the Franchisor of any right or remedy hereunder shall preclude the exercise or enforcement by the Franchisor of any right or remedy hereunder or which the Franchisor is otherwise entitled by law to enforce.

Like the rights of a landlord or a lessor under most lease contracts, and a lender, the franchisor can exercise all its rights one on top of or after the other.

20. Force majeure

In the event that either party hereto is delayed or hindered in the performance of any act required herein by reason of strike, lock-outs, labour troubles, inability to procure materials, failure of power, restrictive governmental laws or regulations, riots, insurrection, war, or other reasons of like nature not the fault of such party, then performance of such act shall be excused for the period of the delay and the period for performance of any such act shall be extended for a period equivalent to the period of such delay, up to a maximum of three (3) months. The provisions of this paragraph shall not operate to excuse the Franchisee from the prompt payment of any fee or other payment due the Franchisor pursuant to the provisions of this agreement.

So, let's get this straight in our own heads. Any delay caused by an act of God or other complicating event or problem beyond the parties' control (as listed) may excuse the franchisee (and franchisor) from performance for essentially the duration of the delaying event plus some grace period. But, no act of God can have a delaying impact that lasts more than three months! Moreover, the franchisee is not excused from prompt payment of fees that are due to the franchisor. The fact that the most important duties and obligations of the franchisee are those same timely payments should not be overlooked. And, given a liberal interpretation of paragraph 6(3)'s right for the franchisor to estimate an amount of sales volume, and hence royalty due, this *force majeure* clause is precious little better than impotent and meaningless to the franchisee.

IN WITNESS WHEREOF the parties hereto have executed this agreement as of the day and year first above written.

RIBS RESTAURANT
Franchisor
Per:

_____

Authorized signatory

NEW GUY ON THE BLOCK LTD.
Franchisee
Per:

_____

BIG BROTHER CORPORATION
Guarantor
Per:

_____

<attach Schedules "A" (list of marks), "B" (description of Premises), and "C" (sublease)>

Chapter 12
Miscellaneous Common Forms

Releases, Guarantees, Assignments, Certificates, Affidavit of Execution,
Power of Attorney and Revocation, Escrow, Indemnity, Nondisclosure

In the other chapters of the latter part of this book, we examined sample contracts of particular and specific types and purposes. A number of other contracts and forms are fairly common, but are not as easily categorized. You will, nevertheless, encounter them with amazing frequency regardless of your line of business. I have aggregated these dispossessed documents into a tidy and useful miscellaneous category.

By no means is this a complete or exhaustive compilation of releases, assignments, and so forth. Rather, what I have tried to provide is a set of typical or common documents that are either very simple and allow for elaboration, or are very extensive and can be simplified. Not that you would be elaborating or simplifying—that would be the work of your legal counsel—but you should know how these basic forms can be altered to account for specific requirements without losing their basic intent and purpose.

Most forms (certificates, assignments, releases, etc.) of the same basic type that you may encounter will have the same general effect despite variations in language. You will notice if you study the few samples in this chapter, that a variety of stylistic formats have been included to give you a rounded idea of how different lawyers will draft these documents to look and sound different. It is important not to lose sight of the fact that the end purpose of each type of document is the same. Specifically regarding these samples, note that they are guidelines only in a universe of options and customizations available to satisfy the specific requirements of the document.[1]

If you have any concern about differences between a document in your possession and the corresponding sample in this book, have your legal advisor sort out the differences and provide you with a proper explanation. I do not recommend the use of any forms provided in this book in acting as your own lawyer. I don't recommend acting as your own lawyer—even if you have been called to a bar association. (There's an old chestnut, the corollary of which would be: A client who represents himself has an idiot for a lawyer.)

Certificate of Independent Legal Advice

I, Leonard Howe, certify that:

(1) Timothy Grayson, the guarantor in the annexed guarantee dated September 21, 1999, between New Products Corporation and Old Money Company Ltd., consulted with me privately and in person prior to executing the annexed guarantee.

(2) I reviewed with Timothy Grayson the contents of the annexed guarantee, and his rights and obligations under it, and at law, and I satisfied myself that he understood those contents, rights, and obligations.

(3) I acted solely for Timothy Grayson in this matter.

DATED this 24th day of September, 1999.

<*signature of lawyer*>

I, Timothy Grayson, am the person named in this certificate, acknowledge having read it, and verify that it is correct. DATED this 24th day of September, 1999.

<*signature of person seeking advice*>

<*attach underlying agreement*>

Sometimes you may be required to provide a certificate that you have been given independent legal advice, say for the purchase of a private equity offering. Elsewhere in this book, I have recommended that it may be prudent to ensure other parties to your contracts provide such certificates so they have no recourse to extricate themselves from the contract on account of mistake, undue influence, etc.

The independent legal advice certificate is very simple and straightforward. The lawyer (Leonard Howe, in this case) certifies that he independently provided an explanation of the contract and its commercial/legal implications to the party that consulted with him (you). The lawyer further certifies that he is not in a conflict of interest position vis à vis any other parties with an interest in the contract.

As if the lawyer's formal certification to his actions were inadequate, the person who consulted with the lawyer must also verify the accuracy of the lawyer's certification. The obvious assurance is therefore that the person who sought the advice in the first place understands the lawyer's counsel.

Renewal Agreement

THIS AGREEMENT made the 15th day of October, 1999.
Between:

Acme Moon Exploration Ltd.

and

Consolidated Cheese Inc.

WHEREAS:

1. The parties entered a contract dated the 1st day of September, 1993, for a joint moon exploration project (herein called the "Contract");
2. The Contract will end on the 31st day of October, 1999;
3. The parties wish to renew the Contract for a further period of three (3) years upon the terms and conditions set forth in this agreement.

NOW THEREFORE THIS AGREEMENT WITNESSES that in consideration of the mutual covenants and agreements herein, and subject to the terms and conditions in this agreement, the parties agree as follows:

1. To renew the Contract upon the same terms and conditions as set out in it, except that the Contract shall have a term commencing on the 1st day of October, 1999, and ending on the 30th day of September, 2002.
2. This renewal agreement and the Contract together constitute the entire agreement between the parties.

IN WITNESS WHEREOF the parties have set their hands and seals.
SIGNED, SEALED, AND DELIVERED in the presence of:
<signatures and seals of parties>

Most, if not all, contracts are written with a finite term, and, as we have seen, with a provision for renewal. Some renew automatically; others require an act by one or both parties to renew. In circumstances in which a renewal procedure and right is incorporated into the original contract, it may not be expressly necessary to create a separate renewal agreement such as this one. For greater certainty (a wonderfully lyrical bit of legal language, in my opinion), however, a renewal agreement such as the sample above should be written—particularly if there are changes to some of the terms in the original agreement.

This particular example renews the original contract on the same terms and conditions. The only change noted in this renewal contract is the specification of the contract's effective dates. It would be equally possible to see a renewal that has several exceptions or alterations to the terms and conditions of the contract it is renewing. The original agreement is attached for reference so that the net effect is to "sign" the original agreement with amendments (most especially the effective dates) again.

Nondisclosure/Confidentiality Agreement

BETWEEN Trustworthy Investment Counsel Ltd.
(hereinafter referred to as the "Company")
– and –
Timothy Grayson
(hereinafter referred to as the "Informed Recipient")

WHEREAS the Informed Recipient and the Company propose to engage in discussions of a preliminary and nonbinding nature relating to certain aspects of the business of the company;

AND WHEREAS it is desirable that the parties set forth their understanding as to any information of a confidential nature which may be disclosed by the Company to the Informed Recipient during the course of the proposed discussions;

NOW THEREFORE in consideration of the mutual covenants contained herein, the sum of one dollar ($1.00) now paid by each party to the other and other good and valuable consideration (the receipt and sufficiency of which is hereby acknowledged by each of the parties hereto), the Company and the Informed Recipient hereby covenant and agree as follows:

1. The Informed Recipient acknowledges that the proposed discussions with the Company may involve disclosure by the Company to the Informed Recipient, of confidential or secret information belonging to the Company and relating to its business or proposed business or to other matters (including, for example, financial and operating statements, ideas, and business plans or other commercial information) all of which would be of interest and value to the Informed Recipient (the "Confidential Information").

2. The Company agrees to advise the Informed Recipient as to which information disclosed by the Company, if any, constitutes Confidential Information.

3. The Informed Recipient shall treat as confidential and, for greater certainty, but not so as to restrict the generality of the foregoing, shall not disclose or cause to be disclosed or publish or cause to be published, any Confidential Information or any other information with respect to any other matter of a secret or confidential nature which may have come into his possession as a result of discussions with or communications from the Company except, however, with the consent in writing by a duly appointed officer of the Company or except with respect to any item Confidential Information that may have entered the public domain through no act of omission to act of the Informed Recipient. For greater certainty, in consideration of the disclosure to it of the Confidential Information, the Informed Recipient hereby agrees on his own behalf and on behalf of each of his employees and consultants, not to make any use whatsoever of the Confidential Information except in furtherance of the assessment referred to in paragraph 1.

   The Informed Recipient shall, where appropriate, require employees and consultants to execute an agreement substantially on the same terms as the within agreement so as to be bound by the terms hereof.

4. Any provision of either paragraph 1 or 2 hereof which is determined to be void and unenforceable shall be severed from all other provisions thereof, and shall be deemed to not affect or impair the enforceability of any such other provisions.

5. The Informed Recipient hereby agrees that all covenants contained herein on his part to be complied with are reasonable and valid, and waives all defenses to the strict enforcement thereof by the Company.

6. The Informed Recipient acknowledges that any violation of any of the provisions hereof may result in immediate and irreparable damage to the Company and agrees that in the event of such violation, the Company shall, in addition to any other rights, relief, or remedy available at law, be entitled to any equitable relief that any court of competent jurisdiction may deem just and fair.

7. The provisions hereof shall enure to the benefit of the successors and assigns of the Company and shall be binding upon the heirs, legal personal representatives, and assigns of the Informed Recipient.

8. The Informed Recipient hereby acknowledges that he has read and understands the foregoing and the implications hereof, and further acknowledges receipt of a duly executed copy of this Agreement.

This agreement shall be governed by and interpreted in accordance with the laws of the Province of Manitoba, Canada.

IN WITNESS WHEREOF the parties hereto have executed this Agreement this 30th day of October, 1999.

COMPANY:

Trustworthy Investment Counsel Ltd.

Per: Authorized signatory

INFORMED RECIPIENT:

Timothy Grayson

This is an excellent example of a functional nondisclosure agreement. I have seen these things drawn up in as little as one page (roughly half the content of what's here), and in as much as seven pages. Given that its purpose is to bind parties to maintain each other's confidence—usually prior to there being a relationship between the two—the longer versions seem to be impractical in every respect. When you get right down to it, nothing, not a contract or otherwise, will prevent someone from divulging a confidence. Thus, the document is really to inform and create a threat of legal action and consequence for betraying a confidence.

The underlying meaning of the document, depending on whether it creates mutual or one-sided confidentiality bonds, is to say: "We are going to exchange confidential information in order to develop this relationship or pursue this line of discussion. You will use this information only as it relates to our discussions and the development of our business relationship, and nowhere else. If you tell anyone else our confidential information we will kill you." A one-page agreement satisfies this intent; a two-page agreement has more detail and describes how we will kill you; a six-page confidentiality agreement is nothing more than an insult to environmentalism.

BOND

Although there is a dollar sign attached to it, this bond has the sense of "my word is my bond" rather than "stocks and bonds." The bond—a surety bond, to be specific—is generally a document that attaches a financial penalty to the (non)performance of the "principal" (the person for whom the surety is being given) named in the bond. A bond requires a surety or sureties. These are people or organizations, such as insurance companies, who agree to make a conditional payment to the named entity in the event that the triggering event does or does not happen, as the case may be within the contract itself. A few specific examples of common bonds are provided below.

Bond for Fidelity of Employee with Sureties

We, Cathryn Grayson of Winnipeg, Manitoba, business woman (the "Employee"), as principal, and Timothy Grayson, of Winnipeg, Manitoba, consultant, and Edward Demkiw, of Winnipeg, Manitoba, retired (the "Sureties"), are bound to Restaurant Restaurant Ltd. of Winnipeg, Manitoba (the "Employer"), in the amount of one thousand dollars ($1,000.00), to be paid to the Employer, its successors or assigns, for which payment we jointly and severally bind ourselves, our and each of our heirs, executors, and administrators, by this instrument.

Sealed with our seals and dated this 21st day of February, 1999.

WHEREAS the Employer has agreed to take the Employee into its employ as a hostess-server, upon the Employee and the Sureties entering into a bond in the above-mentioned sum of one thousand dollars, conditioned as is expressed as follows, for the faithful service by the Employee as a hostess-server:

The condition of this obligation is such that if the Employee shall faithfully discharge her duties as stated above, or if the Employee and the Sureties, or either of them, or either of their heirs, executors, or administrators, shall at all times after this instrument takes effect keep indemnified the Employer, its successors and assigns, against all loss, costs, and expenses which it may sustain by reason of its taking the Employee into its employ, or by reason of any act of or by the Employee while in the employ of the Employer, or otherwise, then in either of these cases this bond shall be void; but otherwise it shall remain in full force.

And the Employee agrees that if as a result of this bond the Sureties, or either of them, shall pay any sum of money to the

Employer, then she, the Employee, shall pay that sum of money immediately to the Sureties, or either of them, together with interest on it at ten percent (10%) per annum commencing with the date payment was made by either Surety.

WITNESS our hands and seals the day, month, and year as first written above.

SIGNED, SEALED, AND DELIVERED in the presence of:

<signature of sureties>

<signature of employee>

<attach Affidavit of Execution>

In the sample above, the bond is made to an employer for the fidelity and proper service of a new employee. Perhaps the business and the new employee's work entails being around and responsible for sums of cash, in which case an employee's fidelity would be of concern. This employee is, upon this document being accepted, "bonded." In this example, two people have provided the surety, binding themselves to keep the employer indemnified from financial damage caused by the employee's actions or to pay the bond value to the employer. Notice how the principal (the employee) is herself obliged to repay the penalty amount to her sureties should they ever be required to make a payment on her behalf.

The people binding themselves are the sureties, thus it is their signatures that are of most concern to the employer. The employee should sign the document because she is a direct party to the contract, with an obligation to the sureties.

Bond Not to Engage in Competitive Business: Vendor to Purchaser

We, John Entrepreneur, of Toronto, Ontario, as principal (the "Principal"), and Mothercompany Inc., of Toronto, Ontario, as surety (the "Surety"), are bound to Falafel-Man Restaurants Inc., of Toronto, Ontario (the "Purchaser"), in the sum of five hundred thousand dollars ($500,000), for which payment we, the Principal and Surety, jointly and severally bind ourselves, our heirs, executors, and administrators, by this instrument.

Sealed with our seals and dated this 16th day of November, 1999.

WHEREAS:

1. The Principal has lately carried on the business of operating a fast-food restaurant themed on a quick-service, dine-in and take-out, falafel-based menu;

2. The Principal has sold the business to the Purchaser in consideration of the sum of one million dollars ($1,000,000) paid to him by the Purchaser and has agreed that he will not, either alone, in partnership with any other person, or as chief officer of a corporation, carry on a similarly-themed falafel-based business within a radius of ten (10) miles from the place of business of the Purchaser for a term of five (5) years from the date of this bond, and that he will not, within this term, solicit the customers of the business either for himself or for any other person, partnership, or corporation; and also that in the event of his failing to observe or carry on the agreement he and/or the Surety will pay the sum of five hundred thousand dollars ($500,000) to the Purchaser as liquidated damages.

The condition of this obligation is such that if the Principal should, either alone in partnership with any other person, or as principal officer of a corporation, carry on the trade or business as described herein, or any branch of it, within the distance before named in any direction from the place of business at 59 Bay Street, Toronto, Ontario, at any time within the space of five (5) years from the date of this bond, or if he should, either by himself or by any other person, at any time within the space of five (5) years solicit the customers of the business to deal with himself or with such other person, partnership, or corporation as he may be connected with; or if he should induce or prevail upon, or attempt to induce or prevail upon, any person to discontinue his dealings with the Purchaser, then in any of these cases, if the Principal, or his heirs, executors, or administrators should forthwith pay to the Purchaser, or its successors or assigns, the sum of five hundred thousand dollars ($500,000), this obligation shall be null and void; but otherwise it shall remain in full force.

The Principal agrees that if as a result of this bond the Surety shall pay any sum of money to the Purchaser, then he, the Principal, shall pay that sum of money immediately to the Surety together with interest on it at the then-prevailing CIBC Prime interest rate plus two percent (2%) per annum calculated from the date such payment was made by the Surety.

WITNESS our hands and seals the day, month, and year as first written above.

SIGNED, SEALED, AND DELIVERED in the presence of:

<signatures of surety and vendor>

<attach Affidavit of Execution>

This bond is specifically for the performance of noncompetition covenants incorporated within the bond (undoubtedly repeated from the sale agreement). Its obvious purpose is to add teeth to the condition that the vendor not compete with the business he has sold to the purchaser. The bond provides a fixed value for liquidated damages that are to be payable by either the vendor or its surety to the purchaser if the vendor should breach the noncompete promises.

While the purchaser may not demand that the original sale be voided due to the breach of the noncompete covenant, which was very likely part of the sale/purchase agreement between the vendor and the purchaser, he will receive some financial compensation. Generally speaking, these types of agreements—with the hefty damages associated—are disincentives to the vendor should he consider reneging on his agreement early or within the geographic boundaries. (Since these are to be liquidated damages, it is conceivable that the vendor might do the mathematics and decide to breach the contract, pay the bond price, and stay in business. He might try this because the payment of liquidated damages dissolves any further rights to other recourse that the purchaser may have.[2])

Most often the terms of this kind of bond are not breached due to the threat of financial penalty. You must bear in mind, however, that the noncompete conditions must be "reasonable" or there may be the potential for their being overruled by a court. In such instance the bond would be ineffective and likely void.

ASSIGNMENT

At one time or another we have all encountered assignments of some sort, be it an assignment of properties, of debts, of accounts, or what have you. The assignment is simply a document that contractually gives the rights and obligations of a *chose* to another party. Assignments can be conditional and dependent; they can be for an entire property, or for only part of it. For the most part assignments are irrevocable. Contractual assignments are generally transactions made willingly; other "assignments" can be forced upon one by a court order. The following assignment contracts provide two examples: one a very basic assignment of an asset, and the other the assignment of something somewhat less tangible.

General Assignment

I, the undersigned, Neil Forrit, of Wadena, in the Province of Saskatchewan, farmer, in consideration of the sum of ten thousand dollars ($10,000) paid to me by Bill Meighen, of Regina, in the Province of Saskatchewan, the receipt of which is acknowledged, assign to Bill Meighen all my interest in <i><description of asset being assigned></i>.

<Special provisions>

IN WITNESS WHEREOF I have set my hand and seal this 29th day of April, 1999.

SIGNED, SEALED, AND DELIVERED in the presence of:

<signature of assignor>

<attach Affidavit of Execution>

This is a simple and basic assignment contract. Party A assigns for a price some thing to Party B. The variables which I have left open (the description of the thing or things being assigned, and any special considerations) are particular to each individual assignment and are infinite in variety. The first variable, the description, need not be elaborate. It could assign all interest in "my business, named XYZ," or "debts owing to me by ABC Co. under a credit . . . ," or any other such thing. The key is that the interest or thing being assigned should be quite specifically identified so there is no doubt about it.

The second variable left open, special provisions, might include any number of provisions that the assignor may attach to the assignment. They could be conditions that must be fulfilled before the assignment becomes effective (e.g., "The assignment will come into effect upon my marriage"). They could be conditions to which the assignee may be subject to complying with on an ongoing basis (e.g., "The assignee must be and remain a resident of Saint John or the interest and rights to this property revert to . . .").[3] With any luck the provisions you see in any assignment that comes before you will be in close to readable English.

Assignment of Assets

> FOR VALUABLE CONSIDERATION, I, John Zinger, of Vancouver, British Columbia, transfer to Bill Meighen Jr., of Victoria, British Columbia, the assets listed in the attached Schedule "A," and I certify and guarantee that I have legal authority to make this transfer; that the balances due on the securities mentioned in Schedule "A" are correctly set out in Schedule "A," and that delivery has been made of the property covered by the securities; that the balances are net, are not disputed by the debtors, and are not past due, and that there are no contra accounts, set-offs, or counter-claims whatever against any of the securities; and that the payment of the balances is not contingent on the fulfillment of any contract, past or future.
>
> I undertake to execute all further documents necessary to carry out this assignment effectually.
>
> I further undertake that entries disclosing this absolute sale to Bill Meighen Jr. will immediately be made on my books and that Bill Meighen Jr. shall have the right to examine and audit the books.
>
> IN WITNESS WHEREOF I have set my hand and seal this 14th day of October, 1999.
>
> SIGNED, SEALED, AND DELIVERED in the presence of:
>
> <signature of assignor>
>
> <attach Schedule "A">
> <attach Affidavit of Execution>

This asset assignment is not all that different from the general assignment, which nicely pertains to assets, except for the added provisions that have been included. The language is fairly straightforward.

Assignment of Contract

> IN CONSIDERATION OF one dollar ($1.00) and other good and valuable consideration, the receipt and sufficiency of which is acknowledged, I, Rollie Stripes, assign to Bill Meighen all my interest in and to the contract dated the 2nd day of September, 1997, made between Rollie Stripes and The Great Big License Co., annexed as Schedule "A," including all rights of action or other rights accruing to me, or which might after this assignment takes effect accrue to me under the contract.
>
> <insert special provisions>
>
> IN WITNESS WHEREOF I have set my hand and seal this 14th day of December, 1999.
>
> SIGNED, SEALED, AND DELIVERED in the presence of:
>
> <signature of assignor>
>
> <attach Schedule "A">
> <attach Affidavit of Execution>

This variation on the theme assigns existing and future rights that may develop with the fulfillment of the contract in question. The assignment itself is not especially different from the basic general assignment except for its specific nature. Notice the somewhat archaic form of providing for consideration in the contract. Less and less frequently do lawyers go through the motion (that fools nobody) of having consideration of "one dollar" to comply with the common law requirement. Since everyone knows it's a sham and pointless, the use of "good and valuable consideration, the sufficiency . . . " seems to be gaining popularity.

I, Rick Blaine, in partial consideration of my employment with Templar Technologies Inc. (the "Employer"), and of the salary or wages to be received by me for the employment, agree:

1. To disclose promptly, fully and in confidence to the Employer or its nominee, all inventions, improvements, or discoveries made or conceived by me during the term of my employment either solely, or jointly with others, in the performance of the employment or with the use of the Employer's time, equipment, material, supplies, facilities, or related to or suggested by trade secret information, other private or confidential matters acquired during the term of my employment, the business of the Employer of the Employer's actual or demonstrably anticipated processes or research and development. All inventions, improvements, or discoveries are defined as "Subject Inventions."

2. (a) Except as expressly provided in paragraph 3, all Subject Inventions shall be the sole and exclusive property of the Employer or its nominee. Accordingly, I specifically acknowledge and agree that I shall have no interest in the Subject Inventions including without limitation any interest in know-how, trade marks, or copyrights, notwithstanding the fact that I may have created or contributed to the creation of same.

   (b) I do hereby agree to waive any moral rights which I may have with respect to the creation of Subject Inventions.

3. On the request of the Employer, or its nominee, assign all my rights, title, and interest in and to all Subject Inventions provided, however, that inventions, improvements, or discoveries produced entirely on my own time and
   (a) which do not relate
      (i) to the business of the Employer or
      (ii) to the Employer's actual or demonstrably anticipated processes, research, or development, or
   (b) which do not result from any work performed by me for the Employer,
   shall remain my sole and exclusive property and are not subject to assignment, but are subject to disclosure to the Employer.

4. On the request of the Employer, to assist it and its nominee, at its or their expense, during and after my employment in every proper way, (a) to obtain for it or their own benefit, patents for Subject Inventions (other than those expressly excluded pursuant to the terms of paragraph 3) in any and all countries, and (b) in any controversy or legal proceeding relating to Subject Inventions, improvement, or discoveries or to the patents resulting from them.

5. That all records, files, drawings, tapes, documents, tools, equipment, and the like relating to the business, work, or investigations of the Employer and prepared, used, or processed by me, or under my control, during the term of my employment shall be and remain the sole and exclusive property of the Employer or its nominee.

6. Prior to leaving employment with the Employer, to deliver promptly to the Employer all the records, files, drawings, tapes, documents, tools, and equipment.

7. I represent that I have no agreement or obligations to others in conflict with the foregoing.

8. The provisions of this agreement shall be binding on my heirs, executors, administrators, legal representatives and assigns.

IN WITNESS WHEREOF I have set my hand and seal this 18th day of September, 1997.
SIGNED, SEALED, AND DELIVERED in the presence of:

<signature of employee>

<attach Affidavit of Execution>

In this example, the thing(s) being assigned are ideas and other products of a person's research, inspiration, and imagination. The terms of this assignment are quite fair inasmuch as inventions not created on the employer's time and with the employer's money, or from the employer's proprietary research, are not assigned to the employer. In some ways it makes sense, because the employer is paying the employee to create such ideas, and since the employer pays, it owns. The employer has also had the employee provide an assurance of assistance regarding the further securing and protection of the assigned inventions. This is extraordinary to the assignment itself, just as would be covenants of confidentiality. Presumably the confidentiality covenants would appear in another agreement between the employer and employee, or would be added into this agreement to create a single comprehensive nondisclosure agreement and assignment.

GUARANTEE

A guarantee is, as the name implies, an individual's legally binding assurance to a third party that a—generally—related party will meet its financial obligations. A guarantee is almost always provided in the lending of money to compensate for a borrower's inadequate credit standing. Most people have run across guarantee requirements when attempting to secure their first car or house loan. Different from the bond, the guarantor (individual guaranteeing the credit) is pledging to put itself into the place of the borrower and fulfill all its obligations, not merely pay a penalty in the event that . . .

Lending institutions such as banks and trust companies have their guarantee forms in place as part of the standard lending package. Others that may provide credit but only on the condition that a guarantor bind itself will tend to use forms similar to that provided below.

Guarantee—Continuing

To: Ma Nee Corporation

FOR VALUABLE CONSIDERATION, receipt and adequacy whereof is hereby acknowledged, the undersigned (herein called "the Guarantors") and each of them hereby jointly and severally guarantee payment to Ma Nee Corporation (herein called "the Lender") of all debts and liabilities, absolute or contingent, matured or not, at any time owing by Mi Por Business Ltd. (herein called "the Company") to the Lender or remaining unpaid by the Company to the Lender and the Company, the liability of the Guarantors hereunder being limited to the aggregate sum of two hundred fifty thousand dollars ($250,000) of lawful money of Canada with interest from the date of demand for payment at the then-prevailing CIBC Prime rate plus two percent (2.0%) per month.

And the Guarantors and each of them hereby jointly and severally agree with the Lender as follows:

1. The Lender may grant time, renewals, extensions, and indulgences as it sees fit without in any way limiting or lessening the liability of the Guarantors under this guarantee.

2. This guarantee shall be a continuing guarantee and shall apply to and secure any ultimate balance due or remaining unpaid by the Company to the Lender.

3. The Lender shall not be bound to exhaust its resources against the Company before being entitled to payment from the Guarantors.

4. Any of the Guarantors may, by notice in writing delivered to the Lender, or by mailing such notice by prepaid registered mail to the Lender, at its last known address, determine his liability under this guarantee in respect of liabilities thereafter incurred or arising but not in respect of liabilities already incurred or arising even though not then matured; PROVIDED, however, that the determination of this guarantee by one or more of the Guarantors shall not affect the guarantee of the others. A notice forwarded to the Lender by prepaid registered mail shall be deemed to have been received by Lender on the second business day after such registration.

5. All debts and liabilities, present, and future, of the Company owing to the Guarantors or any of them are hereby postponed in favour of Lender, and all money received by the undersigned or any of them in respect thereof shall be received in trust for the Lender and forthwith upon receipt, the whole shall be paid over to the Lender without in any way limiting or lessening the liability of the Guarantors under this guarantee; and this postponement is independent of the said guarantee and shall remain in full effect notwithstanding that the liability of the Guarantors or any of them under the said guarantee may be extinct.

6. No lawsuit based on this guarantee shall be instituted until demand for payment has been made to the Company and the Guarantors by registered mail addressed to their last known addresses.

7. This agreement covers all agreements between the parties hereto relative to this guarantee and postponement, and none of the parties shall be bound by any representation or promise made by any person relative thereto which is not embodied herein.

8. This guarantee and agreement shall enure to the benefit of the Lender and its successors and assigns and be binding upon the Guarantors and their respective heirs, executors, administrators, successors, and assigns.

IN WITNESS WHEREOF I/we have set my/our hand(s) and seal(s) this 7th day of June, 1998.
SIGNED, SEALED, AND DELIVERED in the presence of:

<signature of guarantors>

<attach Affidavit of Execution>

Apart from the somewhat obtuse language, this guarantee is fairly simple to understand. The guarantors, whose names would appear at the bottom of the contract for signature, oblige themselves to the lender on account of the company to the maximum extent of a quarter-million dollars. Although the plan would likely be for the guarantors to share the burden of the guarantee, each guarantor is fully liable for the total amount of the credit outstanding if it is called.

The first several terms of the contract serve to ensure that the lender does not prejudice its position with the guarantors by any actions it takes toward the company. Furthermore, the guarantee continues as the company's balance goes up and down and remains outstanding. Paragraph 4 would appear to give any guarantor the right to fix the level of her responsibility and financial liability at any given time, provided that doing so does not affect the full guarantees of the other guarantors. This "determination" of liability by a guarantor only applies to liabilities that have not yet been incurred (i.e., only to future liabilities).

Paragraph 5 is unique among our contract samples, because it actually puts the lender's debts with the company ahead of any debts owing by the company to the guarantors. This makes sense, actually, because there would be little point to having a guarantor's claim precede the lender's. Noteworthy at the end of the paragraph is the promise that the "postponement" will be in effect *even if* the guarantor's obligations under the guarantee are "extinct" (read: ended, done, finished, discharged, paid, void).

POWER OF ATTORNEY

Power of attorney is exactly what the name would imply. It gives the holder (the donee) the power to act on behalf of the person who issued the power (the donor). Some such documents are, as that sampled below, quite broad, permitting the attorney to act in the issuer's stead in every respect. Others are limited in a variety of ways, including the nature of acts for which the power is granted, the time for which the power is granted, and conditions that must arise before the power becomes effective. Most powers of attorney are not granted for consideration and are revocable; some that are granted for a price are generally irrevocable. It would be important to be sure of whether a power of attorney in front of you (either as donor or donee) is revocable or not.

A power of attorney, like many other of these documents that create significant departures from the status quo, requires an Affidavit of Execution. This form, and a description of its use, can be found near the end of the chapter.

Power of Attorney (General authority to act in every capacity)

I, Timothy Grayson, of Winnipeg, Manitoba, author, do hereby appoint Donald Duckworth of Anaheim, California, my attorney to do all acts as fully and effectually as I could do if personally present, and particularly the following acts, the enumeration of which is not in any way to limit the general powers herein conferred, namely:

1. To purchase, sell, make, draw, accept, endorse, discount, transfer, renew, negotiate, and in every way deal with cheques, bills of exchange, promissory notes, deposit receipts, bonds, debentures, coupons, and every kind of negotiable instrument and security.

2. To subscribe for, accept, purchase, sell, pledge, transfer, surrender, and in every way deal with shares, stocks, bonds, debentures, and coupons of every kind and description and to vote and act in respect thereof.

3. To receive and collect rents, dividends, bonuses, profits, interest, commission, fees, salaries, debts, and claims of every kind and to give receipts and discharges therefor and to distrain for rent and interest.

4. To purchase, sell, rent, exchange, mortgage, charge, lease, surrender, manage, and in every way deal with real

estate and any interest therein, and execute and deliver deeds, transfers, mortgages, charges, leases, assignments, surrenders, releases, and other instruments required for any such purpose.

5. To make, assume, purchase, discharge, assign, pledge, and in every way deal with mortgages of real and personal property and to exercise all powers of sale and other powers therein.

6. To purchase, assume, sell, mortgage, pledge, exchange, assign, surrender, give options to purchase and in every way deal with timber licenses of every kind and by whomsoever issued, to work and operate limits, to carry on lumbering and manufacturing operations, and to erect and operate mills.

7. To purchase, assume, sell, mortgage, pledge, exchange, assign, surrender, lease, operate, give options to purchase and in every way deal with mines, minerals, and mining rights.

I, the said Timothy Grayson, hereby covenant for myself, and my heirs, executors, and administrators, to ratify and confirm whatsoever my attorney shall lawfully do or cause to be done in the premises by virtue of these presents.

IN WITNESS WHEREOF I have set my hand and seal this 28th day of February, 1995.

SIGNED, SEALED, AND DELIVERED in the presence of:

<signature of donor>

<attach Affidavit of Execution>

Needless to say, this is a fairly comprehensive power of attorney. One would have to be in a strange circumstance to issue such broad-based powers to another person: perhaps for incapacity or due to an extended stay incommunicado; perhaps because you are required to divest yourself of your interests for some reason or another during a foreseeably fixed period. In the latter case, the power of attorney would generally go along with certain other trust conditions that would prevent the holder (i.e., Donald Duckworth) from acting in a way that might very easily be recognized as not being in your best interests.

This power of attorney's final two powers are probably excessive in any instance in which the person giving the powers does not own a lot of forest land with timber on top and "potential" down below. I've included them because they round out the completeness of the example. In all likelihood, you will encounter powers of attorney limited to specific powers such as the purchase/sale of land, purchase/sale/transfer of shares, act on behalf of another to negotiate a deal, etc.

Revocation of Power of Attorney

WHEREAS I, Timothy Grayson, of Winnipeg, Manitoba, did, on the 28th day of February, 1995, by an instrument in writing, authorize Donald Duckworth of Anaheim, California, to be my attorney, to do and perform all matters and things connected with that as fully as I myself could do.

Now, I, Timothy Grayson, for good and sufficient reasons, revoke the power of attorney and all powers and authority given with that, and all matters and things which shall or might be done or performed by virtue of that.

IN WITNESS WHEREOF I have set my hand and seal this 15th day of March, 1999.

SIGNED, SEALED, AND DELIVERED in the presence of:

<signature of withdrawing donor>

<attach Affidavit of Execution>

This revocation of a previously granted power of attorney, apart from another required Affidavit of Execution, need only make direct and specific reference to the original power of attorney granted that is being revoked. The language is suitably straightforward. Perhaps the only real thing to be concerned about is whether the power of attorney can legally be revoked at all. But that really has little to do with this document, only that it could be of no effect.

RELEASE

A release is an abandonment of an existing claim or right and whatever may flow as a direct result of it, be it to a debt owed, a contractual obligation (to you), or anything else. A release is granted to a specific person or entity and should make clear exactly from what that individual is being released. Since it is a contract that requires consideration, the price for the release must be included (even if "for good and valuable etc.").

General Release of all Demands

> I, Bob Loblaw, of Vancouver, British Columbia, for good and valuable consideration, the receipt and sufficiency of which are hereby acknowledged, release Rowena Crabbe, of Halifax, Nova Scotia, and her heirs, executors, and administrators from all manner of actions, causes of action, debts, accounts, bonds, contracts, and demands whatever which against Rowena Crabbe I ever had, now have, or which my heirs, executors, administrators, or assigns, or any of them, hereafter may have existing up to the present time.
>
> IN WITNESS WHEREOF I have set my hand and seal this 2nd day of January, 1998.
>
> SIGNED, SEALED, AND DELIVERED in the presence of:
>
> <signature of releasing party>
>
> *<attach Affidavit of Execution>*

This particular release is similar to the power of attorney example used earlier, in the sense that it is omnibus. In this case one person is completely releasing another person from all debts and obligations owing to him. More often than not, releases will be made from very specific obligations owing or rights accrued, such as a release from a contract or from performing some promised act. Notice, however, that the release is only for demands in existence up to the time of the release being given.

INDEMNITY

An indemnity is a promise to save some other person or entity harmless from and against any loss that might be created by virtue of that person or thing doing certain specific acts as set out in the indemnity agreement. An indemnity operates in the future, in the sense that it will come into play only if a loss is occasioned.

I have provided two samples of indemnity contracts. The first is an indemnity provided to an officer of a company for undertaking a directorship. The second is an escrow deposit contract, which is an indemnity because it comes into effect if the deal falls through.

Agreement to Indemnify an Officer or Director of a Company

> THIS AGREEMENT made the 15th day of August, 1997, between Big Bob Bramble and Cathryn Grayson.
>
> WHEREAS Cathryn Grayson has, at my request, accepted the position of President and Director of 3B Corporation (the "Company"), and has no financial interest in the Company other than holding one share of stock, which the by-laws require as the minimum qualification of a Director:
>
> In consideration of Cathryn Grayson having acceded to my request, I, Big Bob Bramble, undertake to indemnify and save harmless Cathryn Grayson or her estate against any liability incurred by her by reason of her having acted or acting as a director and officer of the Company notwithstanding any remuneration that may have been given or may be given to her as a director and officer of the Company.
>
> WITNESS my hand and seal the day, month, and year as first written above.
>
> SIGNED, SEALED, AND DELIVERED in the presence of:
>
> <signature of surety>
>
> *<attach Affidavit of Execution>*

This indemnity does not extend to save the director harmless from liability for her actions (meaning "in her own personal capacity"), but rather to save her harmless from actions taken against the company by others that might try to make her a party to the action. Given the precarious state of directors' and officers' liability and the availability of directors' and officers' liability insurance, this indemnity may be limited to relatively insignificant matters. From *big* liabilities, the directors may not be indemnified.

Deposit in Escrow

THIS AGREEMENT made the 25th day of January, 1998, between Wantit Properties Ltd., of Calgary, Alberta (the "Depositor"), and Meighen B. McGee, of Edmonton, Alberta.

WHEREAS the parties to this agreement have executed an agreement, a copy of which is annexed to this agreement, under which the Depositor undertakes to deposit with Lionel Cheatham of the law firm Dewey, Cheatham & Howe (the "Depositary") the sum of one hundred thousand dollars ($100,000) in escrow, as a guarantee of the due performance of the annexed agreement.

NOW THIS AGREEMENT WITNESSES that, concurrently with the execution of it, the Depositor has paid into the hands of the Depositary the sum of one hundred thousand dollars ($100,000) in escrow, to be held and applied as follows, namely:

Upon the demand in writing, at any time, of both parties to the agreement, the escrow deposit shall be paid over as they mutually direct;

Upon notice and demand in writing by either party to the agreement to make payment of the escrow deposit to him, the Depositary shall notify the other party by registered mail, and unless protest shall be made in writing by the other party within twenty (20) days thereafter the Depositary shall make payment as so demanded.

It is intended that the annexed agreement between the parties shall have been fully performed not later than the 29th day of February, 1998. Unless otherwise notified in writing, the Depositary shall on this date pay over the escrow deposit to the Depositor.

The Depositary, by his signature to this agreement, assumes no responsibility except to apply the escrow deposit in accordance with the terms hereof, AND HE SHALL BE INDEMNIFIED by the parties to this instrument against any liability, loss, and expense occasioned hereby.

WITNESS our hands and seals the day, month, and year as first written above.

SIGNED, SEALED, AND DELIVERED in the presence of:

<signatures of all three parties>

<attach underlying agreement>
<attach Affidavit of Execution>

This agreement is included under my heading "Indemnity" for two reasons. First, because the purpose of the escrow deposit is to indemnify the vendor of the property (and escrows are often created for the sale/purchase of real property or other large assets like companies) from a purchaser not fulfilling its purchase obligations. Second, because the actual holder of the escrow deposit (the Depositary) is indemnified from harm arising out of its actions in regard to fulfilling its obligations.

Of particular interest should be that the underlying agreement, which demands the escrow, is annexed to and incorporated into this escrow agreement for reference. Also, the Depositary has specific instructions for how to handle the escrowed funds. Unlike money otherwise paid into trust, the Depositary is contractually directed how to handle the escrowed money. The only contingent act not specified for the Depositary is what to do if the two parties disagree about the payout of the escrowed funds and do not immediately resolve their dispute before the trigger date for completion of the underlying contract. One has to presume that the issue would be litigated and the Depositary would either hold the money until one or either of the parties prevailed or pay it into court.[4]

AFFIDAVIT OF EXECUTION

Affidavit of Execution

CANADA   )

PROVINCE OF MANITOBA) I, _____

) of the _____ of _____

) in the Province of _____

)

TO WIT:) MAKE OATH AND SAY:

1. That I was personally present and did see the annexed instrument and a duplicate of it duly signed, sealed, and executed by *<the person who signed it>*, one of the parties to it.
2. That the instrument and duplicate were executed by the party at the City of Winnipeg, in Manitoba.
3. That I know the party who is, in my opinion, of the age of majority.
4. That I am a subscribing witness to the instrument and duplicate.

SWORN before me at the City of   )

Winnipeg, in the Province of   )

Manitoba, this 20th day of   ) _____

January, 1996.   ) (Signature of Witness)

A Commissioner for Oaths or Notary Public

or a Justice of the Peace in and

for the Province of Manitoba.

My commission expires _____.

The Affidavit of Execution is an oath made on the part of a witness to a signature. A witness is usually required to attest to the signing of any significant contracts. That witness is not merely signing to attest to the fact that ink was placed on the document at the appropriate place by a human. She is supposed to actually know that the person putting the ink on the page is in fact the person for whom the signature space is reserved. When it comes to documents such as powers of attorney and some other forms, as we have seen in this chapter, an Affidavit of Execution may be required on the part of the witness. The witness swears an oath to the effect of the points made in the Affidavit before someone with the authority to administer an oath. If the witness later were to say that she did not see the signature, or some such thing, she has to deal with the nasty little issue of perjury.

Endnotes

Introduction

1. J. E. Smyth, D. A. Soberman, A. J. Easson, 8th ed. (Toronto: Prentice-Hall, 1998). A textbook I have leaned on heavily over the past decade, and one I strongly recommend for further reading.

Chapter 1

1. The judicial ruling on this case, the details of which are not important here, created a fundamental of contract law and is rarely passed over in any introduction to law course. If you want details, get them the old-fashioned way: watch *The Paper Chase*.
2. If the artist, acting in good faith, incurs expenses and expends time (value) to create a painting to fulfill the offer which is later revoked, an award of compensatory damages could quite justifiably be sought and awarded.
3. To bring it all a little closer to home, consider a marriage proposal. An offer is made and, despite the engagement ring, etc., either party can walk away right up to the point of saying, "I do"—the act required to fulfill the contract of marriage.
4. Somebody once told me that God protects children, drunks, and idiots. Apparently the law does as well.
5. The various degrees of capacity etc. are explicitly defined in the *Indian Act*.
6. In this case the advertisement would be an offer rather than an invitation, because the offerees and the conditions of acceptance (who, where, when, etc.) are specific.
7. On occasion the standard form may be interpreted as an offer and the completion and return of the form as acceptance of the offer, particularly where the language of the form would lend itself to that interpretation or the form is customized by the offeror for the offeree (e.g., a "standard" advertising contract that is filled in by the magazine's salesperson for a specific space reservation).
8. On some standard forms—probably not courier or transport bills—business people do make changes by striking out certain terms and/or adding others. The party that created the standard form then has the option of accepting or rejecting the revised terms. In some cases, the invitor will accept the changes. Thus, it pays to read the terms, and not be hesitant to change them—even on a pre-printed, very official-looking standard-form contract.
9. I really do not know if Coca-Cola licenses production and marketing of its product, and would not cast aspersions upon how it conducts its negotiations and legals. I am only using the name "Coca-Cola" because it is my cola beverage of choice.
10. Sometimes there is statutory requirement for offer and acceptance to be in writing, such as for the purchase of a home in Manitoba.
11. The precedent for this is the famous *Carlill v. Carbolic Smoke Ball Company* case that we really do not want or need to get into here, but which makes for excellent legal trivia/arcana.
12. I do not mean to trivialize the formal contract because, as stated earlier, the formal contract drafted by lawyers is designed to shield and protect the parties, and more especially to ensure that all parties understand the deal the same way. However, such a document is not required to fulfill offer and acceptance.
13. Software is not actually sold. Rather, its use is licensed to the user.
14. I believe the legal maxim is actually "Past consideration is no consideration."

15. This gender-specific arbiter of good sense, the "reasonable man," who appears everywhere in the common law, may be the reason why the law is so complicated. If it were a "reasonable woman," I suspect the law would be radically different. But that is another book altogether.

Chapter 2

1. It would likely be enforced in a substantially less savoury way than that prescribed by law. I suspect that the contract would not be voided, but the wronging party would.
2. What the lady did was cause such a media fuss over the issue that both the drycleaner and the leather-cleaning operation came out as bad guys. In the court of public opinion, there is no privity.
3. The manufacturer is nevertheless potentially liable under the tort law of negligence.
4. Such assignments fall under statutory law and questions or concerns about them should be addressed to a lawyer.
5. A statutory assignment is one that is, by the working of the applicable statute law, full and complete; i.e., the assignor is completely extricated from any further benefit or obligation under the agreement.
6. In Manitoba, and possibly in other Canadian jurisdictions, the courts rely on the *Oxford English Dictionary* to define such words.
7. The lesson to be learned here is that it is the *final draft*, the one presented for signature, that should be read and checked most carefully, not overlooking any part of it.
8. J. E. Smyth, D. A. Soberman, and A. J. Easson, *The Law and Business Administration in Canada*, 8th ed. (Toronto: Prentice Hall Canada Inc., 1998), p. 180.
9. An expert's opinion is, however, usually considered as reliable as fact. Your lawyer, for instance, may provide an "opinion" on your legal situation before you give her instructions on how to proceed or enter a service contract with her. She cannot be absolutely certain of the outcome of the situation, because the law is not a science. But, assuming that she has examined the situation thoroughly, her opinion—to you—should be close to fact for your purpose. It is, after all, what you will base your decision upon. The opinion of a property appraiser or coroner could similarly be construed as fact.
10. As I see it, duress is conditional—a threat of future consequences—whereas extortion is actual, active coercion.
11. The contract's terms may continue to have effect beyond the life of a contract, so perhaps we should consider the contract *fulfilled* rather than *ended*.
12. As we will see in later chapters, a lawyer would likely cover this in the contract with *force majeure* and other liability-limiting clauses.

Chapter 3

1. Again, pay no mind to the fact that even in the 1990s some traditionalist lawyers are perpetuating Chaucer's English. "Witnesseth" is more frequently replaced with its simpler, modern replacement, "Witnesses." Either way, it ends up the same.
2. These provisions are the ones that many business people like to see the least. Many of them are "negative" and, for some people, cast a pall on the upbeat mood of the relationship being formed. Since many deals and agreements do not work out as planned, however, paying attention to these terms is probably well worth the time. Otherwise, what may have been dealt with in the contract ends up sending everyone to court. So, when your lawyer seems like a real spoiler, she is doing it because experience shows it is important. Listen to her.
3. The question raised, of course, is "What if the notice that is posted is never received?" Proving that notice was made is the responsibility of the notifier, which is why registered mail or any other delivery that proves receipt is best.
4. What the all-knowing "reasonable man" would consider unreasonable is anybody's guess.

5. This provision may or may not have teeth depending on the unique circumstances surrounding the dispute and the arbitrator's decision. For all intents and purposes, however, it is wise to start with the assumption that both parties have forgone the right to litigate over "interpretation" or "implementation."

Chapter 5

1. The precedent that follows was derived in large part from a sample form in *O'Brien's Encyclopedia of Forms*, printed by and the property of Canada Law Book Limited. *O'Brien's* is one of several sources of legal document forms available to lawyers in Canada.
2. There's an interesting issue here of poor parallel construction of the sentence. Why does the purchaser not agree to "purchase, acquire, buy, accept, and receive" the assets?
3. The important part of the language is that which makes the representation "as far as the vendor is aware." It could be hazardous for the vendor to warranty outright, because it would then be liable even though it was unaware that it was wrong at the outset.
4. The schedule is not provided, although one can refer to Chapter 11 herein for an example of a simple guarantee form.

Chapter 6

1.2.3. The precedent that follows was adapted from a sample form drawn out of *O'Brien's Encyclopedia of Forms*, printed by, and the property of, Canada Law Book Limited. *O'Brien's* is one of several sources of legal document forms available to lawyers in Canada.
4. I have not included a bonus plan example, since it is a schedule referred to and not a contract itself. Besides, bonus plans are as numerous and as different as spring crocuses in Manitoba.
5. See Chapter 11.

Chapter 7

1. This makes me think of an anecdote I once read about accurate language. Two fellows in a hot-air balloon fly into a cloud. When they emerge, they are lost and fairly close to the ground. Seeing a person on the ground, one of them asks "Where are we?" The man on the ground says "You're in a balloon." One balloonist turns to the other and says "That man is an economist." "How do you know?" inquires the other. "Because what he said is accurate, but completely useless." Substitute "lawyer," "banker," or any other occupation in place of "economist" at your will.
2. Here's a skill-testing question: How would you apportion and apply customer credit payment money if you were charging interest at various rates on different credits with the same customer? Extra points if you can generate higher annual profit.
3. The "spread" used to be one of the principal ways banks earned their profits, and since there is an element of risk and effort involved, they deserved every penny. Today, a lot more revenue comes from fees and charges, and from currency trading, mutual funds, etc.

Chapter 8

1. Handbook, Section 3065.
2. J. E. Smyth, D. A. Soberman, and A. J. Easson, *The Law and Business Administration in Canada*, 8th ed. (Toronto: Prentice Hall Canada Inc., 1998), p. 293.
3. In property leasing it is not uncommon for overholding tenants to pay month-to-month rent of double or more than the rent payment during the lease.
4. The term *estate* refers to an interest in land that may include ownership or other, similar rights. *Land*, in

the context of property law, means the real property (the territory of ground itself) and everything both above and below the ground. That is, everything below the ground except mineral rights, oils, etc., almost all of which, in Canada, belong to the Crown—the government—usually of the province.

5. Practically, however, most lease contracts—especially those for space in commercial buildings—contain specific provisions that determine what amount of damage or destruction would provide the tenant with the opportunity to seek rent relief.

6. Most lease contract language contains phraseology to the effect of "Such consent will not be unreasonably withheld," the impact of which is that the landlord cannot be capricious or arbitrary about consenting to the tenant's request.

7. The property lease contract was very generously provided by Shelter Canadian Properties Ltd., of Winnipeg, which owns and manages several commercial and residential properties across Canada. The contract form is for properties in Manitoba, but it is fairly consistent with property leases from other professional property managers across Canada.

8. In other provinces, one would assume that the applicable part of the provincial legislation would be referred to here.

Chapter 9

1. The first insurance policy: "If anything happens, we'll cover it." The second insurance policy: "If anything happens *except* X, we'll cover it," and so on for the next 200 years and beyond.

2. Given the suggested scenario, here is some food for amateur legal thought. Assume the property in this case was damaged by a mechanical "blowout" as described, with a fire being caused concurrently by the same reason. Further assume that the property is then consumed by the fire. I wonder how strong might be the argument that even if the property had not been damaged by mechanical issue, the fire that was started by that mechanical problem would have damaged the property anyway. Thus, the claim for damages to the property should stand.

3. My exclusion's exclusion is my inclusion, maybe? Similar logic led to World War I.

4. Although not impossible, it is uncommon to have medical requirement without "bodily injury."

5. The value of this statement is spurious, inasmuch as the insurer cannot make those kinds of broad impositions. Statute and circumstance would have a great deal of effect in how and when a claim against the insurer can be made. For instance, if the insurer and the other party spent a full year corresponding on the issue without a payment being made, there might be valid cause for a claim to be made after the year has elapsed. A sharp lawyer would, however, make the necessary filings within the prescribed time limit. Furthermore, if the right of action arises out of a judgement or court order, the court would probably have a little something to say on the subject. In any event, it does not really concern you unless you are suing the insurance company, and that would be a breach of contract suit, which is not really covered by this paragraph.

Chapter 10

1. Some larger shareholders may also be directors of a company, in which case, like all other corporate directors, would have a higher level of responsibility and potential personal liability. But, generally speaking, shareholders are responsible only to the extent of their investment.

2.3. The precedent that follows was derived in large part from a sample form in *O'Brien's Encyclopedia of Forms*, printed by and the property of Canada Law Book Limited. *O'Brien's* is one of several sources of legal document form available to lawyers in Canada.

Chapter 11

1. Source: Canadian Franchise Association.

2. The precedent that follows was derived in large part from a sample form in *O'Brien's Encyclopedia of Forms*, printed by and the property of Canada Law Book Limited. *O'Brien's* is one of several sources of legal document form available to lawyers in Canada. Franchise contracts are, apparently, much too confidential to be permitted for reproduction and broad use in a descriptive reference book.

3. It invites the question: What are "normal" business hours—those of the franchised restaurant that is open until 10 pm Sunday? Or, the traditional 9 am to 5 pm Monday to Friday?

4. This formula basically makes the value of the business equal to its book value plus a one-year earnings premium. Generally speaking, that would be "wholesale" for a going concern.

Chapter 12

1. The precedents that follow were derived in large part from a sample form in *O'Brien's Encyclopedia of Forms*, printed by and the property of Canada Law Book Limited. *O'Brien's* is one of several sources of legal document form available to lawyers in Canada.

2. Frankly, I am way out of my depth here. The purchaser could have quite extensive additional remedy, including injunction and other additional cash damages, *if* the actual damages it is or will suffer are substantially more than those anticipated by the liquidated damages. In other words, it is possible that those other remedies available to the purchaser would not evaporate. I suspect that this falls under the rubric of the "court of equity" and is therefore circumstantial. Ask a lawyer.

3. This may or may not be practical in law, inasmuch as it would seem that once you have irrevocably assigned an asset/thing, you no longer control it or the actions of the person to whom it was assigned.

4. Paying out the deposit to the Depositor on the trigger date if the deal did not go through would obviously defeat the purpose of escrowing the money in the first place.

Glossary

Many of the following words, phrases, and terms have been used within this book. Others you may encounter while reading or discussing a contract with a lawyer.

Acceptance	(1) Agreement of an offeree to an offer made by an offeror. (2) An action on the part of the buyer that serves to indicate the existence of a contract.
Accord and satisfaction	An agreement by parties to a contract to substitute a new obligation for an original one that cannot be performed.
Age of majority	The age at which a person is legally recognized as an adult, which varies by jurisdiction.
Anticipatory breach	A breach that is anticipated to happen before the specified time of performance of the obligation.
Assignee	A third party to whom contractual rights and obligations are assigned.
Assignment	The transfer of contractual rights and obligations to a third party.
Assignor	A party to a contract that assigns its contractual rights and obligations to a third party.
Beneficial contracts of service	Apprenticeships and other such contracts of employment *of minors* that are deemed to be in the minor's best interests.
Beneficial owner	A person or entity, which, although not the legal owner, maintains all the other rights over a property (e.g., the owner of a mortgaged house or a car purchased on a loan).
Beneficiary	Someone on whom a benefit is bestowed, for instance under a trust or an insurance policy.
Bilateral contract	A contract in which promises have been traded so that each party is both offeror and offeree.
Capacity (legal)	The law-determined competence and ability of an individual, personal, corporate, or otherwise, to enter into a contract.
Caveat emptor	"Let the buyer beware" (Latin).
Chattels	Tangible personal property that is not real property (i.e., not land).
Choses in action	Rights to intangible property, the value of which is the right or obligation it creates.
Choses in possession	Rights to tangible property, such as chattels and real estate, the value of which is in the possession of the property.
Collateral agreement	A separate contract made alongside and simultaneously with another contract, but not part of the formal written contract. See also *Rider*.
Collateral contract	An implied contract that binds a third party to a contract made between other parties.
Compensation	A money award given to offset loss sustained in performing the obligations of a later-rescinded contract. See also *Indemnity*.
Condition	An essential, major term of a contract.
Condition precedent	A condition or requirement that must be met before the contract may come into effect.

Condition subsequent	An event that, if it happens, ends a promisor's obligation and liability under a contract.
Consequential damages	Damages from a breach of contract that are a step "downstream" from the breached contract, generally arising as a consequence of the injured party's reliance on the promisor's performance.
Consideration	Money or value actually paid for equity in other goods, without which no contract is valid, binding, and enforceable.
Consignment	A shipment of goods from one party to another generally for sale at another location, with title not passing until the goods are sold to the end purchaser.
Constructive fraud	The actions of one party to a contract that permit it to take unfair advantage of the other party or parties and defraud them.
Constructive trust	The right of a third party to a contract to enforce a promise between the parties to the contract, the benefit of which promise accrues to the third party.
Construe	To interpret.
Covenant	A very serious promise, on the order of a "holy oath."
Damages	An award of money by the court to compensate a party injured by another's nonperformance; not a penalty.
Deed	A document under seal.
Discharge (a contract)	To cancel the rights and obligations of a contract, ideally by performance, rendering the contract void.
Duress	Actual or threatened harm used to coerce entry into a contract.
Equitable assignment	Any assignment of rights and obligations that is not a *Statutory assignment*.
Equitable Estoppel	The court's right to bind a promisor to a gratuitous promise where the promisee's reasonable reliance on that promise has caused it harm. See also *Promissory estoppel*.
Estoppel	To stop.
Execution order	A court order giving a sheriff the authority to seize and sell as much of a debtor's chattels and real property as is necessary to settle a judgement debt.
Exemption clause	A provision in a contract that exempts a party from liability for failure to perform one or more of its contractual obligations.
Expectation damages	Damages for breach of contract based on expected lost profits.
Expert opinion	An opinion given by one who is an expert or specialist in a field, and may be considered as a statement of fact by a reasonable person.
Express repudiation	A direct declaration by one party to another that it does not intend to fulfill its obligations under a contract.
Fiduciary	(1) A stronger duty of care bestowed on a party that is a special relationship of trust to another party. (2) A party that bears a fiduciary duty to another party.
Force majeure	A "greater force," beyond the control of the parties to the contract (French).
Frustration, doctrine of	The legal approach to excusing a party from a contract where external forces have significantly altered the nature of the obligation and value originally contemplated.
Garnishing order	A court order requiring an employer, bank, or anyone else who owes money to a judgement debtor to surrender a specific sum from that person's wages or bank account to be applied to the judgement debt.
Good faith	The duty of honest intent to carry out a promise or obligation fully and completely as contemplated.
Goods	Personal property that is not money or *Choses in action*.
Gratuitous promise	A promise made without any exchange of value in return; the promise of a gift.
Guarantee	A conditional promise to pay if a debtor defaults.
Implied term	A contract term not expressly written, but that would have been reasonably included nonetheless.

Indemnity	(1) An award for loss in the recission of a contract. (2) A promise by one party to be solely or primarily responsible and/or liable.
Infant	A person who has not yet reached the age of majority. See also *Minor*.
Injunction	A court order that prevents a party from undertaking a specific act, usually from breaching a contract.
Injurious reliance	A U.S. principle that protects parties injured or harmed by reasonably relying on a gratuitous promise. See also *Equitable estoppel*.
Insurable interest	Exists where a party has a financial interest in a person or thing and would be injured by its loss or damage, and would therefore reasonably insure against such loss or damage.
Interlocutory injunction	A temporary injunction or restraining order pending court judgement.
Judgement creditor	A party that obtains a court judgement for a sum of money.
Judgement debtor	A party that is, by court order, required to pay a sum of money.
Jurisdiction	The laws and the body (i.e., municipality, province, nation) that apply in the circumstances.
Lapse	The termination of an offer due to the passage of a reasonable amount of time or a specified deadline for acceptance.
Legal	In contract, this term encompasses both lawfulness and inoffensiveness to public policy or public welfare.
Liberal interpretation	Interpretation of a contract that infers the intent of the parties into and along with the words used.
Liquidated damages	Damages awarded or specified within the contract for liquidating the contract, such as holding a deposit, to offset the costs of the contract being breached.
Major breach	A breach of a major term of a contract that renders the contract irrelevant and purposeless.
Material (adj.)	Reasonably expected to influence a party's decision to enter a contract; a term of a contract that is fundamental to the contract's purpose.
Material breach	A failure to perform a term of the contract that "goes to its heart" and without which the contract is effectively worthless.
Minor	A person who has yet to reach the age of majority. See also *Infant*.
Minor breach	A breach of a nonessential term of a contract; an insubstantial breach of a major term of a contract.
Miscarriage	Performance of contractual obligations in such a way that the other party or parties would fail to attain the just, right, or desired benefits.
Mitigate	To take action to limit or prevent further injury arising from a breach of contract.
Necessaries	Essential goods and services (e.g., food, transportation, medical treatment) for which a minor entering a contract will be bound.
Negative covenant	A covenant or promise to *not* do something.
Nominal damages	When a court awards a very small sum in damages to indicate a breach against but no valuable loss to the plaintiff.
Non est factum	"It is not my doing" (Latin), where a written agreement is not properly explained and that party neither understands nor voluntarily agrees to the terms of the agreement.
Novation	The substitution of a new contract for an existing one by mutual agreement of the parties to the contract.
Offer	A specific, conditional, and tentative promise from one party to another, subject to the other party's acceptance.
Opportunity cost	When measuring damages this is the economic value lost from not making a similar contract with someone else.
Option	A contract that keeps an offer open for a specified period.

Parol evidence rule	A rule that prevents an agreed term from being added to the final written contract if it was excluded from that final written form.
Part payment	Anything tendered by the buyer and accepted by the seller, after the contract has been formed, which must be deducted from the price.
Part performance	Accepted by the court in lieu of a written contract for contracts *related to land*.
Past consideration	A gratuitous benefit provided to the offeror prior to the offer being made.
Penalty clause	A term within a contract that specifies exorbitant damages in the event of a breach, intended to ensure performance by terror.
Positive acceptance	The act or word of accepting an offer that is positive (i.e., actively confirming) in nature.
Premium, insurance	The price of periodic insurance coverage.
Prima facie	"At first sight" (Latin). Sufficient to establish a fact or raise a presumption of fact prior to investigation.
Privity of contract	The principle that only the parties named to and related by the contract are bound by it.
Promissory estoppel	See *Equitable estoppel*.
Quantum meruit	"What the quantity merits" (Latin); the amount of payment merited by goods or services provided.
Ratify	To acknowledge and promise to perform.
Rectify	To correct a written document in which an error or mistake has been made.
Reliance damages	Damages awarded when the plaintiff incurs a loss in reliance on a contract being performed by the breaching party.
Rescind	To cancel or revoke a contract, and to attempt putting the parties back in their original positions as though the contract had never been made. See also *Set aside*.
Restitution	Repayment or recovery of a loss.
Restrictive covenant	A term of a contract that restricts or restrains proper trade or provision of services.
Seal	Traditionally, a blob of wax impressed with the family arms or signet to execute a document; today, a holdover tradition usually fulfilled with a red adhesive-backed dot or an embossment seal.
Self-induced frustration	A party's attempt to render itself unable to fulfill its obligations and to claim the contract frustrated.
Set aside	Cancel or revoke a contract, and attempt to put the parties in the position they would have been in had the contract never been made. See also *Rescind*.
Set-off	The right to deduct an existing debt from the value of a promise.
Specific performance	A court order that prescribes that the defendant perform a specific act, often the completion of a transaction.
Standard-form contract	A preprinted contract presented to the offeree for acceptance "as is."
Standing offer	An open offer that may be accepted from time to time as required.
Statute barred	A claim that may not be brought to court because the time allowed by the statute of limitations for filing it in court has expired. (Sort of like not making a basket before the shot clock runs out, or not snapping the football fast enough.)
Statutory assignment	An assignment of rights and obligations that, by statute, fully extricates the assignor from further liability or responsibility under the contract.
Strict interpretation	Interpretation of a contract by the strict dictionary definition of the words used (aka "Plain-meaning interpretation").
Subsidiary promise	An implied promise by the offeror that the offer will not be revoked once the offeree has begun its "good faith" performance of its obligations.
Substantial performance	Performance of a contractual obligation that is materially complete despite not being in perfect compliance with the terms of the agreement.

Tender of performance	An attempt to perform one's obligations under a contract.
Third party	A "stranger" to the contract (i.e., not a party to the contract) that is affected by it nonetheless.
Trust	A fiduciary relationship in which one party holds and administers a property for the benefit of another person.
Trustee	A fiduciary, or person, who administers a trust.
Ultra vires	"Beyond the powers of" (Latin).
Undisclosed principal	A party to a contract that is represented by an agent, all of which is unknown to the other party to the contract.
Undue influence	An excessive degree of influence by one party over another to the extent that the latter party's decisions are not its own.
Unenforceable contract	A contract that exists on some levels but may not be enforced by law.
Unilateral contract	A contract in which acceptance is indicated by the performance of an act to fulfill the offer condition(s).
Unjust enrichment	An unfair benefit to a party to a contract; an "unearned" benefit within the intent of the contract.
Vicarious performance	When a third party carries out the obligation of a party to the contract, the party to the contract remains responsible for the third party's performance.
Void	Never formed in law; a void contract is not a contract at all.
Voidable	Able to be voided; is an otherwise properly formed contract that may be set aside, often at one party's discretion.
Waiver	An agreement not to proceed with or to enforce the performance of an obligation/right under a contract.
Warranty	A nonessential term of a contract.